Guide to Housing

Guide to Housing

Mary E. H. Smith
M.B.E., B.A. (Hons.), F.I.H.

Chief Housing Manager to the
Crown Estate Commissioners

SECOND EDITION

THE HOUSING CENTRE TRUST
62 CHANDOS PLACE
LONDON WC2N 4HG

First published 1971
Supplement to First Edition published 1974
Revised Second Edition 1977

© M. E. H. Smith 1971, 1974, 1977

ISBN 0 9502005 3 0   hardback
0 9502005 4 9   paper

Printed in Great Britain by
The Eastern Press Ltd.
of London and Reading

Contents

Contents

Foreword

Advances in policy come about only when public understanding provides a stable base for action. Much of the post-war period has been characterised by a lack of this. One reason is the sheer complexity of the issues involved, but another is the paucity of informed, clear, comprehensible (and comprehensive) information. Most of the increasingly vast literature on housing is as opaque as the web of housing legislation to which it has to refer, or/and as biased as the special pleading of bodies representing the sectional interests which benefit or suffer from current policies.

The level of debate has been typically either esoteric or superficial. The arena has been reserved for specialists on the one hand and the uncomprehending on the other. As a result, the political process has been subverted, and short-term palliatives have followed each other in quick succession. Simple solutions have been popularised, accepted and implemented to the detriment of adequate and well-formulated policies.

There is little hope that this situation will improve until there is a better and wider understanding of the multiplicity of issues which constitute " the housing problem ". This is not a matter to be reserved to experts (or politicians)—though both have important roles to play; it constitutes a major area in which informed debate is fundamental to the formulation of wise policies. Without this, governments will shirk the basic issues—as was done in the 1977 Green Paper.

Of course the issues are complex, difficult and politically delicate to handle. Indeed, in one sense, this *is* the housing problem. The Technical Volumes accompanying the English Green Paper are eloquent testimony to the complexities. But, given a sufficiently informed public, and a broadly based arena of debate, the problems are not incapable of solution.

As I see it, the most important feature of this *Guide* is that it provides a unique contribution to the furtherance of this debate. It presents no panacea; indeed, some may be disappointed that it attempts little in the way of " answers " to the problems it so clearly explains. But this is its virtue. It is as objective an account as one could hope for. It provides a base map of a treacherous terrain. It is precisely what its title suggests: a guide through the labyrinth of housing problems and policies.

In attempting this obvious yet difficult task, Mary Smith has not only filled a gap in the literature, she has done it with a rare skill. Her strength is her ability to set out complexities in a clear and coherent manner. The *Guide* has neither the superficialities of the

Green Paper nor the confusing depths of the Technical Volumes. It steers a middle course, outlining the problems but retaining a sense of proportion. Its strength is that it explains the difficulties clearly. It raises for public debate the very issues which the Green Paper suggests might be conveniently buried. An informed electorate will not allow this to happen.

J. B. Cullingworth.

Toronto, Canada
October 1977

INTRODUCTION
Aim of the Guide

A Guide to Housing was published by the Housing Centre in 1971 to give a concise background to the contemporary housing scene, and the *Supplement to a Guide to Housing* followed in 1974 after certain important changes had taken place in housing.

Since the publication of the *Supplement*, the financial system imposed on public sector housing by the Housing Finance Act 1972 has been changed and transitional arrangements, pending a complete review of housing finance, introduced by the Housing Rents and Subsidies Act 1975; area and house improvement have been given greater emphasis stimulated by the new legislation of the Housing Act 1974, the work of the housing association movement has expanded impressively also through the provisions of the Housing Act 1974, greater attention has been paid to deteriorating social and housing conditions in the inner city areas, the future of the new towns has been re-appraised, and the Community Land Act 1975 has provided the framework for land acquisition for community needs. At the same time, the decline in council building and the reduction in the number of homes let by private landlords have continued, security of tenure has been extended to cover all tenancies (with a few minor exceptions) and home ownership has increased, both in quantity and proportion to other types of tenure; more private property has been brought into social ownership and experiments are being made in co-operatives and other forms of tenure. These changes have taken place during a time of increasing financial stringency and against an inflationary background of rising prices, including rents and rates, of steeply rising building costs and growing problems connected with discordant race relations, vandalism, rent arrears, tenant dissatisfaction and other symptoms of social malaise. The *Guide* has therefore been completely revised to bring the basic facts of housing up to date and to reconsider some of the social and economic problems connected with housing within the context of society in 1976–77.

Housing affects everyone, whether as tenant, landlord, mortgagee, owner-occupier, caravan dweller, applicant on a waiting-list or homeless person. Almost everyone must be aware that there are in many places in this country a lack of good standard accommodation and too many out-dated dwellings. In crude numerical terms, in 1975 there was a surplus of dwellings over

1

households, so that a *national* housing shortage no longer exists, but rather a series of *local* housing needs, differing from place to place, some of them still severe. Housing deficiency has certainly not been overcome, nor bad housing eradicated in the large conurbations and in other congested areas. No-one can feel complacent while families and others are still struggling in miserable conditions—and no statistics or examples can portray adequately the human misery and degradation such conditions entail.

Housing, too, cannot be considered in isolation, but as an integral part of the social scene, and the urgent need for society to create and control its environment is gradually being recognised. Slowly, measures are being taken to control pollution and conserve beauty in buildings and the countryside, to shape and preserve the fabric of villages, towns and cities to make them pleasing and efficient places for living and working.

Today housing is such a complex subject—regulated by an involved system of controls built up in our successive attempts to deal with the symptoms of housing deficiency, governed by illogical and often inequitable financial arrangements, and frequently influenced by conflicting political and selfish interests —that we are in danger of losing sight of the essential that as a progressive, inventive nation we should be able to create conditions within a sensible economic framework whereby we can provide good standard accommodation at reasonable prices in a good civilised environment for all our citizens. And in a democracy, the provision of decent modern housing in pleasant surroundings should be by the co-operative effort of all.

The Milner-Holland Committee concluded that the housing problems confronting our great cities " will not be resolved by market forces or by the provision of more houses alone; they are of a long-term, perhaps permanent, nature ", and that there was a need for " a fully considered development of policy based on an understanding of the whole housing situation ". At the National Conference of the Housing Centre Trust in July 1975, the late Mr Anthony Crosland, as Secretary of State for the Environment, emphasised that there was an astonishing lack of understanding of how the housing system and the current arrangements for housing finance actually work. The revised *Guide* is published by the Housing Centre as an aid to this understanding, at a time when a Green Paper on housing policy is promised which, it is hoped, will show evidence of radical new thinking, and will propose new dynamic policies on housing finance, urban renewal, satisfaction of social needs in housing and other urgent housing matters to point the way to solutions of the many complex problems in housing within an overall housing strategy.

To a certain degree, there is some overlap between chapters in the *Guide*, for example on rehabilitation, but this repetition has been left deliberately to minimise the need to refer back, and to reduce the number of notes and cross-references in the text.

It is hoped that the *Guide* will be of assistance to new members of local authority housing committees, to students in professions concerned with and allied to housing, to experts in one housing sector or profession who need a working knowledge of other aspects, and to all taking an interest in social service and civic affairs; and also that by increasing the awareness of the general public, it will help to create a well-informed public opinion on housing to overcome prejudice and misunderstanding. There is insufficient public knowledge and a lack of communication on housing, and inadequate information available to private citizens and to some local authorities about where the need is greatest and about what remains to be done to relieve housing distress in a so-called affluent society.

The *Guide* is not intended to be a literary discourse on housing, nor to encroach on practical guides which are available to individuals to help them, for example, to buy a house or to obtain a mortgage, or to give advice on interior decorating and furnishing. It treats housing as a subject of social importance to all citizens, and recognises that housing, being so bound up in the lives and domestic affairs of individuals, is one of the great personal social services, in which sociological considerations and management techniques are as important as those of architecture and building. As a basic tool of any housing trade, it aims to provide essential factual information about housing policies, law, administration and practice today, with some pointers to the future. There is a comprehensive bibliography for further study, to which the bracketed figures in the text refer.

The author gladly acknowledges the help received from Housing Centre members at various stages of the *Guide*. Particular thanks are due to: J. A. Balchin, D.P.A. (London), D.M.A., F.C.I.S., F.I.H., for the chapter on new and expanded towns, Bernard Kilroy, M.A., A.I.H., for the one on housing finance, and Margaret Baker, M.B.E., B.A., and Charles Baker, O.B.E., for that on housing associations; and to Walter Bor, C.B.E., R.T.P.I., R.I.B.A., Cleone Christie, A.R.I.C.S., Geoffrey Easton, F.R.I.B.A., and John Hollamby, F.R.I.C.S., who offered advice; and again to Margaret Baker, who has supplied parts of the text and given invaluable advice and assistance in the final drafting.

I am also grateful to Marjorie Cleaver, A.I.H., who has been most helpful in co-ordinating and handling the typescript, putting together the bibliography and dealing with the multifarious details of seeing the *Guide* through to publication. This must have made calls on her time and expertise beyond those of her ordinary duties as secretary of the Housing Centre Trust.

Finally, my personal thanks are due to my daughter, Fiona, and to my mother, Mrs. L. A. W. Land, for their patience and co-operation during the long period of writing and co-ordinating the material.

M. E. H. S.

CHAPTER 1

Historical Background

The origin of the housing problem: nineteenth century to World War I

Probably there has been a housing problem since Adam and Eve were turned out of the Garden of Eden, where there was no need for protection against the elements—although Milton's image of the event suggests that they then at least had no town planning problem: " the world was all before them, where to choose ".

It is unlikely that there has ever been a time in history when we have been able so to arrange our affairs that every household could have shelter against the elements, and a spacious and well-equipped home in which to lead the healthiest and fullest life contemporary society allowed, arranged in such a way that privacy was assured for the occupant and his neighbours. The housing problem as we know it today in Britain, however, has its more immediate origin in the Industrial Revolution. It is to some extent ironical that our well-equipped homes are dependent on a sophisticated technology which can only flourish in an urban civilisation; and urbanisation—the settlement of many people in a small area—has been itself a root cause of our housing problems.

Many of our present housing ills may be traced back to the growth in the population and its concentration in towns during the nineteenth century. In 1801, the population of England and Wales was nine million. In less than two generations it had doubled itself, and by the outbreak of the first world war in 1914 it had doubled again and was over 36 million. New industries drew people into the towns, and places such as Glasgow, Liverpool, Manchester, Birmingham and Sheffield, which were small country towns at the beginning of the eighteenth century, had increased five or tenfold by 1900, and continued to grow. In those parts of the country where industry based on coal and steam was developing rapidly, or where good harbours encouraged trade, towns grew so fast that they came together to form the great industrial conurbations.

Hands were needed for the new industries, and with no cheap passenger transport and the internal combustion engine not yet invented, let alone mass produced, people had to live near the place where they worked. Cheap dwellings were run up quickly by landlords, with no appreciation of the danger to public health from crowding them together without the water supply, town sewerage and house drainage which we take for granted today. There were several cholera epidemics during the nineteenth century, and death rates were high, particularly among the industrial population. Many landlords were interested only in getting what rents they could from poorly paid workers, and local and central authorities were frequently ignorant, indifferent or corrupt. The worst of these dwellings have by now disappeared from our towns. They are described in the enquiries made in the middle of the nineteenth century, in the warnings of medical officers (1), and in the novels and writings of such authors as Charles Dickens and Mrs Gaskell.

Men like Sir Edwin Chadwick, a pioneer of sanitary reform, and Dr Southwood Smith, who had experience of the London Fever Hospital, worked to secure the cleansing and paving of streets, the provision of water and drainage, and control over the construction and ventilation of dwellings. Eventually, the Public Health Act 1875, coupled with the building by-laws, enforced a minimum standard, and limited the building of back-to-back houses without through ventilation—although in some areas such houses continued to be built until much later. " By-law streets " of minimum legal width, usually on a rigid grid-iron pattern, were lined with terraces. We may look upon the worst of them now as dreary soulless places, but at least they were an improvement on what had gone before. The streets in front were drained, and the yard, or sometimes even a garden, behind was an added amenity. Later, piped water, WCs, and better construction and equipment made many such terrace houses reasonably comfortable homes. The fact that the first attack on slums was made from the public health angle is still reflected in housing law.

The first efforts at improving houses themselves were made by enlightened landowners who repaired and improved their tenants' cottages and built new ones to better standards. In the towns, philanthropic trusts were set up to build model dwellings for working people. The first of these, the Society for Improving the Condition of the Labouring Classes, was established in 1830. In 1851, the Prince Consort sponsored a block of dwellings at the Great Exhibition which was to be a model for good landlords and for industrialists to build for their workers. Sometimes model villages were built by industrialists round their new factories to create a proper environment for their employees. At the end of the eighteenth century, Robert Owen had done this at New Lanark, in Scotland, and towards the middle of the nineteenth century another such community was established by Sir Titus

Salt, a Yorkshire woollen manufacturer. Later, the better known Bournville, Port Sunlight and New Earswick were established, and Ebenezer Howard published his book, *Tomorrow: a Peaceful Path to Real Reform,* advocating the " garden city " before the turn of the century (2). The first of the self-contained towns with their own diverse industries, separated from other built-up areas by a green belt, was established by him and his friends at Letchworth in 1903 on land which it was intended should be held permanently in trust for the community by a public utility society.

Meantime, housing improvement had become the concern of Parliament. In 1851, Lord Shaftesbury, perhaps better known for his work to improve conditions in mines and factories, secured the passing of legislation which gave local authorities powers to build lodging houses for the labouring classes, whether single men and women or families, and enabled them to inspect and regulate common lodging houses. The first legislation to deal with slum clearance followed in 1868, the Torrens Act (Artisans and Labourers Dwellings Act 1868), and this was followed a year later by an amending Act which gave local authorities power to build houses to replace the slums they had cleared. The Cross Act in 1875 (Artisans and Labourers Dwellings Improvement Act) provided for the improvement and clearance of large areas. Thus there was legislation on the statute book covering the inspection, closing, demolition and improvement of unhealthy areas and the provision of new accommodation as a public service; but the Acts were complicated, and permissive only. Compensation for the compulsory purchase of property was costly. In 1890, the Housing of the Working Classes Act clarified and consolidated the legislation. It is this Act which is now usually referred to as the first of the true Housing Acts as we know them.

In spite of their housing powers, local authorities had built only about 5 per cent of all dwellings up to the outbreak of the 1914-18 war. Housing associations, including some trusts endowed with charitable funds, pioneered model estates within the bigger cities, but private enterprise was still the main source of supply of houses at low rents.

Any review of this period would be incomplete without a mention of the work of Octavia Hill, one of the outstanding women of the Victorian age who achieved striking reforms, largely by virtue of their own personalities (3). Though less well known than Florence Nightingale in the field of nursing, Octavia Hill had a profound influence on housing. She recognised that a good relationship between landlord and tenant was all important. The one should provide suitable accommodation at a fair price and maintain it well; the other should pay the rent regularly and treat the dwelling properly. She demonstrated her theories by herself managing working-class tenements, in the first instance in a house bought by John Ruskin, and later when working for other enlightened landlords. She herself collected the rents, going down streets which even the police dared not visit. She trained others in her methods, and thereby initiated the profession of housing management. She was interested in people, and believed that people and their houses could not be dealt with separately, thus recognising the importance of housing in social improvement. She promoted community facilities for tenants of the estates she managed, gardens, clubs, outings to the country. Her work extended into what we should now call town planning, and she was active in the foundation of such bodies as the Commons, Footpaths and Open Spaces Society and the National Trust.

The first world war and the inter-war period

During the first world war, the first legislation to control rents was passed, because housing shortage was leading to exploitation by landlords and mortgagees. The Rent and Mortgage Interest Restriction Act 1915 fixed rents, gave tenants security against eviction, and prevented an increase in interest rates on mortgages and the calling in of mortgages. Although this law was intended to be only temporary, in fact some control over rents has existed ever since. There were efforts between the wars to decontrol rents of some houses, when it was felt that the shortage had been overcome, but decontrol was limited to higher rented dwellings, and on the landlord obtaining vacant possession. There were also permitted but limited increases in rent to take account of changes in the costs of maintenance and value of money.

During the period between the wars, local authorities began to play an important part in the provision of houses to let. After four years of war when little or no house building had been undertaken, the nation was faced with a serious shortage of houses, prices were inflated by war conditions, and a strong demand was reflected in the popular slogan " homes for heroes ".

The first of the government reports on standards for new houses, the Tudor Walters Report, named after its chairman, was published in 1918 (4). For the first time an Exchequer subsidy was paid, under the Housing and Town Planning Act 1919, the Addison Act, to bridge the gap between the economic cost of houses and the rents which families could afford. This subsidy was generous, and amounted to the whole of the annual loss on approved schemes, less the product of a penny rate. Almost 176,000 houses were built under this Act, but costs continued to rise, there was a labour shortage, and alternative forms of construction which were tried out generally failed. Two years later this subsidy was withdrawn and shortly afterwards replaced by one limited to a fixed sum per dwelling. Because of experience with this open-ended Addison subsidy, which made the Exchequer liable for an unspecified amount, Exchequer subsidies were given at a fixed rate per dwelling or per person rehoused thereafter, until in 1967 they were made subject to a cost ceiling.

During the whole of the inter-war period, subsidies for house building were available, though the amounts changed. Sometimes subsidies were restricted to house building for letting by local authorities; at others, there were also grants for small houses built by private enterprise. Subsidies, too, were sometimes directed towards houses built for special purposes only: for example, for rehousing tenants from dwellings classified as unfit, and for dwellings built to accommodate overcrowded families. Most subsidies were given as annual payments spread over periods up to 60 years, so that many were still being received in 1972, when a new system involving withdrawal of older subsidies was introduced. Sometimes a fixed proportion had to be paid from the local authority's rate fund to match the Exchequer contribution.

In 1930 (Ministry of Health Circular 1138) local authorities were encouraged to use subsidies to give rent rebates to the poorer tenants who needed them. However, because separate accounts had to be kept for houses built under different acts, such differential rent schemes presented administrative complexities. The difficulty was removed by the Housing Act 1935, which required local authorities to pool all rents and subsidies in a single housing revenue account.

During the first decade after the end of the first world war, legislation was directed primarily to encouraging the building of new dwellings to relieve the general shortage. In the 1930s, however, attention was focused on slums. The Housing Act 1930, the Greenwood Act, directed particularly towards slum clearance, was passed. The country was suffering a severe economic depression at the time and little was achieved, although in 1933 an anti-slum campaign was launched with a five-year programme for local authorities to clear 280,000 slum homes.

This was followed by the Housing Act 1935, designed to secure the abatement of overcrowding. For the first time a penal standard setting up a permitted number of persons per room was introduced. An overcrowding survey carried out in 1936 showed 341,554 houses in England and Wales to be overcrowded according to this standard out of nearly nine million inspected. In some areas, particularly in North East England, 20 per cent of dwellings were overcrowded. In London, too, nine out of the 28 metropolitan boroughs had between 10 per cent and 17 per cent of overcrowded dwellings. The national average was 3.8 per cent (*Report on the Overcrowding Survey in England and Wales, 1936*).

During this period, too, some special assistance was given for housing in rural areas (Housing (Rural Workers) Act 1926). Grants were made for the reconditioning of obsolete but structurally sound cottages.

Between the wars, house production, though slow to get under way, reached a peak of 239,000 for the year 1927–28 when 104,000 subsidised houses were built by local authorities, and 135,000 by private enterprise, 74,600 of which were subsidised.

In the 1930s, building costs and interest rates fell. There was a wide extension of lending by building societies, and private enterprise produced many small homes for owner-occupation. By 1934, over 200,000 houses a year were being built privately, and total production was between 325,400 and 347,000 a year for the five years before the outbreak of war in 1939.

Between 1918 and 1939, altogether about four million new houses were built, of which about 1½ million were built by local authorities for letting, and 2½ million by private enterprise, mainly for owner-occupation. The majority of council houses were two-storey three-bedroom cottages, erected in terraces or pairs, of about 760 sq. ft. floor area, with one or sometimes two living rooms. A few blocks of flats were built in the big cities. Standards were reduced during the economic depression in the 1930s to enable the needs of tenants who could not afford much rent to be met. However, the provision of a fixed bath was made a condition of subsidy soon after the war (Housing Act 1923), and in 1924 it was laid down that this should be in a bathroom (Housing (Financial Provisions) Act 1924). A hot water installation was not, however, general. There were experiments in providing communal amenities, particularly in flats. These included central hot water, water-borne refuse disposal, facilities for drying clothes, communal laundries, club rooms and children's playgrounds. These, however, were exceptional, and many inter-war estates have been criticised for their lack of social amenities.

Although more houses had been built between the wars than earlier estimates had suggested were needed, when war broke out again in 1939 there was still an unsatisfied need for cheap housing.

World War II, 1939–45

At the outbreak of the second world war in 1939, all except the most expensive dwellings were again brought under rent control, rents were fixed, and security of tenure provided.

Apart from about 200,000 houses built for war workers, all house building ceased during the six years up to 1945. 200,000 houses were totally destroyed by air raids, and something like three million received some war damage, about a quarter of a million so seriously as to make them uninhabitable. " First-aid " repairs were carried out to keep houses habitable in tolerable comfort, but scarce materials and labour were not available for anything other than absolutely essential maintenance.

Billeting was used to deal with the housing of people and families who had to be moved to war-time employment, or who were evacuated from target areas, or needed rehousing because they had lost their homes through war damage. It was a patriotic duty for citizens with spare accommodation in areas where it was needed to take in suitable people, and compulsory powers were available if required. Requisitioning powers could also be invoked to ensure that empty houses were put to use.

During the war, public interest was aroused in reconstruction and the planning of a better physical environment to take the place of the unhealthy, congested areas of the older cities and industrial towns, some of which would in any case need extensive rebuilding due to the war damage they had suffered. The Royal Commission on the distribution of the Industrial Population, the Barlow Commission, although set up before the war, reported in 1940 (5). It recommended the continued and further redevelopment of congested areas, the dispersal of population and industry, the encouragement of a balance of industrial development throughout the country, and the appointment of a national planning authority. It was followed in 1942 by the *Report of the Expert Committee on Compensation and Betterment*, the Uthwatt Report (6), and the *Report of the Committee on the Utilisation of Land in Rural Areas*, the Scott Report (7). The Uthwatt Committee recommended the vesting in the State of the rights of development of undeveloped land, and methods of acquiring for the community the enhanced value of land which, it was argued, resulted from community action in developing the district. The Scott Committee made recommendations covering many aspects of development and preservation of amenities in rural areas, including recommendations for improvement of rural housing. This great trilogy of reports provided an outline for town and country planning policy which it was believed would give an opportunity to build a better Britain after the war.

Two advisory plans for the post-war development of London followed. The first, the *County of London Plan, 1943* (8), by J. H. Forshaw and Patrick Abercrombie, dealt with the inner built-up area administered by the old London County Council and the 28 Metropolitan Borough Councils. It defined the social and cultural neighbourhoods, and made proposals for future development based on the principle of creating precincts within the main traffic arteries. Plans for redevelopment of housing areas were worked out at densities of 100, 135 and 200 persons per acre, designed as neighbourhoods which would be provided with community facilities. The second, Patrick Abercrombie's *Greater London Plan 1944* (9), dealt for the first time with the planning of the Greater London Region as a whole, and put forward proposals for new towns and satellites to accommodate the overspill population, which would be displaced by redevelopment at lower densities and better standards of amenity in the central area. Many other cities and towns, particularly those which had suffered extensive war damage, also commissioned advisory plans for reconstruction.

Two other committees with a more direct influence on housing reported in 1944, just before the end of the war. One, the Burt Committee, the Interdepartmental Committee on House Construction, suggested standards of house construction against which were assessed a variety of new methods of house building (*House Construction, 1944*). These were to be used to supplement traditional brick building in post-war conditions of short supply of workers and materials. This committee remained in being during the early post-war years, and continued to assess new systems of building (*House Construction Second Report, 1946 and Third Report, 1948*). Several forms of non-traditional building were approved as suitable for local authorities to finance over a 60 year loan period as " permanent " houses.

The other, the Dudley Committee on the Design of Dwellings, analysed the ways of living of ordinary families in relation to the working core of the house, kitchen, living room, bathroom, etc., and recommended in its report, *Design of Dwellings*, minimum standards which were considerably higher than those of inter-war council houses (10). The three-bedroom five-person house was to have a superficial area of 900 sq. ft., and an outdoor store of 50 sq. ft. There were to be two living rooms (between the wars many " non-parlour " houses had been built with only one). A higher standard of equipment was recommended, the main differences being more fittings in the kitchen, a wash hand basin as well as a bath, a hot water system, and a second WC downstairs.

The report of the Dudley Committee included a report by a study group on *Site Planning and Layout in Relation to Housing* which stressed the close relationship between housing and town planning. It recommended the establishment of residential neighbourhoods not exceeding 10,000 persons, and set out desirable net residential densities according to five types of area in which development was to take place, varying from open areas to central parts of large cities. The land required for housing and community provision for neighbourhoods was analysed.

The plans were made, and hopes were high that post-war reconstruction would be carried out in a way which would ensure that good housing would soon be available to all households.

The post-war period 1945–64

Even before hostilities ceased, a start was made on implementing housing plans which would provide for people eager to return to normal family life after years of living under wartime conditions. A White Paper, *Housing* (Cmnd. 6609), presented to Parliament in March 1945, set out the threefold objectives of a separate dwelling for each family which desired to have one (for which 750,000 dwellings were thought to be needed); the rapid completion of the pre-war slum clearance and overcrowding programmes (a further half-million houses were believed to be necessary for this); and finally, as a long-term objective, a progressive improvement in the conditions of housing, both in standards of accommodation and of equipment. To achieve the last, it was recognised that a continuous programme of new building would be needed.

The programme was ambitious, but the nation was emerging victorious from war and was prepared to think in terms of a housing drive planned as a military operation. The 1945 White Paper proposed that the first two years after the end of hostilities in Europe should be treated as a period of national emergency, when exceptional measures must be taken to meet the housing shortage.

The first concern was to get as many dwelling units into use as possible, whether in existing buildings or new ones; this was to be done by the repair and adaptation of war-damaged houses, by the use of huts and service camps when these were no longer needed for war workers or troops, and also by the production of temporary pre-fabricated bungalows and new permanent houses (Cmnd. 6686, 1945). By the end of 1946, one-third of a million such units had been provided: 80,000 in " prefabs ", 45,000 in conversions and adaptations, 107,000 in repaired unoccupied war-damaged houses, 12,000 in temporary huts and service camps, 25,000 in requisitioned houses, and 52,000 in new permanent houses. About 1¼ million occupied dwellings which had suffered war damage had been repaired (11).

The " pre-fabs " were two-bedroom, factory-built bungalows with a standard plan and equipment. They were financed by the Exchequer and allocated to local authorities who were responsible for their letting and management. Originally steel was to have been used, but those actually produced were mainly built of aluminium; they made no demands on the traditional building industry other than for site work and erection. A few were imported from the United States under lend-lease arrangements. Altogether about 125,000 were erected before the project was brought to an end in 1948. These dwellings were intended to have a 10-year life, but many were in occupation for more than double that time. Although floor areas were small, kitchen and bathrooms were equipped at a high standard compared with most pre-war council housing.

In 1946, the programme for permanent housing was given impetus by the introduction of new higher subsidies for local authority houses (Housing Financial Provisions Act 1946). The Exchequer paid three-quarters of the annual subsidy, and the contribution from the rates was one-quarter, whereas between the wars, the proportions were generally two-thirds and one-third. Additional subsidies were available to meet categories of special need, including areas in which working-class houses were let at unusually low rents, areas where housing would be an exceptionally heavy burden on the rates, houses built on sites liable to subsidence, houses for farm workers, flats on expensive sites, blocks of flats requiring lifts (*i.e.*, those with four or more storeys); also for non-traditional houses using more expensive types of construction, which were encouraged in order to offset the shortage of skilled building labour and of certain traditional building materials.

The national target was set at 240,000 houses a year. 127,541 were completed in 1947, and by 1948 output had reached 206,559. Then, however, it was realised that the building industry had become overloaded; the target was reduced to 200,000 a year, and production was held during the next three years at just over 170,000 a year.

It was a tenet of a strong Labour administration that the government should not only control and plan house production, but also ensure that the allocation of dwellings was on the basis of the most urgent need, and not of capacity to pay. Local authorities were to be the instrument for house production and allocation. The aim was also to create balanced communities in which social classes were to be mixed.

The Housing Act 1949 removed from local authorities the obligation to provide houses for the " working classes " only. Although in practice this term had never been defined in the housing acts, or strictly applied, the implication was that local authorities were now responsible for fulfilling all the housing needs of their areas, and not only those of the working classes.

The 1949 Act also introduced improvement grants payable at the discretion of the local authority to private owners wishing to improve or convert their houses. This meant an extension to urban houses of the type of grant previously available for reconditioning of agricultural workers' cottages. In fact, little use was made of the 1949 Act grants, only 6,000 being paid up to 1953.

Building for sale by private enterprise was severely restricted throughout the period from the end of the war until 1952 when a start was made in easing controls, although the licensing of civil building did not finally come to an end until November 1954. During the period of strict licensing, which was carried out through the local authorities, instructions were given to ensure that the licences to build houses went, and were seen to go, to people in need of a home. The Ministry controlled the number of dwellings to be built in each region. Allocations were made on the basis of the resources of the region, and then broken down into so many dwellings to be built in each local authority area. Private building was the first to be cut when economic conditions made it necessary to reduce output still further.

The standards recommended by the Dudley Committee were adhered to for permanent housing in the first post-war years, although when Aneurin Bevan ceased to be Minister of Health in 1950 the first reduction, the elimination of the second WC in larger houses, took place.

It was the policy of all parties, supported by public opinion, to build as many houses as possible, and the Conservative government which took office at the end of 1951 was committed by election promises to produce 300,000 houses a year. One of the primary reasons for earlier restrictions was the need to economise in imports of soft wood and other materials. The increase in the programme involved relaxing these restrictions even at the expense of burdening the economy with added expenditure outside the country, particularly on imports of timber from Canada and the USA.

Though private building increased from 21,000 houses in 1951 to 60,000 in 1953 and 88,000 in 1954, the main instrument for house production under the new government remained the local authorities, who were encouraged by administrative measures to increase their output. The system of allocations was replaced by one of targets. Local authorities were given the number of dwellings to produce based on local capacity, but were told that if this figure were achieved, they could come back for more. The tight administrative controls over local authority building by the Ministry were also eased and authorities were encouraged to show greater initiative. It was indicated that layouts and designs would be dealt with more speedily if they were prepared by professionally qualified people.

The reduction in standards begun in 1950 continued with a view to making up in quantity what was lost in size and amenity. Floor areas, which averaged 1,050 sq. ft. for a three-bedroom council house at the beginning of 1951, fell to 984 sq. ft. in 1952, 923 sq. ft. in 1953 and 909 sq. ft. in 1954. These reductions were justified on the grounds that designers could, by using ingenuity, produce compact plans and layouts without any loss of amenity. Higher densities would lead to savings in land and the cost of site development, and open plans could be combined with whole house heating, and so would cause little loss of usable living space.

The 300,000 target for house production, which Harold Macmillan as Minister of Housing had pledged himself to reach, was hit in 1953, when 279,000 dwellings were built in England and Wales and 39,000 in Scotland. The following year the figure for England and Wales alone was over 300,000. The problem again became one of avoiding the overloading of the industry and economy. It was difficult to stop private builders, once they had been released from controls. There was a steady increase in their output throughout the 1950s, and the 88,000 houses built in 1954 in England and Wales had almost doubled by 1960 (162,100 houses). This was partly offset by reductions in output of local authorities after 1954, the peak year when 220,924 council houses were built. It was held that the pressure for more houses to overcome the post-war shortage was lessening, but on the other hand, public demand for something to be done about the condition of older houses was mounting.

In November 1953 a White Paper, *Houses: the Next Step* (Cmnd. 8996), was published, setting out the government's proposals for a re-orientation of official policy. It was implemented the following year by the Housing (Repairs and Rents) Act 1954.

The principal innovation was the emphasis to be placed on dealing with obsolete and obsolescent houses. The attack was to be three-pronged. There was to be a renewal of slum clearance, a stepping up of improvement, and encouragement for repairs and maintenance.

The number of houses unfit for habitation included in pre-war clearance programmes in England and Wales was about 472,000 and there were still about 173,500 outstanding at the outbreak of war. 33,700 had been dealt with between that date and March, 1951. It was estimated, therefore, that about 140,000 houses, which had been scheduled as unfit even before the war, were still occupied. The number of houses which had deteriorated into slums in the interval since the pre-war assessment was not known, though the White Paper suggested that it certainly ran into hundreds of thousands. Local authorities were therefore to submit proposals for dealing with them. When the returns were published at the end of 1955, the estimated number of unfit dwellings in England and Wales was 847,100. However, it was later realised that this figure did not give a true picture of the situation, since different local authorities applied different standards in making their assessments. They were influenced inevitably by the general standard in their own area and the numbers with which they felt they could deal.

Policy for slum clearance was based on experience in Birmingham. Under the Town and Country Planning Act 1944, Birmingham City Council had acquired a large area containing some 30,000 sub-standard houses for redevelopment. They could not clear or close them immediately, while the housing shortage remained acute in the area. They had therefore carried out a policy of " make-do-and-mend ". Houses which were to be demolished within about five years were patched up to give tolerable living conditions for the occupants. Those with a life of between five and ten years had work carried out on them at a slightly higher standard, while those which would not be demolished until the second half of a 20 year period were substantially renovated and improved. Local authorities were now given powers and an additional subsidy to acquire houses immediately and patch them up for deferred demolition. Since it is held that a slum house has no value, as it cannot legally be re-let for human habitation, the local authorities paid site value only for these houses.

The second line of policy, for increasing the amount of improvement work to be carried out, was based on an increase in the upper limit of the grant allowed, the raising of the increase which an owner could make in rent to 8 per cent of his part of the cost of the work, and the reduction from 30 years to 15 in the life a house was expected to have to make it eligible for improvement grant. It was judged that the 1949 Act improvement grant had been little used owing to a lack of publicity about it. After the 1954 Act, the Ministry of Housing itself organised a demonstration in London, as did many local authorities in their own areas. Whether due to the more generous assistance available under the Act, or the greater publicity for the benefits of improvement, or the abolition of building licensing and more favourable economic conditions, there was an increase in the numbers of houses improved to over 30,000 in 1955.

The other major innovation of the 1954 Act was that it made the first move since 1939 to deal with repair and maintenance of privately rented houses. When control was imposed in 1939, some dwellings were still let at controlled rents fixed many years before. During the war, it had not been possible to maintain any houses adequately, and the amount which could be spent on repair and maintenance work had been severely limited during the early post-war years by the licensing system. Above all, maintenance costs had trebled as was shown in the report of the Girdwood Committee on the *Cost of House Maintenance*, published in 1953.

Under the 1954 Act, landlords were allowed to increase rents by a figure related to the increase in maintenance costs, calculated on the basis of the difference between the gross and net rateable values. The gross value of a house for rating purposes is the hypothetical rent which, according to the assessment, it would command if the landlord bore the cost of repairs and maintenance. The net, or rateable, value is the gross value less a statutory deduction which the landlord is assumed to require to cover the cost of maintenance and insurance. Thus it was considered logical to relate rent increases made necessary due to increases in the landlord's costs to these figures in which they were supposed to be reflected. The legislation was also designed to ensure that the increased rent was in fact spent on the maintenance of the house. Landlords had to show that their houses were fit and in a good state of repair and that they had spent money on making them so. Tenants who were not satisfied with the conditions of the premises they occupied could apply to the local authority for a certificate of disrepair.

In practice, some 18,000 such certificates were issued in the first six months after the Act was passed, and thereafter the numbers decreased. Undoubtedly, many tenants, of higher standard housing in particular, accepted the increases. High hopes had been expressed that these provisions would encourage landlords to put, and keep, millions of houses in good repair, thus benefiting themselves and their tenants, while at the same time preserving a national asset. However, in practice little was done. Very few of the landlords of the 7¼ million privately rented houses appear to have claimed the increases, possibly because the procedure was too complicated, or the return inadequate, particularly on low rented properties, or because many small landlords had insufficient capital to do repairs, on which in any case they would receive no return until after the work had been completed and the rent could be increased.

Two other provisions of the 1954 Act should be mentioned. The Act exempted housing associations and trusts from rent control (local authorities had never been subject to rent restriction) and it also freed from control new houses and conversions, completed after the Act. Although the first long overdue provision undoubtedly helped housing associations, the second did little to achieve its object of encouraging private enterprise to resume building for letting.

Something, however, was done to encourage owner occupation among people with comparatively low income. In 1954 the government publicised a scheme for a tripartite guarantee by means of which they, the local authorities and the building societies accepted the risk of advancing a higher proportion of the purchase price of a house. It was argued that many purchasers with adequate income to enable them to repay a mortgage found it difficult to deposit up to 20 per cent of the valuation. The scheme was to reduce the proportion of the valuation as a deposit to 10 per cent or 5 per cent for the cheaper houses.

By 1954, housing subsidies were costing the country about £60 million a year. The new subsidised council houses were not all occupied by people in financial need, on the other hand many people who needed better housing could not afford council rents. Costs, and in particular interest rates, had risen since the return of the Conservative party to power in 1951. The Labour government had retained the interest rates at 3 per cent, but by 1956 they had risen to 5¾ per cent. It was believed that the expansion of output during the early 1950s had overcome the most urgent housing shortage, but that there was a need to tackle slum clearance more actively. The New Towns Act 1946 and the Town Development Act 1952, designed to help with the decentralisation of population and industry from the congested centres, were beginning to show results, but is was realised that slum clearance and redevelopment at higher standards of amenity would result in reduced density, and so mean that some of the people now living in the overcrowded central districts of towns could not be rehoused there. A new Act was passed, therefore, the Housing Subsidies Act 1956, justified by its sponsors as a means of reducing investment and spending power, but also of providing economic encouragement to local authorities to concentrate on housing for special purposes.

The 1956 Act reduced the subsidy for housing to meet normal needs at first to £10 a house per year, and gave the Minister power to abolish it, which he did in November 1956, except for dwellings for old and single people. There were, however, subsidies for houses built for rehousing families from slums which were cleared and for housing overspill population in new towns, expanding towns or in schemes in connection with industry. There were higher rates for flats and building on expensive sites. Local authorities were to introduce " realistic " rent policies. Rent rebates, or differential rents, had been recommended by the Housing Management Sub-Committee of the Central Housing Advisory Committee (see Chapter 2) in their report, *Transfers*,

Exchanges and Rents, published at the end of 1953 (fourth report).

By pooling rents and subsidies and also building costs and interest rates, local authorities did not need to balance the historic, economic cost of a particular house or scheme with the rents they charged for it. Houses built when costs and interest rates were low could be let at higher rents, and the rents of the more expensive ones could be reduced. Rent rebate schemes could be used to help the most needy tenants.

Hitherto, there had been a compulsory rate fund contribution which local authorities had to make to their housing revenue accounts proportionate to the Exchequer contribution for each subsidised house. The Housing Subsidies Act 1956 relieved them of this duty.

There was an immediate decrease in the number of houses local authorities completed following this abolition of the " normal needs " subsidy. By 1956, local authority completions dropped to 149,139 in England and Wales compared with nearly 221,000 in 1954 and the fall in output in the public sector continued almost without interruption to 1961, when local authorities built only 98,466. Private building for owner occupation was, however, increasing to overtake council building for the first time since 1945. In 1958 local authorities built 117,438 dwellings and private enterprise 124,087. The trend continued and in 1961, private enterprise built 170,366 houses, 71,900 more than local authorities.

The policy of concentrating local authority housing work on slum clearance was partially successful during the same period. Houses demolished or closed rose from less than 20,000 in 1954 to 47,000 in 1957 and 62,000 in 1961. This was inadequate not only to clear the 850,000 slums which had been estimated as existing in 1955, but also fell far short of the five-year programme to clear 380,000, which local authorities had themselves proposed.

The policy for " realistic " rents was extended to privately let houses, as well as municipal ones—at least that was the intention of the Rent Act 1957, which followed the Housing Subsidies Act in the next year.

The Rent Act 1957 freed the better privately owned houses (those of over £30 rateable value, or £40 in London and Scotland) from any rent control, though there was an encouragement to landlords to offer their tenants a three-year lease. All other privately rented houses remained subject to rent control, but rents were permitted to rise to a new ceiling related to gross value and the extent of the landlord's responsibility for repairs. It was assumed that the poorest houses, which remained controlled, would eventually be acquired by local authorities for slum clearance. All new tenancies, after the landlord had obtained vacant possession, were released from rent control.

The government advocated the Bill on the grounds that it would improve the standard of maintenance of rented property for which old controlled rents were inadequate; maintain the supply of privately owned dwellings to let by encouraging new building for this purpose and discouraging sales to owner occupiers; allow greater mobility of labour; and reduce under-occupation and overcrowding by allowing people to move into houses more suited to their needs rather than encouraging them to cling to statutory tenancies. It was opposed mainly on the grounds that it would merely enrich landlords and enable them to exploit the housing shortage at the expense of tenants.

Another policy to deal with the problem of rents of privately let houses advocated around this time was that they should be taken over by the local authorities, that is " municipalised ". This was propounded mainly by supporters of the Labour party who were prepared to argue that it was undesirable that houses to let should be provided and managed for private gain. Even those who did not oppose such a policy on grounds of self-interest or ideology had grave doubts about the practicability of saddling the public sector with an additional burden of financing and managing millions of older houses, and of virtually reducing all choice of tenure to the alternatives of a council tenancy or home ownership. Whether for these reasons, or because the stock of privately let dwellings was dwindling in any case, it was not until 1974 that social ownership (that is municipalisation and housing association ownership) was actively encouraged (see Chapter 3).

In fact the effect of the Rent Act 1957 varied widely from place to place. It appears to have done something towards improving maintenance in the medium-rented sector. No evidence has been put forward that there was a marked improvement in mobility of tenants, and the privately rented sector continued to decline. In areas of extreme shortage, especially London, fears that it would lead to exploitation were justified. The government introduced an amending Act to safeguard the position of sitting tenants in 1958 (Landlord and Tenant (Temporary Provision) Act 1958). The activities of landlords who exploited the shortage to get rid of protected tenants were personified in the person of Rachman, who operated a racket in North-West London, using bullying tactics to obtain vacant possession and/or high illegal rents.

Housing pressure in Greater London, aggravated by the influx of Commonwealth and other immigrants in certain districts, gave rise to grave concern in the early 1960s, and a government committee under the chairmanship of Sir Milner Holland was set up to investigate the London housing situation, with particular reference to tenant/landlord relationships, including Rachmanism.

The next major piece of housing legislation was the House Purchase and Housing Act of 1959. This had two main objects. One was to encourage owner-occupation by making government loans available to approved building societies in return for their advancing more money for the purchase of older, cheaper houses. These loans were to be made in respect of houses built before 1919, with values up to £2,500.

The second object was to increase the improvement of older houses. For the first time, a new standard grant was introduced which owners could claim as of right if certain conditions were fulfilled. Standard grants were paid as a specified sum towards the cost of installing five standard amenities: a fixed bath or shower in a bathroom; a wash hand basin; a hot water supply; a water closet; and facilities for food storage. The house had to have a 15-year life after improvements were carried out, and contain all five amenities when the work was completed. The old discretionary grants for more thorough-going improvement and conversion work remained in force.

Under the Housing Act 1961, the permitted return on the owner's share of expenditure on improvement work was increased from 8 per cent to 12½ per cent.

The improved conditions, and the introduction of the standard grants, led to increase in the rate at which houses were improved from an average of about 18,000 to over 130,000 in 1960, since when, in spite of a small decline, the numbers of grants approved in England and Wales exceeded 100,000 each year up to 1969, when the Housing Act 1969 gave a further boost to house and area improvement.

The main purpose of the Housing Act 1961, which followed a White Paper, *Housing in England and Wales*, was to introduce a new principle into the subsidy system. The White Paper had taken an optimistic view of the task remaining to local authorities at the time, by suggesting that by the end of 1965 the majority would have dealt with their slum clearance problem. It was recognised that there was still a need for houses for overspill population who could not be accommodated in certain congested areas after these had been redeveloped. Although there had been more than a four-fold increase in the building of small council houses suitable for the elderly, stimulated by the special subsidy of £10 a year for one-bedroom dwellings, it was known that there was still an urgent demand for this type of housing. Conditions in pressure areas, particularly where accommodation in large old houses was being shared by a number of households, were known to be deplorable. The incidence of these problems varied from one area to another, and although local housing authorities were seen as having as their main housing tasks building for slum clearance, for old people, for the relief of overcrowding and other bad conditions, and for overspill, they were to receive subsidy for any approved building which they undertook.

It was argued, however, that those authorities with a large housing stock built at comparatively low cost before 1939 had property which no longer needed to be at a fully subsidised rent, although such property still attracted subsidy under past statutes. Others with few such dwellings, but a currently urgent need for more houses, were in a difficult financial position. The 1961 Act, therefore, provided for subsidies at two basic rates, £24 per house and £8 per house. The rate payable in the case of any particular authority was determined by a resources test. The housing expenditure of the authority as shown in the housing revenue account was compared with the income available to it from rents and Exchequer subsidies, on the assumption that the income from rents equalled twice the gross value of the dwellings for rating purposes. Any authority whose income measured in this way was less than its actual expenditure qualified for the higher basic rate of subsidy; others received the lower one. This method of awarding subsidies gave authorities an incentive to rationalise their rents and use a rent rebate system, so that tenants who were able to afford economic rents would pay them, or something near to them, while those in greater financial need would be helped by the rebates.

These basic subsidies were supplemented by subsidies at the higher rate for housing provided for special purposes, that is for town development and comprehensive development similar to a new town, and to meet the urgent need of industry. Also, authorities whose resources were exceptionally limited could qualify for supplementary subsidies; extra subsidies were available also for building blocks of flats, building on expensive sites, providing agricultural dwellings, or dwellings on land subject to subsidence, or in special materials. Housing associations received the £24 subsidy in all cases.

The 1961 Act included one provision which broke entirely new ground. This was the establishment of a fund of £25 million for making advances to housing associations to provide cost-rent houses. A fund of £3 million was also set up for Scotland. It was argued that houses were needed for those people who did not wish to become owner-occupiers, and were unable to qualify for a new municipal dwelling. This was a pilot project, which became the forerunner of provisions in the Housing Act 1964, to promote cost-rent and co-ownership housing on a bigger scale.

A sub-committee of the Central Housing Advisory Committee, under the chairmanship of Sir Parker Morris, reviewed housing standards and in 1961 issued its report, *Homes for Today and Tomorrow* (13). This proposed that accommodation, design and equipment standards for new housing should be improved to take account of the changes in ways of living. Architects were to be given greater freedom in meeting these standards, which were based on the requirements of households rather than sizes of individual rooms. Publication of the report coincided with one of the frequent periods of economic stringency which continually frustrated housing progress throughout the 1950s and 1960s, so that Parker Morris standards were not made compulsory for local authorities until nearly eight years later (see Chapter 10).

Another White Paper, *Housing* (Cmnd. 2050), issued in 1963, reiterated proposals for increased house production, and a more energetic onslaught on slums and obsolescent housing. Production figures were running at over 300,000 completions a year, and the government hoped that an annual rate of 350,000 would soon be reached. Local authorities were to be encouraged to plan ahead and to use industrialised building systems to supplement traditional building methods. Since long production runs were needed for such systems, authorities were urged to group themselves in consortia which could place large orders. The National Building Agency, a government sponsored body given the task of assessing building systems, was set up to help in the field.

The White Paper was followed by the Housing Act 1964, the main new provisions of which were the establishment of the Housing Corporation with funds to loan to housing associations (called in the Act housing societies) building cost-rent and co-ownership schemes, and the granting of powers to local authorities to declare improvement areas.

The Housing Corporation was allocated £100 million in the first instance from which to make advances to societies which built for letting at cost rents or for co-ownership.

Building societies indicated that they would advance another £200 million; loans were to be two-thirds from a building society and one-third from the Housing Corporation.

The improvement powers given to local authorities by the Act were designed to deal with house improvement on an area basis, and enable them to enforce the carrying out of improvement in such areas. The machinery was rather complicated, and because of the need to safeguard the rights of tenants and landlords, the improvement of an area was a long-drawn-out process. Amendments to the improvement grant provisions already mentioned were complementary to this attempt to improve obsolescent areas.

Trends and developments 1964 to 1972

The Labour government which took office in 1964, with Richard Crossman as Minister of Housing and Local Government, furthered the legislation in the Housing Act 1964. The Minister inaugurated the drive for cost rent and co-ownership housing at a Housing Centre conference in April 1965. During the election campaign, both the Labour and Conservative parties had pledged themselves to step up house production to 500,000 houses a year. The use of industrialised building methods was encouraged to this end. There was also control over large-scale building work other than housing in an attempt to concentrate resources. So far as major legislation in housing and related fields was concerned, however, the government first concentrated on rent control and land.

A short stopgap measure to give security of tenure, the Protection from Eviction Act was passed in 1964 and was followed by the Rent Act 1965 which remains the basis of rent control legislation. In addition to the provisions covering security of tenure and the outlawing of harassment of tenants to obtain vacant possession of a dwelling, it introduced a new principle into rent fixing, that of " fair " rents. For the first time, the rents of privately let dwellings were to depend on valuations made by independent rent officers, but such valuations were to exclude the scarcity element in rent. There was provision for appeal to specially constituted rent assessment committees. This legislation was consolidated in the Rent Act 1968 (see Chapter 5).

A committee was set up in 1969 under the chairmanship of H. E. Francis, Q.C., to review the system of rent regulation under the Rent Acts and to consider the relationship between the codes covering furnished and unfurnished lettings. Their *Report on the Rent Acts* (14), published in 1971 contained much useful information on the operation of rent legislation and its effect on housing at the time. It recognised the difficulties of tenants in stress areas who did not have security of tenure because they lived in furnished lettings. As Mr Francis explained at a Housing Centre meeting (*Housing Review*, May–June 1971, Vol. 20, No. 3), they did not recommend bringing furnished tenancies within the security provisions of the legislation for unfurnished ones because they feared it would do more harm than good by accelerating still more the disappearance from the market of much needed low-rented private accommodation which was already taking place. Lyndal Evans, in a minority report, did not concur in this view. She believed that a distinction could be made between commercial landlords whose tenants should be given greater security and resident landlords who should be able to obtain possession more easily. The committee also made recommendations both designed to encourage landlords to make and keep accommodation available for letting on the one hand and on the other to protect tenants in stress areas. Some of the majority recommendations were subsequently implemented by Part IV of the Housing Finance Act 1972, including progressive conversion of controlled to regulated tenancies and rent agreements between landlord and tenant, subject to a right for either party to apply to the rent officer for a fair rent to be assessed. Much of Part IV of the Housing Finance Act 1972 was repealed by the Housing Rents and Subsidies Act 1975, and protection under rent legislation was extended to furnished tenancies by the Rent Act 1974. The legislation relating to rent control and security of tenure operative in 1976 is dealt with in Chapter 5.

During the same month as the Rent Bill was introduced in 1965, the Milner Holland committee, already mentioned, reported (*Report of the Committee on Housing in Greater London*) (12). This important report highlighted the special problems of London. Its authoritative comments on the shortage of low-rented accommodation of a good standard in certain areas may have reinforced the need to give greater security to tenants. The committee had identified areas of housing stress and suggested that in such areas local authorities should have special powers to exercise control over sales and lettings. It was not until some nine years later however, when the Housing Act 1974 introduced housing action areas, that the idea of special housing powers in special areas was implemented by legislation.

Soon after the Labour government had taken office, a newly created Minister of Land and Natural Resources was charged with the responsibility for land legislation. A Bill was introduced to set up a Land Commission to assemble land required for development and to impose a betterment levy on a proportion of the development value. This proportion was to be increased "at reasonably short intervals". The Land Commission Act 1967 which implemented this policy was a complicated and politically controversial measure and was repealed on a change of government in 1970 (see Chapter 9).

Another piece of legislation affecting housing was the Leasehold Reform Act 1967. This allowed tenants of houses held on long leases to acquire the freehold, or an extended term of 50 years from the end of the existing lease. Provisions covered the price to be paid by a leaseholder for enfranchisement based on the general principle that the bricks and mortar of a house held on a long lease belong to the tenant and the land to the landlord. There are limitations on enfranchisement covering, for example, high-rated houses, certain types of dwellings, the need of a landlord for the house for his own use and provisions for schemes of management for large estates. At the time it was introduced, it was estimated that over one million houses would be affected, but that they were mostly concentrated in South Wales, Birmingham, Lancashire and London. (See also Chapter 9).

During the 1960s, concern was expressed about poor construction of some houses built for sale. The government had been encouraging the voluntary acceptance of standards of construction by house builders through the National House Builders Registration Council (now the National House Building Council), which would reduce the likelihood of such jerry building. (See also Chapter 10). In 1966, local authorities were recommended in MOHLG Circular 19/66 to grant mortgages only on new houses built by a registered house builder, unless its construction had been supervised by a qualified architect or surveyor employed by the purchaser. The Building Societies Association agreed at the same time to recommend their members to impose the same condition on the granting of a mortgage. The NHBRC had a standard specification and an inspection system and also guarantee schemes to safeguard purchasers if major defects developed. These ensured that the necessary remedial work could be done even if the builder concerned had gone out of business. As a result, the majority of house builders sought registration and 95 per cent of them were operating within the scheme by the end of 1969.

In 1967 a change was made in the system of subsidising new building in order to relate the amount of assistance given to interest rates. The Housing Subsidies Act 1967 made subsidies available to the public sector for new housing according to a formula. It was assumed that the " approved cost " of the dwellings provided had been raised by borrowing. The subsidy payable was the excess of the annual loan charges for 60 years on this notional capital sum, calculated at a rate of interest specified by the Minister in an Order laid before Parliament, over the charges calculated at 4 per cent per annum. The rate of interest specified by the Minister was representative of the average rates of interest paid on loans by recipient authorities in the preceding financial year, and was fixed annually. The " approved cost " was the estimated or tender cost at the time that it was accepted, and not necessarily the actual cost, and the Minister had power to limit it to what he considered reasonable and appropriate.

Since this subsidy was based on the actual cost of a particular scheme, its amount varied in direct relationship to capital costs. In order to avoid " an open-ended commitment of Exchequer monies " the cost of housing schemes was therefore limited by a cost yardstick issued by the Ministry. This gave the costs which the Minister would approve according to the densities and sizes of dwellings. It has been retained in use and is described in Chapter 10. In January 1969 it became mandatory for all schemes submitted for loan sanction and subsidies to conform to modified design standards recommended by the Parker Morris committee (see above) and set out in MOHLG Circular 1/68. Prior to this date the standards had been encouraged but were not compulsory.

Payment of additional subsidies under the Housing Subsidies Act 1967 could be made for flats in blocks of four or more storeys, for precautions against subsidence, for houses where the cost was substantially enhanced because special materials were used to preserve the character of the surroundings, for schemes of town development under the Town Development Act 1952 for houses in new towns, and for dwellings on expensive sites. The Minister also had power to give extra financial assistance where otherwise there would be exceptionally high rents or an undue burden on the ratepayers or where there was a substantial transference of industry. There was also a subsidy for hostel accommodation.

Part II of the Housing Subsidies Act 1967 introduced the option mortgage scheme, which was brought into operation in April 1968. This enabled house purchasers to opt for a subsidy in place of tax relief on mortgage interest and so appealed to mortgagors on low incomes who were not paying sufficient tax to make the relief worth while. The subsidy, payable to qualified lenders, reduced the interest paid by the borrower to 2 per cent below the building society rate. It went some way to meet the criticism that tax relief helped those on higher incomes, but not the lower paid house purchasers who most needed financial assistance with their housing costs. It was, however, sometimes difficult for a mortgagor to decide whether he would be better off with tax relief or an option mortgage. Modifications were subsequently made to the option mortgage scheme to take account of higher interest rates and the scheme in operation in 1976 is described in Chapters 5 and 8.

In 1967, the results of the national sample house condition survey carried out by the Ministry of Housing and Local Government and Welsh Office were published. It showed that not only were there still many slums to be dealt with by clearance and redevelopment, but also that many older houses lacking basic amenities were capable of improvement. Further relevant surveys and reports had been published the previous year and in 1968 a White Paper, *Old Houses into New Homes* (Cmnd. 3602), heralded the Housing Act 1969, which provided a new impetus for house and area improvement. This Act and the background to current legislation relating to rehabilitation is dealt with in the first part of Chapter 7, concerned with rehabilitation, as is also the special help given to improvement work in special and intermediate areas from 1971 to 1974 by a higher level of grant being made available in such areas during those years.

Throughout the late 1960s and early 1970s, successive governments, and housing opinion generally, were realising that while the cost of housing subsidies was growing, the aim of providing all households with homes of the right type in the right place at a price or rent they could afford was not being achieved. By pooling the historic costs of houses built when costs were low, the rents of newer council dwellings could be held at a reasonable figure. Yet the system was providing subsidies to some authorities who did not need them, but gave too little to those authorities with the worst problems of slum clearance and shortages. Some council tenants, too, who could have afforded unsubsidised rents, because, for example, there were several wage earners in the household, were enjoying low subsidised ones, while others, perhaps with several dependent children, were having to pay rents which left them with too little to cover other expenditure. Ever since the 1930s local authorities had been urged to use housing subsidies to help through rent rebates those tenants who could not otherwise afford the dwelling they needed. In 1965, the White Paper, *The Housing Programme 1965–1970* (Cmnd. 2838), again urged that subsidies should not be used wholly or even mainly to keep the general level of rents down but to help tenants whose means were small. This was followed in 1967 by MOHLG Circular 46/47 again recommending rent rebates and giving a model scheme in its appendix. Nevertheless, evidence to the Estimates Committee of the House of Commons on Housing Subsidies in the 1968–69 parliamentary session showed that the majority of authorities had no scheme (Report of committee) (15). No form of rent relief related to income had ever been available for tenants of dwellings rented from private landlords. Although the rents of such dwellings were often low because of rent restriction legislation, it was also known that many of the poorest households were in fact living in the privately rented sector. In 1968, however, Birmingham City Council pioneered a scheme under a private Act, the Birmingham Corporation Act 1968, which gave them power to pay rent allowances to tenants in furnished and unfurnished privately rented dwellings. Reporting on the scheme in 1972 at a Housing Centre Conference (*Housing Review*, Vol. 21, No. 1, January-February 1972) the chairman of Birmingham's housing committee said it had run smoothly, but the take-up among tenants who would probably have been eligible had been disappointing.

Central government was very chary of interfering with the autonomy of local authorities in rent fixing and until 1972 only exhortation was used to encourage councils to introduce rent rebate systems. In 1971, the Conservative government published a White Paper, *Fair Deal for Housing* (16), proposing long-term changes in the system of housing finance, including rent rebates and allowances. The following year the *Housing Finance Act 1972* was passed introducing compulsory national rent rebates and allowances schemes for tenants of unfurnished lettings in both the public and the private sector. These were extended the following year by the Furnished Lettings (Rent Allowances) Act 1973 to tenants of furnished lettings. The relevant provisions of the Housing Finance Act 1972 covering these schemes survived when much of the rest of the Act was repealed when a Labour government succeeded the Conservative one in 1974. The schemes are described as they operate now in Chapters 3 and 8.

Prior to the introduction of the Housing Finance Act, there had been a general consensus of opinion that some reform of the housing finance system was needed. When he was Minister of Housing and Local Government, Anthony Greenwood (later Lord Greenwood of Rossendale) writing in the *Housing Review*, (Vol. 19, No. 1, January-February 1970) referred to the " longer term review of housing finance " which he had initiated, and the late Lord Fiske, at the time the Housing Centre's chairman, gave an address at the Centre's Annual General Meeting in the autumn of 1970 advocating far-reaching reforms (*Housing Review*, Vol. 19, No. 6, November-December 1970. " Housing Finance—Is it Time for a Change?"). Housing subsidies from the Exchequer to the public sector amounted to £157,000 million in 1970–71 with an additional £60–£65 million from local authorities' rates funds. At the same time, some £200 million was being foregone in tax relief on mortgage interest. The White Paper, *Fair Deal for Housing* (16), estimated that, if the system then operating continued, subsidies to the public sector would have amounted to £300,000 million per annum within the next 10 years. In fact, they were to exceed this figure long before the 10 years were up.

In spite of the recognition on all sides that something needed to be done, Housing Finance Act 1972 when it came was bitterly attacked by the Labour Opposition both in and out of Parliament. The ideological differences between the two major political parties about the State's duty in relation to housing aligned those against it who wanted to see housing treated as a social service to which all had a right, and which should be paid for primarily out of national taxation; while support came from those who regarded housing as a normal economic service, similar to the provision of food and clothing, with special arrangements made to assist financially people and areas in need. On the more practical side, there were doubts whether or not the new system would in fact distribute the total financial resources available to the nation for housing rightly between the different categories of householders, and among different agencies and areas.

As well as being controversial, the 1972 Act was long and complex. Eight new subsidies were introduced. Some of these were temporary ones to cover the transition to the new system. Others gave financial assistance with the rising costs of new building, with town development and with slum clearance. There were also subsidies towards an authority's rent rebate contributions and to cover the cost, other than the administrative cost, of the rent allowances for tenants of private landlords. There was also a hostel subsidy and new subsidies for housing associations. The latter are mentioned in Chapter 6.

The subsidies towards rent rebates and allowances were criticised adversely by some local authorities because in the first case they required a contribution from the rates and in the second because the cost of administration fell on the general rates. It was argued that they were less housing subsidies than relief of poverty, the cost of which should properly be borne by the national Exchequer. The main subsidies were designed to phase in a system of " fair " rents for the public sector which it was believed would enable the existing subsidies to be withdrawn and the new permanent ones to cover the help necessary for slum clearance and new building. The fair rents which were to be charged were to be fixed on the same basis as fair rents under the Rent Acts. Local authorities were to submit the rents they thought appropriate which would be scrutinised by rent scrutiny boards consisting of qualified persons appointed by the Minister, to ensure uniformity between one area and another. Increases to fair rent level were to be phased. If the increased rent income caused a surplus to show on an authority's housing revenue account, a part of this had to be paid to the Exchequer.

A number of points were made in criticism of the new system. It was held that it removed from local authorities autonomy in fixing rents and put it into the hands of outside assessors with no responsibility to the electorate. It introduced a so-called profit element into a local authority service in that a surplus over historic cost might result. Moreover, part of that surplus had to be passed to the Exchequer. Council tenants were treated unfairly in that they had no direct appeal against the rent assessments, whereas private tenants had direct access to the rent officer and might appeal to the rent assessment committee. The assessment of fair rents (market rent less scarcity value), though the best way so far devised for relating rents to value without allowing shortages to be exploited, was inevitably subjective and, if done in relation to fair rents already existing in the private sector, was not comparing like with like. For example, the large and growing public sector could not be compared with the small and dwindling private sector. Some thought too that the fair rents fixed in the private sector were arbitrary. It was argued that the Act was not comprehensive in that it dealt only with the public sector; it restricted subsidies to council tenants closely to household need whereas tax relief on mortgage interest in the owner-occupied sector was left untouched and was in no way related to financial need. As mentioned above, the omission of furnished tenancies from the provisions for housing allowances, which was criticised when the Act was first introduced, was remedied by further legislation the following year.

A number of authorities initially refused to implement the Housing Finance Act 1972 in England and Wales and its counterpart in Scotland, the Housing (Financial Provisions) (Scotland) Act 1972. There were provisions for commissioners to be appointed to do so in any authority's area where this occurred. In a few cases, commissioners were in fact appointed, although by the end of 1972 most authorities had agreed to fulfil their statutory duties under the Acts. As another method of enforcing compliance, subsidy could be withheld. Under the Local Government Act 1933, moreover, councillors could be surcharged for the amounts lost because the increased rents were not charged. At Clay Cross in Derbyshire, 11 councillors were surcharged and a commissioner appointed. The Labour Party, although officially opposed to refusals to implement an Act of Parliament which had reached the Statute Book by constitutional process, included in their election programme in 1974 promises to repeal the Act. After they were returned to power, the main provisions introducing the fair rent system into the public sector were repealed. Also, the Housing Finance (Special Provisions) Act 1975 was passed to prevent surcharges being made arising out of the Housing Finance Act 1972.

The decade of the 1960s and the first years of the 1970s saw many changes in housing policies and practice. In addition to the housing legislation to which reference has been made above, there were two radical changes made in local government which inevitably had their effect on housing, and which were implemented by the London Government Act 1963 and the Local Government Act 1972. In 1971, the Department of the Environment was set up, combining in one central government department the administration of town and country planning, housing, local government, transport and building, with several ministers and an overlord as Secretary of State for the Environment. Housing output was built up to a record level of 413,700 dwellings a year in 1968, though it subsequently fell. It was realised that the overall national housing shortage of dwellings over households was being met, but paradoxically, symptoms of local shortage and stress became more acute and were manifested in increased homelessness and long local authority waiting lists for council houses. Advances were made in the establishment of Parker Morris design standards for new public sector housing, and of construction standards in the private sector. In the technical field, metric measurements were introduced for all building work. Industrialised, or system, building methods were further encouraged, but the heavy panel systems for high rise blocks of flats lost in popularity, mainly because such housing types were socially unacceptable for family housing. The progressive collapse of the wall of such a block after an explosion due to defective gas equipment at Ronan Point in London served to reinforce antagonism to this form of housing. A series of government advisory reports on such matters as London housing Milner Holland (12), housing management (17), personal social services (18), older houses (19), and the operation of the rent acts (14) promoted debate, and sometimes led to legislation. Many of these reports and the issues they dealt with are of basic importance to housing work in 1976 and have therefore been dealt with in the appropriate sections of the Guide. The main housing legislation relevant and operative now is also considered in greater detail in subsequent chapters.

CHAPTER 2

The Present Position

The review of the historical background to housing policies and problems in the previous chapter is taken up to the early 1970s when several major new legislative provisions were made, and changes in housing policies and practice introduced. Before those which are operative in 1976 are considered in greater detail, this chapter outlines in brief the housing position in that year —the framework of agencies controlling and producing houses, and the quantity, condition and tenure of the housing stock, together with forecasts of housing need and a note on housing finance, which is the subject of Chapter 8. A list of the main statutes affecting housing up to the end of 1976 is given in an Appendix.

The national framework for housing

National housing policy, the responsibility of Parliament, is administered by the Department of the Environment (DOE Circular 1/71), which, as has been mentioned in Chapter 1, also controls town and country planning, local government, and building, with the Secretary of State for the Environment responsible for policy. The Department of the Environment also decided transport policy up to September 1976, when this was transferred to a separate Ministry of Transport, and, at the same time, the Secretary of State for the Environment, in addition to his other duties, was given the responsibility for the development of inner city areas.

The Minister for Housing and Construction is responsible for housing programmes and finance; house improvement; building regulations; new towns; relations with the building and civil engineering industry; building research and development; government accommodation at home and overseas; building for the armed forces, the Post Office, research establishments and the prison service; royal parks, palaces and ancient monuments; and since September 1976, for planning, development control and land, formerly under a planning minister.

The former Ministry of Housing and Local Government had been created in 1951 to take over the housing functions previously exercised by the Ministry of Health (and earlier still by the Local Government Board), and the town and country

34

planning functions which immediately prior to that date had been the responsibility of a separate department. The fact that housing was at one time administered by the Ministry of Health reflects its origin as a public health service in the nineteenth century.

In 1969, a Minister of State for Local Government and Planning had been appointed, with overall responsibility for local government, planning and transport; the Ministries of Housing and Transport had remained in being, but had been co-ordinated under him.

The appropriate central government department for housing in Wales is the Welsh Office, in Scotland the Scottish Development Department and in Northern Ireland the Department of the Environment for Northern Ireland.

The provision and administration of public rented housing in Northern Ireland is unique in the United Kingdom. The administration of housing in Northern Ireland was reviewed in 1969 following the community troubles during the summer of that year and the idea formulated of a central housing authority which would take housing out of politics. The Northern Ireland Housing Executive was set up by the Act of that name, passed in 1971. This set up a nine-man committee, the majority nominated by the Secretary of the Department and some appointed by a Housing Council representing all the local authorities. In October 1971 the former Northern Ireland Housing Trust was taken over by the Housing Executive and during 1972 all local authority housing in the province passed into their control, followed by housing in the new and expanded towns belonging to the development commissions. Thus by April 1973 the Northern Ireland Housing Executive had become the first comprehensive regional housing authority in the British Isles. Unfortunately, the unsettled conditions which have persisted since the Executive was set up have made its task of improving housing conditions there a very difficult one in many areas. The *Fifth Annual Report of the Housing Executive* sets out in detail the achievements of the Executive from 1 April 1975 to 31 March 1976 in the face of a complex range of difficulties.

Legislation affecting England is initiated by the Secretary of State for the Environment, and that affecting Wales by the Secretary of State for Wales, although the two are normally in line. The Secretary of State for Scotland may initiate separate housing Acts to accord with the different Scottish legal system and conditions. Control over housing development is operated through the respective department's administration of statutory powers, and in particular through its power to sanction subsidies and loans for housing development in the public sector (local authorities, development corporations, etc.). The Ministry advises and guides the efforts of local authorities, but as housing agencies they possess autonomy within the Housing Acts in the adminis- tration and management of their housing service, although the Housing Finance Act 1972 temporarily deprived them of their power to fix rents for their properties absolutely, and counter- inflation legislation has restricted rent increases. Under the Hous- ing Acts, statutory housing standards are imposed. Standards of construction are subject to special building regulations which are administered by the local authorities.

Until 1975, the Central Housing Advisory Committee, which was set up under the provisions of section 24 of the Housing Act 1935, advised the Minister responsible for housing on matters of housing policy and practice. The Minister was its permanent chairman and he appointed the members, who were experts in different aspects of housing. From time to time, sub-committees were appointed to examine special aspects of housing, such as management, design of dwellings, and to make recommenda- tions; many of the reports issued by the Central Housing Advisory Committee are listed in the bibliography. There was a separate Scottish Housing Advisory Committee. The Housing Rents and Subsidies Act 1975, however, abolished the Central Housing Advisory Committee.

There had been a housing management adviser to the Ministry responsible for housing from 1944 to 1973. In April 1976 the Department of the Environment appointed a housing adviser to determine the organisation and working arrangements of a pro- fessional advisory unit, to promote good professional practice within housing organisations and to advise the Department on matters relating to its housing policy. A housing services advisory group was set up to provide essential support for the activities of the housing services advisory unit which has its nucleus within the Department.

The Housing Development Directorate also works within the Department of the Environment, carries out research and develop- ment projects, and produces design bulletins, available from HMSO, on all manner of topics connected with housing.

From time to time, the Department of the Environment sets up advisory and study groups to advise on housing matters and on priorities. The following list gives date of establishment and date due to report of groups working at March 1976 (*Hansard*: written answer to Parliamentary Question 17.3.76) it excludes ad hoc and official groups set up as part of the normal depart- mental activity.

Housing Finance Review Advisory Group—est. April 1975—

recommendations of the review were expected to be published in the spring or early summer of 1976, but are not now expected until early 1977. See later under finance.

Working Group on House Purchase Finance—est. October 1975—first stage of the work covered by the group nearing completion in 1976.

Joint Advisory Committee on Building Society Mortgage Finance—est. October 1973—advice provided on a continuing basis.

Housing Services Advisory Group—est. December 1975—advice provided on a continuing basis—see above.

Working Group on New Forms of Housing Tenure—est. November 1975—preliminary report to be considered as part of the housing finance review.

Study Group on Programmes of Social Ownership and Renovation of Council Dwellings—est. May 1975—first report has been produced by the group which is expected to continue its work for an indefinite period.

Working Party on Housing Cost Yardstick—est. June 1975—no fixed date for completion of the work.

Action Group on London Housing—est. September 1971—advice provided on a continuing basis.

Advisory Committee on Rent Rebates and Allowances—est. March 1973—advice provided on a continuing basis.

Mobile Homes Review—est. December 1974—report expected before the end of 1976.

Construction and Housing Research Advisory Council—est. late 1971—advice provided on a continuing basis.

Advisory Group of Chief Officers on Local Authority Housebuilding—est. November 1975—expected to complete work about May 1977.

(Some of these reports have now been published.)

Agencies for housing provision

It is possible to categorise housing in a number of different ways—by forms of tenure, by type of agency which carried out the development, or indeed by its physical form, standard, price, age or condition. In the *Guide* the broad divisions of the public sector and the private sector are used. The former includes local authority housing, housing provided by new town development corporations and by housing associations, dealt with in Chapters

3, 4 and 6 respectively; the latter includes owner-occupation and renting of privately owned dwellings (see Chapter 5).

The public sector

Housing agencies operating in the public sector are (a) the local authorities, (b) new town development corporations, (c) most housing associations, and (d) some special agencies.

(a) Local authorities

At the beginning of 1972, the local authorities responsible for housing were the councils of county boroughs, boroughs, urban districts and rural districts, the 32 London borough councils, the Greater London Council and the Common Council of the City of London. There were 1,400 local housing authorities outside London in England and Wales, ranging in size from Birmingham, with a population of over one million, to rural districts, with a population of only two or three thousand. In Scotland, housing authorities included the large and small burghs, and the county councils in respect of landward areas.

Local government was reviewed by the Royal Commission on Local Government in England (the Redcliffe-Maud Commission) and the Royal Commission on Local Government in Scotland (the Wheatley Commission), both of which reported in 1969. Proposals for reform in Wales were also under consideration at the same date. A White Paper, *Local Government Proposals for Reorganisation* (Cmnd. 4584, HMSO) and plans for local government rationalisation in Scotland and Wales were published in February 1971. The Local Government Act 1972, passed in November 1972, reorganised local government in England (outside London where reorganisation had taken place in 1965), Wales and Scotland, as follows:

England. London remained as set out above, with the Greater London Council and 32 London boroughs and the City of London the primary housing authorities.

Outside London, there are six metropolitan counties and 39 new county areas. The metropolitan counties comprise 36 districts with populations varying from 177,000 to over 1,000,000; and in the new county areas, 296 new districts set up in place of the former 949 authorities. Populations vary from just under 50,000 to over 200,000, but most are around 100,000. The councils of the new districts, some of which have acquired borough status (primarily a prestige designation, not materially affecting their powers and duties) since 1972, are the primary housing authorities, with the county councils having reserve powers.

Wales. Reorganisation in Wales reduced the former local

authority structure with 181 county, borough and district councils (together with over 600 parish councils) to a more uniform system comprising eight county councils and 37 district councils. Again, the district councils are the primary housing authorities.

Scotland. There are eight mainland regions, and two regions based on the Orkney and Shetland Island groups. These regions have 49 district authorities responsible for all usual housing functions.

Local authorities throughout Britain are not only agencies for the provision of housing but also have wide responsibilities over the standard of the housing in occupation in their areas, as described in Chapter 3.

A comparatively new feature of the local authority scene is the Ombudsman system for the investigation of complaints of injustice caused by maladministration in the local government service.

In England, by legislation in 1967, the Ombudsman was appointed to consider complaints of injustice arising from malad-ministration by central government departments, and subsequently Part III of the Local Government Act 1974 made statutory pro-vision for the Ombudsman system to apply to local government, as part of a world-wide movement showing concern for the indivi-dual and his or her difficulty in relating to organisations which seem to be growing larger and larger and more and more remote from the general public.

The statutory framework within which the system operates is that the 1974 Act provides for two local Commissions, one for England and one for Wales. The separate legislation for Scotland is different. In the Commission for Local Administration in England, there are three local Commissioners, together with the Parliamentary Commissioner who is also the Health Service Commissioner, who have the powers of High Court judges with regard to examining witnesses, asking for written material and conducting enquiries. There is no appeal against the Ombuds-man's decision, but at the same time the Ombudsman has no right to impose a ruling on a local authority.

In April 1975 a free booklet, *Your Local Ombudsman*, was issued, giving details of the operation of the complaints service, and later a leaflet. The emphasis in both was that a complaint should go first to the local authority, then to a local councillor, and only then, if the complaint were not dealt with at the local level, should the complainant exercise his right to go direct to the Ombudsman. In the first year, there were 691 planning com-plaints, 488 housing, and 208 education complaints, the rest being relatively minor. The number of housing complaints had risen in

Greater London and the South East and was far greater than in the North; such complaints could be classified as being due to delays, failures and mistakes, and many concerned central heating schemes and improvement grants.

(b) New Town Development Corporations

Under the New Towns Act 1946 the Minister was empowered to appoint development corporations to plan and carry out the development of new towns or the major development of existing towns. Town expansion under the Town Development Act 1952 is an exercise in which two different authorities are involved, but no new development corporation is set up. (See Chapters 4 and 9.)

(c) Housing associations

The housing association movement has a long and interesting history in providing rented and co-operatively owned housing of different kinds to meet multifarious social and general needs. Although housing associations own a numerically small proportion of the housing stock, their work is important in meeting needs for rented housing not always provided for either by local authorities or the private sector, for example, special purpose housing with a strong social welfare element and the less traditional forms of tenure such as co-ownership and co-operative. Except for a few cost-rent and co-ownership schemes, housing associations use mainly public funds and operate within the public sector. The Housing Act 1974 offered opportunities for the expansion of the movement. A general review is given in Chapter 6.

Under the Housing Act 1974, the Housing Corporation (set up by the Housing Act 1964 to make loans to cost-rent and co-ownership housing societies to enable them to meet the whole or part of any expenditure incurred in carrying out their objects) was given much wider powers in relation to the housing association movement which included the establishment and maintenance of a register of housing associations and the supervision and regulation of registered associations. Over 2,000 associations had been registered by 1976, out of a total of 2,620 applications. The extensive powers of the Housing Corporation and the grants and loans available to registered housing associations are also described in Chapter 6.

(d) Other special agencies

Some housing provision is also made by government departments and public authorities. The Ministry of Defence, for instance, provides married quarters for service personnel, and also some housing for key civilians, e.g., at Royal Ordnance Factories; and the Forestry Commission provides estates for housing their employees in remote places. Estates owned by other public authorities, such as the UK Atomic Energy Authority, house scientific and skilled technical staff and other key employees; and public authorities, such as the Crown Estate Commissioners and the Church Commissioners, also own and manage housing estates as well as other property. Some of these bodies use housing associations for their housing work. There are also two large government sponsored housing associations, the Scottish Special Housing Association and the North Eastern Housing Association; see Chapter 6.

The private sector

(a) Privately rented housing

Until after the first world war, most housing to let was provided by landlords as a business undertaking, and the rents charged were determined by the normal process of supply and demand. The standards to which housing accommodation was built were, and still are, regulated by building by-laws and statutory requirements. (See Chapters 1 and 10.) The history of rent control, which was first introduced in 1915, is also described in Chapter 1, and current controls in Chapter 5.

(b) Owner-occupation

The production of new housing in the private sector is now very largely confined to building houses and flats for sale to occupiers. Flat-buying has been steadily on the increase since the sixties. In 1969, 3·8 per cent of UK dwellings mortgaged to building societies were flats or maisonettes; by 1974, the figure had risen to 6·5 per cent; in 1975, it was 7·1 per cent, and by the first three-quarters of 1976, averaged 7·3 per cent. In inner London and in Scotland, flats have long been accepted, but it is only in the last decade or so that the idea of buying such a unit has spread to the provinces.

Most purchasers of houses and flats are able to buy through a mortgage loan secured on the dwelling and paid off over a period of years. Building societies have as their primary function the making of advances to house purchasers on mortgage, though this type of advance is also obtainable from other institutions (insurance companies, banks, etc.), and from local authorities who lend to purchasers of houses for their own occupation. (See Chapters 3, 5 and 8.)

The housing stock

In the past 25 years the number of homes in Britain has increased by 40 per cent to a total of 20 million in 1976. Five million dwellings date from before 1900; of these 1·7 million were built before 1870 and there was a further 1·7 million built between 1900 and the end of the first world war (1).

About 800,000 dwellings are unfit for habitation though structurally sound, while another million lack some of the basic amenities. In terms of these amenities, however, the quality of housing has improved very considerably since 1951, as the following table shows:

Housing Conditions: Possession of Amenities (Great Britain)

*Percentage of all households
entirely without
certain amenities*

	1951	1961	1971
Fixed bath	37·6	22·4	9·1
Water closet: internal or external	7·7	6·5	1·1
Water closet: internal	—	—	11·5
Hot water tap	—	21·8	6·5

*Percentage of all households
sharing certain amenities*

	1951	1961	1971
Fixed bath	7·5	4·4	3·2
Water closet: internal or external	14·9	6·7	4·1
Water closet: internal	—	—	3·1
Hot water tap	—	1·8	1·9

Source: Social Trends, 1973.

Detailed information about the conditions and amenities in older houses was obtained through a sample survey carried out for the then Ministry of Housing by 26 public health inspectors early in 1967, and a second National House Condition Survey was undertaken in 1971. The latter survey showed that of the 17,100,000 dwellings in England and Wales at that time, 1,244,000 (7·3 per cent) were unfit and 2,866,000 (16·8 per cent) lacked one or more of the basic amenities. The following table gives the numbers and percentages of dwellings in England and Wales lacking the basic amenities:

	Percentage	Number in thousands
Inside WC	11·9	2,032
Fixed bath in a bathroom	9·5	1,630
Wash basin	11·9	2,043
Hot and cold water at three points	13·9	2,374
Sink	·5	84

2,747,000 dwellings needed repairs estimated to cost £250 or over. The highest proportion of the unfit houses, 51·8 per cent were rented from private owners and landlords other than local authorities and new town corporations. Proportions of unfit dwellings in other tenures were: owner-occupied 28·5 per cent, rented from local authorities and new towns 4·7 per cent, vacant 13·0 per cent and closed 2·0 per cent (*Better Homes; The Next Priorities*). It has been estimated that about 2·5 million of the houses in need of attention are capable of being improved to the 12-point standard. (*House Improvement Grants. Government Observations on the Tenth Report from the Expenditure Committee, January 1974. Cmnd. 5529.*)

A third survey of the structural condition of houses in England was started in September 1976 by the Department of the Environment. The results of this survey, which covered some 9,000 dwellings in 216 local authorities, will provide valuable information as to the structural condition of the housing stock in 1976. The sample in this survey was about 50 per cent larger than in 1967 and 1971, and will enable broad regional as well as national conclusions to be drawn. The previous surveys covered both England and Wales, but in 1976 housing in Wales was covered by a separate survey.

For the first time, in 1976, it was decided to undertake a social survey of the households occupying the dwellings in the physical survey sample in order to relate information on physical condition to the social and economic circumstances of the occupants.

Improvement and rehabilitation policies and programmes are considered in detail in Chapter 7.

Housing tenure

There has been a marked change during the last half century in the numbers and proportions of houses in the different categories of tenure. In 1914, of the 8·5 million houses in Britain, about 90 per cent were rented privately and 10 per cent were owner-occupied; the number owned by local authorities was insignificant. Figures for housing tenures in the United Kingdom from 1950 to 1975 are shown in the following table:

Stock of Dwellings by Tenure UK

Year ending	No. in thousands	Owner-occupied	No. in thousands	Local authority and new town corporations	No. in thousands	Private rented and other tenures	Total
1950	4,100	29%	2,500	18%	7,300	53%	13,900
1960	6,967	42%	4,400	27%	5,233	32%	16,600
1970	9,567	50%	5,848	30%	3,768	20%	19,183
1975	10,740	53%	6,390	31%	3,220	16%	20,350

Source: *Social Trends, 1974.* Nationwide Building Society Occasional Bulletin 134, 1976.

The diminishing supply of privately rented accommodation has led many who were formerly housed by a private landlord to look to the local authority for the provision of a home. Also, the increase in the number of elderly people, often unable to purchase a home of their own or to maintain and manage their own property, has resulted in many more of the aged being on local authority waiting lists.

To help to meet continued need for rented housing, and to improve housing conditions in the private sector where the highest proportion of unfit houses unlikely to be improved by their owners occurs, local authorities have been encouraged to increase their housing stock through the Labour Government's policy of progressive social ownership of private residential property. At the same time, housing associations have been expanding their activities, both with new development and rehabilitation of older houses, since the passing of the Housing Act 1974.

The dwellings most likely to change categories are, therefore, the older privately rented dwellings, which, if preserved, may be sold for owner-occupation or bought for rehabilitation by a local authority or a housing association or, if demolished, may be replaced by municipal rented dwellings.

The implications and effects of these and other trends in housing tenure are considered in Chapters 3, 5 and 6 which deal with local authority housing, the private sector and housing associations respectively, in Chapter 11 which considers the social aspects of housing, and in Chapter 12 which looks at the future of housing.

Estimate of housing need

In crude terms, in 1975 there was an excess of dwellings over households in Great Britain, as shown in the following table:

Dwelling stock and households UK, in thousands

	No. of households	No. of dwellings
1951	14,554*	13,900*
1961	16,189	16,660
1965	17,960	17,801
1971	18,317	19,457
1975	19,500	20,350

* Great Britain. *Source: Social Trends, 1971, 1974.* Nationwide Building Society Occasional Bulletin 134, April 1976.

The position regionally in 1971 was:

Regional Dwelling Stock and Households, 1971

Region	Households	Dwellings	Percentage excess of dwellings over households
Northern	1,100,460	1,161,000	5·2
Yorks and Humberside	1,649,610	1,736,000	5·0
East Midlands	1,144,950	1,197,000	4·3
East Anglia	569,450	614,000	7·3
South West	1,279,750	1,349,000	5·1
South East	5,915,475	5,929,000	0·2
West Midlands	1,676,660	1,729,000	3·0
North West	2,272,660	2,358,000	3·6

Source: Housing and Construction Statistics, 1972. Census 1971.

Although in all the conurbations except Greater London there is a surplus of dwellings over households, there is in every one a serious problem of overcrowding and homelessness, as the following table for 1971 shows:

Households in Conurbations, 1971

Conurbation	Excess dwellings over households		Number of overcrowded [1] persons	Number of homeless families
Tyneside	16,665	5·6%	40,870	[2]
West Yorkshire	27,975	4·4%	67,700	[2]
Greater London	−115,815	−4·5%	362,515	3,256
West Midlands	12,215	1·5%	118,735	[2]
Merseyside	16,780	3·9%	51,855	[2]
South East Lancashire	32,800	3·8%	78,270	[2]

[1] Overcrowding taken as more than 1·5 persons per room.
[2] Remaining 2,203 families homeless at 31 December 1971 not broken down into conurbations.

Source: Census 1971, Housing and Construction Statistics, 1973, DHSS Report, 1972.

The official estimate for housing need in England and Wales made in the White Paper, The Housing Programme 1965/70 (2), was based on the following needs: (a) to replace unfit houses already identified as slums; (b) to replace old houses not yet slums but not worth improving; (c) to overcome shortage. Additional needs arising annually were: (d) to replace losses due to redevelopment, road widening etc.; (e) to keep up with new household formation.

With regard to (e), the average size of household is decreasing, creating a demand for more homes in spite of a stable population. The dramatic rise in the proportion of smaller households between 1961 and 1971 is shown in the following table:

	% 1961	% 1971
1 Person	11·9	18·1
2 Persons	29·8	31·5
3 Persons	23·4	18·9
4 Persons	19·1	17·2
5 Persons	9·2	8·3
6 or more Persons	6·7	6·0

Source: Social Trends, No. 6, 1975. HMSO.

The increase in the number of elderly people has already been noted—the elderly formed 16·6 per cent of the population in 1973 compared with 6·8 per cent in 1911 and 13·6 per cent in 1951—and the proportion of elderly living alone has increased:

United Kingdom

Percentage of elderly in each sex and age groups who live alone and aged:	Men			Women		
	1951	1966	1971	1951	1966	1971
Males 65–74/						
Females 60–74	6·5	9·0	10·9	15·6	23·1	27·0
75 or over	10·5	14·7	17·7	23·1	31·4	37·5

Source: *Social Trends, No. 5, 1974.* HMSO.

Undoubtedly, many more smaller households would form if suitable accommodation were available, and these " potential " households should be taken into account in any estimate of housing need.

The Secretary of State for the Environment, speaking in Birmingham in September 1976, said that the latest DOE estimate indicated that there would be an increase of two million households between 1974 and 1986. He referred to the difficulty that with the existing housing stock the mix does not always fit local needs. " Even a net housing surplus can only equal equilibrium between need and supply if all the houses are not only of the right size and type, but all in the right place." He suggested that the way to solve real housing needs was to regard housing as " a series of interlinked and interacting local problems, with the amount of public financial support sensitively tuned to the housing needs of each area ".

Calculations by the National Economic Development Office in 1976 for its work on a forward housing strategy produced a figure of 275,000 houses to meet housing need. This allowed for the demolition of about 50,000 slums and 10,000 other properties together with 160,000 homes for additional households, 35,000 to house concealed households and reduce involuntary over-crowding and 20,000 towards more vacancies and second homes.

Final house building figures for 1976 are likely to show the levels of starts on new houses and flats by councils and private firms to be 175,000 and 155,000 respectively, but possible targets for 1977 are estimated to be about 250,000.

The social aspects of changing population structure are discussed in Chapter 11, and the capacity of the building industry to meet housing demand is considered in Chapter 10.

Comparison with EEC countries

The achievements of Britain's housing programme compared to other EEC countries is shown in the UN *Annual bulletin of housing and statistics for Europe—1974*. Britain's success in the field is evident in the fact that while the figures for new houses completed in Britain have decreased substantially since 1970, the number of houses per 1,000 of population has continued to rise (Table I).

Table I. New housing output

	New houses completed (1,000s)			Number of houses per 1,000 inhabitants			Houses built per 1,000 inhabitants for	
	1970	1973	1974	1970	1973	1974	1973	1974
UK	368·2	315·4	290·3	346	355	358	5·6	5·2
France	470·2	517·8	515·8	320·4	–	–	9·9	9·8
Germany	478·1	714·2	604·4	341·3	365	374	11·5	9·7
Italy	377·2	196·2	–	319·4	326·5	–	3·6	–
Denmark	50·6	55·6	48·6	364	386	392	11·1	9·6
N'lands	118	156·3	147·2	289	310	317	11·6	10·9
Belgium	45·9	64·1	–	317·5	383	–	6·7	–
Sweden	109·8	97·5	85·3	–	–	–	12·0	10·5
Ireland	13·6	23·9	25·4	245	248	249	7·9	8·2

Table II shows that in quality our houses compare favourably with houses in countries where more have been built in relation to the population. For instance, Britain's average 4·6 rooms per dwelling compares very favourably with such countries as France which averages only 3·6 rooms per dwelling and even Germany where, although 70 per cent of its new houses were in rural areas (Britain and France produced 71 per cent and 72 per cent respectively of its houses in urban areas), the average is 4·3 rooms per dwelling. The figures indicate that all the EEC countries now provide the vast majority of new houses with bathrooms (assuming that the provision of a fixed bath or shower also indicates a WC as well), although Britain is the only country to provide every new house with a bath.

Table II. New construction 1973–74

	Av. No. of Rooms/ Dwellings	Percentage of dwellings with bath or shower	Percentage of 1–2 dwelling houses
UK	4·6	100	73·1
France	3·6	99+	43·9
Germany	4·3	99·6	39
Italy	4·1		26·9
Denmark	4·8	99+	71·7
Holland	4·8	99	78
Belgium	5·2	99·3	64·7
Sweden	4·4	99·3	45·4
Ireland	5·1	99·2	96·1

Second Homes

The increase in the number of second homes in Britain has been the subject of some controversy since 1971. The total number of second homes in England and Wales in 1972 was between about 300,000 and 350,000; and a report on second homes, *No Place in the Country*, produced by Shelter in 1973, pointed out that there were then nearly 400,000 second homes in Britain. Some 200,000 families owned a second home which they used in addition to their normal residence; another 200,000 families owned or permanently rented a caravan as a holiday home. Between 1960 and 1970 over 20,000 families each year bought a second home and by the end of the century about 10 per cent of households in Britain were expected to have at least two homes.

Views on second homes vary considerably—from angry protests that wealthy outsiders buy up cottages for holiday homes by outbidding local villagers to the detriment of indigenous community life and possibly causing hardship to local people inadequately housed, to the recognition by some local authorities that in the long term they benefit from additional rates on such homes and the local community benefits from the purchasing power of the new residents.

Other reports on second homes include *Second Homes in England and Wales* by C. L. Bielckus, A. W. Rogers and G. P. Wibberley, Wye College, commissioned by the Countryside Commission; and *Second Homes in England and Wales: An appraisal prepared for the Countryside Commission by Dartington Amenity Research Trust*, HMSO.

The use of improvement grants for the modernisation of second homes and the subsequent withdrawal by legislation of grants for this purpose are discussed in Chapter 7 which deals with rehabilitation.

Finance

The main Acts which have affected housing, including housing finance, are listed in the Appendix, and finance is considered in detail in Chapter 8.

As has been described in Chapter 1, the Housing Finance Act 1972 altered the system of subsidies for public sector housing, and later the Housing Rents and Subsidies Act 1975 made financial provision for housing pending a complete review of housing finance for all sectors. It had been generally recognised that reform of housing finance was long overdue to produce a reasonable, sensible and fair system to meet the cost implications of rising standards and ensure that housing aid was distributed to give help where it was most needed. In 1974, the then Secretary

of State for the Environment announced that he had set up a
" searching and far-reaching enquiry " into housing finance to
be carried out by the DOE. The aim was to go back to funda-
mentals, " to get beyond a housing policy of ' ad-hoc'ery ' and
crisis management " and to find out precisely what needed to be
done if the desperate social problems of housing were to be solved.
The finance review advisory group received a vast amount of
evidence and advice from many bodies connected with all aspects
of housing, including the Housing Centre whose evidence is summarised in Chapter 8. The review was subsequently extended to
cover the much wider field of housing policy and the Secretary
of State for the Environment announced in 1976 that a Green
Paper on housing would be produced. Speaking in Newcastle
in September 1976, the Secretary of State said the review covered
a wide field, including the role of central government, the form
of subsidy arrangements, the part local authorities and housing
associations had to play and so on, and was set against the background of all the changes in housing which have occurred since
the war. It is understood that the Green Paper will be a consultation paper embracing housing policy as a whole and forming
the background to the government's promised overall housing
strategy.

CHAPTER 3

The Local Authority
Housing Service

The increasing involvement of local authorities in the general improvement of housing and the provision of new accommodation as a public service has been traced in Chapter 1. The removal by the Housing Act 1949 of the obligation on local authorities to provide houses for the "working classes" only, widened the housing activities of the authorities by implying that they were in future to be responsible for fulfilling all the housing needs of their areas, and not only those of the working classes.

In 1968, however, the *Report of the Committee on Local Authority and Allied Personal Social Services* (1: 18), under the chairmanship of Mr Frederick Seebohm, recognised that adequate housing was one of the foundations on which an effective family service must be based, and developed the concept of "a comprehensive housing service", by which local authorities should take the broadest view of their housing responsibilities and be concerned with housing in all sectors and with differing ways of assisting housing difficulties. The committee recommended that local authorities should provide centres for housing guidance and advice to which the public, as well as workers in statutory and voluntary social agencies, could turn. They believed that local authorities should be able to give advice to anyone who sought it, that they should cover the whole field of housing activity, public and private, offering advice on mortgages and lending money themselves for house purchase to less traditional borrowers, such as tenants' co-operatives, housing associations or self-build groups. The committee pointed out that if the proposals in the White Paper, *Old Houses into New Homes* (Cmnd. 3602, 1968), were adopted—and these were subsequently embodied in the Housing Act 1969, and extended in the Housing Act 1974—local authorities would be encouraging proper adaptation and repair on a bigger scale, and, as comprehensive housing authorities giving a full housing advisory service, they would have to know much more about the *total* housing situation in their areas and the trends and developments which bear upon it.

The report of the Cullingworth committee, *Council Housing: Purposes, Procedures and Priorities*, 1969 (1: 17) endorsed the view of the Seebohm committee: "Essentially this means a new approach on the part of the housing service: instead of dealing with ' applicants ', the housing department has to become a truly local and community service seeking to establish local needs and assist in meeting them. We are fully aware that this may lead to the housing advice service recommended by the Seebohm committee. This requires fuller consideration, but lies outside our terms of reference ".

The White Paper, *Local Government in England: Government Proposals for Reorganisation* (Cmnd. 4584, 1971), and plans for local government rationalisation in Scotland and Wales, emphasised the importance of housing as a local authority function, and, in giving the new districts the responsibility for housing, stressed that the accurate assessment of housing requirements and the provision of housing and housing advice to the individual was of such paramount importance that the service should be operated as close to the citizen as possible.

In 1973, the White Paper, *Widening the Choice: The Next Steps in Housing* (Cmnd. 5280) further reinforced the point that local authorities should take the broadest view of their statutory housing functions. This was more recently emphasised in *Race Relations and Housing* in September 1975 (Cmnd. 6232), which stated, " The Government has made it clear that it looks to local authorities to take the broadest view of their statutory responsibilities and powers, taking into account private as well as public housing; to respond to the housing needs of their area by formulating and pursuing social policies for new building and older housing, and for managing and allocating their own housing stock; and to be ready to give advice (directly or through voluntary housing aid centres) on housing matters to those in need or in ignorance of the help available to them ".

This chapter, therefore, considers housing as a local government service in the widest context and outlines the main housing functions of local authorities in that context.

The reform of local government, which took effect in London in 1965, and in the rest of England and in Wales and Scotland in 1974, has been described in Chapter 2. As explained there, the primary housing authorities are: in London, the Greater London Council and the 32 London boroughs and the City of London; outside London, the councils of the districts, with the county councils having reserve powers; in Wales, the district councils; in Scotland, 49 district authorities within 8 mainland housing regions and 2 regions based on the Orkney and Shetland Island groups; while in Northern Ireland, the Northern Ireland Housing Executive is the comprehensive regional housing authority.

Housing functions of local authorities

The Institute of Housing's report, *The Comprehensive Housing Service—Organisation and Function* (June, 1972), set out the main housing functions of local authorities as follows:

1. To consider the housing conditions of the district with respect to the provision of housing accommodation.
2. To provide housing accommodation through the erection and acquisition of houses, or through the conversion, alteration or improvement of properties acquired by the council. (This function has been extended by the Housing Act 1974 and the government's municipalisation programme discussed below.)
3. To acquire, develop or dispose of land and houses for housing purposes and to agree arrangements for over-spill.
4. To arrange for inspections to be carried out from time to time to ensure that there are satisfactory standards of repair, maintenance and sanitation in housing accommodation.
5. To exercise powers and duties as to clearance areas and orders, unfit houses, overcrowding, houses in multiple occupation, improvement of dwellings and other general powers and duties relating thereto, by:

> (a) securing the effective treatment of unfit houses, including making of demolition and closing orders;
> (b) arranging for the inspection of housing to secure the detection and abatement of over-crowding;
> (c) providing financial assistance to persons wishing to improve their houses;
> (d) arranging improvements to groups of houses and tenement accommodation;
> (e) exercising powers in relation to the designation of general improvement areas. (Renewal strategies under the Housing Act 1974 provide for housing action areas, priority neighbourhoods and general improvement areas.)

6. To provide temporary accommodation for those in urgent need through homelessness or emergency.
7. To exercise powers in relation to housing associations, housing societies and trusts.
8. To provide mortgage advances.
9. To exercise powers contained in legislation for improving tenancy relations in private dwelling houses, including the powers to initiate prosecutions for offences.
10. To exercise powers of management including collection of housing revenue, allocation, sale, letting, maintenance and repair of dwellings vested in the council as a housing authority.
11. To exercise powers in relation to the employment of directly employed labour.
12. To assess rents in respect of all council owned housing accommodation and to operate rent rebate schemes in

relation thereto, and also the rent allowance schemes for needy private tenants.

13. To exercise powers of maintenance, repair, letting and management of shops and garages which are vested in the council as a housing authority.

14. To maintain estate amenities.

15. To provide a comprehensive housing advisory service.

16. To exercise all the powers and duties conferred by or under any Act, statutory instrument and regulation, on the council as housing authority.

Housing conditions and estimation of needs

The powers of the local authorities to provide and manage housing accommodation are contained in Part V of the Housing Act 1957, which consolidated earlier legislation and is known in housing as the " principal act ". Sections 76 and 91 place a specific duty on local authorities to consider housing conditions in their areas, to carry out surveys from time to time of the housing needs of those areas and to frame proposals for the provision of any necessary new housing. Section 70 of the Housing Act 1969 extended these responsibilities by requiring the authorities to seek out unsatisfactory housing conditions, as well as to deal with matters brought to their attention by outside agencies.

The authority has to know the housing requirements which it is intended to meet. The appraisal of the condition of the housing stock and the assessment of the overall housing need in each area should be based on a thorough survey of the whole housing problem of the area, which will take into account the existing stock of houses, the degree of obsolescence—including the extent and urgency of the problem of decaying areas, tenement blocks and multi-occupied dwellings—and the number of potential households; and will estimate how many units of each size of accommodation are needed, with the waiting list serving as a useful, though not a complete guide. (Figures on a waiting list may be out-of-date because applicants may not have notified the authority when they have found accommodation for themselves; the basis of the list may make it an inaccurate guide to housing need, e.g., the rules may exclude anyone who cannot satisfy a 10-year residential qualification; the list is usually simply an indication of the number of people who might want council accommodation when it is available in a certain place and if the rent is right.) Some inter-war schemes, for example, concentrated too much on the three-bedroom house to the exclusion of accommodation suited to households consisting of young married couples, old people and large families. Households vary in size during their life cycle as a unit, and there must be sufficient variety of accommodation to satisfy their different needs at different times. A family cannot always be fitted into a house tightly as into a glove during all stages of its life, and some degree of under- or over-occupation will be inevitable at times, although this may be mitigated if there is variety of accommodation together with a flexible transfer system. Further, modern society requires a much larger number of small houses and flats, suitable for small households for all ages, than has been provided previously—only 14 per cent of the country's housing stock in 1975–76 was in units for one or two persons, whereas 50 per cent of households came into this category. The size of the average household has been affected by changing social conditions—more and more elderly couples and single persons of all ages have or are seeking their own separate accommodation, so that in any given area the total number of dwellings needed may increase although the total population may not. DOE Circular 24/75, *Housing Needs and Action*, emphasised that much greater attention ought to be given by local authorities to the needs of small households, both by making fuller use of the existing housing stock and by devoting a larger proportion of new building to smaller dwellings, and DOE Circular 61/75, *The Housing Cost Yardstick*, included a new cost allowance for smaller dwellings: both circulars are discussed further in Chapter 10. Greater provision of accommodation specifically designed for elderly persons and for the physically handicapped may also be needed in certain areas, e.g., in high-amenity districts which attract retired people. (Chapter 11, which considers the social aspects of housing, looks in more detail at the provision for special needs.) Moreover, many other factors, such as changes in population trends and in industrial development in an area and in neighbouring areas, will affect housing demand. A regular review, perhaps every three years, of the estimate of housing need is, therefore, essential. Long-term forecasting is always very difficult as the values of some of the factors are liable to fluctuations, e.g., falls in the average age of marriage, decline in the birth-rate, changes in the rate of voluntary migration from or to an area, unexpected arrivals of immigrants from abroad, changes in living standards, and decline or upgrading of any particular neighbourhood.

By 1976, it was generally recognised that housing needs of different areas varied very widely both in degree and, as described above, in type. In the autumn of 1976, the Secretary of State for the Environment announced in a speech at Birmingham that he hoped to introduce a new system of housing investment plans by 1978 " linked to a system of single housing capital allocations to replace the present complicated and compartmentalised arrangements ", and promised discussions with local authorities about " the whole of their housing needs " in this connection. Little is known at the time of writing about the details or full implications of such a policy, but knowledge of what an authority's comprehensive housing needs are seems likely to become even more important if it is implemented.

Professor J. B. Cullingworth discussed the desirability of all housing authorities having to produce housing needs assessments, which he called Housing Policies and Programmes (HPPs) in two papers at Housing Centre conferences, reported in *Housing Review*, January–February 1976, Vol. 25, No. 1 and *Housing Review*, July–September 1976, Vol. 25, No. 4. The Scottish Development Department had made considerable progress with the preparation of official guidance on the matter between 1971 and 1976, including carrying out a pilot study in the Dundee area which was published in 1976, *Local Housing Needs and Strategies—A Case Study of the Dundee Sub-Region* (1). Also, a series of four articles on the subject by members of the Department working in this field were published in *Housing*, Vol. 12, Nos. 6, 8, 10 and 11 for June, August, October and November– December 1976. Similar studies to the Dundee one have been carried out by some local authorities in England and publications by the Centre for Urban and Regional Studies, Birmingham University and the Scottish Housing Advisory Committee also offer guidance (2, 13, 14, 15).

The provision of housing

Local authorities will generally provide new or reconditioned housing to satisfy three basic demands in their areas: a demand arising out of shortages; a demand for additional housing to meet the growth of households and demographic changes, e.g., the present increasing demand for accommodation for smaller house-holds, and to cater for special needs, such as for the elderly and the disabled; and a demand for dwellings to replace those lost through slum clearance, area improvement (as in housing action areas and general improvement areas where some renewal of housing may be appropriate and where rehabilitation may result in a loss in the overall number of separate units) road works and other redevelopment. In 1976, the provision of new housing development was being used less frequently in some areas than rehabilitation, which is described later in this chapter and discussed in detail in Chapter 7.

When it is known what is needed, and some new development has to be undertaken, a suitable site for a project must be acquired. In some areas, where no undeveloped land is available, the local authority will usually have to consider redevelopment as an alternative to rehabilitation. Local authorities have power to purchase land either by agreement or compulsorily—and the Community Land Act 1975 places significant new responsibilities and duties on local authorities with regard to the forward acquisition of land. The Act is discussed in Chapter 9, but it is relevant to mention here that after the " First Appointed Day ", i.e., 6 April 1976, authorities were required to identify all land which is needed for " relevant development ", in accordance with the needs of the community, for up to 10 years ahead, and prepare five year rolling programmes for its acquisition. When land has been brought into public ownership, authorities may either develop it themselves or make it available for development by private development agencies, and a combination of these methods may be used as expedient. Land for private housing will generally be made available freehold to the eventual houseowner, with the builder/developer operating under a building licence.

Local authorities may ease pressure on their housing resources by making arrangements for the dispersal of population from overcrowded areas, e.g., by overspill procedures; and local authorities in areas where demand for housing is not so great, or revitalisation is needed, may operate a town expansion scheme to attract population from outside their area. These policies are discussed in Chapter 4 which deals with new and expanded towns.

Design

The design of the scheme may be carried out by the architect's department of the local authority, or by a consultant. The latter procedure is more usual in the case of smaller authorities, or where large authorities wish to spread the work load and benefit from a variety of approach.

The design of local authority housing is affected by the " cost yardstick " which sets the maximum cost of dwellings for which Exchequer subsidies will be paid in any local authority scheme, and by the housing standards, based on the Parker Morris recommendations, contained in the report, *Homes for today and tomorrow* (1: 13), which were made obligatory from 1 January 1969 for all council housing sanctioned (MOHLG Circular 36/67). The design and standards of dwellings, the effect of the cost yardstick, and the relationship between design and maintenance are considered in Chapter 10.

On the layout itself, the housing manager should agree the brief with the housing architect and the landscape architect at an early stage for all the practical implications, including, from an appearance and maintenance point of view, all such external features as grassed areas, shrubberies, situation of footpaths, garages, play areas and other communal requirements; and internal design, planning and amenities, with special reference to particular needs of different sections of the population.

Normal construction procedure is for competitive tenders for the scheme to be invited from building contractors, although other methods, e.g., by design/build contracts, are being tried in an effort to speed up construction.

Construction and layout are also considered more fully in Chapter 10.

Acquisition and improvement of properties

To secure an " immediate increase " in local authority housing stock, DOE Circular 70/74, W.O. 111/74, *Local Authority Housing Programmes*, sets out a series of initiatives designed to achieve this end. Public expenditure on housing was increased substantially, by £350 million in the public sector in 1974–75, to allow local authorities to make an early increase in their programmes of building to rent; to enable local authorities with urgent housing needs to acquire some of the many thousands of unsold, completed or virtually completed houses in the private sector; and for a start to be made on programmes for social ownership of rented housing in the worst areas of housing stress. Circular 70/74 said the extension of social ownership of rented accommodation could best be achieved by local authorities drawing up plans for the progressive expansion of such ownership, bearing in mind the initial need to concentrate on the immediate relief of housing stress, the need to safeguard tenants from threats of eviction and harassment, and the problems of homelessness. The categories of properties to be acquired were then: (1) acquisition made in pursuance of a confirmed compulsory purchase order or to meet a statutory obligation to acquire a particular property; (2) acquisition, particularly in areas of acute housing stress, of tenanted property where the local authority had clear evidence that tenants were in need as a result of bad housing conditions, including threat of harassment and risk of becoming homeless; (3) acquisition of properties which had been standing empty for six months, or of properties with vacant possession in areas in which there was a serious overall shortage of housing and the acquisition of which would be for the purposes of housing essential public service employees or the homeless; (4) houses previously sold by a local authority which they were re-acquiring under the terms of a pre-emption clause imposed on the original sale; and (5) acquisition on behalf of, or in order to sponsor, a housing association or a tenants' co-operative.

Many local authorities, particularly those in areas of housing stress, put in hand extensive programmes of purchase of properties and, encouraged by the government's emphasis on the improvement of older houses (in DOE Circular 70/74, WO 111/74), set about improving the condition of their own earlier housing. Section 105 of the Housing Act 1974, however, provided that a housing authority might not incur expenses on the conversion and improvement of dwellings in its ownership (including dwellings bought under schemes for municipalisation of privately rented accommodation) except in accordance with proposals submitted by the authority to the Secretary of State and approved by him. Approval might be given subject to such conditions as appeared to the Secretary of State to be appropriate. The effect was to subject all expenditure of this description to the Secretary of State's approval, irrespective of whether improvement or conversion schemes were financed with the aid of Exchequer subsidy, or from a local authority's own resources.

A letter to each local authority from the DOE in March 1975 announced a cutback on conversion and improvement of substandard houses in public ownership. This, following closely on a circular requesting local authorities to cut back on maintenance and repair (which in England and Wales was costing over £200 million a year compared with £126 million in 1971–72) was seen by many local authorities as highly damaging to the preservation of the housing stock.

In May 1975 the Secretary of State for the Environment announced in DOE Circular 64/75, *Housing Expenditure Changes*, that an extra £60 million would be allocated for expenditure under section 105 of the Housing Act 1974 " to ease the position for certain authorities facing the worst problems " in improving older housing—but a local authority's special needs still had to be proved to the DOE's satisfaction. Together with another £40 million, which was to be used to maintain for another year the 1974–75 high level of local authority spending on purchase of older housing, this money came from a £100 million cut in the money available to local authorities for home loans.

DOE Circular 33/76 helped to bring back into balance the money available for the acquisition of, and the money available for the improvement of, local authority housing. Local authorities had often been restricted in their programmes of acquiring housing because their section 105 allocation would not have been sufficient to cover its improvement. In January 1976 local authorities were told that permitted expenditure on renovation would be reduced from £285 million in 1975–76 to £270 million in 1976–77, and programmes submitted by councils were as much as halved. In general, Circular 33/76 widened the categories of houses available for municipalisation as compared with those laid down in Circular 64/75, but did not get back to the very wide categories set out in Circular 70/74. The new categories came as a result of recommendations of the Study Group on Programmes of Social Ownership and Renovation of Council Dwellings (3), and were:

(a) acquisitions made in pursuance of a confirmed compulsory purchase order to meet a statutory obligation to acquire a particular property;

(b) acquisitions of any dwellings in housing action areas, priority neighbourhoods and general improvement areas declared and notified to the Department to meet the objectives of those declarations;

(c) acquisitions of properties which had been standing empty for at least two months in areas where there was a serious overall shortage of housing or where the purpose of acquisition was to relieve homelessness;

(d) re-acquisitions of houses previously sold by a local authority;

(e) acquisitions of properties for use as hostels; provided that

(i) the total cost of a single transaction involving a number of dwellings did not exceed £100,000, and

(ii) the rateable value of the acquired dwelling (or where a house was acquired for conversion the existing rateable value divided by the number of dwellings to be provided) did not exceed by more than 15 per cent the average rateable value of comparable dwellings already provided by the council. This did not apply to category (e) above.

Although the above categories and provisos were designed to allow local authorities to acquire without reference to the DOE, any other properties could be "municipalised" providing approval could be obtained from the Department. The circular indicated that such applications were likely to be treated favourably if they concerned properties, tenanted or empty, near housing action areas and priority neighbourhoods, which were needed for temporary rehousing while the improvement and repairs were carried out, or for rehousing any residents permanently displaced from these areas.

In one of its most useful provisions, the circular stated that "the capitalised costs of initial works on acquired property may be treated as municipalisation and will not be required to count against an authority's section 105 allocation provided that: (1) the work is commenced before 31 December 1976 or 12 months from the date of acquisition, whichever is the later, and (2) the dwelling has been in the authority's ownership for not more than five years from the date of the commencement of the work ". An example of what this directive could mean in practice was estimated by the Minister of Housing and Construction, who, referring to Islington council, said that although its rehabilitation expenditure under section 105 was reduced from £22 million to £12 million, it was entitled to spend another £9 million from its municipalisation budget.

Powers and duties relating to sub-standard housing conditions

Local authorities have wide powers and duties in the exercise of control over the standard of housing in their areas, which are summarised in nos. 4 and 5 of the list of functions given above. The Housing Act 1974 has further increased local authorities' comprehensive responsibility for general housing conditions, and encouraged comprehensive action to remedy housing and environmental obsolescence.

(a) Unfit houses

The law relating to unfit houses and slum clearance is contained mainly in Parts II and III of the Housing Act 1957. The matters to be taken into account in determining whether or not a house is unfit for human habitation are defined in section 4 of the Housing Act 1957, as amended by the Housing Act 1969, as follows:

repair
stability
freedom from damp
internal arrangement
natural lighting
ventilation
water supply
drainage and sanitary conveniences
facilities for preparation and cooking of food and for the
    disposal of waste water.

The addition of internal arrangement of a dwelling to the list of matters to be taken into account in determining fitness was recommended in a report, *Our Older Homes: a Call for Action*, which was produced by a sub-committee (chaired by Dame Evelyn Denington) of the former Central Housing Advisory Committee (1: 19). The recommendations were implemented by the Housing Act 1969.

Any back-to-back house is specifically deemed to be unfit, but in all other cases it is a matter of fact whether or not the house is so far defective in one or more of the defined matters as to be not reasonably suitable for occupation in that condition.

By section 18 of the Housing Act 1957, parts of houses, including underground rooms, are deemed to be unfit by the same criteria as for houses (section 4 of the Housing Act 1957, as amended by the Housing Act 1969) mentioned previously, but the action in all cases is limited to the making of a " closing order ". Underground rooms are defined as being rooms where the surface of the floor is more than 3 ft. below the surface of the parts of the street adjoining or nearest to the room, or more than 3 ft. below the surface of any ground within 9 ft. of the room. Any underground room with a ceiling height less than 7ft. is declared to be unfit as is any such room which fails to meet the requirements of regulations made with the Minister's consent for the purpose of securing the proper ventilation and lighting and the protection thereof against dampness, effluvia or exhalation.

Having determined that a house is unfit, local authorities have various courses of action open to them, one of which they must take. Local authorities can act under the Public Health Acts which to some extent overlap with the Housing Acts in this respect. Under the Public Health Acts, they have power to enforce the abatement of a nuisance by the owner. This provision is often used when dealing with sanitary defects in old houses, but it is not appropriate, for example, when dealing with extensive defects which cannot be remedied " at reasonable cost ". If local authorities consider that houses can be made fit at reasonable cost, they can serve a repair notice on the owner and compel him to do the necessary work specified in it; often informal representation is adequate however. There is no legal penalty for non-compliance, but local authorities may themselves carry out the work in default and recover the expense. An owner has a right of appeal to the county court against a repair notice on the grounds that the house is not unfit, that the required works are not relevant, or that the house cannot be made fit at reasonable expense. The powers of local authorities when premises are deemed capable of repair at reasonable cost are listed in section 9 (1) of the Housing Act 1957. If an appeal is allowed and it is determined that the house cannot be made fit at reasonable expense, the local authority may purchase by agreement or by compulsory purchase order in certain circumstances; a demolition or closing order must be made.

Before local authorities require an owner to demolish or close his house at his own expense, the owner can negotiate; he can, for example, undertake to make the house fit even though the expense is not reasonable. If, however, nothing is done, a demolition order is made, subject to provisos that a closing order is substituted where demolition would injure adjoining properties, or if the building is of architectural or historical interest; a closing order may also be used to close part of a house for use as a dwelling—for example, an underground room.

Local authorities also have a third way of dealing with the matter. They may purchase the dwelling at site value and patch it up for temporary use under " deferred demolition " procedure. This procedure is used where housing shortages are so acute in an area that closing or demolition would cause hardship and homelessness.

Houses may be judged to be unfit not only because of intrinsic defects but also because they are " by reason of their bad arrangement, or the narrowness or bad arrangement of streets ", dangerous or injurious to the health of the inhabitants of the area.

The obligation of local authorities to rehouse occupants of closing and demolition order premises and several other categories, and to pay home loss and disturbance payments, are detailed below.

(b) Clearance areas

Under section 42 of the Housing Act 1957, local authorities have a duty to define and declare a " clearance area " where groups of unfit houses occur and where this is considered to be the most satisfactory method of dealing with the conditions, subject to (1) availability of suitable accommodation in advance of demolition for displaced persons; and (2) availability of sufficient resources for implementation of such an order. Having declared a clearance area, local authorities may make an order for demolition of the buildings in it by the owners. Such clearance orders, however, are only used for small groups of houses where authorities do not intend to develop the site. The more usual procedure for dealing with slum areas is by means of a compulsory purchase order on the site as a whole. This enables authorities to acquire all the site satisfactorily. Maps have to be prepared and the properties shown on them coloured differently according to whether they are (a) unfit or (b) fit but included because the site has to be developed as a whole. The main reason for this differentiation is that compensation is paid on a different scale, according to the category into which the individual properties fall. By section 42, the compensation payable on acquisition of an unfit house is basically its site value.

The general principle underlying compensation for compulsory acquisitions by a public authority is that an owner should receive fair value for his property with no allowance for the fact that acquisition is compulsory and may, for example, be against his will. In other words, a willing seller as well as a willing buyer is assumed. It has long been accepted that an unfit house which cannot be made fit at reasonable expense has no value, and the owner of such a house thus only receives site value. (If the cleared site is more valuable than the site with a house on it, the owner will not receive this extra value, since it is argued he should not be able to make a profit from the action of the local authority in clearing it.) There are, however, exceptions to this rule that slums have no value, which have been made largely to mitigate its severity. First, payments may be made for good maintenance. If a house, though unfit, has been well maintained in whole or in part, the owner, or the tenant if he is responsible for the maintenance, may receive a payment calculated to a formula laid down in the Acts. Secondly, compensation for the owner-occupier of an unfit dwelling is increased in a way which will bring it up to full market value. There is, however, a qualifying period during which an owner-occupier must have been resident, in order to discourage collusive sales from landlord to tenant. Payments must be made to displaced persons who qualify.

Part IV of the Land Compensation Act 1973 amended the general law of compulsory purchase, and Part V the law relating to planning blight under which an owner might require the acquisition of his interest where he desired to sell and the market value of the interest had been substantially reduced by impending events of specified kinds.

Market value continued as the basis for compensation but new terms were available in all cases where the valuation date was on or after 17 October 1972. Under Part IV of the Act, a statutory right was given to 90 per cent of compensation to be paid in advance on or after entry into property being acquired. The compensation payable on the acquisition of an unfit house was limited to its site value, with a further payment of eight (formerly four) times the rateable value, subsequently adjusted to $3\frac{1}{8}$ times the rateable value where the relevant date on which the rateable value was determined fell on or after 1 April 1973 (Housing (Payments for Well Maintained Houses) Orders 1973, and DOE Circular 54/73, WO 97/73), if the house had been well maintained, provided that the total sum did not exceed the property's market value; or half of this if only either the interior or the exterior had been well maintained. The new statutory right under the Land Compensation Act 1973 to compensation in respect of injurious affection caused by new development for certain people from whom no land was taken, and who were debarred from bringing an action at common law for damages for nuisance, applied to claimants in respect of works coming into use on or after 17 October 1972.

The Land Compensation Act 1973, as amended by the Housing Act 1974 and the Housing Rents and Subsidies Act 1975, made provision for home loss payments, subject to a minimum of five years' residence, farm loss payments and disturbance payments to persons displaced from land in consequence of compulsory acquisition, or of a clearance, demolition or closing order, or an undertaking that a house would not be used for human habitation, passed or given under the Housing Acts, or by an improvement notice or improvement work to a dwelling acquired by the authority or a housing association.

Home loss payments, a new concept introduced for the first time in the Land Compensation Act 1973, were designed to compensate for the upheaval of a forced move from one's home, in so far as money could do so; they are paid subject to a minimum residence period of five years, and the amount is related to the rateable value of the home with a minimum of £150 and a maximum of £1,500. Caravan dwellers also qualify for payments if there are no other suitable sites on which they can park their homes. Disturbance payments, which had been discretionary before the Act, became mandatory, provided the occupants had been in residence on a specific date. These payments are related to reasonable renewal expenses and actual losses sustained. A special provision was introduced to allow payment of the expenses of modifying a dwelling for a disabled person who had to move from one which had been adapted to his needs.

Under the Land Compensation Act 1973, section 39, as amended by the Housing Act 1974, people displaced from their homes by acquisition, redevelopment or improvement are entitled to rehousing if suitable alternative residential accommodation on reasonable terms is not otherwise available to them. This qualified entitlement to rehousing does not apply, however, to a resident whose property is acquired in consequence of a blight notice served by him, to a trespasser, or to a person who has been permitted to take up temporary residence pending demolition. In some circumstances, too, an owner occupier who has borrowed money from a local authority for the purpose of obtaining "accommodation in substitution of that from which he is displaced" also loses his entitlement to be rehoused. This statutory duty to rehouse is also extended to people displaced from a caravan on a caravan site in cases where neither suitable residential accommodation nor a suitable alternative site is available.

DOE Circular 103/72 pointed out that an authority might well rehouse people not covered by statutory liability. If a householder is displaced by another authority's acquisition, the housing authority for the area in which he was living would be regarded as the appropriate one to rehouse, though the acquiring authority would have to indemnify against any loss. The obligation might be discharged by the offer of a council tenancy. Where a displaced occupier did not wish to become a council tenant, the housing authority could discharge its obligation by making a loan for house purchase.

Attention was paid to mortgages for owner-occupiers displaced by development, as the government believed that this type of borrower should have a very high priority for mortgage finance. Local authorities were urged to make advances on the most helpful terms possible to displaced owner-occupiers and were given discretionary power to grant interest-only mortgages. Advice was given on arrangements with the Supplementary Benefits Commission to meet interest charges. Councils were reminded that displaced owner-occupiers might be offered council houses which were available for sale.

The former practice of some authorities of reducing the compensation payable to displaced owner-occupiers who were rehoused in council accommodation was made illegal by the Act. DOE Circular 103/72 emphasised the need for making advice and help available to the ordinary man in the street on these matters.

(c) Overcrowding

The Housing Act 1957, sections 76–90 and Schedule 6 places upon local authorities a duty, in certain circumstances, to survey and report on overcrowding and the need for new housing, and a duty to enforce provisions to control overcrowding. The reduction in size of many households, noted earlier, has greatly reduced the incidence of overcrowding, although it still occurs in areas of acute housing shortage, and among large families.

The overcrowding standard takes into account the number of rooms (that is, living rooms and bedrooms) and their size. This gives a " permitted number of units " for each house, which is compared with the number of " units " which the residents comprise. An adult counts as one unit, a child under 10 but over one year old as a half-unit and a child under one year old does not count at all. If the household represent more units than the " permitted number ", then the house is overcrowded. Even if the numbers are satisfactory, the house is statutorily overcrowded if the situation necessitates adults of opposite sex, not living together as man and wife (and this does not necessarily mean legally married) sleeping in the same room.

Local authorities may authorise temporary use in excess of the " permitted number " by licence. A landlord commits an offence if he does not satisfy himself reasonably when letting that the accommodation will not be overcrowded; or if after written notice that the occupier is committing an offence he fails to take reasonable steps to secure abatement. He is liable to a penalty for not recording in a rent book the " permitted number ", or for not notifying the local authority when overcrowding comes to his knowledge. Private landlords can seek the advice of the local authority on the suitability of any letting offered, including the rent.

Overcrowding existing at the time when the Act was passed was not regarded as penal; nor is subsequent overcrowding caused by the natural growth of the family. It is an offence for an over-crowded occupant to refuse unreasonably the offer of suitable accommodation, for example made by or through the local authority.

If a tenant has, by taking additional occupants into the home, caused it to be overcrowded, thus committing an offence, and if the tenancy is a controlled or regulated one, the landlord, having given notice to terminate the tenancy, can insist that the court give him an order for possession. (Ordinarily, in the case of con-trolled and regulated tenancies, the court has discretion concerning possession orders, and does not grant them readily.)

Special provisions apply to houses let in lodgings whereby local authorities may determine the number of persons who may sleep in any particular room or preclude its use as a bedroom. Allowance can be made for age of residents. There is a right of appeal against a local authority's decision as well as a penalty for contravention.

The provisions with regard to overcrowding in the Housing Act 1957 repeat those in the 1935 to 1936 Acts. Owing to the acute shortage of housing in many areas since the Second World War, formal use of the provisions and powers is often impracticable, especially where there is severe housing stress and transient occupants. The penal overcrowding standard is low by modern standards and differs from standards used for letting by most local authorities, housing associations and responsible landlords.

Section 19 of the Housing Act 1961 provides for the limitation of the number of persons or households who may occupy a house when in multiple occupation, the limit being given by way of formal direction and based on facilities available to the occupants.

(d) Multi-occupation

Multi-occupation, often an intractable problem in areas of housing stress, occurs, according to the Housing Acts, in " houses let in lodgings or occupied by members of more than one family ". The 1971 census showed 270,800 dwellings in multiple occupation in England, over 152,000 of which were in Greater London. The census figures, however, do not reflect the wide range of con-ditions encompassed by the term " multiple occupation ", ranging from the worst of rooming houses to quite satisfactory, well-equipped " bed-sitters ". Further, where two or more families live together and take a main meal together, the census treats them as one household, thus in many cases underestimating the problem of multi-occupation, which has increased in recent years as a result of both economic and social factors.

Although there were for many years powers to require the adequate provision of services and amenities if they did not exist already, these were not very effective until new measures were introduced under the Housing Act 1961. Under this Act, local authorities were given power to apply a code of management to houses in multiple occupation; to insist on the provision of additional facilities and of adequate means of escape from fire; to carry out works in the case of default by the owner and to recover the cost from him; and to make a direction limiting the number of persons who might live in a house or part of a house in multiple occupation—sections 12–20, Housing Act 1961. Section 12 of the Act allows local authorities to make a Management Order in respect of a house in multiple occupation which they feel is in an unsatisfactory state because of failure to maintain proper standards of management. The Management Order is made to apply the Houses (Management of Houses in Multiple Occupation) Regulations 1962, which require the person managing the property (i.e., the owner/agent or other person in control of the house) to maintain proper standards of management. Briefly, these standards include: the good order and repair of the water supply, drainage, gas and electricity supplies, lighting, heating, all rooms and services in common use, and the yards and out-buildings; the cleanliness of staircases, and common parts; the proper storage of refuse; the general safety of the occupants. The Housing Act 1969, section 60, provides that where a house in multiple occupation cannot be wholly made to comply with means of escape in case of fire requirements at reasonable expense, but where conditions are such that if part of the house were not used the remainder would or could be made to comply at reasonable expense, local authorities may negotiate and accept an undertaking that the part will not be used. In the absence of such an undertaking or in the event of contravention of an undertaking, a closing order can be made.

The Housing Act 1969 contained further powers to deal with multiple occupation. Under previous legislation, local authorities could not limit or regulate multi-occupation until after it had actually occurred. Under the 1969 Act, authorities can make regulations before multi-occupation takes place and can be given powers to make registration with the local authority a pre-requisite of new multiple occupation. In order that local authorities may also assist owners to provide satisfactory amenities in houses let in lodgings, special improvement grants (see Chapter 7) are available for the provision of the basic amenities, even if they may not be for the exclusive use of any one family in the house.

Powers to control multi-occupation, although they are backed by heavy penalties, often prove difficult to implement for several reasons. Overcrowding is generally more prevalent in multi-occupied houses than elsewhere, and authorities are often limited in what they can do because of shortage of accommodation in their area; it may be very difficult to put effective pressure on absentee landlords, and also the occupants may be intimidated by fear of eviction.

(e) Abatement of nuisance, remedy of individual defects in premises and other powers

Sections 91–94 of the Public Health Act 1936 places a duty on local authorities to inspect from time to time for the detection of nuisances. Statutory nuisances which may be dealt with summarily are listed and include among other matters " any premises in such a state as to be prejudicial to health or a nuisance ". The responsibility rests with the person by whose act, default or sufferance the nuisance arises and continues, except that any defect of a structural character is specifically the responsibility of the owner. Local authorities must serve an abatement notice, and in default of compliance make a complaint to a justice of the peace. The Public Health (Recurring Nuisances) Act 1969 strengthened the powers of local authorities regarding nuisances recurring on the same premises by giving discretionary power to serve a prohibition notice.

Specific provisions for remedy of individual defects in premises are mainly contained in the Public Health Acts and By-laws. The Public Health Act 1936, for example, places a duty on local authorities to require the proper provision of drainage, replacement or provision of additional WC accommodation, maintenance of a water supply to a flushing apparatus for a WC, sweeping and maintenance of common courts; as well as many other requirements. The Public Health Act 1961 includes a power to deal with wholly derelict buildings and a power to require suitable food storage accommodation for any separate dwellings.

Local authorities also have powers which are designed for drastic and immediate action when and where necessary. The Housing Act 1964, section 73 (amended by section 63 of the Housing Act 1969), gives local authorites power to take over the control of premises for a period not exceeding five years by the making of a " control order " in cases where (a) action has or could be taken under sections 12–15 or 19 of the Housing Act 1961; and (b) it appears that it is necessary to make the order to protect the safety, welfare or health of the persons living in the house. Provision is made for entry to the premises and for taking immediate action to protect the safety, welfare and health of the occupants, and for preparation and service on the owner(s), within eight weeks, of a formal " scheme of works " which the local authority would have required to be carried out under any enactment and which constitute works involving capital expenditure.

(f) Rehabilitation

Rehabilitation as an integral part of national policy for upgrading all housing and as a process in urban renewal, often as an alternative to wholesale clearance, is discussed in detail in Chapter 7. Here a summary is given of the functions of local authorities in promoting and carrying out rehabilitation, including providing financial assistance to persons wishing to improve their homes.

By virtue of government legislation from 1949 onwards, financial assistance from the Exchequer both to house owners and local authorities has been available for conversions and improvements. The amounts and details of grants made, which have been changed under different Acts in an effort to encourage more improvement work, are given in Chapter 7, together with details of local authority powers and duties, summarised below, regarding the improvement of older housing areas and the social conditions in them.

Apart from the improvement of their own older houses, local authorities are concerned under the 1969 and 1974 Housing Acts with the improvement generally of houses within their area, and in particular with the rehabilitation of defined areas of older housing. Already before the Housing Act 1969, some local authorities—for example, Leeds C.B.C.—had adopted a procedure whereby they approached all the owners in an area, encouraging them to carry out improvement work with grants and loans. If owners found this impossible, they were asked to sell their properties to the local authority, who themselves carried out the work and thus gave the occupants the benefits of improved living conditions.

There were provisions under the Housing Act 1961 for encouraging work of this kind in what were designated general improvement areas. They were not very much used, however, and the Housing Act 1969 introduced new area provisions and provided an Exchequer subsidy towards the improvement of the environment.

The Housing Act 1969, as amended by the Housing Act 1974, provided for the declaration of general improvement areas when the local authority considers that living conditions ought to be enhanced by way of improvement of the amenities of an area or of dwellings or both. Such areas must not include clearance areas but may be adjacent to or surrounding clearance areas, and if the Minister excludes any such land from the compulsory purchase order confirmation, it will be included in the general improvement area unless the Minister specifically directs otherwise. Similarly, the general improvement area may surround a housing action area but not include it. A priority neighbourhood may, however, be included.

The Housing Act 1974 provided for the declaration of housing action areas and for the first time specifically brought the social conditions of the area into consideration. General improvement areas and priority neighbourhoods may be included.

The standard amenities required by the Housing Act 1969 are described in Chapter 7. It is relevant to note here, however, that section 89 of the Housing Act 1974 enables a tenant of a dwelling which is not provided with all the standard amenities (fixed bath or shower, sink, wash basin, hot and cold water and WC), and which is not situated in a general improvement area or housing action area, to apply to the local authority to exercise its power to require the installation of the missing facilities. The person having control of the premises has to be notified that the application has been made and may make representations thereon. The application may be rejected if in all the circumstances it is not considered that the improvement should be effected. Improvement notices are served and procedures followed as for compulsory improvement in housing action areas if it is considered that the dwelling should be improved, and reasonable expense is a qualification for action.

Circular 160/74 dealt in detail with housing renovation grants and compulsory improvement notices. DOE Circular 13/75, WO 4/75, Housing Act 1974: *Renewal Strategies*, and DOE Circular 14/75, Housing Act 1974: *Housing Action Areas, Priority Neighbourhoods and General Improvement Areas*, emphasised that gradual and sensitive renewal, framed " to meet the housing needs of the people in the area " (as the task of local authorities was defined in the Housing Act 1969), would enable local authorities to treat housing areas as " living urban organisms ", with schemes responsive to particular physical and social needs. Circular 13/75 directed in the light of the Housing Act 1974 all housing authorities to undertake a thorough review of their policies in relation to older dwellings, and expressed the Minister's view that local authorities would commit themselves to a policy of " flexible, co-ordinated and continuous renewal "; while Circular 14/75 gave information, advice and guidance on the statutory provisions in the Housing Act 1974 relating to housing action areas, priority neighbourhoods and general improvement areas. The comprehensive renewal plan worked out by the local authority should include within its scope both privately-owned and community-owned housing, and the declaration of the various areas, as defined above, must be justified against overall assessments of needs, priorities and resources. Further details are given in Chapter 7.

In March 1976 the Department of the Environment gave added stimulus and encouragement to local authorities to undertake improvement programmes, rather than redevelopment schemes, by approving their largest ever compulsory purchase order for rehabilitation. The order affected 153 run-down Victorian houses in Islington which will be rehabilitated for the benefit of the residents.

Harassment

Local authorities have powers to prosecute for harassment of tenants and DOE Circular 15/73 (WO 34/73) drew the attention of local authorities to the increase in the maximum penalties for harassment and unlawful eviction. The Criminal Justice Act 1972, section 30, provided that from 1 January 1973, on summary conviction of harassment, an offender is liable to a fine of up to £400, or up to six months' imprisonment, or both; and on conviction on indictment, to an unlimited fine, or to imprisonment for up to two years, or both. The circular also referred to the need for local authorities to appoint tenancy relations or harassment officers in areas of housing stress. Such officers should have an outgoing role and their work should include conciliation as well as investigating complaints. The appointment of such officers by many authorities already was welcomed in the circular in view of the importance of local authorities being able to act swiftly and effectively through them in areas where tenant and landlord relationships come under strain.

The circular also emphasised that local authorities should inform all tenants concerned of their rights at the time of approval of a house improvement grant for private tenanted accommodation. This could be done, the circular suggested, by sending tenants copies of the DOE's leaflets, *Private Tenancies—New Measures in the Housing Finance Act 1972*, and *Protection under the Rent Acts*, which had been distributed to local authorities.

Powers in relation to housing associations

Advancing money to housing associations constitutes a very important housing function of local authorities outside the housing revenue account (see below), and such advances are not subject to the limitations applied to advances for house purchase to private individuals. It is government policy that local authorities should assist housing associations by making available the necessary capital finance on a self-financing basis. The Housing Act 1974 provided the financial framework for the rapid expansion of the housing association movement. This framework and the ways in which housing associations can borrow from local authorities and the Housing Corporation are described in Chapter 6. Briefly, local authorities borrow the sums required to finance relevant house construction schemes and lend the money to associations at a rate of interest sufficient to cover both the authorities' borrowing costs and the cost of administering the transactions. Because housing associations enjoy different house-building subsidy arrangements from local authorities, and because relatively small rate fund charges normally arise from the arrangements, some authorities look to housing associations to provide a considerable amount of rented accommodation in their areas. Housing associations are often involved in housing action areas, where opportunities are taken to involve residents in neighbourhood schemes and to create flexible ongoing management and maintenance programmes.

For 1976–77, however, although the government has added a further £20 million to the public expenditure figures for local authorities' lending to housing associations, their funds are heavily committed to paying for the next stages of development of past approvals. The combined total of approvals by local authorities and the Housing Corporation will be considerably less than in the previous year. In housing action areas, the contribution of housing associations will be restricted if the appropriate local authority's unit-allocation to housing associations is absorbed elsewhere.

Advances for house purchase

Local authorities also have powers to make advances to assist house purchase, and power, with the approval of the Secretary of State for the Environment, to make certain guarantees to building societies. Under section 43 of the Housing (Financial Provisions) Act 1958, they can make advances to any person for the purpose of acquiring, constructing, converting, altering, enlarging or improving houses. This power may be used in respect of houses or buildings inside or outside the local authority's area. Other statutes under which local authorities have powers to make advances are the Small Dwellings Acquisition Acts 1899–1923, as amended; these Acts are permissive, and have been much used. Circular 20/64, however, pointed out that the Housing Act powers are wider and more flexible. The Housing (Financial Provisions) Act 1958, as amended by the House Purchase and Housing Act 1959, also empowers a local authority, with the approval of the Secretary of State, to guarantee the repayment to a building society of any advance made by the society to any of its members for the purpose of enabling them to build or acquire houses, whether within or without the area of the council. In certain circumstances, the Secretary of State may undertake to reimburse the authority with one half of any loss sustained under the guarantee.

Throughout the later 1960s and 1970s there have been periodic restrictions imposed on expenditure by local authorities in the interests of the national economy as a whole. Since there are other sources of mortgage loans open to purchasers for owner occupation, notably the building societies, governments have restricted the amounts local authorities may lend to individuals for this purpose. A series of circulars have indicated that the limited funds available should be allocated mainly to those borrowers who are least likely to be able to obtain an adequate loan elsewhere. Local authorities have thus become largely lenders of last resort, providing mortgage loans up to 100 per cent of the valuation of the dwelling, to certain categories of borrower regarded as having priority need, for example the homeless, people high on a council's waiting list or displaced by new development, and people wishing to buy older property which would not attract a building society mortgage. Additionally, since 1974, they have been permitted to lend to first-time purchasers of new dwellings. Because of the shortage of building society funds in the early part of 1974, the 1974–75 lending was exceptionally high. However, in 1975–76, as has already been mentioned, to enable local authorities to make adequate progress in improving unfit housing acquired by them, and to provide for continued investment by local authorities in the improvement of their own housing stock, £100 million was switched by the Secretary of State from lending. It was, therefore, necessary to restrict local authority lending to the priority borrowers mentioned above and most local authority schemes are currently suspended. The £100 million " switch " is a good example of the way local authorities' plans are compulsorily changed at short notice. It is likely that further restrictions will occur in future years, bearing in mind the priority of applying the available restricted resources to the provision of public housing and the improvement of the existing stock.

Arrangements were made in 1976 for building societies to lend to some borrowers of the kind normally catered for by the local authorities, as described in Chapter 5.

Housing finance is discussed in detail in Chapter 8.

Housing management

The initiation of the profession of housing management by Octavia Hill has been described in Chapter 1; over the years the profession has adapted its methods to meet changing needs in housing, and management functions have widened. Functions involved in a modern, fully comprehensive housing service are described later, but routine management has included the following: control of waiting lists; letting of properties; organisation of rent collection and control of arrears; maintenance of accounts and records; administration of rent rebate schemes; maintenance and repair of properties, possibly by direct labour; social welfare in relation to housing management; and the general care of estates, with emphasis on establishing and maintaining a good relationship between landlord and tenant.

The value of "improved and enlightened management of properties", both publicly and privately owned, was given official recognition over 40 years ago in the *Report of the Departmental Committee on Housing, 1933*. The first detailed official advice was contained in the first report of the Housing Management Sub-Committee of the former Central Housing Advisory Committee, *The Management of Municipal Housing Estates* (4), which was sent to all housing authorities in 1938, accompanied by a ministerial circular, advocating that, as far as practicable, there should be a single officer to whom the tenants would normally look as the medium of communication between themselves and the local authority, and asking that housing authorities should send a report giving details of their housing management organisations. In 1945, authorities who had not recently reviewed their general arrangements for housing management were asked to do so immediately. Subsequently the most comprehensive advice on the organisation of housing management was given in the eighth report of the Housing Management Sub-Committee, *Councils and their Houses* (*1959*), which was decidedly in favour of what it called "the unified form of housing management", wherein all the functions which bring the landlord and tenant into association should be the responsibility of one committee and one department.

The recommendations of the Seebohm Committee in 1968 and in the Cullingworth report with regard to the establishment of separate housing departments operating a fully comprehensive housing service have already been mentioned. In 1973, the Bains Report, *The new local authorities: management and structure* (5), stated " . . . a Chief Housing Officer or Director of Housing should be responsible for the total housing function, including management, assessment of need, improvement, slum clearance, and any advisory service . . ." using the services of the appropriate specialist officers of other departments.

In November 1975 the Minister for Housing and Construction, speaking at the Institution of Housing's annual conference, referred to the new kind of housing service needed: "Housing management has gone into a new orbit. . . . The need for a comprehensive housing organisation in local authorities is stronger than ever and its tasks must range from the strategic one of developing a total approach to the needs of the whole district in all sectors of housing, to providing a housing advice service for all comers, to dealing with the everyday problems of Mrs. Smith in the top floor flat."

The Institute of Housing, in its Year Book, 1976, emphasises the need for highly skilled and experienced housing staff with a qualified director of housing or housing manager in charge of a comprehensive housing department. It sets out in broad outline its views on the duties and functions of such a chief officer and describes comprehensive housing management, based firmly on modern management techniques, as involving research, advice and administration as follows:

1. Examination of the housing conditions of the area, estimation of housing demand, including the requirements of special groups such as the aged, physically handicapped and the homeless; and the assessment of housing supply, including the physical condition of existing dwellings and the size and scope of the building and acquisition programme of all the agencies involved.

2. Research required to assess housing need to ensure that all available resources are used to the best advantage of the community at large.

3. Briefing architects to include advice on all types and mix of dwellings and the social, management and maintenance aspects of layout and design, taking into account community requirements and preferences.

4. Overall responsibility for the local authority housing programme, including development of estates, slum clearance, redevelopment, rehousing and demolition.

5. Advice on and management of all housing authority properties, estates and ancillary amenities, temporary accommodation and areas awaiting redevelopment; including rent collection and accounting; recovery of arrears and possession; the establishment of a sound relationship between the tenants and the housing authority as landlords; and the fostering of good social relationship and community development.

6. Allocations of housing accommodation, and the administration of suitable arrangements to facilitate transfers and mutual exchanges between occupiers of all types of accommodation.

7. Assessment of fair rents and the administration of the rent rebate/allowance schemes.

8. Repairs and maintenance of local authority dwellings and other estate properties.

9. Housing welfare and liaison with social services.

10. Advice on and the administration of schemes for the sale and purchase of houses, including home loan schemes for purchase, repair and improvement.

11. Administration of a housing aid and advice service to individuals, including advice on Rent Act and Housing Act matters, landlord and tenant relationship, house purchase and mortgages, property improvements and resettlement in other areas.

12. Responsibility for any necessary action in connection with overcrowding, multiple occupation or essential repairs and improvement to residential property whether in public or private ownership.

13. Advice and assistance to housing associations and societies.

14. Liaison between housing authorities, including new and expanded towns.

15. Responsibility for encouraging the good management, maintenance and rehabilitation of all housing stock in the district, including co-ordination of action in general improvement areas and, in both publicly and privately owned properties, fostering participation in such matters by tenants and other interested parties.

It is recognised that some of these duties will call for the expertise of officers employed in other departments, and appreciated that whether such officers should be transferred or seconded to the housing services department, or whether they should retain semi-independent status as separate branches within the directorate of housing services, is a matter for local arrangement. The chief officer should encourage the provision of comprehensive training schemes within his establishment for new entrants to the housing service.

Housing management has to relate to a comprehensive housing service, embracing all aspects of housing provision. The constant challenge to the housing management profession must be in ensuring that housing management policies and methods in all areas are based on continuing research and reappraisal, are flexible and are responsive to changing social needs. Tomorrow's housing managers must assume a wider sociological outlook to meet the modern, much wider interpretation of need, and to act as catalysts for rehabilitation schemes in twilight areas and in housing action areas which by their very nature will house many who deliberately seek to avoid participation in any public action, and must be ready to operate complicated financial procedures, and keep up to date with advances in technical and sociological processes, in cost control and financial techniques. The implications for the organisation of housing departments were discussed in the

Institute of Housing's report, *The Comprehensive Housing Service —Organisation and Functions*, published in June 1972.

There is increasing emphasis on tenant participation in management. Several factors, including the extension of housing activity by local authorities, considerable criticism of management and maintenance policies of local authorities, increasing vandalism and alienation on estates, more standardisation between public and private housing—in rent levels, for instance—together with the extension of the concept of participation by the public in local government schemes which affect their lives, e.g., in planning, present a prima facie case for extending tenant involvement in the management of publicly-owned housing, and possibly ultimately for passing control of housing and its environment to the users, where this is practicable and, most important, genuinely desired by them. Colin Ward, author of *Tenants Take Over* (6), sees in dweller control the answer to the social failure of so many housing projects in this country—the result of this failure is seen in vandalism and neglect because tenants have no stake in the property they occupy. Various experiments in tenant participation are being carried out, e.g., by area committees in Lambeth, by considerable delegation in the GLC development at Thamesmead, and the St Mary's joint management sub-committee of the Greenwich housing committee. Others are listed in research by Ann Richardson, University of London Goldsmith's College, into tenants' participation schemes in practice, the research being sponsored by the Centre for Environmental Studies and the Department of the Environment. If schemes for tenant participation are to work for the benefit of the community and the nation as a whole, and achieve a real form of participation, they must be broadly based on genuine co-operation between the local authority, or housing association, and the majority of tenants. The beneficial effects cannot be judged unless or until the concept is essayed on a comprehensive basis by progressive local authorities, and the results researched and evaluated.

Alternative forms of tenure are also being explored. The report (7) of the working party under the chairmanship of Harold Campbell on tenants' co-operatives and other forms of social ownership, tenure and management, and methods by which opportunities may be provided for individuals to share in the ownership and management of their homes, are considered in Chapter 11, which deals with the social aspects of housing. It is relevant to note here that equity sharing schemes are being operated by Birmingham, and by the GLC in Hertfordshire, and that Lewisham Borough Council is studying the feasibility of erecting a small housing scheme using the self-build system designed by the architect, Walter Segal.

The implications for training of housing personnel (which is exclusively the responsibility of local authorities and housing associations, although the Local Government Training Board has been nominally responsible for the oversight of quality and quantity) of the operation by local authorities of a fully comprehensive housing service and of alternative approaches in management and tenure, is considered in Chapter 12 which looks at the prospects for housing in the future. Here too the need for a much wider context in housing than a purely local authority corporate one— with closer contact, realisation and a sense of common purpose between local authorities, voluntary agencies, community associations and government bodies—is discussed.

Maintenance

Maintenance, which reports of the former Central Housing Advisory Sub-Committee have included as one of the basic elements of management, covers all matters affecting the repair and upkeep of houses and flats and the care and supervision of their environment. Local authorities may have their own labour force to execute maintenance and/or they may employ contract labour. Whichever is used, maintenance work should be planned and organised to achieve speedy execution of necessary repairs so that an estate will not deteriorate to the point where tenants become dispirited and apathetic. The co-operation of the tenants in keeping the property and its environment in good condition is essential and this is more likely to be achieved, and a good landlord/tenant relationship established, if the landlord's policy on repairs is clearly explained to the tenants and seen to be effective in action.

Many authorities are experiencing difficulty in finding and keeping a speedy and efficient labour force for repair and maintenance work both contracting and direct labour. The problems in the building industry, where some 350,000 building workers, including those normally working in the manufacture and distribution of materials, are out of work, are discussed in Chapter 10. The Defective Premises Act 1972 described in Chapter 10, became effective on 1 January 1974 and must make local authorities look more closely as to how they are observing their responsibilities as landlords under section 32 of the Housing Act 1961. Complete and regular inspections of all council-owned property are essential in order that repairs and maintenance to fabric and fittings can be achieved to meet this legal obligation. The cost of maintenance and repairs has been rising steeply, and this, as well as social considerations, may encourage more local authorities to introduce much more freedom of action by their tenants over the appearance of individual houses and estates.

Allocation of local authority housing

Local authorities have a statutory duty under the Housing Act 1957, section 113, to give preference in allocating dwellings to people living in slums or overcrowded houses, to those who have large families, or who are living in unsatisfactory conditions. As previously mentioned, they must also provide accommodation for people displaced under slum clearance procedures and in certain other circumstances. A circular on homelessness, issued in February 1974, (DOE 18/74; DHSS 4/74; WO 34/74) placed additional housing priorities on local authorities, and promoted a fresh approach by local authorities to homelessness but made no change in statutory responsibilities. Although all homeless people whether families with children, adult families, or single people should be helped, even if the homelessness seemed to have been self-inflicted, the circular stated that in areas of housing stress there must be priority groups who must have first claim on the resources of local government. These groups, for whom local authorities should provide accommodation themselves, or help those concerned to find accommodation in the private sector, were families with dependent children living with them or in care; and adult families without children, or individuals who become homeless in an emergency, such as fire or flooding, and were temporarily unable to fend for themselves; or who were vulnerable because of old age, disability, pregnancy or other special reason. The prevention and relief of homelessness was regarded as a function of local government as a whole and not of either housing authorities or of social services alone. The circular urged local authorities to phase out communal and non-self-contained accommodation for homeless families as quickly as possible and said that if its guidance were followed, bed-and-breakfast accommodation should become increasingly unnecessary. The function of housing aid centres in decreasing homelessness is mentioned below.

Policy for the allocation of council housing depends on its availability, and suitability. In areas of housing shortage, local authorities have to select tenants according to an assessment of the degree of their housing need; but there may be difficulties in accommodating special groups, e.g., the elderly, the single, rootless, one-parent families, if not enough accommodation of the right size and amenity is available. Further, allocating council housing to those in greatest need does not necessarily have the greatest impact on housing stress—only too often bad housing conditions are merely perpetuated by another family moving in to the accommodation vacated. In areas where the pressure on housing is not so great, consideration of urgent need may not be of such importance. It is normal practice for local authorities to maintain a list of applicants for accommodation, which will indicate the number, size or type of households who may be desirous of council accommodation when it is available and if the rent is right. As has already been indicated, however, waiting lists are not in themselves a reliable indication of future housing needs, but if the list is kept reasonably up to date, it can at least serve as the basis for estimating trends. Because applicants are becoming more aware of their needs and aspirations it is not unusual even in an area of great housing stress to find a very high refusal rate when offers are finally made, and the standards of some estates are declining because only those who are desperate and/or have low standards will accept them.

Some authorities in whose area there is a scarcity of council housing have made various requirements for admission to the waiting list, a minimum period of residence in the area being common. Government advice on the criteria used for the assessment of housing need has discouraged the practice of requiring a residential qualification from applicants for housing. Section 22 of the London Government Act 1963 expressly forbade the practice, yet all London boroughs adopted a formula which circumvented its intentions; and the report, *Council Housing: Purposes, Procedures and Priorities, 1969* recommended that local authorities should not be allowed to impose a residential qualification for admission to a housing list (1: 17). The London borough of Hammersmith has eliminated the residential qualification for admission to its waiting list—see " Why Hammersmith scrapped residential qualifications ", by Derek Fox, Director of Housing, in *Municipal Engineering*, 16 May 1975. It was reported in 1976 that this had not resulted in excessive applications being received.

Factors which give rise to housing need include: overcrowding; the lack of basic facilities, such as a kitchen, or bathroom; the involuntary separation of some members of the family; the condition of the present dwelling; ill health; the unsuitability of the location of the present dwelling in relation to the particular family's needs; and the threat of eviction. When households have been evicted and are homeless, they must be given shelter by the local authority, as mentioned above. Social service authorities are under a duty to provide temporary accommodation for the homeless in accordance with section 21 of the National Assistance Act 1948, as amended by the Local Government Act 1972. Circular 18/74 rested implicitly on the proposition that while help for the homeless calls for the co-operation of all local authorities and departments, it is housing authorities who can best—possessing as they do the relevant resources, powers and expertise— provide and manage accommodation for housing the homeless (*Homelessness—A Consultation Paper*, DOE, WO and DHSS,

April 1975). Legislation to make housing authorities responsible for the homeless was expected to be introduced in 1977. (See also Chapter 11.)

Housing aid centres

The recommendation of the Seebohm committee that local authorities should provide centres for housing guidance and advice was mentioned at the beginning of this chapter. A number of local authorities inaugurated housing aid centres with the basic concept of trying to examine each individual housing problem in depth to see what housing solutions could be found as an alternative to providing local authority accommodation, but at the same time helping to prevent homelessness, social deprivation and increasingly expensive council building. Many housing aid centres were initially very successful in advising, guiding and even motivating people towards house purchase as a method of solving housing needs, but unfortunately market conditions are denying this solution to many people. The centres, especially in areas of housing stress, are finding that an increasing proportion of time is taken up with guidance in tenancy problems, both to landlord and tenant, which often prevents hardship and possible evictions (8).

Rents

The Housing Act 1957 empowered local authorities to fix such reasonable rents and grant to any tenant such rebates therefrom, subject to any terms and conditions, as they say fit. They were charged to review rents from time to time and make such changes, either in rents generally or in particular rents, or in rebates where these were granted, as circumstanuces might require. The traditional independence enjoyed by local authorities in working out for themselves how to fix rents for council housing was challenged in 1968, when the government referred council house rents to the Prices and Incomes Board. The Board found this independence incompatible with the prices and incomes policy, and its recommendations in the report, *Increases in Rents of Local Authority Housing* (1968, H.M.S.O., Cmnd. 3604) led to legislation which restricted the increase in rents which local authorities could make for a limited period. (Prices and Incomes Act 1968; Rent (Control of Increases) Act 1969.)

The Housing Finance Act 1972, which is described in Chapter 1, applied the principle of fair rent (introduced in the Rent Act 1965 for private unfurnished dwellings) to every housing revenue account dwelling of every local authority and new town corporation. The rent of each dwelling was to be assessed, therefore, by reference to the character, location, amenities and state of repair, but disregarding the value due to any local shortage of similar accommodation. Council house rents were no longer to be influenced by the state of the local authority's housing revenue account, the size of its building programme or the amount of rebates granted to its tenants; nor were rents expected to bear the cost of slum clearance or the community benefits connected with housing. The procedure for determining the fair rents was laid down in the Act, and provisional assessments of rents were to be submitted to a rent scrutiny board.

The Housing Rents and Subsidies Act 1975 repealed certain provisions of the Housing Finance Act 1972, and replaced them with a new system of rents and subsidies. It ended the 1972 Act system of fair rents in the public sector (except for housing associations), including the rent scrutiny board machinery and the mandatory increases to fair rents for local authority and new town corporation tenants, and restored to local authorities the power to fix rents. The new subsidy system provided by the Act (summarised below) was aimed to help new building, the acquisition of land and housing, and the improvement of existing housing. The Act also helped people to form housing co-operatives by agreement with the local authority or new town corporation with the approval of the Secretary of State and enabled grants to be paid to co-operatives which were registered with the Housing Corporation.

After a rents standstill in 1974–75, however, a short period of local freedom of decision in fixing rents has been cut short by the White Paper (Cmnd. 6151) *The Attack on Inflation* which deals specifically with rents and subsidies. The government accepts that the pay policy requires the commensurate action on local authority rents; that is, that in 1976–77 rents rise no faster than the rise in prices generally. The White Paper estimates on this basis that rises from the spring of 1976 averaging about 60p per week are necessary. As no " real " improvement in the balance of local authority housing accounts results from such a rise, the government is providing up to £68 million extra in subsidy.

Local authorities have been urged ever since the 1930s to use housing subsidies to help, through rent rebate schemes, those tenants who could not otherwise afford the rents of the dwellings they needed. Such a scheme was defined in 1967 as one where a standard rent was fixed for each dwelling and the tenant could apply for a rebate related to his income and family responsibilities (MoHLG Circular 46/67). A differential rent scheme was described as one where all tenants were required to declare their income, and rents were then fixed on a scale related to income. The Ministry of Housing recommended rent rebate rather than differential rent schemes, and put forward a model rent rebate scheme. Detailed figures submitted to the Estimates Committee of the House of Commons for 354 urban districts in 1967–68, however, showed that 232 had no rebate schemes, and of the rest 84 gave rebates totalling 25 per cent or less of the subsidy (1: 15).

As described in Chapter 1, Part II of the Housing Finance Act 1972 required every housing authority to introduce by 1 October 1972 a rent rebate scheme for their own tenants, and every local authority, except the Greater London Council, to introduce by 1 January 1973 a rent allowance scheme for private tenants living in unfurnished accommodation in its area. The Furnished Lettings (Rent Allowances) Act 1973 gave effect to the extension of rent allowances to certain tenants of furnished lettings, and the Rent Act 1974 simplified the procedure and brought the two kinds of tenancies, furnished and unfurnished, into line for rebate and allowance purposes. (See section 25 (1) of the Housing Finance Act 1972, and DOE Circular 137/74, WO 212/74, *Rent Act 1974: Rent Rebate and Rent Allowance Schemes.*) In London, the rent allowance schemes are administered by the London boroughs. " Housing authority " is defined in section 104 (1) of the 1972 Act as a local authority or a new town corporation, and " local authority " as the council of a county borough, London borough, or county district, the Greater London Council or the Common Council of the City of London. Subject to sections 20 and 21 of the 1972 Act, rent rebate and allowance schemes must conform with the provisions of, and be not less generous than, the model schemes prescribed by the Act.

Schedule 3 to the 1972 Act sets out details of the computation of rebates and allowances. Under the scheme, every tenant eligible for a rebate has a needs allowance calculated to take account of the size and composition of his family. The amount of the needs allowances are varied from time to time by regulations made by the Secretary of State with the consent of the Treasury, and he must refer his proposals in this matter to the Advisory Committee on Rent Rebates and Rent Allowances, as described below. Needs allowances have been increased several times since the passing of the Act, and in November 1976, currently governed by S.I. 1976 1470, were:

Individual	£23·05
Married couple	£32·75
Individual and dependent child	£32·75
Each dependent child	£5·35

Housing authorities may make their schemes more generous provided that the overall cost of doing so does not exceed the cost of operating the model scheme by more than 10 per cent.

The Act provided for the setting up of a committee, the Advisory Committee on Rent Rebates and Rent Allowances, to advise the Secretary of State on any question relating to the operation of rebate schemes and allowance schemes in general, or of particular rebate schemes or allowance schemes, or to the advisability of varying the provisions of Schedule 3 or Schedule 4 to the Act (Part I of Schedule 3 deals with computation of rebates and allowances, as summarised above; Part II with persons receiving supplementary benefit. Schedule 4 deals with procedure for operating rebate and allowance schemes.) The advisory committee can consider particular schemes, but it is not part of its function to act as an appeal body against decisions taken by local authorities on individual applications.

Local authorities are obliged to give publicity, as detailed in the Act, for their rent rebate and allowance schemes and all landlords who granted a new tenancy of a dwelling to a private tenant on or after 1 January 1973 had to furnish to the tenant in writing and in a convenient form the statutory particulars of the allowance scheme currently operated by the local authority in whose area the dwelling was situated. Subsequently, all landlords were required to insert a prescribed form of words referring to the availability of a rent allowance in every rent book.

Legally, the tenant must see that the rent reaches the landlord or his agent who is under no obligation to collect it or to send a reminder or a demand for it. In practice, however, especially for local authorities who own large number of properties, many let on weekly tenancies, it is in the landlord's interest to ensure that the tenants have every facility for paying their rent, and rent collection forms a major part of the work of a housing office. Door-to-door collection, which provided the main point of contact between the tenant and the landlord—and this contact was an integral point of the Octavia Hill school of management, mentioned in Chapter 1—has been abandoned in many areas for security and other reasons, including less need for welfare contacts with very many tenants, a wider spread of income groups in local authority housing, less poverty, better education and wider dissemination of information, and the absence of many housewives from the home during the day. Many other systems, and combinations of systems, including payment by Giro and banker's order, now operate.

Rent arrears are increasing rapidly, particularly in urban areas (see *Behind with the rent*—A study of council tenants in rent arrears, by the National Consumer Council, 1976). Most inner London boroughs have rent arrears to the order of 4 per cent of annual debit, and three have exceeded 10 per cent. The use of the ultimate weapon of eviction as a method of control of rent arrears was restricted by DOE Circulars 83/72 and 18/74. Qualitative research on this subject (carried out for the IMTA (now CIPFA) in 1969) indicated that the effect of using this weapon was not as widespread or long lasting as was generally supposed. The local authority has an obligation to rehouse tenants after eviction. Rent arrears appear to be very much a symptom of modern urban society, and to a great extent the more urban the local authority the greater arrears are likely to be. Most forms of rent collection now entail positive action on the part of the tenant to get the rent to the landlord, and natural inertia can only lead to increasing arrears. In some case, remedies such as rent guarantees from the social services are used to prevent arrears accumulating. Greater involvement by tenants in management and increasing variety of tenure, including some form of social ownership, combined with more co-operation with tenants on an individual casework basis, may achieve an amelioration of estate management problems, including rising rent arrears.

Rates

General rate is a levy on property made by the rating authority over a prescribed area to meet the cost of local government services.

The rate is calculated at an amount in the pound and levied on the rateable value of every hereditament within the area, with some exceptions, such values being determined by assessments prepared by Valuation Officers of the Commissioners of Inland Revenue. The assessments of a whole rating area are made up in the Valuation List and the rating authority is required to keep this list open for inspection by any ratepayer in the country. Proposals for alteration or amendment of the values can be made by the rating authority, as well as by the owner or occupier or " by any person aggrieved ". If the proposer is still dissatisfied after his proposal has been considered, an appeal can be taken to a local valuation court and thereafter to the Lands Tribunal.

The deposited lists show the gross value and the net annual value of dwellings, the latter being the same as the rateable value, except in certain cases. The basis for the assessment of gross value is the rent which a tenant might reasonably expect to pay in the open market, assuming that the normal conditions prevail, the tenant paying the usual tenant's rates and taxes, and the landlord being responsible for the repairs and insurance, and other expenses necessary to maintain the property in a state to command that rent. To arrive at the net annual value, deductions meant to represent the cost of repairs and insurance are taken from gross value in accordance with a statutory table set out in the Second Schedule of the Rating and Valuation (Miscellaneous Provisions) Act 1955.

Under the Rating and Valuation Act 1925 it was laid down that a revaluation of property should be carried out quinquennially, but in fact no new lists were made from 1934 (1935 in London) until those which came into operation on 1 April 1956. From that date, provision was made for lists to be deposited every five years. In fact, the next revaluation took effect from 1963, and then not until 1973. In the ten years 1963–64 to 1972–73, the amount collected in rates rose from £894 millions to £2,268 millions, an increase of more than 150 per cent, while average rate poundages rose from 45p to 92p, more than double. The increase in the average gross rate income required by local authorities throughout England and Wales was estimated to be up by about 11 per cent over the previous year in 1973–74, and it has continued to rise. The proportion of the general rate going to housing, however, is low in comparison with other services.

In the White Paper, *Better Homes; the next priorities*, the government proposed to give powers to local authorities to charge full rates on empty properties, as opposed to the previous 50 per cent limit. This was to discourage owners from keeping accommodation, particularly houses, empty, often with a view to financial gain; and the proposal was implemented by the Local Government Act 1974.

Residential ratepayers may qualify for rate rebates, and special " revaluation " relief was announced by the government in March 1973 to help householders who faced a large rates increase as a result of the property revaluation. Complicated arrangements for calculating the relief to be paid to householders whose rate bills for 1973–74 had increased by more than 10 per cent as a result of revaluation were set out in DOE Circular 34/73, WO Circular 71/73.

There has been considerable criticism of the rating system during recent years, and the 1973 revaluation aroused much controversy and gave rise to very many appeals against the assessments. The government set up a committee under the chairmanship of Mr Frank Layfield, QC, to review local government finance, and the committee's report was published in May 1976 (9). Briefly, the committee recommends the introduction of local income tax in addition to rates to help finance local government services and strengthen local democracy. It believes that the basis of assessment should be changed from the rent value of the rated property to capital value. The new system would cost about £100 million to run and involve the employment of an extra 12,000 Inland Revenue staff.

Water rate is a charge by the water authority on the occupier of premises for the supply of water and is usually a percentage chargeable on the net annual value of the property as it stands on the current valuation list. The government has introduced legislation to exempt from this charge properties not connected to public sewers (mainly where drainage is to cesspools); and adjustments were made for 1974–75 and 1975–76 by allowance from the 1976–77 rate payments.

Accounts

Local authorities must by law keep a housing revenue account, into which is paid the revenue from rents and exchequer subsidies, and any subsidies allocated from the general rates fund (compulsory for subsidised housing until 1956). The largest item in expenditure is the repayment and interest on loans raised to cover the capital cost of housing; other outgoings are the cost of management and repairs.

The housing revenue account must be in balance at the close of each financial year. If there is any deficit, it must be made good from the rates, i.e., by a rate fund contribution, or by an additional one if there is already one which has been budgeted for. If there is a surplus, this must be carried forward to the next financial year, unless it is applied to making good any rate fund contribution made in the preceding nine financial years.

Local authorities also have to keep a housing repairs account. The purpose of this is to equalise as far as practicable the charges for repair and maintenance of dwellings by transferring an annual sum to the account. A contribution from the housing revenue account must also be made to meet any deficit in the repairs account at the end of the previous financial year. Actual expenditure on repairs is paid for out of the housing repairs account.

Thus, the main items of expenditure and of revenue must be brought within these accounts, but there are marginal items which authorities may charge to the housing revenue account, or to the general rate fund. It is usual to argue that items which are for the benefit of council tenants only are properly within the housing revenue account, but that other items which benefit the citizens of the area at large are properly a rate fund affair—for instance, the maintenance of the housing list may be regarded as the latter (10, 11).

Local authority expenditure which does not form part of the housing revenue account can be classified under five separate, although overlapping, groupings: house improvement and renovation grants; housing action areas and general improvement areas; slum clearance functions; advances for house purchase; and other housing, including loans to housing associations.

Legislation relating to government subsidies which bore a major part of the cost of servicing the capital needed for the housing programme before 1975 is summarised in Chapter 1. New systems of housing subsidy were provided, as an interim replacement for previously existing legislation pending a further review, in the Housing Rents and Subsidies Act 1975. The new system, intended to remain in operation until the major reconsideration of housing finance started in 1975 is completed, consolidated and carried forward subsidies existing in 1973–74 and provided for additional subsidies based mainly on the capital cost of new construction, improvement work and acquisitions. In 1975–76 there has been paid additionally a special element of subsidy to provide a measure of relief to rents immediately after the year of rent freeze in 1974–75 and a similar special element is being paid in 1976–77 to provide relief from the effects of restricted rent increases in the year of " £6 " incomes limit. The rates of the new subsidies are fixed in advance and entitlement does not depend upon rent income. This is a corollary of the government's decision to give back to local authorities freedom to determine for themselves what distribution as between rents and rates of their housing costs, after subsidy, they consider reasonable.

In more detail, the subsidies payable under the Housing Rents and Subsidies Act 1975 are as follows:

(1) The basic element is the aggregate of the subsidies paid under the Housing Finance Act 1972 (residual, transition, rising costs and operation deficit subsidies) for the year 1974–75.

(2) The new capital costs element meets 66 per cent of new loan charges on admissible capital costs ranking as " reckonable expenditure " and calculated at the authority's average loans fund rate of interest for the year. The admissible capital costs include expenditure on the acquisition of land for housing, the acquisition of existing dwellings (and essential repairs to them), new house-building schemes and the improvement of dwellings.

(3) The supplementary financing element takes into account the higher costs of re-borrowing by reimbursing 33 per cent of the excess on an authority's reckonable loan charges in 1975–76 and subsequent years over the comparative figure for the previous year which are attributable to admissible capital costs incurred in any year before 1975–76.

(4) The special element subsidy is based on a formula designed to give help to those authorities whose costs rise above an agreed threshold after making certain notional assumptions to their accounts. The basic purpose of the subsidy is to recompense authorities for additional costs arising from national policies which restrict local freedoms—the achievement of a national policy on the extent of changes in rent levels being a prime example.

(5) The high cost element, payable from 1976–77, is to assist those authorities whose capital cost per dwelling (averaged over

the total housing stock) is so much above the national average as to be a marked disincentive to further building.

(6) Rent rebates subsidy is paid at the rate of 75 per cent of the standard amount of rent rebates.

Problems of local authority housing finance are discussed in Chapter 8.

Sale of council housing

Local authorities can sell their own houses to their tenants, or indeed to anyone wishing to buy. This power, under the Housing Act 1936, was originally subject to the consent of the Minister in each case, but with certain conditions as to the minimum selling price, rent limits and other relevant matters; it also covered the disposal of houses on long leases.

The extent to which local authorities should sell council houses is controversial, and in 1968 became a political issue. It was argued that authorities in areas where there was a severe shortage of rented housing should not reduce their stock in this way, and the Minister withdrew his general consent to council house sales. Consent was renewed, however, by MoHLG Circular 42/68 in the case of the majority of housing authorities, but others in the conurbations of Greater London, Merseyside, South-east Lancashire and the West Midlands were allowed to sell only up to one quarter per cent of their houses in any one year. MoHLG Circular 54/70, issued by a Conservative government, withdrew the limitations on the sale of existing council houses, and in 1976 the position remains that councils may sell their houses at current vacant possession market value, provided this is not below cost, with a discount of up to 20 per cent and certain restrictions on resale. Some new Conservative-controlled councils in 1976, however, were proposing to promote the sale of council houses on a large scale, and the proposal was that tenants should be able to buy their homes at the current market price less 30 per cent after three years' occupation; long-term tenants would be allowed a bigger concession, which could amount to a 50 per cent discount after 20 years tenancy.

It appeared that generally throughout the country the sale of council houses and flats reached a peak in 1972–73 when some 45,000 were sold, but the figure for sales fell rapidly to 5,000 in 1974. The reduced interest may have been due to changes in political control in some councils in the spring of 1973, when incoming Labour groups abandoned Conservative policy allowing tenants to buy; but also high prices may have pushed mortgage payments beyond the limit for many potential applicants.

In 1976, the position of the Secretary of State for the Environment was as stated in May of that year, that, " Whether selling is right or wrong must depend on local circumstances and above all on the effect it would have on housing shortage and housing need ".

Local authorities were encouraged to build reasonably priced houses for sale by DOE Circular 60/73 (WO 112/73), *Building for Sale by Local Authorities*, but such schemes were not to produce work for direct labour departments. Subsequently, DOE Circular 52/74 (WO 95/74), issued by the Labour government, explained that the government was concerned that the restrictions on the use of direct labour might reduce the capacity of local authorities to build lower-priced houses for sale where local need was not being met; direct labour departments were, therefore, to be allowed to tender (16).

The future of public sector housing

This chapter shows the very wide powers and functions of local authorities in the housing field and the complexity of their operations. It shows too how their housing activities are affected by political considerations and how their plans and programmes often have to be forced into changes of direction by government policy changes, e.g., by the implications of section 105 of the Housing Act 1974.

The purpose of the Housing Centre conference on the future of public sector housing, held in February 1976, and reported in the March–April issue of *Housing Review* (Vol. 25, No. 2, 1976), was to bring together those involved in the field to consider current issues; i.e., of costs and standards for new building and rehabilitation; the balance between redevelopment and rehabilitation; the worsening problems of older housing estates (usually built in previous periods of constraint on housing expenditure and restrictive subsidies)—and, worse still, some rapidly deteriorating newer estates; and the possibilities of various forms of devolution to tenants, including management committees and co-operatives. Both the papers and discussion at the conference revealed many areas of concern and produced far-ranging proposals for remedying defects in public housing and improving the housing stock generally.

Public expenditure cuts in 1976 included two key reductions in housing—£146 million in 1977–78 taken from the money councils can lend to home buyers, and the ending of the open-ended commitment to council house-building. DOE Circular 80/76 conveyed to local authorities that limited public funds should be concentrated first on policies for renewal and rehabilitation in stress areas, and secondly on special local requirements and particular social needs; in fact, that " selective intervention " should provide the recipe for future policies.

Circular 80/76 gave priority in housebuilding to authorities listed in the Annex of the circular, which are considered to have special problems of housing stress. It is made clear, however, that representations from other authorities wishing to claim similar treatment will be considered. Other priorities will include: pockets of housing stress within other authorities, instances of special need such as industrial development, or town development, and particular social needs. The remainder of the programme will be allocated in respect of general needs.

The Secretary of State for the Environment has expressed the government's deep concern about the future of inner city areas, and has indicated that an overall review of policies for the urban areas, together with future policies on dispersal, will be undertaken. Further, a new basis for housing finance, including an overall capital ceiling for local authority housing expenditure to replace separate control of rehabilitation (under section 105 of the Housing Act) and new housing is to be introduced in 1978. These proposals are examined further in Chapter 12.

CHAPTER 4

New and Expanded Towns

BETWEEN THE WARS, the housing needs of the bigger industrial towns and cities were met in the main by building where the only land was available, on the outskirts. Sometimes local authorities even built housing estates beyond their own boundaries. The influx of new workers from areas of economic depression, the natural growth of population, the demand for more spacious and higher standard living conditions, both at home and at work, all combined to produce ever larger cities which sprawled out beyond their former limits, while at the same time the process of slum clearance and central redevelopment created a demand for both housing and industrial accommodation, which somehow had to be met. The resulting suburbs were for the most part little more than dormitories, work and entertainment having to be found still in the inner area. The journey to work became progressively longer and transport more congested. In spite of efforts to preserve a green belt of undeveloped land around the large cities, such as London, the towns and suburbs in the main manufacturing and business areas coalesced into the large conurbations we know today.

The idea of the " garden city ", that is, a new virtually self-contained community, where people live and work and shop and play, had been put forward before the end of the nineteenth century by Ebenezer Howard. The town was to be built on land held in communal ownership, so that it could be planned and developed to benefit all the citizens, and any profits could be devoted to enhancing the amenities for their welfare. Ebenezer Howard founded Letchworth Garden City in 1903, to be followed by Welwyn Garden City in 1919. They were pioneer projects based on voluntary efforts, and though successful, their contribution to the need was small in scale.

In 1940, the Royal Commission on the Distribution of the Industrial Population, in the Barlow Report, stressed the economic and strategic disadvantages of the concentration of industries and industrial workers in densely populated areas, particularly in Greater London. The report also suggested that the necessary dispersal could be achieved by the enlargement of small towns or the creation of new ones. In 1942, the whole matter of land ownership and valuation was studied by the Uthwatt Committee (*Final Report of the Expert Committee on*

93

Compensation and Betterment). During the war, too, Professor Patrick Abercrombie produced his plan for Greater London which contained proposals for new towns and for the expansion of existing towns, outside the " green belt " around London (see bibliography Chapter 1). Professor Abercrombie proposed eight new towns and this gave great stimulus to the new town idea. (In the event eight London ring new towns were designated although only two corresponded with Professor Abercrombie's proposed locations.)

In 1945 therefore, a New Towns Committee (the Reith Committee) was set up, and in three reports made recommendations for the implementation of proposals for new towns. The New Towns Act 1946 gave effect to most of the recommendations, and provided for the establishment by the Minister of Town and Country Planning of government-financed and appointed development corporations for the development of new towns. This Act was followed by the Town Development Act 1952, by which development was to be by the exporting and importing authorities themselves (see below). The 1952 Act is still the relevant statute for expanding towns but the New Towns Act 1946 has been replaced by an updating and consolidating New Towns Act 1965.

The primary objective of both these measures was to secure the redistribution of population and employment to relieve the severe overcrowding and congestion in large towns, and to create balanced communities of limited size. There were considerable differences in the means by which the objective was to be achieved. Whereas new towns are developed as a result of direct action by the government, expanded towns are achieved by co-operation between the " exporting " authority from which the population comes, and the " importing " authority in which population can be accepted, and where the provision of housing and industrial expansion are possible.

A secondary objective was to achieve economic growth as well as to relieve congestion. New towns in the North East and North West and Scotland have helped to bring work into these regions and so relieve unemployment and retain population. Then following the 1964 South-East Study (1) with its forecast of " major population growth ", new centres or growth points, were proposed, e.g., at Milton Keynes, Peterborough and Northampton and subsequently in Central Lancashire. Since 1946, 33 new towns have been designated in the United Kingdom, eight known as the London ring new towns, 13 elsewhere in England (four of them also assisting the London overspill problem), two in Wales, six in Scotland and four in Northern Ireland. The Northern Ireland towns are now the divided concern of the Department of Housing, Local Government and Planning for Northern Ireland, the Northern Ireland Housing Executive and the appropriate local government authority. Four " completed " London ring new towns (Crawley, Hatfield, Hemel Hempstead and Welwyn Garden City) are now the concern of the Commission for New Towns but the remainder are still being developed under the aegis of the development corporations.

Up to December 1975, the population of these 33 towns had been increased by one million; 350,000 dwellings had been built (two-thirds by the corporations themselves) and 250,000 industrial jobs had been created plus jobs in commerce, public services etc. Some of the " greenfield " new towns started out from small existing populations, e.g., Harlow (4,500 at designation) and Stevenage (6,700) but more recent designations have been of larger areas embracing one or more established towns and setting much larger population targets than were conceived in 1946 when the maximum anticipated population was 60,000. Thus Peterborough which had a population of 81,000 at designation in 1967 has a " target population " of 180,600. Central Lancashire New Town (which embraces Preston, Chorley and Leyland) started with an existing population of 235,000 and a target of 420,000. The aggregate population target for all 33 towns is over 3 million. Over the 30 years of new towns there has been new thinking about town size, distance from the conurbation, self-containment and catchment areas for employment, recreation etc., and this has affected the choice of new designated areas.

The development of a new town

Planning

The Secretary of State for the Environment designates the area of the new town by making a Statutory Order after which a master plan is prepared by the development corporation. Both stages are subject to public inquiry at which objections to the proposals are heard and considered on the report of the inspector conducting the inquiry. The master plan (comprising a comprehensive written statement and a land use plan) sets out the broad principles of development, its phasing, and the estimated final population. The development corporation is empowered to acquire the necessary land by agreement or by compulsory purchase.

The development corporation role is a creative and co-ordinative one. It plans the development of the whole town, and, while not responsible for the provision in every case, considers every factor which affects urban life—for example, roads and sewers, water supplies, electricity and gas services, education, public health, sites for factories, and, of course, housing. The corporation itself has usually provided the majority of the houses, shops, offices and factories, and many other facilities necessary to the creation of a new community. The local authority and private enterprise also provide some of the housing, and many of the communal facilities are provided by other public authorities or private undertakings, for instance, schools by the education authority (usually the county council), and hospitals by the area health authority, cemeteries, crematoria, leisure activities by the local authorities, usually on land provided and serviced by the corporation and sometimes with financial or technical assistance from the corporation. The development corporation keeps in touch with all organisations involved to supply information where necessary, and to co-ordinate all development.

A principal aim has been to balance employment and housing, if not within the town's boundaries, at least within those of the town and its hinterland. Most existing new towns have not found it easy at first to attract industry and a great deal of time and effort has had to be devoted to this. Houses, however urgently needed, are of little use without jobs; and on the other hand, factories moving to a new town want to be assured that there will be houses for employees. Changes in the economic situation can lead to a reduction in jobs, and so upset the balance. Sometimes, too, conflicts of interest have arisen because the Department of Industry has understandably given priority to the " special areas " when encouraging industrial movement. These need more work but not more population. In contrast, for new towns designed to relieve the housing pressure, it is important that both jobs and families, in balanced proportions, should be moved.

Members of a development corporation are nominated by the Minister. Normally there are nine members (including the chairman and deputy chairman) but the present government has taken power in the New Towns (Amendment) Act 1976 to increase the number to 13, if required.

Corporate management methods have always operated in new towns where the corporation appoints its own staff, at the head of whom is the general manager (sometimes styled managing director or chief executive). While the corporation's role is a creative one, and as such has officers of the appropriate professions serving it, it has a management and maintenance function also, and therefore employs estate staff, housing managers, building surveyors and landscape maintenance managers as well as planners, architects, engineers, quantity surveyors etc. and the supporting financial, legal and administrative staffs. The corporation supplements its direct staff resources by employing consultants (e.g., on the preparation of the master plan) and offers the services of its own staff and that of its consultants to other local and statutory bodies and industrialists etc. associated with the development of the town.

Finance

Main sources of finance are three-fold. Apart from limited bank overdrafts, all borrowing by corporations must be from the government via the National Loans Fund. Perhaps 70 per cent of all capital expenditure on new towns is obtained this way. The second source is from local or national government or nationalised bodies providing the associated services. The third is private enterprise in the provision of housing for owner-occupation, industries, commercial buildings and shops where initial finance is not provided by corporations. In the early years of a new town it may be difficult to attract private capital but later on, in the interests of reducing public expenditure, every effort is made to attract private investment.

Loans to the corporation are fixed-interest repayable on an annuity basis over 60 years at rates obtaining at the time of the loan. There is a statutory limit on government on the amount of advances to corporations. The limit in the New Towns Act 1946 was £50 million. Successive Acts have brought the figure to £2,000 million.

Control over corporation spending is by reference to quin-quennial programmes, annual budgets and, for some proposals, individual schemes. In addition the Department of the Environment specifies a standard form of accounts which has to be submitted annually (after audit by professional auditors) together with an annual report by the corporation on its activities over the financial year. Both are then published and presented to Parliament by the Secretary of State. The accounts, though of standard type, distinguish the forms of expenditure and income so as to provide a separate analysis of housing expenditure to correspond to the housing revenue account of a local housing authority. Besides these statutory accounts, each corporation submits annually to the Secretary of State a set of management accounts which are used for forward planning of the national new towns programme as well as for internal control purposes by each corporation.

Rents

Section 42 of the New Towns Act 1965 empowers the Secretary of State to make grants to corporations in addition to normal Exchequer subsidies. This is in recognition of the fact that corporations have no rate income, so the grant is paid in lieu so far as the housing revenue account is concerned. Except for the period during which the Housing Finance Act 1972 applied the concept of " fair rents " *inter alia* to new town housing, the rents of corporation housing have been fixed at a level which, with subsidies and section 42 grant, are sufficient to balance the housing revenue account.

Corporations are not allowed to use any of the profits from commerce or industry to reduce the rents of their houses. They have no pre-war houses to aid their rents pool, and, in the early years of a new town at least, rents tend to be somewhat higher than those of local authority estates in the area. Rent rebate schemes cushion the effect for households with lower incomes. By section 33 of the Housing Repairs and Rents Act 1954 houses provided by development corporations are not subject to the Rent Acts.

Allocation of Houses

The Department of the Environment has laid down guide-lines as to who should be eligible for corporation housing in new towns. In so far as the new towns around London are concerned, for instance, priority must be given to families coming from London who are in established housing need, or council tenants, or tenants of housing association property. The applicant must obtain work in the new town or close to it, unless of course he or she is retired or is a single parent obliged to stay at home to care for the children. Perhaps the biggest problem of new town development and town expansion is the matching of work and workers. It would be simple if the only housing priority was for skilled men irrespective of their housing need. But equal emphasis is placed on housing those with need irrespective of their employment skills. So two conflicting objectives must be brought together and the types of employment encouraged that will offer opportunity to skilled and unskilled workers alike. Great efforts have also to be made to ensure that jobs of the right kind are made available in the new town or receiving areas at the same time as the housing. In 1953, the Industrial Selection Scheme was instituted by the then Ministry of Housing and Local Government to ensure that families with a housing need are given priority of opportunity for employment and housing in new and expanding towns; under this, exporting authorities keep an industrial selection list of people resident in their areas willing to move, and whom they would be prepared to nominate.

In London, all applicants on London borough council waiting lists and tenants of the Greater London Council, London borough councils and housing associations are eligible and can apply directly to the GLC for registration. The scheme operates in conjunction with the Department of Employment through employment exchanges. Applicants are given a trade classification which forms the basis for selection. Employers notify the local employment exchange of their requirements, having confirmed with the importing authority that housing is available, and if vacancies cannot be filled locally, the exporting authority is informed and submits details of suitably qualified persons. Interviews are arranged at their nearest exchange, and names are then submitted from which the employer can choose. There are many inherent difficulties in getting the scheme (now known in London as the " New and Expanding Towns Scheme ") to work efficiently and quickly, and ways of improving it are constantly being investigated.

Exceptions to the London rule can be made where a man moves with his factory to a new town from elsewhere, or if he is recruited for a job which cannot be filled by the Department of Employment by someone from London. Exceptions are also made for professional people, such as teachers, doctors and civil servants. The London new towns have been criticised for not doing enough for Londoners in urgent housing need. The reason for the number of non-Londoners housed is that industry attracted to new towns tends to employ a high proportion of highly skilled men who are nationally in short supply and cannot necessarily be obtained from London. Once an industry is established, it is necessary to man it and if the requisite skills cannot be recruited either locally or from London, employers must look elsewhere and need to be able to offer housing by the corporation if they are to attract the employees required. This points to the need for a diversification of employment from the outset—in types, sizes, and skills—if the town is to be shielded from economic recession and the workers are to be found from all walks of life. As the new town matures, its own population throws up fresh demands for work and housing. As regards work, the aim is to find employment for those leaving school or for housewives seeking jobs after their children have grown up. This reduces the demand for in-migrant workers and especially for the unskilled. As a result the new town is even less able to offer help to London's unskilled. As regards housing, it is of great importance that housing is available for the town's second generation. If they are forced away because of lack of housing, more in-migrants must be sought. It is to everybody's advantage to house the new generation of households on the spot and help to consolidate the town's social composition. The statutory responsibility for housing the second generation is of course the local authority's, but corporations accept that much of this demand arises from their activity in bringing the initial families into the town and there is a moral obligation to cater for the children when they marry and set up house.

The parents of new town residents are also housed in new towns when they retire. This has proved very successful, as it helps both young and old. Further, it often deals with urgent housing problems, frees local authority flats, and reduces, if only slightly, the inevitable imbalance of the age structure in the new town.

Because of these and other demands on the housing stock, the proportion of new town houses offered for in-migrant workers declines significantly. In the early years about 80 per cent of dwellings might be used for such workers from the conurbation concerned but after 20 years the proportion will be less than half that. This is no ground for criticism. That would be justified if an attempt was made to maintain a high in-migrant proportion at the expense of meeting locally generated housing needs.

Social problems of the newcomers

A new town presents special opportunities and difficulties in the building of a new and, so far as possible, balanced community. In some cases, where a nucleus already exists, the new and the old communities must be integrated. Social provision must keep pace with population growth: if they do not, the exaggerated allegations about "New town blues", and "Neurosis in new towns", which have featured in newspaper headlines might have some justification. Unfortunately, although new towns are given some priority in resource allocation, finance for these facilities is often forthcoming at a slower rate than house production and the new populations are denied the facilities they need. In addition some young housewives have a difficult time at first, and face loneliness and depression; they miss the old, familiar surroundings, and the support and social contacts of their parents and relations and feel the lack of shops and buses. There is much that development corporations (and councils of expanding towns) can do to help, particularly in the early stages; "authority" must show that it cares, must listen to complaints, discover grievances and find temporary solutions to problems until permanent solutions are possible. A temporary hair-dressing salon in a caravan, a clinic in a church hall, garages converted into a temporary church, a mobile library, are all examples of the earliest makeshift measures. Information as to what is being and will be done, and encouragement of self-help, are vital. Many keen and active people move to new and expanding towns, as is shown by the success of many voluntary ventures, such as pre-school play groups and nursery schools. In most of the new towns, which attracted younger married men who moved with the industry, the population included a very small proportion of elderly people, but, as explained above, accommodation is now frequently provided for older relatives, and the general age-structure changes in any case with time. Much of the success of a new town depends on the staff of the public relations or social development departments and the housing management staff; they must be given time and opportunity to do the job.

In recent years there has been a movement towards dual use of premises so as to maximise the return on social investment. Schools have community centre " wings ", churches are ecumenically provided and sometimes so used. Corporations are allowed within fixed limits to assist financially the provision of amenities, large and small, which might otherwise be beyond the early rate resources of the local authorities.

Future ownership and management of new town housing

The long awaited measures for settling the future of new towns are now in hand. Crawley and Hemel Hempstead, which were considered finished, were handed over in 1962, and Welwyn and Hatfield in 1966, to the New Towns Commission, which was set up to take over the new towns when completed. The original intention of the 1946 Act had been for completed towns to be handed over to the local authority, but this was amended by the New Towns Act 1959 as the judgment of the government of the day was that it was premature to make the hand over, and moreover there might be other forms of control more appropriate in view of the government investment that had gone into the new towns. The New Towns Commission was an interim piece of machinery.

A change of government led to the appointment of Professor J. B. Cullingworth and Miss V. Karn in 1966 to advise on ownership and management of housing in the new towns. Their report (2), published in 1968, was not very definite on the issue of transfer to the local authority of corporation rented housing, and no government action on this aspect was taken at the time. It had also examined the possibility of the transfer of some corporation housing to housing associations and co-operatives, the transfer of some housing to the local authority, and the retention of some by the development corporation or *ad hoc* successor to it. Professor Cullingworth examined the issue of what is a " normal " pattern of housing tenure in a town, and found that while local authority ownership of housing to let is normal, its extension to near monopoly, which would result if all development corporation housing were transferred to the local authority, would not be normal. The advantages and disadvantages of the various types of tenure are intensified in new towns owing to the concentration of property in the hands of the development corporations.

However after two further changes of administration, the government in 1974 announced its intention of transferring rented housing and related assets of new towns nearing completion and of the New Towns Commission to the appropriate local authorities. A proposed scheme was put forward by the Stevenage Working Party (comprising officers of the Department, the Stevenage Borough Council, and the Stevenage Development Corporation) in 1975 and on this was based the New Towns (Amendment) Act introduced in the Commons on 12 March 1976 as a bill of that title and becoming law on 15 November 1976. It is envisaged that the housing assets of the New Towns Commission and those of the older new towns still building will be transferred to the local authorities from 1 April 1978 onwards. A consultation paper issued on 31 December 1974 by the government proposed that, with this transfer, the function of the New Towns Commission should change, to concentrate on the industrial and commercial aspects of new towns, which it was not intended to transfer to local authorities.

New Towns (Amendment) Act 1976

The new Act provides for the Secretary of State to direct any new town corporation and the new town local authority, in respect of a town designated at least 15 years previously, to prepare and submit a scheme for the vesting in the local authority of all completed housing and related assets (garages, neighbourhood shops, estate greens and open spaces etc.) belonging to the corporation. The transfer will take effect from the 1st April following the approval of the scheme. The Act provides for transfer by instalments if necessary, but it is expected that there will be two transfers—existing housing on the 1st April vesting day and the balance of the housing assets when the development corporation is itself wound up.

The houses in the second transfer will, however, have already been handed over for management purposes to the local authority as and when they are completed, to ensure unified housing management of the total stock. The financial basis of transfer will be on outstanding debt and transfer of subsidies. But the section 42 grant to corporations will not be transferred because this might result in a heavy rate burden; the Act provides for Exchequer grants in the first years of transfer after which these special grants would be phased out. The financial mechanics provided by the Act are designed to secure that the transaction will result in no financial gain to either the transferring corporation or the receiving council.

Although only the older new towns will be immediately affected, the Act is cast to provide for transfers in all new towns as the years pass and, if corporation and authority agree, for suggestions to be made to the Secretary of State for a direction to prepare a transfer scheme even before the 15 years have expired. The transfer scheme will contain proposals to give corporations nomination rights for new dwellings and vacated dwellings so that they will possess the same facility for offering accommodation to priority categories of housing demand to whom they will still have a continuing obligation.

Circular 5/77, *Transfer Schemes under the New Towns (Amendment) Act 1976*, 60p, of 17 January from the Department summarises the contents of the Act and offers guidance as to the preparation of the transfer scheme, a model of which is appended to the circular.

Sale of houses to tenants

One other feature of the Cullingworth/Karn report of 1968 (2) was the argument that if the wishes and aspirations of the families in new towns were to be taken as a guide, there should be a greater opportunity for owner-occupation. The proportion of houses occupied by their owners in new towns is considerably below the average for the country as a whole. Moreover, it was suggested that for economic reasons private capital needed to be attracted to new towns.

Corporations were therefore allowed to provide housing for rent or sale and some preliminary steps were taken towards sale of existing houses to sitting tenants. But more positive steps in the latter direction were called for by the government of 1970. It looked beyond redressing the balance by new building: it called on corporations to exercise the powers (already possessed by local authorities) to sell existing houses to sitting tenants. The price was fixed at market value with vacant possession less a standard 20 per cent. reduction. Tenants' response was immediate and 24,000 houses were sold between then and 1973 when escalating prices and the mortgage famine stemmed transactions which were in any event brought to a halt by the new government's decision in 1974 not to permit further sales. The reason given was the shortage of rented housing to meet existing demand. In some new towns there was subsequently little evidence of shortage and in the summer of 1976 Ministers agreed to consider, in towns meeting specified criteria about supply and demand, allowing a resumption of sales to future tenants. But a shift in tenure proportions has already been achieved. In Stevenage for example, the 1971 Census showed that only 10 per cent. of occupants were owners. The 1976 figure is over 35 per cent. though still far short of the national average for all housing of 52 per cent. owner-occupation.

Whatever their attitude to sales of existing housing, governments of all shades of opinion agree that balance between housing tenures is important. Successive Ministers urged that new towns should achieve a 50 : 50 ratio of rented housing (by corporation, local authority and housing association) to owner-occupied housing. In the early stages of a new town the emphasis is usually on rented housing provision with private housing following on to adjust the balance. In the older new towns, the balance has never been achieved, though a major step towards it was taken during the period when sales to sitting tenants were allowed. At present, with the pressure for more rented housing, the Secretary of State has asked corporations to ensure that 75 per cent. of new provision is of rented houses but he has indicated a readiness at the appropriate time to revert to the 50 : 50 aim previously held.

The role of the new towns

Since 1975 there has been much debate about the significance of new towns in today's situation which is so different from that which obtained in the late 1940s and 1950s. The prevailing argument is that no more new towns need to be designated and that the rate of development of existing ones should be reappraised. The grounds are that national population has fallen and with it the need to provide overspill housing on the scale previously envisaged; that the big towns are losing population and jobs at a faster rate than desirable or convenient, leading to loss of revenue, urban obsolescence etc.; that some of the nation's resources now being used on new towns could be diverted to urban renewal of existing towns; and that new towns are sometimes wasteful of land, especially agricultural land that the nation cannot afford to lose. The government has already abandoned the new town proposals for Stonehouse, and recent statements by the Secretary of State for the Environment have suggested that development programmes at such " third generation " towns as Milton Keynes, Peterborough, Northampton, Warrington and Telford might be substantially curbed. The smaller programmes at the older new towns may be less affected because the extra investment involved is relatively small since it builds on and benefits from the capital already invested in creating the town.

Few question the contribution the new towns have made to housing, planning and industrial growth. The question now is whether, in times of limited potential investment, the country can afford *not* to use it on trying to stem the loss of industrial output and an industrial labour force in the existing towns and cities where so much of the infrastructure is now being under-utilised. To use it on new towns only exacerbates the inner city problem.

The new town machinery

Although further new towns are not therefore likely, there has been some discussion on using the machinery of new town creation for major urban renewal in this country and also for the building of new towns overseas. A new company is being created under government aegis to sell the unique British experience in this field. And suggestions are frequently made that the London Docklands Area—now the concern of a local authority joint committee (drawn from the GLC and five London boroughs)—should also be turned over to a development corporation. Overseas adventures may have some future but it is unlikely that local government would welcome the government "interference" which is associated with the idea of new town corporations which, after all, are government agents.

The Community Land Act 1975

An outline of the above is given in Chapter 9 which considers planning and land. The experience of the new towns in land assembly and co-ordinated development is quoted by Ministers as being the pioneer basis for the government proposals for the legislation on land. The provisions of the Act are extremely complicated, but new town corporations are local authorities for the purposes of the Act, even though they may still prefer to operate under the New Towns Act 1965. Land transactions by corporations will lie outside the Community Land Account and there are no shares of any surpluses available to the local authorities.

Expanded towns

By the end of 1949, the eight London new towns had been designated and also two in the North of England, one in Wales and two in Scotland. The next step in the implementation of the proposals contained in the Barlow report for the dispersal of industries and industrial workers was put forward in December 1949 in a memorandum from the then Minister of Town and Country Planning, and carried the new town concept further by suggesting the expansion of existing small towns within the South East region by linking them with sectors of London. As in the case of new towns, the purpose of " expanded " towns was to accommodate the " overspill " population and industry resulting from the reduction in residential density, and the redevelopment of the congested areas, in the inner parts of London.

They were to be developed as balanced self-contained communities in which the inhabitants would find work as well as homes. The Town Development Act 1952 provided the powers, financial and otherwise, for the expansion of existing small towns, and later the Housing Act 1961 extended them to include large towns.

Town expansion policy related the problem of the large congested areas to that of the many smaller rural and urban districts who were anxious to improve the opportunities, amenities and services available to their inhabitants but had insufficient resources to be able to do so. The Act made provision for the councils of the larger " exporting " areas and the smaller " receiving " areas to enter into agreements, whereby houses would be built and factory sites made available in the receiving areas for overspill population with industry to move in hand in hand. Thus, the over-congested areas could be relieved (without the expenditure and time involved in the building of new towns), while, at the same time, new population, new industry and new vitality would be injected into those areas whose life was threatened with stagnation.

Under the 1952 Act, arrangements with the receiving areas can be by means of either nomination or agency agreements. In a " nomination scheme " the exporting authority nominates the tenants but the receiving authority is fully responsible for the development; in an " agency scheme " the exporting authority underwrites the development on an agreed programme and provides the necessary initial finance.

The exporting authority's point of view

In theory, the Town Development Act 1952 should enable the exporting authority to relieve congestion and proceed with development plans within its boundaries; in practice, there have proved to be many difficulties. The first task for the exporting authority is to find areas which are suitable for the reception of overspill, and whose councils are willing to take part in an overspill scheme. An acceptable receiving area must have sites for housing and industry, capable of being developed at a reasonable cost; it must have adequate water supply, gas and electricity, sewerage and other essentials, or these services must be expandable; transport facilities must be available for commercial and individual needs and schools, shops, medical, fire, police and all the other services must be capable of growth to meet the needs of the newcomers. Distance from the exporting town seems less important than good communications, reasonable facilities and an attractive environment. Inevitably, not all the areas who might like to take part in an overspill scheme can fulfil these essential conditions, and of those who can, many are not easily persuaded to do so. Despite government subsidy and such financial and technical assistance as they may get from the exporting authorities and from their own county councils—whose approval on planning and other grounds is, of course, essential—many small towns who contemplate receiving overspill are understandably nervous of shouldering what, to them, is a heavy financial burden and one which for a considerable time will bring little return. They may also be fearful of the effect of a vast influx of strangers on their own character and identity. To the exporting authority, concerned with its own urgent and vast housing problems, progress may indeed seem desperately slow.

Here, as with new towns, one of the major difficulties is that of attracting industry. Naturally the smaller authorities do not want to encourage an influx of population which will merely compete for the limited number of jobs which already exist in the area. They want instead population accompanied by industry, providing new opportunities, teaching new skills, and making for a more prosperous and balanced economy. Until recently it was thought no advantage to the exporting authority to lose population if industry did not go too, and strenuous efforts, especially in London, were made to encourage industries to move to expanding towns. By this means areas within the city could be redeveloped and non-conforming industries " winkled out " to the city's and the industrialists' advantage as well as to that of the expanding town. Now there has been a reaction, and even London, where the GLC has been the most forthcoming of all exporting authorities, is calling for a halt to the export of firms. Still some may be anxious to move. The advantages of decentralisation for industrialists are that land is much less expensive, the building of new houses should ensure a supply of labour, living and working conditions would be more pleasant, and the escape from the long and tiring journey to work should help improve the health of employees and employers and so improve productivity. Disadvantages to industrialists may be the loss of long-established contacts in their present premises; the expense and loss of production consequent upon the move; and so on. Many industries that have moved out of congested areas have benefited and have reported favourably on their progress in new surroundings.

Recruitment of workers to these industries is through the same Industrial Selection Scheme described for new towns. Priority for those in housing need has to be reconciled with priority for those with the right industrial skills. This is no easy task. Neither is that of balancing supply with labour demand as factories are completed and block housing demands arise. A hiatus in either programme can lead to factories without workers or houses without tenants, and in smaller expanding towns can present a severer headache than arises in the larger new towns.

The receiving authority's point of view

Many small authorities are faced with the urgent need of strengthening their economy and bringing new life to their areas. In many places there is no opportunity of suitable employment for able children who may thus be forced to leave their homes and towns—and as farming becomes more mechanised there are fewer jobs on the land. An injection of new industry and of new blood is needed to prevent stagnation and decay.

Town expansion under the 1952 Act can give new employi opportunities to the receiving authority and improve social fac... ties and amenities, but to be successful each expansion must be an exercise in real co-operation between the exporting and receiving authority. Only by close co-ordination of programmes and activities will the problems described above be avoided. The newcomers have their problems too. Many will have moved from familiar streets where, even if housing conditions were overcrowded or unsatisfactory, friends and relations have been close at hand. They may feel lonely and friendless in their new surroundings. Children, however, often help to break down barriers, and generally the whole family takes its place quickly in the general pattern of the town, especially if there are good public relations and social welfare facilities available.

Financial aspects

The principle underlying the Town Development Act 1952 is that local authorities should themselves take the initiative in carrying out schemes of this kind, the government's role being to provide additional financial assistance where necessary and to assist in eliminating procedural or legal difficulties between the authorities and to stimulate the necessary movement of industry. The Act confers few new powers on the receiving authority since most of the work can be carried out under existing powers in the Housing Acts and the Town and Country

Planning Acts. The financial position is that the receiving authority will make itself responsible for providing the land and services and for building the houses. It will provide the factory sites and may, indeed, build the factories and let them out at profit rentals.

For approved schemes, the Minister pays both the normal Exchequer housing subsidy and in addition an " expanding town subsidy " (Housing Rents and Subsidies Act 1975, section 4). The latter is paid for 10 years and is currently fixed at 12 per cent. of capital loan charges plus one-tenth of capital costs met out of revenue. There is now no statutory obligation for exporting authorities to make a contribution towards the costs of receiving authorities in respect of these subsidised dwellings; but those exporting authorities anxious to make the scheme a success are likely not only to make such contribution but also share the burden of unremunerative expenditure in the early years of development. In addition, the Minister, having regard to the resources of the authority, may make contributions towards the expenses of the receiving authority in acquiring the land, preparing the site, providing, extending or improving main water supply, sewerage, or sewage disposal services, payments to main water suppliers, and payments to river boards and drainage authorities in respect of expenses incurred by them in carrying out work resulting from the new development.

Expanding town as an alternative to new town

There is no clear-cut criterion on which the New Towns Act rather than the expanding towns legislation should be used to enlarge an existing town. Major expansion could clearly involve expenditure beyond the largest local authority resources—as would also lesser expansions carried through at an abnormally fast rate. Much depends on whether the expansion is part of national or regional economic planning strategy or is locally generated. So Peterborough, forming part of the strategy for the South East, was treated as a new town but Basingstoke (a partial substitute for the ill-fated " Hook " (GLC New Town)) was an expanded town. The democratic difference was that Basingstoke had control of its destiny—the type, scale and rate of developments in the town; but Peterborough was much more subject to government and corporation initiatives. To try to bridge this difference, Peterborough, Northampton and Warrington, though to be developed under the New Towns Act, were styled " Partnership Towns " and arrangements were introduced to ensure that the local authorities (county and district) had a fuller say in the development of their towns. The government, profiting from the success of these arrangements, proposed in the consultation paper of 1974 that the principles of partnership shall be applied as far as practicable in other new towns. One measure already taken has been to increase the local government representation on corporation boards and this is a reason for the recent enlargement in the membership numbers of corporations.

Past achievements

Starting from 1952, the progress with expanding towns to June 1975 may be summarised as follows. Nine English major exporting towns (including London) have been involved but only two on a diverse scale. The GLC have had agreements with 28 towns to expand and Birmingham 12, the other seven exporting towns having 21 between them. In total 250,000 dwellings are planned of which more than a third have been completed. Some of the towns expanded are as big as the medium-size new towns, e.g. Swindon (now Thamesdown) and Basingstoke, whereas others are quite minor in scale but significant all the same for the small town being enlarged.

The future

The reappraisal of the role of new towns now in hand affects the towns; also, as indicated earlier, cities have lost employment and population too fast for their comfort, although only a small part has been by planned overspill. The loss of the remainder is more difficult to control; but planned overspill can be constrained. If doubts have been expressed about the *new* towns draining off the resources of the conurbations, they are redoubled for *expanding* towns. This is because the exporting authority is bearing major expenditure for expanding towns which it is spared in the case of new towns. It is also finding most of the industry by exporting it to the expanding town while the new town draws its employers over a wider area. Understandably, therefore, the Greater London Council has taken the view that there should be no more expanding town agreements and their existing expansion schemes should either be phased out or be stretched out—all with a view to saving money, population and jobs in the hope that these could improve and stabilise the capital instead of denuding it.

Conclusion

Although it appears that there is to be a downturn in, and maybe even an abandonment of, new and expanding town activity, that comes not from the failure of the achievements of these towns but from the disappearance of the circumstances that gave rise to the need for them in the earlier post-war years. The new towns (and it applies in no small degree to the expanding towns) have been rightly hailed as a great social experiment pioneered in Britain and now being emulated in Europe and the world. It is also the most successful town planning operation achieved in this country. But more important still, these towns and the people who live in them are an abiding witness to what can be done when central and local government combine to improve the quality of life for their citizens.

CHAPTER 5

The Private Sector in Housing

The activities of private enterprise in housing can be divided into two quite separate categories—those of the developer engaged in the construction of new houses for sale for owner occupation, which have increased considerably since the end of the war, and those of private landlords owning and letting properties, which have declined sharply in recent years, as has been shown in Chapters 1 and 2. Private enterprise building, when encouraged by the government, is a "growth industry"; private landlordism, which has been subject to controls of varying severity over the last 60 years and more, tends on that account to be financially unprofitable, and new building to let is no longer carried out except perhaps for a few luxury accommodation flats, although even in this field building for sale is replacing building for letting.

The rate of private housebuilding

Before the second world war, the private sector of the industry played a large part in the housing drive. About 2½ million houses were built by private enterprise between 1919 and 1939. Particularly good results were achieved in Great Britain in 1936–37, when 281,683 houses were built for sale without direct subsidy. The government of the day concentrated the available financial resources on slum clearance, and other types of subsidised house-building were discontinued. Some of the houses built in the 1930s for private sale may have been shoddy, but the majority were solidly built and they were cheap—well within the reach of the average skilled man in employment. By 1939, the demand for houses, except for those living in the slums, was considered by some to be well on the way to being met. During the war, private house-building naturally had to take second place to the need for building for military purposes. As described in Chapter 1, the controls then necessary were continued after the war by the Labour government, which operated a strict licensing procedure over all works of construction, and imposed a ration of private to publicly built houses which at one period was as low as 1 to 10. Indeed, so tight was the licensing procedure that in 1950, the last full year of Mr. Attlee's Labour government, only 27,358 out of 198,171 houses built in Britain were for sale, the rest being for

112

renting in the public sector. The change to a Conservative government in 1951 was followed by the progressive abolition of the licensing system, and the last controls were removed in 1954. The removal of controls made possible a rapid expansion in private enterprise house-building. For example, whereas 22,551 houses had been built by private enterprise in Great Britain in 1951, 113,457 were built in 1955. In 1964, 373,676 new homes were completed, of which 218,094 were built for sale by private enterprise and 155,582 were for letting by public authorities. This was the peak year for building by private enterprise for sale until 1968 when 221,993 such new houses were built.

After the change of government in 1964, there was a significant alteration in the proportion of houses built for private enterprise and public authorities. The government decided that the annual rate of house-building should be raised to 500,000 new units by 1970 (subsequently reduced by 16,500 in the years 1968 and 1969) of which total public authorities should be producing " somewhere near 250,000 ", so that the public sector of housing should have " an even faster growth of building " than the private sector in the next few years.

This policy decision, in conjunction with the economic circumstances of the period 1965 to 1967 and certain fiscal and legislative measures taken by the government, meant that the steady increase in private sector house-building experienced between 1951 and 1964 (except for 1962 and 1963) was halted and indeed reversed from 1965 to 1967, and only increased again in 1968. 218,094 houses were completed for sale in 1964—but only 213,799 in 1965, 205,372 in 1966, 200,438 in 1967. The improvement in 1968 to 221,993 was attributed partly to the large number started in the previous year to avoid betterment levy on development value of land (see Chapter 9) which it was known would be introduced. Completions in the private sector fell again to 181,703 in 1969, when the public sector completed 185,090. Thus the 50 : 50 balance of the two sectors was nearly achieved. Fewer houses and flats were finished in Britain in 1970 than in any year since 1963; and the number started in 1970 in the public and private sectors was the lowest since 1961; only 170,300 dwellings were completed in the private sector, the lowest figure since 1960.

The total numbers of dwellings completed in Great Britain for the years between 1971 and 1975 inclusive varied around 300,000, from 350,600 in 1971 to 313,200 in 1975, the lowest figure being 269,500 in 1974. Private sector completions represented rather over half of the totals, the highest figure being

196,500 in 1974. There was a slight improvement in 1975 to 150,900, but the better total for this year was mainly due to more completions in the public sector which for the only time during these five years topped the private sector with 162,300 completions.

Completions in both sectors were slightly higher in 1976 at 314,600 than the year before. Private sector completions increased over the previous year by 800 to 151,700. Although in the private sector there were more starts than in the previous year, there was a substantial fall in the last quarter of the year for which starts were 25 per cent lower than the previous quarter.

It has been shown in Chapter 2 that the average size of households is decreasing, creating a demand for more smaller homes. The following table of new dwellings in the private sector, however, shows that private house-building has in fact marginally increased the supply of larger units, for which demand was still active.

Houses and flats completed: by number of bedrooms

For private owners	1 bed.	2 bed.	3 bed.	4 bed. (or more)
1970	2·3%	20·8%	68·0%	8·9%
1973	2·6%	16·8%	68·3%	12·3%

Housing and Construction Statistics No. 12, HMSO, 1974.

Housebuilders have indicated that the demand for new private houses is declining. In a survey conducted by the House-Builders Federation in 1976, 12·3 per cent of more than 300 firms questioned indicated that demand was decreasing, although 10·5 per cent replied that there had been signs of an improvement. Noting factors which were limiting the supply of new houses, 70 per cent of the firms cited the inadequacy of the profit margin available on current development projects. The lack of economically priced building land was reported by 75 per cent of the respondents as a likely restriction to output; over 45 per cent saw it as a serious problem in the future. "Serious difficulties" over planning permission were reported by 80 per cent of the firms—these seemed to have been particularly worrying in the London and southern regions.

Improvement grants to private owners

Improvement grants are described in detail in Chapter 7. From the modest beginnings of the 1949 Housing Act, which first introduced subsidies for improvements generally, great progress has been made in the reduction of the number of dwellings lacking basic domestic facilities. There has been a succession of measures (see Chapter 7) to induce, and sometimes enforce, landlords and owner-occupiers to raise the amenity standards of dwellings. The obstacle has been that part of the cost has to fall on the owner (if there is a tenant it is passed on in increased rent) who may not be so willing to have the increased amenity as authority would wish. Nevertheless, a high proportion of owners of older dwellings, particularly owner-occupiers, have taken advantage of improvement grants, and the number of households with the exclusive use of a fixed bath, for instance, more than doubled between 1951 and 1971, to 14·5 million. Census data, however, when dealing with households without the exclusive use of bath/shower, hot water or inside water closet, shows that the owner-occupier of the older house which originally lacked these amenities has usually taken steps to remedy the defects, whereas the private landlord has not.

House prices and mortgages

The price of houses has risen steadily since the war until 1972 when the increase was the biggest on record. The average cost of a new house across the whole country went up by £52 a week. According to figures published by the Nationwide Building Society, the price of a new house rose on average by 47 per cent and of an existing one by 40 per cent; in the eastern regions, the average increase was 70 per cent. The average price of a new house was £8,725, and this figure, modest by the standards of some regions, would have been higher if it were not for the inclusion of Northern Ireland, where prices rose by only 10 per cent, and Scotland, where a 21 per cent increase was recorded. The most expensive new houses were in London and the South-East; the average price there being £13,205.

Although house prices continued to rise in 1973, the rate at which they did so was considerably less rapid than in the preceding year. During the year as a whole, prices of new houses rose by 12 per cent and of modern secondhand houses by just over 14 per cent (Nationwide Building Society's *Occasional Bulletin 118*). However, nearly all the increase occurred during the first three-quarters of the year, and during the last quarter the increase in the price of new houses was only 0·5 per cent, modern secondhand house prices showed no increase at all, while the older type of properties increased in price by 2 per cent.

Many factors, at work on both sides of the supply and demand equation, contributed to the 1972 inflation of house values.

Demand increased for economic and psychological reasons. Availability of building society finance and the government's temporary abandonment of credit restrictions made borrowing easier. Psychological pressures, resulting from the "roof-over-our-heads" philosophy, subtly cultivated by successive governments, the property developers and sections of the press, and to some extent by the "bogey" that rents would rise after the Housing Finance Bill became law, induced many households to rush to buy: and the growing rate of formation of separate households increased the number of such buyers. The resultant rise in demand was not matched by a rise in supply with the result that prices of accommodation rocketed upwards.

Supply is affected by several factors, including the difficulties of the building industry in maintaining a continuing and efficient programme against a background of wage inflation and rising costs of materials, and, basically, by the scarcity of land available for building and society's inability to cope with the resulting land prices. The problem of land availability and the implications of the Community Land Act 1975, passed to help to solve the problems of land scarcity and high price, are considered in Chapter 9.

Since 1973, the prices of houses have risen less steeply—the table in the next section shows the average price of dwellings in the years 1971 to 1975.

The results of a survey by Nationwide Building Society indicate that house prices rose by only 8 per cent in 1976, despite a record level of lending in the region of £6,000 million. In the previous year, when societies lent about £1,000 million less, house prices rose by between 12 and 13 per cent. The low rise in 1976 is due to a rapid deceleration in the last three months of the year, when prices rose by only 1 per cent.

Regional variations in rises are massive. Those areas where prices are already comparatively high, e.g., the South, South-West and South-East, saw the smallest rises. New property went up at around 10 per cent, but even so did not match the increase in building costs over the same period.

Mortgages

The vast majority of houses for sale are disposed of direct to individual members of the public, who normally purchase by means of a mortgage from a building society, who will make a loan available on the basis of the householder's ability to make repayments out of income. Although most mortgages are advanced by building societies, local authorities may give mortgages, as described in Chapter 3, especially on older type properties which might not attract building society finance; insurance companies may also finance house purchase, and to a much smaller extent, money may come from banks and other sources.

Most building societies are affiliated to the Building Societies Association, which recommends to its constituent members the interest rate which they should charge on their mortgage loans, and also the investment rate they should offer depositors. Most, but not all, affiliated building societies follow these rates; and at the end of 1976, the lending rate was 12¼ per cent. The period for repayment of mortgage loans is variable, though 25 years is most usual. However, the average length of a mortgage is only about seven to nine years, because so many mortgagors move from one house to another.

People who pay income tax do not pay tax on the interest paid on mortgage loans, subject to a ceiling of £25,000, as mentioned later. This did not assist people with incomes too low to be taxed, but from 1 April 1968 home buyers were able to choose between receiving the normal income tax reliefs or taking advantage of a new option mortgage scheme already referred to in Chapter 1. This scheme provided for a subsidised mortgage rate of 2 per cent below the current building society recommended rate, with a " floor " of 4 per cent.

The scheme was adjusted later, so that from 1 January 1970 the subsidy was based on a sliding scale varying from 2 per cent less than the normal rate, when this was 6 per cent, to 3 per cent when it was 9⅝ per cent and over. The choice is not an easy one for many people. Wealthy mortgagors will benefit more from the tax relief; the least well off will do better to opt for the subsidy; but many home buyers were faced with a difficult decision. Only one choice was permitted when the scheme was first introduced, and people's financial circumstances alter.

A mortgage crisis occurred early in 1973 when withdrawals of savings with building societies rose to a record height. The Building Societies Association revealed that during March 1973, for instance, withdrawals amounted to £412 millions. Eliminating interest paid to savers, the net receipts of societies were £30 millions during the month compared with nearly £100 millions in the first two months of that year. These figures explained the Building Societies Association's decision to defy intense government pressure and increase the rate of interest charged on home loans from 8½ per cent to what was then a record 9½ per cent as from April 1973. Subsequently, after hot and lengthy debate, the government details of terms on which a temporary bridging grant of between £15 millions and £18 millions would be available to building societies were announced. This controversial decision to subsidise the building societies out of the already-budgeted expenditure of the Department of the Environment enabled societies to keep the mortgage rate below double figures for a short time. The grant was available to building societies in Great Britain on certain conditions. It was not payable for new mortgages in excess of £13,000 or for existing mortgages where the outstanding mortgage balance was in excess of £13,000; for new mortgages for second homes; for existing or new further advances on the same dwelling except for extension or improvement; and for mortgages for dwellings wholly let, under construction for sale, or for business or other properties which included some residential accommodation.

A sudden fall in short-term interest rates helped the building societies over difficulties in attracting savings and societies were soon reporting a marked improvement in their position. The crisis did, however, produce some new thinking on the part of the government who felt that in future efforts must be made to exercise some control over the flow of building society funds on to the house market in order to moderate the cycle of surfeit and starvation. It was argued that under such conditions the money does more to get prices up than houses built. It was hoped that the instruments of control, which would have to include a special government account where surplus funds could be invested at times of plenty, would be prepared for the next time of crisis; but the setting up of such a stabilisation fund would still leave the problem of house prices, rather than mortgage rates, unsolved.

Talks with the building societies about the creation of a stabilisation fund which would be used to iron out the peaks and troughs of the building societies' cycle were started to try to achieve a more steady flow of finance for new houses which would produce a higher average level of new completions at a somewhat lower cost. It was realised that such a fund would need the injection of money as a pump-priming operation to start it off, and the channelling of " other types of finance," including City funds, were mentioned. Any such arrangement as the latter, however, would add a further cross-subsidisation of the house-owner to the existing system, and the subsidies would not be available to the three-quarters of the population who are not repaying mortgages.

Further details of mortgages as a source of funds for housing are given in Chapter 8 which considers many aspects of housing finance in each sector.

The table given in Chapter 2 shows that an increasing proportion of households have embarked upon home ownership over the past 25 years, and in 1975 the proportion was 53 per cent. Property prices and high interest rates have made home ownership increasingly costly, however, and, therefore, not possible for the poorer section of the population. The following tables illustrate that, whereas in 1971 a man on average weekly earnings could just about purchase an average price home, by 1975 home ownership would only be possible if he were prepared to buy a cheap, old house (for which a building society mortgage might not be available) or if he were able to make a very substantial deposit.

Weekly earnings cf. Mortgages Available and Average Price
of Dwelling

	1971	1972	1973	1974	1975
Mortgage interest rate	8½%	9½%	11%	11%	11%
Average weekly earnings	£32·3	£36	£40·9	£46·5	£59·2
Maximum loan on average weekly earnings	£5,038	£5,616	£6,380	£6,045 [2]	£7,695 [2]
Average price of dwellings	£5,631	£7,374	£9,222	£10,990	£12,144 [1]

[1] Third quarter of 1975.
[2] Calculated by Halifax Building Society but on different basis from 71–73 figures.

The Building Societies Association insist, however, that people can still afford to buy, and do, and the proportion of owner-occupiers continues to increase. In modern society, there are many more wives in paid employment than formerly and wife's earnings are taken into account by building societies.

At the end of 1976, Mr. Leonard Williams, chief general manager of the Nationwide Building Society, however, commenting on the figures in the survey referred to earlier, claimed that buyers were in a good position, despite a lack of building society funds for purchase. " House prices have risen little more than half the rate of inflation as measured by the retail price index during the year. Over the past three years house prices have increased by about 27 per cent, while earnings have increased by more than 70 per cent. In consequence, despite the recent increase in the mortgage rate to 12¼ per cent, the average first time buyer can now more easily afford to buy a home than three years ago." These statistics, however, discount effects of the house price boom of 1972. Similar figures for the last six years reveal that there has been a 154 per cent rise in prices, compared with a 146 per cent rise in average earnings.

The property " boom " has caused other complications and distortions in the private sector. For instance, it was generally assumed that house and flat prices would continue to rise, and the possibility of a fall in the more expensive sectors of the market was completely overlooked. Many people in receipt of substantial incomes and thus tax liabilities took out mortgages to secure the benefit of tax relief on the assumption of a capital gain on their private houses. In the event, many of these people have since found that their incomes have been severely cut back and have been unable to meet the interest charges. This resulted in a situation where prices of large expensive houses in some cases rose from, say, £50,000 to £150,000 during 1972–73, since when prices have fallen back, in some cases, below the original £50,000. This dramatic fall has been helped by the fact that tax relief is no longer available on interest on new mortgage loans over £25,000 and by the general recession.

During 1976, many expensive properties have been sold to Arabs and thus a new market has built up. As far as the heart of London is concerned, this carries considerable risks in the formation of wealthy Arab areas which may tend to encourage the indigenous population to move further out, coupled with the additional risk that if the present " fashion " becomes unfashionable, the market could again collapse.

Further, many of the people who bought flats which they had previously rented are now finding themselves in difficulties. When they purchased, they assumed capital gains would be forthcoming and that they would at the same time be able to control their outgoings to a greater degree than they might have anticipated through the " fair rent " procedures (see later in the section on the private rented sector). However, during the last three years, the horrific inflation in fuel costs, rates, service charges and mortgage interest charges has drastically altered the situation. Despite this fact, some Rent Act tenants continue to purchase long leases/freeholds from their landlords although at much more favourable terms.

Building standards

Ever since Disraeli's Public Health Act of 1875, local authorities have been making by-laws or taking statutory power to fix minimum standards affecting building. With the exception of London, which is covered by other legislation, these by-laws have been codified into National Building Regulations. These deal with health, safety and fire precautions and represent a minimal protection to the house purchaser. Nor is the law of consumer protection entirely satisfactory in this regard. The old Common Law adage, *caveat emptor,* applies generally, and the purchaser indeed often buys at his own risk. The man who employs an architect to design a house specially for him and to supervise its construction has someone professionally qualified to watch his interests and see that the work is carried out satisfactorily.

The vast majority of new private houses, however, are bought directly from the builder who has built them on the speculation of finding a buyer. In the event of such a house developing defects, the purchaser's remedies will depend entirely upon the terms of the contract. There will normally be a " maintenance clause " entitling the buyer to obtain rectification of defects discovered within the first six months, but that may not be enough.

However, the main protection for the house purchaser is to ensure that the house which he buys is built by a firm registered with the National House Building Council. This body was set up as the National House Builders Registration Council in 1936 on the initiative of the National Federation of Building Trades Employers. However, it is not a builders' body. One third of its council members are builders, two-thirds represent other interests. It keeps a register of house-builders and requires all on the register to submit to various safeguards in the interests of purchasers. These safeguards apply whatever the price of the house, and the register is intended for all house-builders, whether they build expensive houses or cheaper ones. NHBC inspectors visit building sites during the construction of the houses to see that the construction standard is up to the Council's specifications—which are higher than the Building Regulations. The Council also gives the purchaser financial protection against the bankruptcy of the builder before or after the house is completed and protection against major structural defects occurring within 10 years. In 1966, the Building Societies Association recommended to its members that participation in the NHBC scheme should be a condition for advancing a mortgage on a new house; and simultaneously, the Minister of Housing asked local authorities, in Circular 19/66, to restrict their loans on new houses in the same way. Building standards are considered further in Chapter 10, together with changes introduced by the NHBC in 1975.

It is relevant to note here that the recession in 1976 has resulted in severe damage to the construction industry—to developers, private and public, architects, quantity surveyors, engineers and contractors. Current building costs do not reflect the inflation that has occurred. Building costs in 1976 are lower than they should be if contractors are to maintain adequate profit margins and as soon as there is recovery there is likely to be vast inflation. Nonetheless, even though building costs are held back by excessive competition, unit costs in London generally exceed market values and thus substantial inflation in property prices is likely to precede a recovery in the construction industry which cannot, at any event, recover rapidly. The Development Land Tax (see Chapter 10) is also likely to deter entrepreneurial activity.

The private rented sector

Ever since 1915, a series of Rent Restriction Acts have removed the incentive to developers to build new homes for private renting. Not only are rents controlled or "regulated," but also no depreciation allowance or tax relief on sums set aside for amortisation or a repair reserve is available to the developer. The Milner Holland Report (1.12) in 1965 illustrated how the British taxation system operated to discourage the provision by private enterprise of accommodation to let, and adversely affected the tenants of privately owned property, particularly at the lower rent levels. Indeed, tenants of private landlords, if they paid a rent which would give the landlord a reasonable return in relation to other investments, would have to pay more than the rent of a council house or the equivalent of mortgage interest. If they pay a controlled rent, and there are still many houses which may only be let at rents fixed many years ago, the dwelling is likely to be an old poor one on which the minimum of repairs and maintenance has been carried out. Many of the poorest households live in such low rented accommodation, but the value they receive for their rent in standards and amenities is also often very low. The statistics for the United Kingdom already given in Chapter 2 reveal the decline in privately rented accommodation during the 25 years between 1950 and 1975. Not only have the numbers of such dwellings decreased by more than half from 7·3 million to 3·2 million, but whereas in 1950 they represented 53 per cent of all dwellings, in 1975 the proportion was only 16 per cent. The following table, given in answer to a Parliamentary question, shows estimated numbers of privately owned dwellings available for letting in England and Wales, divided into London and the rest of England and Wales, in 1961, 1966, 1970 and each year thereafter until 1975:

Dwellings rented from private owners
Greater London and the remainder of England and Wales:
1961–75
millions

	April				End of year			
	1961	1966	1970	1971	1972	1973	1974	1975
Greater London	0·93	0·77	0·73	0·72	0·71	0·69	0·67	0·66
Remainder of England and Wales	3·72	3·18	2·63	2·56	2·48	2·41	2·34	2·25
England and Wales	4·65	3·95	3·36	3·28	3·19	3·10	3·01	2·91

The explanation of the decline lies partly in the rapid extension in house building for sale by private enterprise and for letting by local authorities since 1945 and also the fact that an increasing number of private landlords sold their houses once they gained possession of them, thus reducing the pool of privately rented accommodation. Nor did the Rent Acts of 1957 and 1965 (see Chapter 1) succeed in halting the decline in privately rented accommodation, although it was hoped that the first would do so. Since its passage, about a million houses have passed out of the privately rented sector. It was the policy of the Labour Government in 1964, expressed in the White Paper, the *Housing Programme, 1965 to 1970,* to seek a remedy for the shortage of rented accommodation in an increase in public sector building, rather than in a revival of private land-lordism, which, it was held, experience had shown could not overcome the shortage.

The law relating to private landlord and tenant relationships is extremely complex, and the main legislative provisions can only be summarised here. In November 1975 the government announced that a review of the Rent Acts and the means by which they were administered was to be carried out. A list of the principal Acts affecting landlord and tenant relationships in the private sector is given at the end of this chapter, and the review of the Rent Acts is considered in Chapter 12.

The Rent Act 1965 completely revised the law relating to rent restriction and introduced a new principle into rent fixing for unfurnished letting, that of regulated rents, usually called " fair rents." Its main provisions for unfurnished letting may be summarised as follows:

(a) The security of tenure granted by earlier Acts was extended to every unfurnished tenancy of a dwelling house of up to £400 rateable value in Greater London or £200 in the rest of Great Britain on 23 March 1965 or, in the case of a new dwelling house, as soon as it first appeared in the new valuation list. These limits which represented new assessments made in 1963 (and so differed widely from amounts quoted in earlier Acts before revaluation) covered nearly all property in the country except for luxury accommodation (but see below Counter Inflation Act 1973). Unfurnished tenancies newly brought within the provisions for rent control by the Act are known as " regulated tenancies."

(b) A new machinery was set up for reviewing the rents of unfurnished regulated tenancies. Rent officers were appointed by counties, county boroughs, London boroughs and the City of London in England and Wales, and by government itself in Scotland. Their task is to bring together landlord and tenants where they cannot reach agreement about the rent, and to register a " fair rent " for the property. An appeal lies from the rent officer to a rent assessment committee, of which the personnel are chosen by the Minister. The committee then fix a " fair rent " from which there is no appeal except on a point of law. The rent is registered and cannot be altered for a period of three years, except on a change of circumstances or on special grounds.

(c) The Act nowhere defines a " fair rent." In determining a fair rent, the rent officer and the rent assessment committee are to have regard to all the circumstances (except personal circumstances of the landlord and the tenant) and in particular to the age, character and locality of the dwelling and to its state of repair. Any scarcity value will not be taken into account. The fair rent covers all the payments made by the tenant to the landlord for the use of the dwelling apart from rates.

(d) Tenancies already controlled under the earlier Rent Acts continue to have their rents determined according to the provisions of the Rent Act 1957, but see Housing Finance Act 1972 below. The Minister was given power to transfer existing controlled tenancies into regulated tenancies by Order, but this has not been exercised.

(e) Where the Minister is satisfied that every part of an area no longer needs the protection of rent regulation above a certain rateable value, he may release from regulation any dwelling house which he feels need not be regulated any longer.

(f) It was made a criminal offence to evict a tenant whose tenancy has come to an end otherwise than by a court order.

(g) It was made a criminal offence to harass a tenant with the intention of driving him out or deterring him from exercising his rights as a tenant. Local authorities have power to prosecute for such offences. See Chapter 3 for penalties for harassment and unlawful eviction.

The Rent Acts from 1920 onwards were consolidated into the Rent Act 1968, except for section 16 of the Rent Act 1957, covering the minimum length of notice to quit for property let as a dwelling (i.e., a minimum of four weeks' notice on either side, covering weekly, fortnightly and monthly tenancies) and Part III of the Rent Act 1965 which deals with harassment and protection from eviction. (In January 1976 the Secretaries of State for the Environment and Wales implemented one of the provisions in the Housing Act 1974 by issuing regulations setting out the information which must be given in a notice to quit. The new regulations, which apply both to protected tenancies and to Part VI contracts, are set out in the Notices to Quit (Prescribed Information) (Protected Tenancies and Part VI Contracts) Regulations 1975 (S.I. 1975 No. 2196).

The Housing Act 1969 enables landlords of dwellings, where at all times since 25 August 1969 all the standard amenities specified in the Act, i.e., bath, wash-basin, sink, hot-water supply to these, and W.C., all to an approved standard of design and construction, have been provided, and those where works to provide any standard amenities lacking on 25 August 1969 had begun before that date, to have controlled tenancies converted into regulated tenancies. The landlord can apply to the local council for a qualification certificate and on receipt of such a certificate can apply to the rent officer for a fair rent to be assessed to replace the controlled rent.

In 1969, the Labour government set up a committee to examine the workings of the 1965 Rent Act, and asked that particular attention should be paid to the operation of the Act in areas of housing shortage and to the relationship between the codes governing furnished and unfurnished lettings. Its five members were led by Mr Hugh Francis, QC, as chairman. The report of the Francis committee, *Report of the Committee on the Rent Acts,* was published in 1971.

The Housing Act 1972, Pt. III, simplified administrative procedures for conversion of a controlled tenancy to a regulated one under the Housing Act 1969. Much of Part IV of the 1972 Act, however, which implemented some of the majority recommendations of the Francis Committee and provided that rent-controlled dwellings which were not brought into rent regulation by being improved could be converted into regulated ones by phasing depending on rateable values prior to 1973, was repealed.

The Counter Inflation Act 1973 brought within the protection of the Rent Act 1968 tenancies with ratetable values up to £600 in Greater London and £300 elsewhere in England and Wales; and as from 1 April 1973 the upper limit of the new rateable values which are protected is £1,500 in London and £750 elsewhere in England and Wales. This measure, extended by the Rent Act 1974, widened the protection of the Rent Act 1968 to about 16,000 more unfurnished residential tenancies in the private sector, or in other words, to about 80 per cent of such tenancies formerly excluded from its protection by virtue of their rateable values.

In February 1974 the Labour government froze residential rents until the end of December, thus fulfilling one of its election promises. The freeze was eventually lifted on 11 March 1975, by which time the Housing Rents and Subsidies Act had received the Royal Assent and many private landlords had disposed of their assets. The Housing Rents and Subsidies Act 1975, which was intended to be a temporary measure until the government had completed its housing finance review begun in 1974, provided for phasing of all rent increases on registered rents (Schedule 2) and halted the decontrol provisions under the Housing Finance Act 1972 whereby properties became regulated purely by reference to their rateable value.

Almost all the large property companies moved out of residential investment in the period 1966 to 1973, and those that did stay in the residential market moved more and more to furnished lettings.

Furnished lettings

The Rent Act 1974 extended the area of security of tenure to tenants of furnished accommodation where there was no resident landlord. On the passing of the Act, there were 750,000 furnished tenancies and during the passage of the Act through Parliament there were a number of evictions in an effort to avoid protected tenancies. Furnished and unfurnished lettings now operate under the same code; furnished tenants can ask the rent officer (or the Rent Tribunal in the case of a resident landlord) to fix fair rents, assessed on the principles established under the 1968 Act, the Furnished Lettings (Rent Allowances) Act 1973 extended rent allowances to certain tenants of furnished lettings, and the Rent Act 1974 brought the two kinds of lettings, furnished and unfurnished, into line for rebate and allowance purposes (see Chapter 3). The landlord can only obtain possession—and on specific restricted grounds—with a court order. The " protection " now given by legislation means that the court can only give possession for very limited reasons, and the Rent Tribunal can only suspend it where there is a resident landlord or in other special cases; only where there is board provided with a furnished letting does the normal protection not apply. With this control of furnished accommodation since 1974, investment in residential property has virtually ceased.

Furnished lettings in the private sector range from one-room accommodation in family houses and furnished flats in multi-occupied properties to blocks of commercially-run furnished flatlets. Generally, in areas where there is not a scarcity of housing, furnished lettings have provided temporary homes for people who have a reason for living in the area for a short time, but do not want the expense and inconvenience of providing their own furniture. They have undoubtedly satisfied a need in the housing field. In areas of housing shortage, however, where unfurnished lettings are usually less profitable than furnished lettings, many properties are often multi-occupied in furnished lettings both by single people and families who cannot find unfurnished accommodation to rent. Lettings may be seriously overcrowded and deficient in sanitary amenities, and local authorities, although empowered under the Housing Acts to take restricting or remedial measures, may not have the resources of staff or alternative accommodation to act.

Because the 1965 Act did not extend security of tenure to furnished accommodation, some landlords in areas of acute housing shortage were able to evade its restrictions. Furnished tenants, with the knowledge that their landlords could evict them with only minimal delay while a court order was obtained and implemented, were not likely to complain about bad conditions, harassment, overcrowding or even high rents. The supply of unfurnished tenancies in London and some other crowded cities dwindled, while many premises were converted to furnished tenancies. In a report on London's homeless, Professor John Greve blamed this growth of furnished accommodation (with its insecurity of tenure) for much of the increase in homelessness (1). Since 1974, however, as described above, tenants of furnished as well as unfurnished accommodation have security of tenure under the Rent Acts.

The Rent Act 1974 has been condemned for leading to further homelessness and drying up the supply of homes for the very people the Act was designed to protect, especially in the furnished sector. The statistics already given, however, show that the decline in the number of privately rented dwellings from 1966 to 1975 was steady and unaffected by recent rent legislation.

Diversity

The private sector houses a wide variety of people, in furnished, unfurnished and service lettings, and the following table shows its present composition:

England and Wales

Tenure type		Households *(million)*
Unfurnished { regulated		1·1
{ controlled		0·4
Furnished (resident and non-resident landlords)		0·5
Provided by employers/rented with shop or business		0·8
		2·8

There is much more mobility among tenants of furnished accommodation than of unfurnished where the majority have lived in their homes for many years; and the former tend to be much younger and more affluent than the latter. More than 40 per cent of tenants in unfurnished accommodation are over 65 and over 50 per cent are in the lower income groups; whereas over half the heads of households in furnished accommodation are under 30 and belong to higher than average socio-economic groups, and more than 40 per cent are single.

Similarly, landlords vary considerably, from the elderly person owning one or two properties as an investment often made many years ago or acquired as an inheritance, to the large company landlords.

Physical condition of privately-rented housing stock

It has been noted in Chapter 2 that the highest proportion of unfit houses, 51·8 per cent, are rented from private owners and other tenures than owner occupation, or rented from local authorities and new town corporations. The 1971 England and Wales House Condition Survey found that 70 per cent of the privately rented and tied dwellings were built before 1919. 40 per cent lacked one or more of the basic amenities; 30 per cent were in substantial disrepair; and just under 25 per cent were statutorily unfit for human habitation.

Section 32 of the Housing Act 1961, which is referred to in Chapters 1 and 3, made landlords generally responsible in their lettings to which the section applies (i.e., any lease of a dwelling house granted after the passing of the Act, being a lease for a term of less than seven years; and "lease" includes an under-lease, an agreement for a lease or underlease, and any other tenancy, but does not include a mortgage) for structural and exterior repairs, and repair of installations for the supply of water, gas, electricity and sanitation (including basins, sinks, baths and sanitary conveniences) and for space and water heating. The Act also introduced special provisions to deal with houses in multiple occupation, including power for local authorities to apply a management code, to require works of repair, etc., to reduce overcrowding, and to register houses let in this way. The Defective Premises Act 1972, which came into force on 1 January 1974, altered the law with regard to responsibility for repairs and maintenance in several respects—these are described in Chapter 10.

Inflation and the rising cost of maintenance and repair have made it extremely difficult for landlords of controlled tenancies to keep property in a decent state of repair. The Housing Rents and Subsidies Act 1975, s. 10, provided that the rent of controlled tenancies could be increased by 12½ per cent of the cost of repairs. Notice of such increases must be given to tenants in the form scheduled in the Rent Control (Notice of Increase) Regulations 1975 (S.I. 1975 No. 315). Landlords have found, however, that the small increases obtainable in most cases does not justify all the work of implementing the provision.

Further, on regulated tenancies, private landlords point out that while fair rents have risen by about 25 to 40 per cent over the past three years, the cost of living and the housebuilding cost indices have risen by 54 per cent over the same period, while average earnings have risen by almost 64 per cent. Further, the phasing provisions mean that a landlord has to wait for two years before the full fair rent is obtained, and even then the rent will usually be below the level needed to keep pace with inflation.

Legislation on service charges has also created difficulties in the management of privately rented accommodation, especially with regard to the complex and expensive County Court procedures which may become necessary. Section 124 of the Housing Act 1974, for instance, extended sections 90 and 91 of the Housing Finance Act 1972 by providing that the services represented by a service charge recoverable from the tenant of any maisonette or flat which is not held by a protected or statutory tenant must be provided to a reasonable standard and that the amount paid to provide the service must also be reasonable. A landlord can no longer pre-empt decisions on questions of quality and reasonable charge by a provision in the lease for the agent's certificate in respect of the amount payable for services. Disputes on such questions are to be submitted to the High Court unless there is an arbitration agreement within the meaning of section 32 of the Arbitration Act 1950. Where a landlord proposes to carry out works which are estimated to cost more than £250 and are chargeable to services he must obtain at least two estimates; and where any work is estimated to cost more than £2,000 the landlord must also consult with a tenants' association, or if there is none, with the individual tenants before the work is put in hand (except in cases of emergency). Tenants also have the right to inspect details of service charges.

Rent allowances

All private tenants—unfurnished, as provided for in Part II of the Housing Finance Act 1972, and furnished in the Furnished Lettings (Rent Allowances) Act 1973—can apply to the local authority for a rent allowance (and residential rate-payers may also qualify for a rate rebate). The operation of rent allowance schemes in 1976 is described in Chapter 3.

Where by virtue of section 1 (1) of the Landlord and Tenant Act 1962 as amended by the Rent Act 1968 (provision of rent books for tenants whose rent is payable weekly) a landlord is under a duty to provide for a private tenant of a dwelling a rent book or other similar document, he must insert the statutory particulars of the allowance scheme currently operated by the local authority in whose area the dwelling is situated in any rent book or similar document issued to the tenant. Subsequently, a prescribed form of words referring to the availability of a rent allowance had to be inserted in every rent book. The current regulations are The Rent Book (Forms of Notice) Regulations 1976 (S.I. 378/1976). They came into force on 1 June 1976, but are made under the Landlord and Tenant Act 1962 as amended by the Rent Act 1968.

The future

It is recognised that the private rented sector has catered for various groups who need ready access to accommodation at short notice and who are unable to rent from a local authority or housing association or to buy for owner-occupation. These include mobile workers and their families, students, trainees and other young people, the newly-married and those suffering from family break-up. As has been shown, rented accommodation in the private sector is decreasing rapidly and until this downward trend is halted or an acceptable way of fulfilling the role once played by the private landlord is found, the existing stock of housing will not be put to its fullest use in meeting housing needs. Various alternative schemes of tenure are being studied, including sale and leaseback arrangements between local authorities and landlords, systems involving landlords and their managing agents, shared equity schemes and landlord/local authority or housing association co-operatives. New forms of tenure and the future of the private rented sector generally are considered further in Chapter 12.

Principle legislation affecting landlord and tenant relationships in the private sector

Security of tenure and rent fixing

The Rent Act 1968 as extended and amended by subsequent enactments, including:

Sections 80 and 81 of the Housing Act 1969.

Part III, IV and Sections 90 and 91 of the Housing Finance Act 1972.

Section 14 of the Counter-Inflation Act 1973.

Section 18 of the Housing Act 1974.

The Rent Act 1974.

Sections 7 to 11 of the Housing Rents and Subsidies Act 1975.

Paragraph 16 to 23 of Schedule 8 to the Rent (Agriculture) Act 1976.

Protection from eviction

Part III of the Rent Act 1965 (harassment and unlawful eviction).

Section 16 of the Rent Act 1957 (notices to quit).

The Protection from Eviction Bill, which seeks to consolidate these provisions, was introduced on 21 December 1976.

Related enactments

The Accommodation Agencies Act 1953 (charges for accommodation exchange services illegal)

Part II* (multiple occupation) and Sections 32 and 33 (landlords' repairing obligations for short leases) of the Housing Act 1961.

The Landlord and Tenant Act 1962 (rent books).

Part IV* of the Housing Act 1964 and Part IV* of the Housing Act 1969 (multiple occupation).

Parts VII* (improvement grants) and VIII (compulsory improvement) of the Housing Act 1974.

*In so far as these provisions relate to rented housing.

CHAPTER 6

Housing Associations

Previous chapters have dealt with the provision of housing by local authorities and new town development corporations within the public sector, and with owner-occupation and private renting which form the private sector. Housing associations make up the only other important type of agency providing new dwellings and owning and letting existing ones. They are a part of the public sector in that they employ public funds and are entitled to Exchequer subsidies, though a few cost rent and co-ownership societies are differently financed and are sometimes regarded as within the private sector. All associations are, however, non-profit making, as are local authorities, but unlike local authorities they are not the creatures of statute law with specified housing powers and duties. Under the Housing Acts, local authorities must assess the housing needs of their areas and make provision for the supply of any deficiencies, which they often, but not necessarily, do by the building of council housing or municipalisation of privately owned housing. Housing associations must conform to the appropriate statutes when they provide housing to be eligible for subsidy and loans from public funds, but that they provide it at all is a voluntary act. Thus the housing association movement is frequently described as the " voluntary " housing movement. It has also been called " housing's third arm ".

Housing associations resemble local housing authorities and new town development corporations in that they build and improve new subsidised housing for letting. Thus they supplement and complement council and new town housing, letting their accommodation to households in housing need, many of them often nominated by the local authority from applicants on their housing lists.

The fundamental difference between housing associations and private agencies is that the former are non-profit making. As with local authorities, any excess of income they receive from rents, and from any subsidies to which they are entitled, over their costs in providing, managing and maintaining their houses and any ancillary services must in general be used for the purposes of the association.

Housing associations do not normally build for sale and so differ in this respect also from the largest part of the private sector which supplies the home ownership market. The main exceptions

132

are the self-build associations (see below) but other associations, like local authorities, may sell their houses, and some have done so, when the accommodation is no longer needed for letting, or if a choice of tenures is required in a particular development.

Housing associations should not be confused with building societies whose main housing function is the supply of loans on mortgage for house purchase. Only co-ownership and self-build societies cater for a somewhat similar market to that of the owner-occupied private sector, but they do so in a different way. Members of a co-ownership society pay a rent, to entitle them to occupy a particular house or flat, but they are in fact co-owners of the whole of the property belonging to the society. Self-build associations resemble the old terminating building societies in that when their schemes are completed the houses are usually sold to the individual members.

Thus, housing associations may be regarded as forming a separate type of agency, with its own characteristics, some of which are common to them all, although others are peculiar to certain types of associations or to individual ones. Before these characteristics are defined further, or housing association work is described, it will be helpful to see how the housing association movement evolved.

Evolution of housing associations, 1830–1914

Housing associations have a longer history than local authorities as housing agencies, having been the first in the field in providing social housing. They were not called housing associations at the time, but for the sake of brevity this term, which has became the generic one, is used throughout this chapter for all non-profit housing bodies. The earliest such body, the Society for Improving the Condition of the Labouring Classes, was originally established as the Labourers' Friend Society in 1830. It began its housing work in 1844 and survived well over a century until the 1960s when it was taken over by the Peabody Trust.

This society and another one, the Metropolitan Association for Improving the Dwellings of the Industrious Classes, which started work at about the same date, had as an objective the building of dwellings as models to private landlords and enlightened employers in the provision of housing for lower paid workers at low rents. Under the patronage of the Prince Consort, such model dwellings were erected at the Great Exhibition in 1851. During the second half of the nineteenth century, societies and model dwellings companies built cottages and tenement blocks superior in standard of accommodation and construction to the mean, often jerry-built, hovels which were being run up for the families of low paid workers in the growing industrial towns at the time. The Metropolitan Association, although having a commercial character, limited its dividends to 5 per cent, and any surplus derived from rents was to be used in extension of its objects. The main contribution of the model dwellings companies to housing improvement seems to have been the conscious attempt to build to better standards rather in the creation of a special type of agency.

Although the Labourers Dwellings Act 1855 authorised the incorporation of dwellings companies, it was not until 1866 that the Labouring Classes Dwelling Houses Act extended the powers of the Public Works Loan Commissioners to make advances to such companies and associations. Some progress was made, but the next big impetus to housing improvement came with the endowment of the Peabody Trust in 1862. George Peabody, like many other Victorian philanthropists, was a colourful figure. An American, born of poor parents, who started life as a grocer's apprentice, he prospered first in America and later in London, where he settled down already a rich man, gave up his American business and started banking. In addition to his benefactions to American charities, he made gifts totalling half a million pounds (a sizeable sum at that time) to ameliorate the condition of the poor of London, suggesting to the trustees of the fund that the money should be used for " the construction of such improved dwellings for the poor as may combine in the utmost possible degree the essentials of healthfulness, comfort, social enjoyment and economy ". The fund was intended to be " progressive in its usefulness " by charging rents which would produce a fair return on the endowment to finance further building. Although the 5 per cent return which George Peabody regarded as appropriate was never achieved, by the end of the first 20 years of its existence the Peabody Trust owned 3,500 dwellings housing over 14,600 people. Sites cleared under slum clearance powers by the Metropolitan Board of Works (forerunner of the LCC and GLC) were developed by the Trust and by 1914 it owned 6,400 dwellings, twice the number which had been built by the metropolitan borough councils at that date.

Other charitable housing trusts were endowed during the prewar period, the Guinness Trust (1889) and Samuel Lewis Trust (1906) operating then in London. The Sutton Housing Trust, endowed with £2 million under the will of Richard Sutton in 1900, owned and managed by 1976 over 12,000 houses and flats in industrial towns throughout England. Around the turn of the century, the Bourneville and Rowntree Trusts were set up, and housing associations, mostly then called housing trusts or public utility societies, were used to develop housing at the new town of Letchworth. At Bourneville, the co-ownership principle was used to give the occupants a stake in the ownership and management of the estate.

Public utility societies were recognised as housing agencies in the Housing, Town Planning &c. Act 1909, and borrowing rights from the Public Works Loans Commissioners were extended to those registered under the Industrial and Provident Societies Act 1893 with limited dividends.

Evolution of housing associations, 1919–39

After the first world war, housing subsidies from the Exchequer were introduced for the first time. Under a series of Housing Acts, local authorities produced one-and-a-half million dwellings for letting between 1919 and 1939. Private builders, building mainly for sale, but at that time also for letting, erected two-and-a-half million new dwellings during the same period. The charitable trusts and public utility societies continued with their work, but their output did not expand on the scale of that of the local authorities and speculative builders. New societies were formed, when it was realised that in spite of the new council houses the slums remained to be cleared and the housing of the poorer families was still a disgrace to the nation. These societies were eligible for subsidies and often borrowed capital by appealing for loans from people of good will at low interest rates, varying from 2 per cent to 4 per cent, and they also continued to seek gifts and endowments. In 1919, local authorities were empowered to assist in the promotion and financing of housing associations and these powers were extended during the inter-war period. Associations carried out a variety of housing work. Some managed older houses in towns, while some, sponsored by special industries, built houses for the workpeople, often on a co-operative basis. Others built flats and houses for the poorest families or made arrangements with local authorities to rehouse families from slums and over-crowded dwellings. They not only built and managed the dwellings, but often carried out local surveys of the housing conditions in their areas, which were used as housing propaganda. Although these early surveys may appear amateur today, they were influential in building up support for the anti-slum campaign of the 1930s and were the forerunners of the more scientific surveys and enquiries to which we are now accustomed (6).

The main contribution made by housing associations to housing reform in the inter-war period was less in their capacity as producers of housing than in propaganda and experimental work. Their combined output was a tiny proportion of the house production of the period; indeed it is difficult to find reliable figures for their output, but they could justifiably claim to make up in quality for the lack of quantity. They often pioneered such amenities as children's play areas, nursery schools and central hot water systems, at a time when to heat water in a copper and transfer it by a rotary pump to the bath was regarded as a reasonably high standard. They employed trained housing estate managers and often associated welfare services and social centres with their schemes. Some encouraged the tenants to take an active part as co-operators in schemes. Local authorities were also raising the standards of design and equipment, but considering the small numbers of dwellings erected by housing associations, it is remarkable how many of them included some especially progressive feature.

In 1935, a central organisation, the National Federation of Housing Societies, (now National Federation of Housing Associations (NFHA)) was set up, recognised and grant-aided by the Minister of Health, then responsible for housing.

Evolution of housing associations: 1945–60

After the second world war, local authorities were charged with the primary responsibility for housing provision, and in the immediate post-war years almost all house-building was carried out by them for renting. Later, as licensing restrictions were eased and finally abolished, private enterprise built for sale to owner-occupiers. Housing associations found it extremely difficult to undertake new building, since they were not exempted from rent control under the Rent Acts until 1954 and their financial position in the economic conditions of the period was steadily deteriorating.

There were one or two directions in which they could expand their work. Three special types of associations which became active were industrial housing associations, self-build societies and associations providing accommodation for the elderly, whether as their sole output or part of general housing provision.

Soon after the war some industries were expanding rapidly in places where they had not previously had large undertakings, or which had been developed for war production with workers living in temporary accommodation or billeted in other people's homes. In such areas, the local authorities were often already committed to building for normal housing needs and to allocating any new tenancies according to criteria which gave priority to household need and often also to previous residence in the area. Some industries sponsored industrial housing associations in these places, by putting up much of the capital required for the building, often at preferential interest rates. By so doing they ensured that their employees, and key workers coming into the district, could be nominated as tenants of the houses and have a chance to settle down. The housing associations, as separate non-profit-making organisations, were eligible for subsidies and also for loans from the local authorities. Although the company which sponsored such an association normally nominated the tenants from its employees, tenancies were not tied to a particular employment.

During the early post-war period of acute housing shortage coupled with high building costs, there were many young families, some of them with skills in the building crafts, who joined together to build their own houses. By the 1950s, there were a number of such groups in operation, and such self-build societies continue active in 1976.

Housing associations also became more active in the 1950s and 1960s in providing housing for old people. Greater longevity, better health in old age and better pensions and social security for retired people created an increasing demand for suitable dwellings where the elderly could live independently. Some of the existing charitable trusts and associations and many small new local associations experimented with conversions and the building of groups of bungalows and flatlets for old people, who could live completely independently in self-contained dwellings, and also those who could manage for themselves if they had some support from a warden or house mother in temporary illness or emergency. Such associations were often sponsored by voluntary bodies such as church organisations, the British Legion, Rotary and Soroptimist clubs, Old People's Welfare Councils and the WRVS. Many were charities and could receive gifts. Later, the National Corporation for the Care of Old People, and Voluntary and Christian Service (better known as Help the Aged), provided promotion capital for the Hanover Housing Association and Anchor Housing Association respectively to operate on a national scale.

Generalising about housing associations is unwise because they have been and are so varied, but broadly their main contribution during the first two post-war decades was in continuing their former practice of seeking out and meeting special needs. It is doubtful whether this was a conscious policy on the part of the housing associations themselves—they were in any case only very loosely associated in their National Federation. It was partly a reflection of government policy which, while encouraging local authority building to let and later private enterprise building for sale, largely ignored housing associations beyond leaving local authorities the option of making loans of 100 per cent of the cost of new schemes and of passing on Exchequer subsidy and adding rates subsidy in appropriate cases. A few of the larger associations, including the early charitable trusts, had no difficulty in expanding in co-operation with local authorities who appreciated their help, but much of the crusading spirit which the voluntary housing movement had originally generated evaporated in the face of an active and largely successful policy of using local authorities as the main agency to provide houses for letting.

Evolution of housing associations: cost rent and co-ownership, 1961–75

Councils were so successful in housing provision, and private landlords were so discouraged from building for letting, or even remaining in the market at all if the houses they owned could be sold for owner occupation, that towards the end of the 1950s people wanting to rent a modern house, or indeed to rent at all, could virtually only do so from the local authority. Concern was felt over the reduction of choice in housing to the alternatives of renting a council house or buying for home ownership, and over the lack of provision for households who wanted to rent rather than buy, but who did not need the subsidised rents in the public sector.

For this reason, a pilot project for building houses to rent at cost without profit to the developers, but also without subsidy to the tenant, was launched under the Housing Act 1961. Under section 7 of this Act and the Housing (Scotland) Act 1962, s. 11, loan capital amounting to £25 million for England and Wales and £3 million for Scotland was made available from public funds. The government looked to the housing association movement to operate the scheme, but separate new housing bodies had to be set up for the purpose, although several were sponsored by existing housing associations. The advances were made direct from the Ministry of Housing and Local Government and the Scottish Development Department to the new societies with the NFHA acting as administrative agents. No subsidy was available and local authorities took no special part beyond that of administering the necessary planning and building regulations as with any private developer.

By the end of 1963, the whole of the funds available had been taken up and some 7,000 new houses and flats had been built and let at cost rents in various parts of the country. The government was encouraged to launch a more ambitious scheme and legislation was introduced to make further provision for this kind of housing.

The Housing Act 1964 provided for an entirely new government agency, the Housing Corporation, which had the primary duty to encourage the formation and growth of a special type of housing association called in the Act a " housing society ". Housing societies were to provide houses and flats either for letting at cost rents, as under the 1961 Act pilot scheme, or on the basis of group ownership by the occupiers. At a conference organised by the Housing Centre Trust in 1965, a few months after the Housing Corporation had been established, the Minister of Housing at the time, Richard Crossman, stated that the new provisions were to meet " a shortage of one particular kind of housing namely accommodation to let at moderate rents to people who could not afford to become owner occupiers ". He described these people as " young energetic people, scientists and technologists, who had to move about the country ". It was thought they could afford the cost rents. They were not likely to be eligible for housing by the only other agencies building to rent, the local authorities, new town development corporations and older housing associations who were concentrating on subsidised housing as a social service.

Capital for building under the 1964 Act by housing societies was raised by mortgage loans to cover the full cost. Normally two-thirds was lent by a building society and one-third by the Housing Corporation, who were initially provided with a fund of £100 million for this purpose.

One of the difficulties which housing associations operating under the 1961 and 1964 Acts had to overcome was that of finding finance for abortive promotion work, or even for any such work, since the amounts which the Corporation would advance for this purpose were severely restricted. Partly to overcome this difficulty they were encouraged at the time by the government and the Housing Corporation to form themselves from groups of professional people who would be able to recoup some of such expenses from professional fees for the work. This shortsighted policy of introducing self-interested motives into part of the voluntary housing movement was soon recognised as being open to possible abuse and was abolished by restrictions under the Housing Act 1974.

The main difficulty for cost rent associations, however, was that, as costs rose, the rents required to cover outgoings, even without any profit element, became too high for the tenants, especially by comparison with subsidised rents and restricted rents for older privately owned accommodation. In consequence, the co-ownership society came to be used more generally. Members of these societies could secure the same reliefs as are available to owner-occupiers either in the form of tax relief on mortgage interest, or more generally the society itself could obtain a reduced rate of interest, the option mortgage rate (see Chapters 5 and 8) and pass on the benefit to occupiers in lower rents.

By March 1976 the Housing Corporation reported that loans for 43,000 co-ownership dwellings had been approved, mostly prior to the Housing Finance Act 1972, which widened the scope of Housing Corporation lending. By 1974, however, the Housing Corporation had reported that co-ownership societies were also finding the payments required from tenants too high. Approvals for this type of work consequently fell and by 1975–76 no new ones were being given.

General housing association work 1960–72

Even during the period between the 1964 and 1974 Acts cost rent and co-ownership work was only a small part of all housing association work, and one which was somewhat separated from the main stream of the housing association movement which had begun to make greater progress in its traditional field of social housing.

Already during the inter-war period, some housing associations had specialised in the improvement and conversion of older houses. During the 1960s, they looked to this field of activity again, particularly in what had come to be called the areas of housing stress. The problem of the homeless was increasing. Families who could not be housed by the local authority for lack of suitable vacancies or fear of allowing immigrant households to " jump " the legitimate queue of applicants could sometimes be helped by housing associations who could offer an improved older dwelling. New associations were formed to buy and convert suitable property. Indeed, until agreed areas of operation had been worked out, it seemed that too many were springing up and by competing with one another for the purchase of properties were forcing up prices.

The special role of housing associations in improvement work was recognised in legislation when the discretionary grant was fixed at a higher limit in cases where a housing association was acquiring a property for conversion or improvement. Under the Housing Subsidies Act 1967, s. 12, and the Housing Act 1969, s. 21, they were made eligible for a special subsidy for improvement, which in most cases was more favourable than the discretionary grant, also available to the private owner, which they could obtain as an alternative.

All new housing associations face the problem of covering their promotion costs, as mentioned above in the case of cost rent and co-ownership societies. Promotion work, which is often highly complex even on small schemes, requires expert salaried staff. Housing associations unlike local authorities, have no general rate fund behind them and they must cover the management costs of the organisation by other means. Prior to the 1974 Act, they often had to meet the initial costs of purchasing sites and houses and starting development before loans were advanced or rents received. There were a number of ways in which these costs were met by associations working in the field of social housing, such as sponsorship of an association by a single endowment or donation, or by the help of established national charities often working through local groups, as mentioned above in the case of old people's associations. In order to assist this kind of expense for associations who were housing the homeless, a special appeal was initiated by Shelter, the National Campaign for the Homeless, which by 1970 had collected over £3 million in donations, many of them small, and used them to help certain housing associations, in particular those catering for poorer households with young children in the stress areas. Shelter made a special appeal to young people, who collected much of the money. It also sponsored special projects for area development, for example in Liverpool and Bradford, and a housing aid centre in London.

Housing associations also received greater encouragement from the local authorities during the late 1960s and early 1970s, many of which showed a readiness to lend them capital: for instance, the Greater London Council increased its allocation for this purpose which had been running at about £7 million prior to 1969–70 to £25 million a year for the next three years.

A government advisory committee was set up in 1968 under the chairmanship of Sir Karl Cohen to investigate the future role of housing associations. It never reported though the evidence submitted to it was published by DOE in 1971 (5).

The Housing Finance Act 1972 introduced a new principle into public sector housing finance which profoundly affected housing associations. The aim was to allow low rents to rise in relation to the value of each dwelling, to relate subsidies more closely to the financial needs of each household through a national system of rent rebates and allowances (see Chapter 3), and to withdraw progressively subsidies still being paid under previous Housing Acts. The 1972 Act subsidies for new work by housing associations started at 100 per cent of the deficit between the approved costs and the permitted rents and were also to be phased out over a 10-year period during which it was thought permitted rents would rise sufficiently to make the schemes viable.

For reasons explained in Chapter 1, the rent fixing system introduced for council housing was repealed on a change of government in 1974, and the Housing Act 1974 introduced a new subsidy system for housing associations. However, for housing associations the rent fixing system introduced in 1972, which is similar to that for fair rents for privately rented houses under the Rent Act 1965, has remained; so also has the arrangement for withdrawal of pre-1972 subsidies, but the new provisions under the 1974 Act offset some of the difficulties of withdrawing subsidies.

The Housing Finance Act 1972 also widened the lending powers of the Housing Corporation to allow it to lend to any housing association and not only cost rent and co-ownership ones. It also made subsidies payable direct through the central department, DOE, and not as previously on application and at the discretion of the local authority

The 1972 Act provisions regarding subsidy created so much uncertainty about the future viability of new development that most associations undertook no new schemes under these provisions. The NFHA and others, including the Housing Centre Trust (see Memorandum on Housing Association Output, *Housing Review*, Vol No. 4, July-August 1973) made representations and by the end of 1973 a Bill providing for a different form of subsidy was introduced. Although the Conservative government fell before it could be passed, the measure had been broadly agreed by the main political parties, and the new Labour government introduced a Bill in very similar terms soon after taking office, which became the Housing Act 1974. This gave housing associations a better chance to continue and expand their work effectively than they had had for several decades.

Terminology and definitions

From the foregoing it is clear that the housing association movement has grown in a very haphazard way, and its evolution does not fall into any clear or tidy pattern. Confusion can easily arise over the meaning of the terms " housing association ", " housing society " and " housing trust ". The term " housing association " was first used in statute law in the Housing Act 1935 and this has become the generic term. A housing association as defined in section 189 of the Housing Act 1957, and section 189 of the Housing (Scotland) Act 1950, as amended by the Housing Act 1974 is " a society, body of trustees or company established for the purpose of, or amongst whose objects or powers are included those of, providing, constructing, improving or managing or facilitating or encouraging the construction or improvement of, houses, or hostels as defined in section 129 (1) of the Housing Act 1974 being a society, body of trustees or company who do not trade for profit or whose constitution or rules prohibit the issue of any capital with interest or dividend exceeding the rate for the time being prescribed by the Treasury, whether with or without differentiation, as between share and loan capital ". For many years the rate specified by the Treasury for this purpose has been 5 per cent, but this method of raising capital is so little used that even Treasury officers scarcely remember what the rate is.

Housing trusts are sometimes classified separately from other housing associations, for example, in section 5 (3) of the Rent Act 1968, in which a long definition broadly defines a housing trust as a body which is required by its constitution to devote all its funds to working class housing or, if having wider powers, it does in fact so devote them. (So far as exclusion from the Rent Acts is concerned, however, there are other provisions involved, including, since the Housing Act 1974, registration by the Housing Corporation.)

Section 1 (7) and (8) of the Housing Act 1964 defined a housing society, which would be eligible for loans from the Housing Corporation (that is a cost rent or co-ownership society), as one which:

" (a) is registered under the Industrial and Provident Societies Act 1893; and

(b) does not trade for profit; and

(c) is established for the purpose of, or amongst whose objects or powers are included those of, constructing, improving or managing houses being

(i) houses to be kept available for letting, or

(ii) where the rules of the society restrict membership of the society to persons entitled or prospectively entitled (whether as tenants or otherwise) to occupy a house provided or managed by the society, houses for occupation by members of the society ".

Under the Housing Finance Act 1972 co-operatives and co-ownership societies were not eligible for subsidies but were made so by the Housing Rents and Subsidies Act 1975.

Until 1975, a housing co-operative was referred to in statutes as a housing association with rules restricting membership to tenants and precluding the granting of tenancies to persons other than members. The term " housing co-operative " was however introduced into housing law by the Housing Rents and Subsidies Act 1975, Sched. 1, para. 9, to define a body with which a local authority with the approval of the Secretary of State may make an agreement to carry out housing functions without forfeiting subsidy. Such a body need not be a housing association. but it is likely that it would fall within the basic 1957 Act definitions

After the Housing Act 1974, the term " registered housing association " has come to be used to distinguish housing associations registered by the Housing Corporation (see below

Registration by the Housing Corporation). However, when encountering this term it should be interpreted in relation to its context, since it is also used to denote incorporation by the various means open to housing associations and the term "registered 1965 Act association" is used in the Housing Act 1974 itself to denote an association registered under the Industrial and Provident Societies Act 1965.

To be eligible for registration by the Housing Corporation a housing association must conform with the definition in section 13 of the Housing Act 1974. This requires it to be a registered (not exempt) charity or a society registered under the Industrial and Provident Societies Act 1965. It may not trade for profit and it must be established to, or have power to, provide, construct, improve or manage (a) houses kept available for letting, or (b) houses to be occupied by its members, whether as tenants or otherwise (that is members of a co-operative, co-ownership or self-build association), or (c) hostels. Any additional powers or purposes must be within those set out in the section, that is, providing land or buildings for the ancillary requirements of the tenants or occupants of the association's houses, providing amenities or services for their benefit either exclusively or with others, encouraging and advising on the formation of other associations eligible for registration, and providing services for and advising on the running of registered associations.

Fuller details of the statutory definitions and varied terminology applied to houses associations is contained in *Housing Associations* by C. V. Baker (1), which also covers in considerable detail the information outlined in this chapter.

Types of housing association

Housing associations may be categorised according to the type of constitution under which they operate, the main way in which they finance their schemes, the type of work they do. There is a good deal of overlapping between these categories— old people's associations could, for example, be endowed charities, be registered under the Industrial and Provident Societies Acts and employ loans from local authorities and the Housing Corporation, be a form of co-ownership relying on investment by tenants—the main consitutional differences are defined first.

The majority of housing associations are registered under the Industrial and Provident Societies Acts with the Registrar of Friendly Societies; not less than eight people, one of whom is the secretary are required to effect registration in this way.

Some of these are recognised as charities and, as such, obtain exemption from taxes. Other associations are incorporated under the Companies Acts. Charitable trusts may be subject to special deeds or instruments defining their duties and subject to the jurisdiction of the Charity Commissioners.

The NFHA, with the approval of the Registrar of Friendly Societies, has evolved various model rules which are suitable for use by the different types of association for registration purposes. These rules are not, however, appropriate to the cost rent and co-ownership societies obtaining advances under the the Housing Act 1964, for which the Housing Corporation has its own model rules.

The main categories of housing associations, differentiated primarily according to the type of work they do, are as listed below, although many may undertake work in more than one of these categories (2).

(a) *General family associations*

The largest group of housing associations affiliated to the NFHA are placed under this heading. More than half are registered as charitable trusts, including the older endowed charitable trusts. The group includes associations whose main work is both in new building and in improvement and conversion. Many of these associations provide also for old people, the disabled or other special categories of household as well as families with children.

(b) *Old people's housing associations*

Housing associations under this heading are the second largest group categorised by the NFHA. Most have charitable status and many are quite small, owning perhaps one group of bungalows or a flatlet scheme for 10 or 30 people. Others own a large number of small schemes throughout the country. Many were sponsored by religious and other philanthropic organisations. Most provide sheltered housing for renting where there is support from a warden in purpose-built grouped bungalows or flats, and some adapt and convert large dwellings or other buildings. Some associations also provide extra care, such as one or more main meals, or set up residential homes giving full care and attention for the infirm. A few have experimented with tenant investment for occupiers in higher income groups who can contribute capital, perhaps as the result of the sale of an owner-occupied house, in return for a life tenancy.

(c) *Industrial housing associations*

Industrial housing associations consist of those promoted by the employers or employees of certain industries, to house the employees. Some have obtained loans for capital development from sponsoring firms at favourable interest rates and some are co-operatives. This is one of the smaller groups of associations although it includes some associations with large numbers of houses, such as the Coal Board Housing Association which took over a number of colliery housing associations after nationalisation of the coal mining industry, and that formed some 45 years ago to house workers in the Great Western Railway. As mentioned above, some large firms found housing association machinery useful in providing accommodation when they needed to attract key workers into a new area, such as, for example, the English Electric Co. (later General Electric Co.), most of whose property was later transferred to the Sutton Housing Trust for general family housing, United Steels, and British Airways who set up the British Airways Staff Housing Association, a housing co-operative. However, at the time of the Housing Finance Act 1972, it became policy not to approve subsidy where accommodation was intended to meet the needs of individual employers and, although under the Housing Act 1974 housing for essential workers whose needs would not otherwise be met is eligible for subsidy, this category of association is showing little expansion in the 1970s.

(d) Self-build housing associations

These associations, usually called societies, are formed by groups who build their own houses with their co-operative labour. It was estimated by NFHA in 1975 that over 10,000 houses had been built by more than 1,000 associations since the first self-build society was formed in 1949. The houses are usually sold to the members, but sometimes have remained the property of the association and been let to members. Equitable arrangements are made whereunder the prices charged to each member are related to the hours of labour he has put in. Self-build societies are able to borrow from local authorities or the Housing Corporation to enable them to purchase land and materials. When the houses are completed members arrange their own mortgages in the normal way and purchase the houses from the association enabling it to repay its loan and wind up. Since little or no labour costs have to be included in the purchase prices of the houses, these are usually as low or lower than valuation. As a result mortgages to cover the whole of the price are usually readily available (12).

(e) Cost rent housing associations

The group of cost rent associations set up under the Housing Act 1961, s. 7 and the Housing (Scotland) Act, s. 11, are described above. There are under 50 of them and, since the fund is now exhausted, the number will not increase further. Cost rent associations, called societies, set up to operate under the Housing Act 1964 with loans from the Housing Corporation, are more numerous, though they ceased to be able to offer new viable housing after a few years and are no longer being formed in 1976.

There are also a few associations operating without subsidy with loans from local authorities or building societies, for example where a group of residents of a block of flats or houses have formed an association to take them over from a private landlord. In some such cases, co-operatives are formed.

(f) Co-ownership housing associations

Co-ownership housing associations, mostly called societies, provide houses or flats to be occupied exclusively by their own members, who own collectively the dwellings they occupy individually. Usually the society got the equivalent of the option mortgage subsidy (see Chapters 5 and 8), but no other subsidy, on the interest on the loan. Co-ownership societies may be set up by the members who wish to occupy the dwellings when they are completed, but those operating under the Housing Act 1964 and borrowing from the Housing Corporation were usually initiated by sponsoring societies, whose members were replaced on completion of each scheme by members who were the occupiers. Each scheme thus formed a separate society. Sponsoring societies may, and often do, continue to act as managing agent.

A very few co-ownership societies obtained funds under the Housing Act 1961 pilot project. Some operate under rules based on a model drawn up by the NFHA, which enables them to borrow capital through a local authority or some other source than the Housing Corporation. The largest group of co-ownership societies comprises those which obtained capital from the Housing Corporation and which use its rules.

All co-ownership society members are responsible for the estate and elect the committee of management. In the case of NFHA associations, each member may be asked to put down, as a loan, about 5 per cent of the cost of the dwelling he is to occupy, which reduces the amount to be borrowed elsewhere. A returnable deposit may be required against possible decorative repairs being required on leaving. A co-ownership member's rent repays his share of the collective mortgage and covers interest on the society's outgoings and the cost of maintenance, repairs, management and insurance. If the co-owner moves away, the society returns any loan capital, or returnable deposit, or both, which is due. If he has been resident for a qualifying period, he may also receive a payment in respect of the repayment of the principal, which has taken place during his occupation and a proportion of any appreciation in the value of the dwelling he has occupied.

A type of co-ownership being evolved in 1976 was described in *Housing Review,* Vol. 25, No. 4, July-September 1976, " Equity Sharing—The Possible Panacea " by Alan Edgar and Harry Defries. In the scheme described, the association always retains in its ownership a small minimum proportion (say, 10 per cent) of the equity of each dwelling and is able to give a small proportion (also say 10 per cent) to each occupier; thus ensuring that both association and occupiers have an essential minimum interest. The occupier, if he so wishes can purchase the whole or a part of the remainder of the equity, if necessary obtaining his own individual mortgage for this purpose. Rent is paid to the association to cover (a) the appropriate proportion (depending on the proportion of the equity acquired by the occupier in each case) of the association's loan charges; and (b) the cost of management, maintenance and other outgoings. On leaving the scheme, the occupier sells his own part of the equity. The scheme was being found viable without any direct subsidy for an older block of flats, the majority of which contained sitting tenants. One of the advantages claimed for it is that of enabling people to get a foothold on the owner occupation ladder (17, 18).

(g) *Co-operative housing associations*

Co-ownership housing associations are co-operatives in the accepted sense of the term, but in housing association terminology housing co-operative is generally used to describe an association where the tenants have no individual stake in the equity or a stake limited to a share repayable on leaving at its original par value. This type of co-operative is more precisely termed a " non-equity " or " par value " co-operative. It is not new, but has not hitherto been widely used in Britain. It has been usual for all tenants, though it is not always made essential, to hold a share in the association on which interest may be paid within the limit set for housing associations. All members of a co-operative are ultimately responsible for the estate and elect the management committee.

A Working Party on Housing Co-operatives, set up by the government, published its final report in 1976, advocating the wider use of co-operatives to encourage a greater sense of involvement and responsibility by tenants of rented houses (14). DOE Circular 8/76 (WO 15/76) endorsed this view and described the way in which " management co-operatives " (those which merely take over responsibility for some management functions) and non-equity co-operatives might be sponsored and supported by local authorities, housing associations and others. It has been held that the majority of tenants on an estate made a housing co-operative should be supporters of the co-operative principle, but the interests of non members can be safeguarded. In 1976, however, this type of co-operative housing whether promoted by local authorities or housing associations, was still in an experimental stage (13, 15).

(h) *Special purpose housing associations*

In addition to the housing associations building for the old, some others concentrate their activities in providing accommodation for special classes of households. Many have charitable status if this is appropriate to their function, or are co-operatives, or neither. They include those providing for single people, students, disabled people, members of a particular ethnic origin, refugees, single parent families, agricultural workers, discharged prisoners and so on. Some housing associations have repaired and let short life property awaiting redevelopment in close co-operation with local authorities. Others have provided hostels for, for example, battered wives, which are run by other voluntary bodies.

(i) *Government sponsored housing associations*

Although termed housing associations, these bodies, which were brought into being to supplement the housing work of local authorities in certain regions, are not housing associations in the general sense of the word. The Scottish Special Housing Association and the North Eastern Housing Association were formed between the wars to operate in what were then termed special areas, that is, areas severely affected by economic depression. They built houses for workers with funds advanced by the Commissioner for Special Areas, thereby relieving local authority rate funds. Their boards were appointed by the government. Later, the work of the Scottish Special Housing Association was extended under the Housing Acts and it continues to carry out functions outside the scope of normal housing association work. For example, it has duties in respect of non-traditional methods of construction, research and development and uses its own direct labour organisation. By 1976, it owned and managed about 86,000 dwellings.

Further development by the North Eastern Housing Association was regarded as unnecessary following the reorganisation of local government and in 1975 it ceased building. By this time, the association owned and managed 18,415 houses and flats to which the local authorities in the region nominated all the tenants. The members of the Association have formed a separate association, the North Housing Group Ltd., operating in the same way as any other non-statutory association.

The other government sponsored association was the Northern Ireland Housing Trust, which was set up after the second world war to build and manage housing in the province. It too was very successful, owning some 48,000 dwellings by 1971 when it was merged in the Northern Ireland Housing Executive which was made responsible also for the housing functions of all local authorities. It had a high reputation for its standards of design and management.

Registration and control by the Housing Corporation

Since housing associations are eligible to use public funds and since they operate under varied constitutions, it came to be recognised that some emblem of probity and competence in housing work was required to show which associations should be accepted for certain privileges and at the same time to reduce the risk of any undesirable bodies penetrating the voluntary housing movement and abusing such privileges. Provisions in the Housing Act 1974 require the Housing Corporation to maintain a register of housing associations.

Housing associations are statutorily eligible for registration if they conform with the definition in section 13 of the Housing Act 1974 (see Terminology and definitions above) and if they also satisfy the criteria which the Housing Corporation is required to establish. The Corporation is advised on the criteria and on registration matters by the Housing Associations Registration Advisory Committee, a statutory committee appointed by the Secretary of State. The criteria were issued in January 1975. They recapitulate the relevant law but go beyond this in setting out other requirements, some of them involving subjective judgments, which the Housing Corporation expects to be satisfied. Nevertheless, in practice it seems that few applications have not been accepted on the existing records of those associations who have applied and some 2,000 were on the register by the end of 1976.

Only those housing associations which are registered are eligible to receive Exchequer subsidies and are entitled to certain tax privileges. Also only registered associations, and unregistered self-build societies, are eligible to receive loans from local authorities and the Housing Corporation. The tenancies of unregistered associations are not excluded from Rent Act protection.

Once on the Housing Corporation's register, which must be open for inspection at its head office, and has been published, an association is subject to considerable legal control under the Housing Act 1974. It may not sell, lease, mortgage, charge or dispose of land except with the Housing Corporation's consent, unless it is a charity which already needs the consent of the Charity Commissioners who will themselves consult the Housing Corporation. This applies to all grant-aided land, even if held by an unregistered association. It also still applies if an association is deregistered, which can only occur if it ceases to be a registered charity or industrial and provident society, or ceases to exist. The Housing Corporation has statutory power to investigate suspected misdemeanour or mismanagement of a registered housing association, and, on this being substantiated, has powers to replace committee members, transfer property, and petition for the winding up of the association.

The Corporation's consent is not required for short leases and so does not hamper normal letting. It has power to transfer property in the event of a registered association winding up and must give its consent to amalgamations or transfers between associations. The Charity Commission must consult the Housing Corporation before agreeing to changes to the objects of registered associations which are charities.

The Housing Act 1974 prohibits any payments by an association to members, except proper payments under its rules, which allow, for example, payments to co-owners on their relinquishing a tenancy. The Housing Corporation may also specify maximum fees payable to association members and conditions of any contract involving them. Committee members must declare any interest they have in any contract of the association and are liable to prosecution on failing to do so. Legislation to prohibit payments such as fees to members altogether has been forecast. In the meantime, they are discouraged by administrative means.

Financing of housing association work

The most significant contribution to the work of housing associations made by the Housing Act 1974 was its introduction of new subsidies. The Housing Finance Act 1972 had brought associations within the rent fixing system of the Rent Act 1965 (see Chapter 5) and provided for the phased withdrawal of the subsidies being paid under earlier Acts. As already mentioned, the new building subsidies it introduced were ineffective, and provisions covering them were repealed. Subsidies under the Housing Act 1974 are paid on the principle of covering the deficit between the costs of providing housing and the income from the permitted rents which may be charged. The wider implications of the system are discussed in Chapter 8 on Housing Finance. The following notes outline how the system works in practice.

Rents

Although housing associations are within the fair rent system an association could, if it wished, fix a rent at any amount a tenant was willing to pay. In practice it is unlikely to do so, since this could be altered on application for a fair rent to be fixed. In any case, only registered rents would be taken into account for subsidy. Except in the case of co-ownership societies which are outside these provisions, rents are therefore fixed and registered by the rent officer in the same way as for privately let housing and there is the same right of appeal to the rent assessment committee. The registered rent then becomes the rent limit for the tenancy, unless it is more than 75p a week in excess of the existing rent, in which case the limit can only be increased by up to 75p a week in any one year until it reaches the registered rent. This phasing applies even when the rent includes a sum in respect of services. Registered rents may be revised on application at three-year intervals and it might be that because of the phasing an association's rents would never catch up with the full fair rent. An addition may be allowed in calculating housing association grant (see below, housing association grant) to compensate for loss due to phasing, where, for example, an association acquires property with a continuing tenancy. If there is a change of tenancy, the full fair rent may be charged, except where the tenancy passes to a member of the tenant's family residing with him. This may lead to anomalies where a tenant of long standing is paying less for the same accommodation than one who has moved in recently. It may also cause difficulties with transfers within estates.

Loans

Housing associations are dependent on loans to cover their capital costs. Their main sources are local authorities and the Housing Corporation who have power to lend to registered associations and unregistered self-build societies. There is no reason why associations should not borrow from other sources,

and building societies have lent them money on mortgage. Associations have also raised bridging loans or loans to provide working capital, from banks and similar lenders. Loans from public
funds are usually made at rates related to those paid by local
authorities, or building society lending rates, and are for 40 or
60 years, the latter more commonly now, for new building
projects, and for 30 years or less for acquisition and improvement of older houses. A small additional percentage (for
example, ⅛ per cent), or a lump sum (1 per cent of the total loan
in the case of the Housing Corporation), may be charged for
administration expenses.

Subsidy withdrawal

Prior to the Housing Finance Act 1972, most housing
associations were receiving Exchequer and sometimes rate fund
subsidies under authorised arrangements with local authorities
for periods intended to run for up to 60 years, and were
applying them in reduction of rents. It was assumed that by
allowing fair rents to be charged these subsidies would become
unnecessary and provisions were made for their phased withdrawal at the rate of £20 per house per year, termed the
withdrawal factor. The subsidies payable on the coming into
force of the Act, and subsequently the amount still due after
some withdrawals have been made, is termed the "basic
residual subsidy." There is also a "special residual subsidy"
relating to schemes approved but not completed during the
limited period of the transition to the new subsidy system.
Owing to the rent freeze, it was necessary to cancel withdrawals
for the year 1974–75 and this was done by the Housing Act
1974, but withdrawals of these earlier subsidies subsequently
continued and if as a result housing associations are faced with
costs they are not able to meet, these are covered by revenue
deficit grant, see below.

Subsidies under the Housing Act 1974

The new subsidies introduced by the Housing Act 1974 are
(a) housing association grant (HAG), (b) revenue deficit grant
(RDG), (c) management deficit grant, and (d) hostel deficit
grant. All are payable only to registered housing associations.

(a) Housing association grant (HAG)

Housing association grant (HAG) may be paid by the Secretary of State under the Housing Act 1974, s. 29, to registered
housing associations, other than co-ownership and self-build
associations, to cover the net deficit arising from any housing

project whether of new building, or acquisition, improvement or repair of existing accommodation. Application is made through the local authority if the authority is to provide loan finance or through the Housing Corporation in all other cases. It is payable as a capital sum, but payments on account may be made as construction work progresses.

HAG is available for projects of low-cost, rented dwellings designed to meet housing needs which are established by associations in liaison with local authorities and the Housing Corporation. DOE Circular 170/74 (WO 274/74) set out six categories of projects which should have priority. These may be summarised as follows:

(a) projects in housing action areas, general improvement areas and priority neighbourhoods or elsewhere to relieve housing stress, or homelessness;

(b) projects to meet special needs, including needs of the elderly, the disabled, single people and others with special housing problems where there is a shortage of suitable accommodation;

(c) projects in other areas to meet local needs and shortages;

(d) projects to maintain the stock of rented housing;

(e) projects to prevent serious structural deterioration or environmental degeneration;

(f) projects to meet high demand which would not otherwise be met, such as accommodation for essential workers.

In 1976, owing to the national economic situation and the cutback in funds available for housing, the priorities were interpreted more stringently.

The amount of grant is the difference between the approved cost of the project, including the cost of management and maintenance, and the estimated receipts from the fair rents fixed. For new building projects, design standards are the same as for local authority subsidised housing and construction costs must be within the DOE's cost yardstick, see Chapters 3 and 10. Costs above the approved costs, including those due to design standards above the minimum, may be allowed if the housing association can meet the excess from its own resources but will not be eligible for HAG. Loss due to decanting of tenants, and disturbance and home loss payments (see Chapter 3) for which housing associations are liable, and capitalised interest on a project until the majority of the dwellings are let, are all eligible for HAG, as are the administrative costs of acquisition and development, and management and maintenance costs, for which allowances are fixed by DOE and revised from time to time. The method of calculation of HAG is set out in DOE Circular 52/75 (WO 94/75) and the rates of allowances are also given in circulars published periodically as revisions are made.

For works of improvement and conversion, HAG is available within cost limits. These are higher for acquisition and works than for works only, vary for different regions, and for different sized units according to the number of persons each unit will accommodate. They are thus more sensitive to the nature and location of the project than are the grants for improvement work by private owners. The minimum standards are the same as those for all grant-aided improvements (see Chapter 7).

HAG is available for hostels, though DOE Circular 170/74 does not encourage this form of provision " with a full range of catering and other services " under housing as opposed to social service legislation. Standards, but not cost limits, are set out in DOE Circular 170/74, Appendix F, which also gives guidance as to the calculation of HAG in relation to the accommodation costs, excluding furnishing and services. Subsequently, DOE Circular 12/76 (WO 14/76) gave cost yardstick allowances for shared accommodation for single working people on the lines and to the standards set out in DOE Design Bulletin No. 29, *Housing Single People 2*, see Chapter 11.

(b) *Revenue deficit grant (RDG)*

Revenue deficit grant (RDG) is a rather unusual subsidy which was introduced during the passage of the Housing Act 1974 through Parliament, following representations by the NFHA. It was originally intended that HAG would look after the needs of new schemes and that further subsidies would not be necessary, except in those cases covered by management deficit grant described below. It was realised that housing associations, which would be operating between income and expenditure limits fixed at figures largely outside their control, would inevitably come to grief if the cost of running their housing and the permitted limits of the rents they could charge could not be made to balance by any means legally open to them. RDG is paid towards an association's deficit at the discretion of the Secretary of State where he is convinced that the association is obtaining the maximum permitted income; that management and maintenance expenditure is reasonable; and that the association has not got sufficient income from other sources to make RDG unnecessary. It has to be claimed within 15 months of the accounting year in question and the claim has to be supported by audited accounts. It relates to deficit on all the workings of an association and not on a single scheme.

Charitable or other income earmarked for a particular purpose is not taken into account, but this is a matter which has given rise to some misgivings; associations who have charitable monies should be specific about the purpose for which they are to be used if they are not to be absorbed into meeting a general deficit which would otherwise be covered by subsidy. Rent freezes, increases in interest rates, and fuel and other service costs have in fact proved the necessity for this subsidy.

(c) *Management deficit grant*

Management deficit grant is available to registered housing associations which provided cost rent housing without subsidy before they were subjected to rent limitation from 1 January 1973. It represents a payment towards the deficit arising from income from the letting of dwellings and expenditure necessary to their proper management in the financial year for which it is payable. Like RDG, it is discretionary and does not necessarily cover the full deficit.

(d) *Hostel deficit grant*

Hostel deficit grant resembles RDG, though its calculation has to take into account that charges are not fixed by a statutory system. It may be related to a single hostel separately from the other operations of an association.

Subsidy towards warden's services in sheltered housing

Social service authorities have made annual grants under the Local Government Act 1958 towards the provision of appropriate services supplied as an integral part of a housing project, for example towards the cost of wardens in sheltered housing. Some authorities are taking the view that RDG should come to the rescue if these subsidies are withdrawn, but this was being contested in 1976. In new schemes, an addition to the normal management and maintenance allowance ranks for HAG in respect of wardens' services and the cost of running communal facilities in sheltered housing

Development by housing associations

Housing associations are subject to the same planning and building regulations and controls as are private developers and to similar standards and cost yardsticks as apply to local authorities (see Chapters 3, 9, and 10). The Community Land Act 1975 and the Development Land Tax Act 1976 affect them as buyers of land, but should not cause special problems. The NFHA have published guidance on the implications of these

Acts for housing associations (10). Land purchased by housing associations will only be recognised for HAG and public loan finance if it is acquired at or below the district valuer's valuation. This has caused difficulties and delays leading to loss of sites when associations have been competing with purchasers who are not so restricted, but recent land legislation, with its powers of intervention by the local authority except on very small sites, may ease this. Local authorities and the Housing Corporation can, and frequently do, assist over site acquisition. Associations should, however, make their own assessment of the suitability of sites for the development they wish to carry out, since it is they who will be letting and managing the housing and who are responsible for the success of the estate.

Housing association projects have to be submitted to and approved by the lending authority and the DOE. Efforts are being made to simplify these procedures, but a glance at the Housing Corporation's Practice notes, published in 1976, indicates that they are still quite formidable. However, the detailed checks and counterchecks must be accepted as part of the price to be paid for the use of public monies without which reasonably low rented housing could not be produced. As the authorities and the Housing Corporation gain confidence in the associations with whom they work, it is to be hoped that such difficulties will be ironed out.

Housing associations usually employ architectural and other professional consultants for their development work, though those associations actively engaged in it normally employ at least one officer on their staff qualified to handle building contracts and supervise progress in co-operation with consultants. Some large associations, in particular those carrying out much improvement work, are able to maintain teams of designers and technically qualified people within the organisation, who often acquire special expertise in dealing with the type of property being handled. The NFHA collaborate with the National Building Agency on technical matters affecting housing associations, and both bodies together and separately have published guidance documents listed in the bibliography (11).

Housing association management

Housing associations generally have a reputation for a high standard of efficient and sensitive management. Maintenance standards are good and rent arrears are generally low, though in this regard associations generally—those catering for the very poor and for the socially inadequate are an exception—have some advantage over local authorities in that they can be more discriminating in selecting tenants. Associations are sometimes criticised for employing a high proportion of management staff in relation to the number of tenancies, but this criticism often overlooks that the management staff of a housing association does not have at its call the expert and general administrative services of staff in other departments of the town hall that a local authority housing manager can call upon. Also, the specialist associations mentioned above may require to spend time on welfare aspects of housing, notwithstanding their general reliance on the statutory or voluntary social services. Perhaps the major advantage housing associations enjoy as regards management is that they do not normally have enormously large estates to care for and are therefore able to establish a more intimate approach.

Under section 5 of the Rent Act 1968, and section 18 of the Housing Act 1974, the tenancies of registered housing associations are excluded from protection under the Rent Acts with a few exceptions. Provision on these lines, first made in 1954, was at the time important to enable associations to charge rents which would cover their outgoings and so make their work viable. Since they were brought within the fair rent system in 1972, housing associations are no longer able to charge rents they themselves have fixed, but as responsible landlords they have been left with the power to obtain possession of their dwellings after due notice to quit has been served and a court order made. As with most local authorities, this power to evict is rarely used and then only as a last resort in dealing with an unsatisfactory tenant.

Tenant selection and nomination rights

Housing associations providing subsidised accommodation for letting normally select their tenants according to the recognised criteria of housing need, having regard to their own individual objects. Those providing for special categories, for example, select from the type of household within such category. In some cases their constitutions may oblige them to do so.

After the Housing Finance Act 1972, it became a condition of sanction for local authority loans to housing associations that the mortgage agreement should entitle the authority to nominate at least 50 per cent of the tenants of the scheme. In some cases the authorities demanded the right to nominate all tenants. No rigid nomination quota is laid down in the 1974 Act arrangements. DOE Circular 170/74 suggested that " a significant proportion of nominations " should be accepted from the local authority, at the same time stressing that housing associations should be able to preserve the flexibility they enjoy in tenant selection, in particular by housing people who, though in serious housing need, have little or no expectation of being offered local authority accommodation in the near future. In January 1976 a letter to all local authorities (H5/1041/1) again stressed the value of housing associations being left free to house those who, because they lacked residential qualification or for other reasons, could not obtain council housing. It is indicated that where virtually all places, or on the other hand few or none, are reserved for local authority nominations the scheme would not be acceptable for HAG. Nevertheless, local authorities advancing capital for schemes may make nomination rights a condition of doing so and when a loan is obtained from the Housing Corporation, it will normally require some arrangement about nominations to be made with the local authority. Housing associations are free in the last resort to choose their own tenants and to refuse to offer a tenancy to those referred to them by the housing authority if they are inappropriate. Many associations go to great lengths to select those who are in greatest need of the type of accommodation they can offer.

Conclusion

It is evident from the outline review in this chapter of housing associations and their work that they are somewhat hybrid bodies of quite strongly differentiated kinds. Some are motivated by a form of self-help, such as some co-ownerships and co-operatives. The majority inherit the philanthropic, or in more modern terms " socially responsible ", approach to housing improvement of the earlier reformers. All are managed by responsible committees serving in a voluntary capacity, a type of service which attracts people with an interest in public work, and above all in housing, who perhaps do not wish to involve themselves in party politics. Officers serving associations are also often attracted to work within a movement which is broken down into a comparatively large number of not very large units, and is doing a job which can therefore be seen as a whole.

House production by housing associations is still very small compared to that of the two main agencies, the local authorities and private enterprise building for sale, but since the 1974 Act it has been growing. In 1971, 10,000 new houses were completed and just under that number started. Although in 1975 only 13,652 were completed, there were over 30,000 under construction at the end of June 1976. The Housing Corporation's Annual Report of 1975–76 recorded that approval had been given during the year for loans covering 38,000 houses, apart from those being financed through local authorities. Unfortunately, the cuts in national housing expenditure in 1976 mean that lack of finance, rather than of capacity, will reduce output again in the immediate future. Approvals of improvement grants for housing associations were running at about five or six thousand a year from 1971 to 1975.

About the time the 1974 Act was introduced, there was criticism of housing associations for being too numerous and too small. Some are small and there is a danger in this if it means they are unable to command the services of members with the necessary management and professional skills. On the other hand, it is becoming generally recognised in all spheres that increase in size does not necessarily mean increase in efficiency. If one scheme of housing for the elderly is what is needed in a small place, it may well be better promoted and managed by a group of local people, provided continuing responsibility can be assured. Even some larger associations working on a nationwide basis enlist the help of local representatives. It is necessary nevertheless to ensure that several associations engaged on the same kind of work are not competing in one area, and local authorities have taken an active part in zoning areas of activity for the associations with which they are prepared to co-operate. Another recent development within the movement itself has been the formation of associations providing grouped development services for a district.

The flexibility and readiness to experiment which has led to the varied forms of housing provision and tenure by housing associations was being called in aid in 1976 to promote new forms of co-ownership and community leasehold housing. It was hoped these might enable schemes to be promoted combining the individual mortgages and capital, which would give occupiers a share in the equity, with an element of subsidisation, which would ensure continuing social ownership of the project as a whole. Subsidies for such schemes would, however, be less than the 75 per cent or so of capital cost usually required to finance housing association rented housing in 1976. At the same time the tenant and management co-operatives described above were being regarded as a way of involving council tenants more closely in the management of their estates. A Co-operative Housing Agency was set up by the government under the aegis of the Housing Corporation in order to encourage all types of co-operative housing. Unfortunately, the national economic situation was such that it had scarcely been formed before cuts were announced in the funds available for all housing association work, and it has yet to be shown how these proposals will develop.

It is usually held that the main role of the housing association movement is to complement and supplement that of local authorities. This is reflected in official policy in defining the priorities associations have been given for their work, in particular that of providing for special groups and needs not otherwise being met. In stress areas, where there is little question that any available help with housing improvement is needed, associations are supplementing the work of local authorities, a role which was reflected in the special place they are given in legislation for HAAs (see Chapter 7). However this may be, it is to be hoped that housing associations will maintain their characteristic versatility, flexibility and enthusiasm. So long as they do, they should continue to make a significant contribution to housing.

(For further reading see bibliography references 1–18).

CHAPTER 7

Rehabilitation

In Britain council houses have usually been financed on the assumption that they will remain in use for 60 years, though there are very many houses in the country older than this. Even within the last 60 years there have been three major reports on housing standards—the Tudor Walters, the Dudley and the Parker Morris reports (see bibliography for Chapter 1) and after each of these a higher space and equipment standard has been adopted as the minimum appropriate for a new dwelling. Indeed, technological advance has gathered speed over the centuries and is expected to do so even more in the coming decades. It is arguable, therefore, that the rate of obsolescence in housing will continue to accelerate, making the demand for improvements continuously more insistent.

Throughout their period of life, houses get altered and re-equipped, so that if the basic structure is sound they are adapted to the changing needs of the occupants. This kind of work is only carried out, however, if the economic return to the owner justifies it, or if owner-occupiers are able and willing to pay for it to increase their comfort. The acute housing shortage concentrated attention in the earlier post-war years on new building. Nevertheless, special financial incentives to carry out improvements were introduced as early as 1949, although they were not extensively used by comparison with those for new building and clearance and redevelopment, for which financial arrangements were generally more favourable in the public sector. Indeed, it was not until the beginning of the 1970s that improvement, not only of housing itself, but also of older residential areas, was given priority in legislation and administration over redevelopment and even new development.

Improvement from 1945 to 1959

It is recognised that houses must not be let for occupation unless they are fit for human habitation, and there is a responsibility on all landlords to keep them so fit, but it was accepted that landlords could not be expected to install new modern amenities at their own expense during the course of a tenancy to bring the dwellings up to the standard at which new ones had to be built. Financial assistance from public funds was, therefore, granted for house improvement and conversion to encourage

162

modernisation and reduce the charge which had to be paid by the occupier or passed on as rent to a tenant. Even before the rent legislation which now operates, increases in rent after improvements were limited to a percentage of the owner's costs. It is usually accepted that such assistance began after World War II, with the grants for improvement which local authorities could make at their discretion under the Housing Act 1949. In fact, very similar provisions under the Housing (Rural Workers) Acts were available between the wars for reconditioning cottages in rural areas.

The 1949 Act grants were known as discretionary because they were made at the discretion of the local authority for the area. They amounted to half the cost of approved work within certain limits, and local authorities as well as the Exchequer had to make an appropriate contribution towards them. Many authorities were reluctant to press for their use for this reason, or because they had already as much housing work as they could deal with to provide dwellings for normal needs or for redevelopment. Nevertheless, between 1949 and 1958, 160,000 discretionary grants were approved, 10,000 of which were taken up by the local authorities themselves.

House and area improvement from 1959 to 1969

The House Purchase and Housing Act 1959 introduced a new type of grant, the standard grant, which could be claimed by an owner as of right for installing certain amenities, and, if the necessary conditions were fulfilled, the local authority had no discretion in respect of granting it. Discretionary grants remained for more thorough-going work for houses which had a future 30 years of life.

Standard grants were limited in amount in relation to the cost of supplying five standard amenities—originally a fixed bath or shower, a wash hand basin, a water closet, a hot and cold water supply, and a ventilated food cupboard—and were available where the dwelling had a future life of about 15 years or over. (Later, the ventilated food cupboard was omitted and the amenities increased to seven by the addition of a sink and a hot and cold water supply at this and the bath and basin.) When the work was completed, the house had to have all the amenities, and the amount of grant available was related to those which were formerly lacking and provided as a result of the improvement.

The 1959 Act resulted in an increase in the number of improvements carried out. For example, in 1960 some 131,000 grants were approved, of which 64 per cent were standard grants. Although the discretionary grant approvals remained at about the same rate for some years, standard grants began to fall off

towards the end of the 1960s. This may have been due partly
to the reduction in the number of dwellings eligible for grant,
but also may well have been because the maximum amount of
grant remained the same from 1959 to 1969, although costs were
rising all the time. Moreover, associated repair and decoration
work, unless made necessary by the improvement, was not eligible
for grant aid, and had to be paid in full by the owners themselves.

There was a change in legislation regarding improvements in
the Housing Act 1964, which empowered local authorities to
designate improvement areas, if within such an area there were
50 per cent or more dwellings which lacked at least one of the
five standard amenities. The idea of improvement areas as well
as slum clearance and redevelopment areas had been recognised
under earlier legislation, but the 1964 Act was designed to
encourage local authorities to compel the improvement of all
houses in a particular part of their area. It was hoped that in this
way the whole of an area could be given a lift to a better
standard. The 1964 Act, however, gave no special financial help
with environmental improvement, but concentrated on the
internal improvement of the houses themselves. A few local
authorities implemented these provisions, but the procedures
under the Act were cumbersome and slow, so that there were
never more than just over 100 improvement areas designated in
any one year.

There were various adjustments to make improvement grants
more attractive during the 20 years between 1949 and 1969, and
quite a lot of spasmodic public relations work, which included
demonstration improvements and conversions sponsored by the
Ministry of Housing and Local Government itself, followed by
a series of local authority demonstrations in different towns and
various other exhibitions and publicity projects by some of the
industries concerned. This was important since improvement
grants were intended primarily for privately owned houses, and
private owners had to be told about them and encouraged to
use them. Most grants approved were for older houses owned by
their occupiers, and some for privately let houses, such houses
forming a sizeable, though already decreasing, proportion of all
stock at the beginning of the period.

In 1966, two important Ministry of Housing and Local Government publications focused attention not only on house improvement but also on the improvement of the whole residential
environment. The first of these, the report of the Denington
Committee, a sub-committee of the Central Housing Advisory
Committee, *Our Older Homes: A Call for Action* (1), examined
standards of fitness and made recommendations for an active
policy for improvements. In the same year, the Ministry published

The Deeplish Study: Improvement Possibilities in a District of Rochdale (4). This described a survey of an area of older housing and argued that the existing population would be better served if the area were dealt with by improvement rather than clearance and redevelopment. It was believed that, helped by grants, the owners would be prepared to put their own resources into improvements to the housing if the environment were also rehabilitated. A pilot project was carried out in the area to improve the streets by traffic management, planting, introducing better paving, street lighting and so on.

In 1967, moreover, the national sample house condition survey organised by the Ministry of Housing and Local Government and Welsh Office revealed that not only were there 1·8 million houses in an unsatisfactory condition which could not be rescued, but that a further 4·7 million were in need of major repair and improvement work. At long last improvement was recognised as of major importance to a comprehensive housing policy. In 1968, a White Paper, *Old Houses into New Homes* (Cmnd. 3602), promulgated a policy for improvement and promised legislation which reached the statute book in the following year as the Housing Act 1969.

Improvement under the Housing Act 1969

The Housing Act 1969 gave a new complexion to housing improvement work. The amounts of the discretionary improvement grant and the standard grant were increased to avoid an economic advantage to either new development or improvement. A third type of grant was introduced, the special grant for installing the standard amenities in houses in multiple occupation where self-contained units were not provided. Grants could be used for approved works of repair and replacement up to one-half of the cost of the whole. The Minister had power to increase the amount of the grant over the limit in special cases where there was good reason for it and he did this for the London area. There was also a higher limit allowed for houses of three or more storeys. Local authorities, the New Towns Commission, new town development corporations and housing associations became eligible for help with acquisition of houses for improvement or conversion as well as with the improvement work itself, the grant being increased by a small amount in such cases. Housing associations were also able to use a special subsidy of three quarters of the annual loan charges on the approved cost of improvement and conversion work, an arrangement which generally worked out more favourably than if the grant available to private owners was used.

The Housing Act 1969 was the first legislation to provide an Exchequer subsidy for environmental improvement as well as the improvement of the house itself. This was a new conception. The 1969 Act also altered the provisions for area improvements.

The general improvement areas (GIAs), which local authorities were asked to designate under the 1969 Act, were to be areas which had a potential for upgrading. They were to be free from disadvantages of position as residential areas, and not have a significant proportion of the dwellings so far deteriorated as to make rescue impossible save by clearance and rebuilding. Guidance was given in MOHLG Circular 65/69 on the assessment of the relative economic advantages of redevelopment or rehabilitation as applied to different cases, based on the standard of the result and the useful life of the dwellings. Since no compulsory powers were available, other than compulsory acquisition which was not at the time favoured, local authorities were advised to seek areas for treatment as GIAs where the local population were favourably inclined towards it, or at least ready to be interested. Public participation, already being sought in other kinds of work on behalf of the community, was essential for the success of GIAs. Although local authorities were exhorted to seek out and promote appropriate areas to become GIAs, other non-governmental bodies or even individuals could themselves carry out surveys and put forward proposals for areas to be designated. The result was a series of pilot projects in different parts of the country which were well publicised in the DOE's Area Improvement Notes, a series of specialist advisory publications on all aspects of improvement, and officially and unofficially sponsored demonstrations, films, talks and reports. It became evident that improvement schemes, and perhaps GIAs in particular, owed their success to the personalities of one or more promoters, often living and working in the areas, whether as architects, social and community workers, or improvement officers appointed by the local authority or a housing association, no less than to an active corporative effort by all the departments involved at the town hall.

Following the 1969 Act, there was a substantial increase in the numbers of all types of improvement grants approved. In 1969, 108,900 grants had been approved in Britain and in 1971, 198,000. There was also a marked increase in the numbers being taken up by local authorities themselves.

By the end of 1971, a further fillip was given to rehabilitation by the passing of the Housing Act 1971. This gave further assistance to areas of high unemployment by increasing the proportion of the grants in such " development and intermediate areas " from 50 per cent to 75 per cent of the cost of the work. Also the Exchequer contribution to the grants was increased from 75 per cent to 90 per cent of the annual loan charges for 20 years. The provisions were to apply for the limited period of two years only, from June 1971 to June 1973, but were later extended by the Housing (Amendment) Act 1973 by a further year to work completed by June 1974. Again there was a marked increase in the number of grants approved to 368,068 in Britain in 1972, of which 185,172 were in development and intermediate areas, and 453,496 in 1973, of which 236,533 were in development and intermediate areas. There was a fall to 300,482 in 1974 when the additional help for these areas came to an end.

After the 1969 Act, local authorities themselves took up an increased number of grants mainly to modernise their older estates, nearly 104,000 and 118,000 being approved in 1972 and 1973 respectively. The declaration of GIAs gathered momentum and, in 1972, 275 were designated in England and Wales comprising 89,122 dwellings, followed in 1973 by 247 comprising 63,185 dwellings.

Some abuse of grants created problems, particularly in London. Evidence was put forward that, in areas of housing shortage, houses were being improved with grant and then sold at a high figure or let as expensive flats, perhaps furnished or with services, to those who could afford the high rents. The Housing Centre summed up improvement grant problems in stress areas in a memorandum submitted to the Minister for Housing and Construction in January 1973. (*Housing Review*, Vol. 22, No. 2, 1973.) The favourable results of the 1969 Act were listed as the increase in the numbers of dwellings being improved and converted, the increase in the number of good small dwellings where these were needed, and the increase in GIAs and environmental improvement. The main disadvantages were summarised as being the decrease in the number of dwellings, including larger family dwellings, available for letting to the indigenous population at rents which they could afford, the use of public funds towards improvement of dwellings subsequently sold for profit, and the added incentive to seek vacant possession from tenants who were inadequately protected against eviction, which could lead to homelessness. The memorandum reminded the Minister that special powers over stress areas had been suggested eight years previously in the Milner Holland *Report of the Committee on Housing in Greater London* (see bibliography Chapter 1) and asked him to implement them. It also advocated the extended use of compulsory purchase orders by local authorities to further improvement work in stress areas without creating hardship for existing tenants.

Housing Act 1974

Major new developments in a policy for stress areas were heralded in 1973 in a White Paper, *Widening the Choice: the next steps in housing* (Cmnd. 5280) and measures to implement

such a policy were set out in a second White Paper, *Better Homes
—the next priorities* (Cmnd. 5339), presented to Parliament the
same year. The Conservative government introduced a Bill early
in 1974, but this government fell before it could be passed.
Fortunately, this measure had been largely agreed by both main
political parties and the Bill, substantially on the same lines,
introduced by the new Labour government, was passed though
Parliament rapidly and came into force as the Housing Act 1974.
This Act contains the main provisions for improvement of houses
and older areas at the date of going to press.

The main innovation, so far as improvement work is concerned,
introduced by the Housing Act 1974, was in the use of the
concept of rehabilitation to deal with the worst areas of housing
stress. Hitherto, it had been assumed that the worst housing
conditions would have to be dealt with by means of slum clearance
and redevelopment. GIAs were, and still are, areas where the
majority of the houses are fundamentally sound and their inhabitants have confidence in them and the environment, but where,
nevertheless, houses and environment are old and need improving.
The housing action areas (HAAs) and priority neighbourhoods
(PNs), provided for under Parts IV and VI of the Housing Act
1974, are intended to be areas of housing stress where both the
social and physical conditions create unsatisfactory living conditions. They are substantially those areas identified previously by the
Milner Holland committee as requiring special treatment. Partly
because the worst slum property was disappearing and because
greater emphasis was being put on social as opposed to physical
conditions, and partly because of the unpopularity of much
redevelopment, it was now proposed to deal with such areas by
putting more emphasis on improvement.

Although improvement is encouraged within HAAs by more
favourable grants, and indeed may be made compulsory, the
provisions governing such areas extend beyond those concerned
with physical improvement work to houses and environment.
They include, for example, controls over changes in forms of
tenure. Local authorities, having designated an HAA, may see as
the objective for it a holding operation to ameliorate conditions
for a period pending eventual clearance and redevelopment. DOE
Circular 13/75 suggests, however, that in most cases an early
and demonstrable improvement of conditions generally should
be produced which will lead to a stable future for the area. This
could lead to a changeover to a GIA for which higher environmental grant is available and which could enable a higher standard
of improvements to houses to be secured. Some redevelopment
might also be found desirable and appropriate.

The main policy objectives of the rehabilitation provisions of the 1974 Act were set out in DOE Circular 160/74 (WO 266/74), in which local authorities were asked to regard the rehabilitation of existing houses as an integral part of their housing programme. The circular advised that renewal of residential areas should be based on a comprehensive strategy consisting of a mixture of clearance and redevelopment by a variety of agencies; appropriate infill; acquisition and renovation by the local authority, housing associations or co-operatives; voluntary grant-aided improvements and repair; compulsory improvements and repair; and environmental treatment.

The legislative framework for rehabilitation, covering HAAs, PNs and GIAs together with house improvement, is dealt with in the following sections of this chapter. It is set out in some detail because of its direct relevance to individual occupants and owners in the older residential districts, as well as to the local authorities and housing associations who must operate within it.

Housing Action Areas (Housing Act 1974, Part IV)

HAAs are intended to be those areas where (a) the " physical state of the housing accommodation in the area as a whole ", and (b) " the social conditions in the area " are such as to be unsatisfactory and can be most effectively dealt with within a period of five years so as to secure (a) the improvement of the housing accommodation in the area as a whole, and (b) the well-being of the persons for the time being residing in the area, and (c) the proper and effective management and use of that accommodation. (Housing Act 1974, section 36 (1) and (2)).

A report to the above effect may be prepared by the authority for the area itself or by other persons or organisations who appear to the authority to be suitably qualified. DOE Circular 14/75 suggests that people and organisations, other than officers of the authority, submitting reports might be neighbourhood councils, residents' associations, housing associations or other voluntary bodies; consultants; or other persons with relevant knowledge. The circular specifically mentions that authorities should welcome the contributions of housing associations and others in identifying HAAs, as means of relieving their own staff. However, any person or organisation thinking of acting in this way should consult the local authority at the earliest stage. This is advisible, partly because whether a report is acted upon will depend not only on the suitability of the area, but also on the resources available to take the necessary action. If a report is not acted upon, local authorities should give their reasons to the person or body submitting it.

A report need not be an elaborate document nor contain precise figures, but should gather together relevant information. DOE Circular 14/75 sets out the type of information regarded as relevant. DOE Area Improvement Note 10, *The Use of Indicators for Area Action* (5), advises on the sources of data and their use in selecting areas for special action as HAAs, PNs or GIAs.

Local authorities are required by section 36 (3) of the 1974 Act to have regard to the guidance of the Secretary of State in declaring HAAs, and this is set out in paras. 11 to 16 of DOE Circular 14/75. It covers the assessment of physical conditions—numbers of houses unfit, lacking amenities, etc.—and social conditions, and the extent to which physical and social factors combine. Social conditions should be assessed principally on the following indicators, though it is recognised that not all will be relevant in every area:

(a) the proportion of households sharing cooking facilities, a bath, water closet or other facilities;

(b) the proportion of households living at a density of over 1½ persons per room (or any other overcrowding measure relevant to the area);

(c) the proportion of households living in privately rented accommodation; and

(d) the concentration of households likely to have special housing problems, for instance old-age pensioners, large families, single parent families, or families whose head is unemployed or in a low income group.

Before declaring an HAA, authorities must be satisfied that they have sufficient resources to secure a significant improvement in five years. If resources are insufficient to cover all potential HAAs, then guidance is given as to the assessment of priorities and phasing of declarations. Resources are defined as:

(i) financial resources, taking into account severe restrictions on expenditure likely during the next few years;

(ii) staff;

(iii) resources, money and staff available to registered housing associations working in the area;

(iv) the local capacity of the building industry; and

(v) rehousing or decanting space for people temporarily or permanently displaced by improvement work.

Although the appropriate size of an HAA will depend on particular circumstances, local authorities are advised that a range of 200–300 houses is likely to prove satisfactory for the intensive action required. PNs can be declared to prevent deterioration in adjoining areas.

Finally, local authorities are advised that HAA procedures are not appropriate to areas where a large proportion of the houses are already in their own ownership. These should be dealt with, if necessary, under other improvement powers.

An area defined on a map and declared to be such by the local authority becomes an HAA immediately. The authority must however send its resolution, the map and report and certain other information to the Secretary of State to enable him to assess the desirability of the declaration. This must include a statement which will enable him to judge what housing association support will be available in the action to be taken, a provision which reflects the view of Ministers and Parliament that housing associations should play an important role in HAAs. The Secretary has power within a limited period to cancel or modify the area.

The local authority must as soon as may be after the declaration of an area publicise it by means defined in section 36 (4) of the Housing Act 1974. These are the placing of advertisements in two or more newspapers circulating in the area identifying the area and naming a place or places where the map and relevant documents can be inspected. Any alterations made to the area or its cancellation by the Secretary of State must also be publicised.

In order to provide local authorities with a means of identifying tenanted property which is being bought and sold and in which tenants are at risk of displacement, a system of notification operates in HAAs. Owners must notify the authority of notices to quit, the termination of tenancies by the effluxion of time and disposals of property. Since it is a criminal offence not to comply with these requirements, local authorities must inform owners of these obligations and of the name and address of the person to whom representations must be made. The local authority must respond to such notifications within four weeks. They need not do so by an offer to buy the property or a compulsory purchase order. Other appropriate action may be taken, such as an offer of a renovation grant, the suggestion of an agreement to nominate a tenant, a control or management order, or, in the case of a notice to quit, informing the tenant of his rights.

The statutory provision which makes the well-being of the people living in an HAA one of the requirements for its declaration emphasises the social objectives of the legislation. DOE Circular 14/75 stresses the importance of enlisting public participation and of keeping households informed of plans for action and progress. Advice is proffered on methods of overcoming problems of communication, particularly in areas where there are households not accustomed to reading or speaking English or who have little knowledge of housing law or landlord and tenant procedures. Local teams and offices, and demonstrations of improved houses are recommended.

The objective of the action programme of seeing a significant improvement in five years must influence the work undertaken in an HAA. Although quick results should not prejudice continued progress, local authorities should guard against applying standards which are too high to be practicable or acceptable to the inhabitants because they are too costly or cause too much disturbance. Another objective of HAA treatment is the avoidance of the break-up of existing communities, which may require that special categories of households, such as old people, large families, single parent families, etc., who have close ties with the area and do not wish to leave it, should have suitable types of accommodation made available to them. For example, single people requiring " digs " or " bedsitters " may be satisfactorily housed in accommodation which is not self-contained, though for families with children decent self-contained homes should be the objective. The 1974 Act makes provision for improvements to a reduced standard (see below), and local authorities have powers under the Acts of 1957, 1961, 1964 and 1969 for dealing with individual unfit houses and the control of multiple occupation also available to them for use in HAAs.

Following a recommendation of the *Tenth Report of the House of Commons Expenditure Committee on Improvements* (3), the Secretary of State was given powers to call for reports on progress to enable HAAs to be monitored. DOE Circular 14/75 asks for such reports to be made and indicates what they should cover.

Local authorities have special powers applicable in HAAs, including that given in the Housing Act 1974, section 43, to acquire land to secure the objectives for which the declaration was made as set out in section 36 (2), see above. DOE Circular 14/75 lists some circumstances where such acquisitions might be appropriate and where, if the property could not be acquired by agreement, the Secretary of State would be prepared to consider compulsory purchase orders. These include cases where a house is in disrepair or lacking in standard amenities and those responsible are unwilling or unable to rehabilitate; where multiple ownership prejudices the improvement of a group of dwellings; where tenants have been subjected to harassment (whether technically an offence or not); where a house in multi-occupation is badly managed; and where housing is being kept empty or unoccupied. Priorities for acquisitions are to make the best use of housing in stress areas by bringing unoccupied property into use, by relieving overcrowding, or providing rehousing space for improvements elsewhere; and to facilitate improvement, particularly where multiple ownership makes full-scale improvement impractical or where compulsory improvement procedures are not effective or unlikely to be so. If local authorities acquire houses, however, it is important that they should be dealt with promptly and local authorities should therefore be sure that they have the resources to do so before embarking on extensive acquisitions.

General consent was given subsequently for land acquired under HAA powers to be treated for subsidy and loan sanction as if it were acquired under Part V of the Housing Act 1957, which brought such acquisitions into the local authority housing revenue account.

Part VIII of the Housing Act 1974 virtually re-enacted provisions for compulsory improvement which had been repealed by the Housing Act 1969 and these are available in HAAs and GIAs. They apply to tenanted dwellings, but only to owner-occupied ones if the failure to improve prevents the improvement of a dwelling which is let in the same building or adjacent. The procedures are still somewhat complicated. The authority must be satisfied that the dwelling is without one or more of the standard amenities and is capable of improvement to the full or reduced standard at reasonable expense, and that " housing arrangements " are satisfactory, or unnecessary, for the tenant while the work is being carried out. Home loss or disturbance payments under the Land Compensation Act 1973 may also be involved (see Chapter 3). A prescribed provisional notice must be served on the person having control of the dwelling: an undertaking that improvement will be carried out may be accepted, or, if necessary, an improvement notice requiring the work to be done must follow. A local authority may act in default. The person having control of the dwelling and the tenant have a right of appeal on certain grounds to the county court and the owner has a right to the appropriate grant for the work and to a loan from the local authority. He may also serve a notice on the local authority requiring them to purchase his interest in the dwelling.

In order to encourage improvement work to be carried out in HAAs, the various grants for it are payable at higher rates than elsewhere, up to 75 per cent of the allowable cost, and up to 90 per cent in cases of hardship. Cases of hardship are not defined in the Act and local authorities have to make their own judgments. Some guidance is given in DOE Circular 160/74, where it is suggested that criteria to be taken into account are eligibility for supplementary benefit and rate rebate, and a state retirement or disability pension as a principal source of revenue. Grants for repair work only are only available in HAAs (see below " Repairs Grant "). There is a grant for environmental work in HAAs on land not in the authority's possession. Subsidy towards environmental work is however only 50 per cent of up to £50 per unit of housing accommodation in the area, a good deal less than the £200 per unit available in GIAs. It is the intention that there should be a greater concentration on house improvement than environmental work in HAAs.

Conditions attached to the letting and occupancy of dwellings after improvement with the aid of grants are obligatory for HAAs, PNs and GIAs and the period during which a dwelling must be held available for letting is seven instead of five years in an HAA. These conditions are set out in greater detail below in the section on " Grant Conditions ".

Priority Neighbourhoods (Housing Act 1974, Part VI)

The main purpose of the legislation applying to PNs is to prevent the deterioration of the housing position in or around stress areas in which immediate action is impractical, and to avoid stress conditions rippling out from such areas where action is being taken, normally by declaration as an HAA. The conception is that PN procedures can be used as a holding operation for areas which cannot be dealt with immediately either as HAAs or GIAs. The provisions for their declaration and for control and action in them are broadly similar to those for HAAs, but do not require an urgent five year programme of action. There is no time limit set for the completion of action in PNs, but they are declared for an initial five year period and may subsequently be renewed for further five year periods. They thus come up for review every five years and it is the intention that they should be dealt with more radically as HAAs or GIAs, as appropriate, as soon as practicable.

The criteria for the selection of PNs are similar to those for HAAs. Local authorities must have regard to the physical state of the housing and also to the social conditions. These must be unsatisfactory and the authority must be satisfied that PN powers are required to improve the conditions and manage the housing in the interest of the community. PNs must also surround or have a common boundary with an HAA or a GIA. Stress is laid on the significance of a high proportion of houses in the area being owned by private non-resident landlords. Detailed guidance as to the criteria to be used in identifying PNs is set out in DOE Circular 14/75 and WO Circular 5/75.

The special powers which operate in PNs are the same as those which apply in HAAs regarding the acquisition and use of land and the notification system, but there is no grant for environmental work and the more favourable grants for house improvement work do not apply.

Local authorities are warned in the circulars that the declaration of a PN will arouse expectations of improvement and that they should be able to demonstrate that such expectations are well founded, otherwise the loss of confidence which may result may be more harmful than if no declaration had been made. They must also be assured that they can operate the notification system fairly and effectively. It is pointed out that the declaration of a PN may actually inhibit improvement work, since people in the area will not be entitled to the more favourable grants which apply in HAAs and GIAs and may postpone action in the expectation of these becoming available later. However, if owners are already reluctant to apply for grants in a potential PN, or if the value of the other powers, such as the notification system, outweigh this consideration, a decision in favour of a PN may be desirable.

General Improvement Areas (Housing Act 1974, Part V)

As previously explained, the legal provisions for General Improvement Areas were first introduced in the Housing Act 1969, with a special grant for environmental improvement; but the Housing Act 1974 made some alterations. GIAs differ from HAAs and PNs in that improvement in them is perhaps seen more in physical terms than in relation to the management of the housing to improve social conditions. The criteria for selecting GIAs remain broadly unchanged since the 1969 Act and lay emphasis on their consisting of fundamentally sound houses, capable of providing good living conditions for many years to come. The areas should be unlikely to be affected by redevelopment or major planning proposals, and should contain stable communities without a preponderance of privately let houses. The inhabitants, many of whom will be owner-occupiers, should have confidence in putting their own money into the houses. DOE Circular 14/75 reiterates earlier advice that areas should be avoided where the environmental conditions have so far deteriorated that even after improvement they would not give satisfactory living conditions. On the other hand, since rateable value limits are fixed for owner-occupied houses eligible for improvement grants (see below " Improvement Grants "), the numbers of houses in the area within such limits should influence their choice. A GIA must not contain a clearance area, but it may adjoin or surround one. There may, however, be some individual unfit houses in a GIA which cannot be dealt with by improvement, but which can be dealt with by clearance procedures. Indeed, it is suggested in DOE Circular 14/75 that the sites of such houses may be useful in improving the environment generally if they are used for open space or play areas, etc. GIAs may also be contiguous with HAAs and PNs, which, as already stated, may become GIAs at a later stage in their treatment if this is found appropriate. As in the case of HAAs, areas containing 200–300 houses are regarded as of an appropriate size for a GIA.

The procedure for identifying GIAs, the report by a suitably qualified person or persons and so on, remains substantially as under the Housing Act 1969, but revised provisions under Part V of the Housing Act 1974 and its Schedule 5 give the Secretary of State power to prevent the confirmatory resolution which is required before an area actually becomes a GIA. DOE Circular 14/75 states that these powers were taken to prevent the misuse of public funds " by excessive, premature or inappropriate declarations ". The Secretary of State's directions as to the information he requires in order to reach a decision as to whether a GIA should be confirmed or not are given in the same circular. This includes the numbers of dwellings in the area classified as to age, standard, etc. and rateable value; the number of dwellings in other GIAs and HAAs already declared by the authority which remain to be dealt with, and the progress made with environmental improvement; the public participation which has taken place and is and will be taking place; and the staff resources which the authority can make available during the initial two years of the project. The implication seems to be that authorities should not undertake more improvement work than they can carry through.

A higher level of improvement grants is available in GIAs than generally. There is no provision to raise the percentage further in cases of hardship in GIAs as in HAAs. Repairs grants (see below " Repairs Grants ") are available in GIAs, as in HAAs, but not elsewhere.

Since it is the intention that GIAs should consist primarily of houses which after improvement will provide satisfactory living conditions for a considerable time, improvement to a high standard with the help of improvement grant is likely to be desirable, but the other grants which allow a reasonable standard to be achieved are all available in them and the full standard could be achieved by degrees. Local authorities are warned that there may be householders who do not want or cannot afford the higher standard, for example old people, who have managed without modern amenities in the past and who fear the disturbance of the construction work, and young people whose financial resources have already been stretched in the process of acquiring a home.

Compulsory powers are available to local authorities in GIAs, as in HAAs, to acquire properties for improvement and to require improvements by the owner. It is suggested that owners will be discouraged from improving their own houses if some in the area are allowed to deteriorate into a dilapidated state. On the other hand, it remains official policy to use compulsory acquisition only as a last resort and to use persuasion wherever possible rather than impose compulsory improvement.

The importance of public participation and support to the success of GIAs, and indeed to all area and house improvement, can hardly be overstressed. The official literature and circulars are bespattered with exhortations to this effect and with advice as to early and continuing contacts with the local community, how demonstrations and technical assistance can help, and how the wishes of the local people regarding environmental work should be met. Even the legal provisions are designed to ensure co-operation between the authority and the residents; for example, after the declaration of a GIA as well as a HAA, certain publicity for it is prescribed and people in the area must be informed of the name and address of the person to whom inquiries and representations should be made. Initiative for area improvement work has not, however, always come from the same direction, that is from the local authority. Local action groups, housing associations and residents' groups have promoted improvement projects. Experience of alternatives to local authority managed area improvement, however, also illustrates the importance of securing a consensus of support among the community affected (9).

House Renovation Grants

Government policy to implement the Housing Act 1974 provisions by concentrating resources on improving the worst housing conditions first have been applied not only through area improvement, but also through renovation and conversion grants and the ways of using them. It had been suggested that public funds were being abused or wasted on raising the standard of housing which was already satisfactory, including that of some older housing on council estates, rather than concentrating them on essential work on manifestly substandard dwellings. The financial difficulties (in maintaining and improving houses) faced by many landlords under rent legislation as well as by low income owner-occupiers, and most of all the blighting effect of closures and the delays and social disturbance of clearance and redevelopment, have led to improvement procedures and renovation grants coming to be regarded as just as important as redevelopment as a means of securing the gradual progressive renewal of all but the worst slums. Moreover, strategy is being aimed not only at tackling physical conditions but also at securing social improvement, as is reflected in some of the provisions for HAAs and PNs and also in controls over the use of individual dwellings after they have been improved with grant. Also, just as it is suggested that HAAs and PNs may progress to the higher environmental standards of GIAs, dwellings improved to reduced standards may qualify for an improvement grant to a higher standard at a later stage. There are practical advantages in such a policy where occupants, perhaps elderly people, are unwilling to have improvements to a home they are satisfied with, or which they cannot afford, but there is also a danger, of course, that to carry out a comparatively small job in two stages may itself be rather wasteful.

Although grants for house renovation are especially important to the treatment of HAAs and GIAs (PNs to a lesser extent as these are primarily a holding operation), they are available outside these areas. They are paid in a different way for work carried out by local authorities themselves on property which they own, by housing associations and by private owners. Local authorities receive Exchequer contributions under section 79 of the Housing Act 1974 for the provision of dwellings by conversion or the improvement of dwellings in circumstances similar to those in which they would pay an improvement grant to an owner other than themselves. The contribution is a sum payable annually for 20 years from completion equal to 37·5 per cent of the loan charges on the eligible expense. Ceilings governing eligible expense have been kept in line with the ceilings for grants to private owners (S.I. 1975 No. 729). Acquisition and improvement by housing associations is eligible for housing association grant and in this case too there are ceilings of eligible expense. The matter is dealt with in greater detail in Chapter 6 on Housing Associations.

Grants for private owners, whether landlords or owner-occupiers, are paid by the local authority to whom the applicant must apply. The local authority receives Exchequer subsidy towards such grants, amounting to a percentage of the annual loan charges on the expense for 20 years after completion of the work. The proportions are 90 per cent if the grant is made for a dwelling in a GIA or HAA and 75 per cent if it is elsewhere. This amount can be altered by statutory order.

Applications and payment of grants

Directions and specifications to local authorities as to applications for grants, which have statutory force, were set out in Appendix A of DOE Circular 160/74, as amended by DOE Circular 13/76. Model forms are given in Appendix C of the same circular.

Grants will not normally be entertained for work started before the application has been approved. They are also generally prohibited for work on dwellings built after 2 October 1961 except where plans were approved before that date which meant that the dwelling was completed without one of the standard amenities; nor will they be paid for work which has already been approved for grant. This restriction does not however prejudice applications to bring previously grant-aided dwellings to a higher standard by additional work, as explained below. When approving an application the local authority may make a condition of payment that the work is completed within a stated period, not being less than 12 months. If, however, the authority is satisfied that additional works are required, the time may be extended.

Applications for grant must include plans of the dwelling before and after the proposed improvement or conversion, a specification of the work to be done, certificates of future occupation of the dwelling and, in the case of a dwelling to be available for letting, a statement as to what housing arrangements, if any, are to be made for existing tenants during and after improvement. There must be a statement that the dwelling was provided before 2 October 1961 or, in the case of conversion, that the building was erected before that date, and a statement of rateable value. The statement of rateable value applies only in the case of an application for an improvement grant and a statement as to housing arrangements is not required for special grant. In addition to this prescribed information, local authorities in practice require additional data, including an estimate of the cost of the work.

Grants may be paid after completion of the works or by instalments, provided such instalments do not exceed a half of the cost of the works when completed. Arrangements may be made for payment to be made direct to the builder. If someone carries out work to his own house, grant will not normally cover the notional cost of his labour.

If a grant application is refused, the local authority must state its reasons for doing so.

Loans by local authorities for improvement work

Local authorities may make advances to owners on mortgage to help them finance their part of the cost of improvement work. In the case of compulsory improvement, they must make such a loan if they are satisfied that it will be repaid. They may also make an advance to enable an owner to pay off a previous mortgage if this will meet the housing needs of the applicant. DOE Circular 160/74 points out that this may be helpful where an owner is unable to get a further advance from his original lender. Local authorities may also grant maturity mortgages which allow interest only to be paid and the capital sum repaid only at the end of the loan period. This, DOE Circular 160/74 suggests, may be particularly helpful to old people. The interest payments may in appropriate circumstances attract social security benefits.

Types of renovation grant

There are four types of grant available under the Housing Act 1974:

(a) improvement grants,
(b) intermediate grants (formerly standard grants),
(c) special grants,
(d) repairs grants (available in HAAs only).

Their main characteristics and differences are outlined under these headings in the sections below.

Amounts of grant and appropriate percentages

The amount of grant which the owner may receive depends on the type of grant and the work to be done and also on the appropriate percentage of the eligible expense. The appropriate percentage depends on the location of the dwelling and was fixed by section 59 of the Housing Act 1974 as follows:

(a) 75 per cent where the premises are in a HAA;
(b) 60 per cent where they are in a GIA;
(c) 50 per cent anywhere else.

These rates may be varied by order. In the case of a dwelling in a HAA, the local authority may increase the proportion up to 90 per cent if the applicant could not otherwise finance the work without undue hardship (see above " Housing Action Areas "). In the case of improvement, special and repairs grants, local authorities may approve grants at lower percentages than the maximum appropriate ones, but if they do so they must state their reasons.

The eligible expense on which the appropriate percentage will be paid by way of grant is so much of the estimated expense which is approved by the authority which falls within the relevant limits for the different types of grant as set out below. If applicants satisfy the authority that additional works are required to achieve the appropriate standard which could not have been foreseen, a higher expense may subsequently be approved.

Grant conditions

The Housing Act 1974 introduced a number of conditions applying to the use of dwellings after improvement or conversion with grant. These conditions are more stringent than those under former legislation and are intended to prevent public monies being used to improve or convert houses as a business proposition without ensuring that the benefit is enjoyed by the occupier.

As previously mentioned, applications for grants other than special grants must be accompanied by a certificate as to future occupation and, unless the future occupation conforms with the statutory conditions, grant will not be made. These conditions are:

(a) If the house is, or is to be, owner-occupied, it must be available throughout the first year and for four years afterwards as the applicant's main residence, or he must certify that it will be so occupied within one year and for the next four years. This enables a house to be improved with a grant prior to a move, say for retirement, but it prohibits grants being used for second homes or holiday homes. If after the first year it is not used in this way, it may be let as a residence or made available for letting.

(b) If the house is to be available for letting, then it must be let, or be available for letting, as a residence and not for holiday, or be occupied, or available for occupation, by a member of the agricultural population in pursuance of a contract of service (a tied dwelling).

(c) If the dwelling is in a GIA, a HAA or a PN and is let, the local authority must impose further conditions, which they may impose also elsewhere if they so desire. In no case may they impose any other conditions. These are:

(i) that the dwelling must be let, or be available for letting, on a regulated tenancy, or for furnished accommodation a contract to which Part VI of the Rent Act 1968 applies;

(ii) that the owner will after due notice and within the specified time furnish a certificate to the effect that this condition is being fulfilled;

(iii) that the tenant will on the owner's request furnish him with the necessary information to enable him to fulfil (ii) above;

(iv) that if on the certified date of the completion of the works there is no rent registered for a regulated tenancy under the Rent Act 1968, and no application for such pending, an application will be made to the rent officer, or the contract referred to the Rent Tribunal within 14 days;

(v) that such an application or referral will be diligently proceeded with and not withdrawn;

(vi) that no premium shall be required as a condition of the grant, renewal or continuance of the lease or contract.

Certain dwellings—parsonages, dwellings on glebe and charitable lands, and dwellings in which a housing association has an interest at the date grant was approved—are exempted from these conditions.

The conditions as to dwellings which are let will generally last for five years, seven in the case of premises in a HAA, from the date certified by the local authority as that on which the work was completed to their satisfaction. They are enforceable also during that period on someone who buys the dwelling or other successors in title. They are registrable in the local land charges register. If there is a breach of the conditions, the amount of the grant with compound interest is repayable on demand to the local authority. The local authority has discretion, however, not to demand such payment in full or in part. On payment of the sum demanded, or voluntary payment of a like sum, the conditions will cease to apply. Thus, some one who has received a grant may, as it were, buy himself out of the conditions, if circumstances change and he so wishes.

Improvement grants

Improvement grants are available at the discretion of the local authority for what are described in DOE Circular 160/74 as " works normally of a high all-round standard for the improvement or conversion—plus repair—of properties with a good life ahead of them ". They are not available for improvement or conversion of dwellings for owner-occupation with rateable values in excess of the limits specified by the Secretary of State. These limits are £300 in Greater London and £175 elsewhere in England and Wales (S.I. 1974 No. 1931).

Section 61 (3) of the Housing Act 1974 defines the conditions which must be fulfilled for the dwelling on completion to reach the required standard as: —(a) that it must have all the standard amenities for the exclusive use of its occupants; (b) that it must be in good repair (disregarding the state of internal decorative repair) having regard to its age, character and location; (c) that it must conform with the structural standards and be provided with the services and amenities specified from time to time by the Secretary of State; and (d) must be likely to provide satisfactory housing accommodation for a period of 30 years. If it appears to the local authority, however, that it is not practicable at reasonable expense to reach the standard required under the first of these requirements, they may reduce it. They may also substitute a shorter period of not less than 10 years.

The standard amenities, listed in Schedule 6 to the Housing Act 1974, are the same as those relating to intermediate grants and are given below under that heading.

The standards specified by the Secretary of State were given in DOE Circular 160/74, as follows:

On completion of the works the dwelling must

    (i) be substantially free from damp;

  (ii) have adequate natural lighting and ventilation in each habitable room;
  (iii) have adequate and safe provision throughout for artificial lighting, and have sufficient electric socket outlets for the safe and proper functioning of domestic appliances;
  (iv) be provided with adequate drainage facilities;
  (v) be in a stable structural condition;
  (vi) have satisfactory internal arrangement;
  (vii) have satisfactory facilities for preparing and cooking food;
  (viii) be provided with adequate facilities for heating;
  (ix) have proper provision for the storage of fuel (where necessary) and for the storage of refuse; and
  (x) conform with the specifications applicable to thermal insulation of roof spaces laid down in Part V of the Building Regulations in force at the date of the grant approval.

The Secretary of State has power to prevent the approval of improvement and intermediate grants of a specified description unless his consent has been obtained. In DOE Circular 160/74 he does this in respect of:

  (i) an application which includes works for insulating a dwelling against heat loss. This prohibition is modified, however, in the case of elderly or disabled people who could not meet the cost of thermal insulation of roof spaces without grant-aid.
  (ii) An application for a grant if an improvement grant had been paid already within 30 years to bring the dwelling up to the full required standard. This does not apply where a previous grant has been in respect of a reduced standard, when the amount of the grant will be modified to take account of the previous grant paid.
  (iii) An application for a grant for conversion of premises which do not at the time comprise a dwelling. This is to prevent the use of grant for conversions where the rateable value limits do not apply, though consent would be given if the local authority confirm that the conversion would assist them as a housing authority and that in their view the applicant should receive help from public funds. DOE Circular 13/76 subsequently removed this restriction from the use of grant to aid conversions of non-residential premises where the resultant dwellings would be used for letting and not owner-occupation.

The amount of the grant is the appropriate percentage of the estimated expense which does not exceed the relevant limit. If an intermediate, or repairs grant, or a former standard grant, has been made within 10 years of an application for an improvement grant, the limit will be reduced by the amount of eligible expense on the former grant (or a corresponding amount in the case of a standard grant). This provision is relevant to the idea of progressive improvement to a higher standard discussed in relation to HAAs and GIAs. Not more than 50 per cent of the estimated expense (or such other percentage as may be prescribed) may be allowed for repair and replacement. Some guidance is given in DOE Circular 160/74 as to the extent of repairs and replacements justified for grant purposes, which could include re-roofing, replacement of ineffective damp-proof courses, suspect electrical wiring and defective rainwater pipes and guttering. Apart from redecorations made necessary by the improvements, internal decorative repair should generally be excluded.

The relevant limits of improvement grants, which may be altered by the Secretary of State, were fixed by S.I. 1974 No. 2004 at £3,200, or £3,700 where the dwelling has been provided by conversion of a building of three or more storeys. These limits may be increased in particular cases such as those of buildings of special architectural or historic interest.

DOE Circular 160/74 gives guidance as to eligibility for grant of certain types of works. Local authorities will vary in their interpretation of such guidance, however, and applicants would be well advised to make inquiries from the responsible officer at the local authority at an early stage and before making a formal application.

(a) Enlargements and extensions would not normally be eligible for grant except for a first bathroom or a more adequate kitchen. An exception might be an additional bedroom for a household who had to live in an isolated position for reasons of employment.

(b) Fire escapes are acceptable where their absence poses a threat to safety, and particularly in cases of conversion into separate flats.

(c) Electric wiring in conjunction with other improvements or the installation of electricity supplies for the first time would attract grant as improvements. Renewal of existing wiring is regarded as replacement.

(d) Space heating would normally only attract grant when linked with other conversion or comprehensive improvement work.

(e) Parker Morris standards are intended for new building. The required standard for improvement in section 61 of the Housing Act 1974 (see above) is however a minimum, and local authorities should consider sympathetically higher standards for fittings and equipment which can be achieved within the maximum eligible expense, if they consider them worth the cost.

(f) Water and drainage facilities within the curtilage of the dwelling are eligible for grant-aid if they are required to supply an improvement, where existing provision is inadequate and where piped water is introduced for the first time. A septic tank or cesspool would rank for grant where connection with main drainage is not practicable. Replacement mains or changeover to mains supply would normally only be eligible if they were part of a comprehensive improvement.

As mentioned above, improvement grant is available for thermal insulation of a dwelling for an elderly or disabled person. As the result of an amendment during the passage of the 1974 Act through the House of Lords, grant can cover " works required for the welfare, accommodation or employment " of a registered disabled person " where the existing dwelling is inadequate or unsuitable for those purposes ". This provision relaxes many of the restrictions on the availability of grants. For example, standard amenities could be duplicated if an existing one were inaccessible to the disabled person, and grant could be given even to new homes. This provision has not however been widely used, and the grant for roof insulation for elderly and disabled people even less so. This may be due to inadequate knowledge about the grant and failure to publicise it.

Intermediate grants

An intermediate grant (the former standard grant) can be claimed as of right, provided the applicant satisfies the local authority that the conditions will be fulfilled. It can only be claimed however in respect of one or more of the standard amenities listed below which are not already provided, or are not accessible to a registered disabled person by reason of his disability, and have not been provided in the dwelling for at least 12 months. This last condition is designed to prevent abuse of grant to replace old equipment by taking it out immediately prior to the application.

After the completion of the work, the full standard, or a reduced standard, must be attained. The full standard is defined in the Housing Act 1974, section 66 (2). It means that:

(a) the dwelling must be provided with the standard amenities for the exclusive use of its occupants; and

(b) it must be in good repair (disregarding internal decorative repair) having regard to its age, character and location; and

(c) it must conform with the Secretary of State's requirements as to thermal insulation (i.e., requirements applicable to roof spaces in Part F of the Building Regulations 1972 (DOE Circular 160/74));

(d) it must be in all respects fit for human habitation (defined in Housing Act 1957, section 4, and amended by Housing Act 1969, section 71 (see Chapter 3)); and

(e) it must be likely to be available as a dwelling for 15 years (or such other period as the Secretary of State may specify).

The local authority must dispense with the requirement for all standard amenities to be provided for the exclusive use of the occupants of the house if they are satisfied that it is not practicable to do so at reasonable expense except where the building is multiply occupied and they could require the works under a notice under the Housing Act 1961, section 15. They may also reduce the standard of repair, thermal insulation and fitness if these cannot be provided at reasonable expense, and they may also substitute a shorter period than 15 years. If any or all of these modifications are made, the dwelling will have been brought to the reduced standard.

The standard amenities and maximum eligible amounts are given in Schedule 6 to the Housing Act 1974, as follows:

Description of Amenity	Maximum eligible amount £
A fixed bath or shower	100
A hot and cold water supply at a fixed bath or shower	140
A wash-hand basin	50
A hot and cold water supply at a wash-hand basin	70
A sink	100
A hot and cold water supply at a sink	90
A water closet	150

A fixed bath or shower must be in a bathroom, unless this is not reasonably practicable but it is reasonably practicable to supply it with hot and cold water. It may then be in any part of the dwelling other than a bedroom. The water closet must, if reasonably practicable, be in, and accessible from within, the dwelling, or, where the dwelling is part of a larger building, in that building so as to be readily accessible from the dwelling. These standard amenities are the same as those required for improvement grant purposes, see above, and with modifications for special grants, see below.

The total eligible expense for an intermediate grant is ascertained by adding the amount the local authority regard as proper for the necessary repair and replacement required, not exceeding £800 (or some other figure specified by the Secretary of State), to the amounts for the provision of amenities up to the maximum eligible amount for each amenity provided. The standard of repair should not exceed the full standard set out above for intermediate grant. Grant will be the appropriate percentage (see above) of such eligible expense.

Special grants

Special grants, given at the discretion of the local authority, are for the provision of the standard amenities in a house in multiple occupation, that is a house occupied by persons who do not form a single household in accommodation which is not self-contained. Local authorities have regulatory powers under the Housing Acts 1961 and 1964 to improve conditions in such houses, see Chapter 3. Special grants are not intended to encourage new multiple occupation, but to relieve bad conditions where they exist and where there is no immediate prospect of thorough-going conversion into self-contained houses and flats. They should at least achieve the standard which the local authority requires under its regulatory powers and may, where appropriate, bring it above that level. DOE Circular 160/74 mentions their value in helping an owner who is already known to have heavy mortgage commitments and where the authority intends to limit the number of people who may live in the house and require additional amenities to be installed. It is known, for example, that some land-lords have stretched their finances in order perhaps to provide themselves with a home and then sometimes crowd the house with lodgers to enable them to meet their outgoings.

The standard amenities and maximum eligible amounts in relation to them are the same for special grants as for interme-diate grants, as set out in the first part of Schedule 6 to the Housing Act 1974, see above under Intermediate Grants. However, special grant will not be given for a bath which is not in a bathroom and no requirement is made about the location of the WC. Special grants cover only repairs associated with the provision of the standard amenities within the limits set. They cannot be used for repairs and replacements generally.

The amount of a special grant will be the appropriate percentage (see above) of the eligible amount, that is the approved expenditure on the amenities provided subject to the maxima for the different amenities set out in the schedule. The authority may, of course, approve more than one amenity of one kind in this case.

Repairs grant

This grant was first introduced in the Housing Act 1974 and has no predecessor. It is to enable a dwelling to be brought into good repair (disregarding the state of internal decorative repair), having regard to its age and character and the locality in which it is situated. It is only available in GIAs and HAAs and then only at the local authority's discretion. Moreover, repairs grants can only be approved if the authority is satisfied that the applicant would not otherwise be able to finance the work without undue hardship. In assessing hardship, local authorities are referred in DOE Circular 160/74 to the same guidance as is given for awarding 90 per cent grants in HAAs. The standard of repair after completion of the work is left to local authorities, but it is suggested that it could be similar to essential repairs, such as those required by a compulsory repairs notice under section 9 of the Housing Act 1957. A repairs grant cannot be obtained if any other renovation grant is made.

The amount of the grant is the appropriate percentage of the approved cost of the works subject to the limit on eligible expense of £800. The Secretary of State has to approve a higher eligible expense in a case or description of cases.

Compulsory improvement at the request of a tenant

The Housing Act 1974 provides for an occupying tenant to require a local authority to compel improvement of a dwelling which is without one or more of the standard amenities, whether or not it is also in a state of disrepair, provided it was built before 3 October 1961. He must make representations in writing to the authority. If they are satisfied that the dwelling is capable of improvement at reasonable expense to the full standard or reduced standard, and that it ought to be and is unlikely to be so improved unless they exercise their powers, then they must do so. The procedures are similar to those described above for compulsory improvement within HAAs and GIAs.

Design aspects

Since older houses requiring improvements may have been built to very different designs in the first place, and some may have been altered since they were first built, the planning and construction of the work required to bring them up to the relevant standard, or to convert them into a different type of dwelling or a number of separate dwellings, may have to be tailored to suit almost every individual case. Nevertheless, certain types of plan are common in particular regions and towns and, especially where groups or streets of houses of the same type are being dealt with as one project, type plans, with perhaps minor adaptations, may be used. DOE's Area Improvement Note 4, *House Improvement and Conversation* (5) is helpful in showing typical plans of older houses before and after treatment. Nevertheless, the care for detail, which often makes one new housing scheme stand out as more attractive and convenient than another, is no less important for improvement. It may sometimes be necessary to compromise on standards, but those advocated in the DOE Bulletins on house planning, on safety in the home, on kitchens, on bathrooms and so on, if applied when amenities are being installed in an existing house, may make all the difference to the convenience and satisfaction of the occupier (see bibliography Chapter 10). Environmental improvement, too, should strive towards standards for traffic and car parking advocated in the relevant DOE Design Bulletins and Area Improvement Notes (5) (see also bibliography Chapter 10: 12, 18, 19). The introduction of some open space for children's play and general amenity are matters in which public participation, as well as the best possible standards, is specially important.

Do-it-yourself improvement work may appeal, particularly to owner-occupiers, not necessarily those who will be eligible for grants. Some publications designed to help individual improvers, whether they undertake the building work themselves or not, are listed in the bibliography (8, 9), including one by the National Home Improvement Council, a non-profit making organisation who are championing the cause of improvement and can give advice. The work of voluntary groups in HAAs has already been mentioned. An inspiring account of self-help work in Macclesfield is described in *Housing Review*, September-October, 1975, Vol. 24, No. 5, by the architect, Rod Hackney, who lived in the area and helped his neighbours to transform their homes and the neighbourhood through improvements carried out by themselves.

Some local authorities have been able to use prefabricated kitchen and bathroom units for large scale improvement, particularly when dealing with early interwar council houses where baths were originally provided in the kitchen. Large scale improvement of houses in a single ownership, whether by local authorities or housing associations, presents special problems, such as those of decanting and rehousing the existing tenants; it also offers opportunities to speed up the work by rationalisation and thus save expense. For example, caravans or mobile homes have been used to house tenants while the work is being done. A series of publications on these matters were issued by the NBA as advice to housing associations working in the improvement field, but are helpful to local authorities also (6).

A frequent difficulty when dealing with older houses is that of damp penetration, particularly where the house was originally built without a damp proof course. This has been overcome successfully by systems working on the principle of osmosis, applied by specialist firms.

Progress and Improvement in 1976

In 1975, there was a further substantial fall in the numbers of renovation grants approved in Britain to 159,139, compared to 300,482 the previous year. Figures seemed to be running at between 30,000 and 40,000 a quarter at the beginning of 1976. This decrease in the use made of grants may have been due to the imposition of more stringent conditions for improvements to privately owned houses by the Housing Act 1974, to restrictions by the Secretary of State on local authority expenditure on conversion and improvement under section 105 of that Act, which required him to approve it, or to the effect of inflation on costs and economic stringency generally. By the end of the second quarter of 1976 altogether over 1,000 GIAs had been declared, containing well over a quarter of a million dwellings. Grants had been approved in respect of about a third of them. By the same date, 137 HAAs had been approved.

To sum up, legislation and administration in 1976 reflected the growth in the popularity of rehabilitation of housing. Considerable social antipathy to some redevelopment projects had built up in the 1970s, and is discussed elsewhere in the Guide. The worst slums had been cleared before this date. In the short term, improvement is relatively cheap compared with new building. It may cause less disturbance to existing communities. All these considerations and the attachment people have always felt for the neighbourhoods they know and the homely domestic architecture with which they are familiar have reinforced the case for improvement rather than clearance and redevelopment. Although rehabilitation to modern space standards of occupation and open space provision often means some overspill from congested areas, just as a clearance and redevelopment does, the movement of population is generally more gradual and so less traumatic. Nevertheless, the long-term cost benefits of the two methods should be appraised. The officially designed model for doing this, referred to above as having been issued after the 1969 Act, was critically examined in *Housing Review*, July-September 1976, Vol. 25, No. 4, in an article by D. Green and J. Kirkwood, who concluded that it remained a useful tool for comparing economic aspects of the choice. However this may be, successful action by local people to secure improvement rather than redevelopment of out-dated areas, and the voluntary movement into those which have been gentrified, are all evidence that popular sentiment at all income levels is in favour of housing improvement in 1976.

CHAPTER 8

Housing Finance

GENERAL PROBLEMS OF PERSPECTIVE

" Whimsical " is how a previous Secretary of State, the late Mr. Anthony Crosland, described our housing finance in a major speech explaining why he had set up a fundamental review of the system (1).

The confusion begins even in defining the subject because of the difficulty of seeing the system in its totality. Each of us, according to where parts of the system touch our interests, tends to concentrate on parts of it. Do we mean measures of *spending*, either nationally or on individual houses? Or how that expenditure is *funded* by mortgages or loans? Or how *payment* is made for it by individuals? Or how these payments are reduced by *subsidies*, either generally (i.e. automatic) or means-tested?

Through whose eyes do we see parts of the system? The eyes of central government? Or through those of an agency providing housing, whether developer or local authority? Or through the eyes of an individual, whether householder, ratepayer or taxpayer?

From whatever point of view, housing finance is important. After food, shelter is the biggest item of personal expenditure, taking on average more than 13 per cent of individual budgets, more than £1 in every £8 of gross income. Housing subsidies of all kinds are equivalent to some 15 per cent of income tax, or more than £2 per week from each household. Housing accounts for 10 per cent of all public expenditure. Loans for private house purchase account for a third of the annual funds flowing through all the financial institutions apart from banks.

Not surprisingly, therefore, housing finance is inextricably involved in a delicate web of financial inter-relationships: with taxation policy, incomes policy and social security; with economic policy, because housebuilding is a principal regulator of demand and, therefore, of employment; with the balance of payments, because of the import or the energy content of materials used in housing; with monetary policy, because changes in the money supply are quickly reflected in the volume of lending and the costs of borrowing; with investment policy, because capital for industry is raised on the market as is capital for property.

This degree of overlap is surely an important explanation of why the programme for the DOE's review of housing finance, originally announced in November 1974, has constantly slipped from its scheduled date of report, the end of 1975, until it is not now due until the summer of 1977.

This economic sensitivity is heightened by a personal sensitivity, even defensiveness, because reform involves intrusion into the home by one of the two popular bogeys, the tax collector or the landlord. Because it is known that the government is anxious to cut down public spending, there has been widespread anticipation that any reform will entail increased outgoings at a time of a relative standstill on incomes, after a period when the proportion of income spent on housing has already increased on average by a third, from 10 per cent to between 13 and 14 per cent (2, 3).

It is easy to see the electoral liability. It is seemingly never the right time to introduce changes. Since the review was first announced, Ministers found it necessary both to allay fears that mortgage tax relief would be reduced and to defer rises in council rents. Unlike expenditure on fuel and transport costs, expenditure on housing, it seemed, would be cushioned from the other unpalatable measures to combat inflation.

On the other hand, a tide of opinion in favour of change has been rising from the growing realisation that by holding down unrealistically the levels of payments by individuals for housing, the housing problem has been aggravated and its solution has become more costly to the nation as a whole and, therefore, to its citizens. If subsidies are enjoyed universally, we are either all financing each other out of taxation or out of foreign borrowing for which we all have to pay in the end. To reverse the process by increasing personal expenditure on housing in an equitable manner need not entail disproportionate increases for any one group within the community.

The existing tendency for *ad hoc* responses to particular interest groups is not conducive to any but short-term remedies which in time give rise to other problems. The remedies proposed must be truly appropriate to the ills they are to cure and their positive advantages made clear to those they affect. If rents must go up, it must be according to a more logical and better understood system of fixing them. If public borrowing must be cut, it must be shown that the different components of public expenditure funds can be more efficiently used. If the privileges of owner-occupiers are to be reduced, it must be demonstrated that they have over-heated demand and so caused prices to rise. Similarly, the package of reforms for each sector by itself must be part of a complete package which covers the relationship between housing sectors and other parts of the economy.

Another essential requirement of change is the recognition that the housing system itself and each particular part of it has been moulded by historical circumstances. These cannot be ignored and forced into theoretical straitjackets. Each sector has its own special strengths which should be maximised and weaknesses which should be minimised; it would be counter-productive to force upon them, without good reason, characteristics which belong to another sector.

Three essential conditions for a successful review of housing finance emerge from this background, as the HCT said in its *Evidence for the Housing Finance Review.* The review should, firstly, be comprehensive and deal with all sectors of housing. Secondly, any new system adopted should be introduced gradually by means of a phased programme over (say) 10 years and, thirdly, it must be acceptable on a non-partisan basis. The main reasons for these conditions are set out below.

Firstly, a comprehensive case. Changes in one sector immediately affect other sectors and may distort them. Inflation affects the different sectors, and even different parts of each sector, in quite different and arbitrary ways. Most lobbying stems from immediate, though none the less real, anxieties by interested groups—e.g., builders, building societies, local authorities—and the government is often persuaded to react in *ad hoc* ways. This piecemeal response leads to one anomaly being replaced by another.

Secondly, a phased programme. When dealing with so basic a commodity as housing, and one which forms such a major item in each household's budget, savings, effort and emotional attachment, any programme of reform should be gradual. A phased programme over the short, medium and long term, say, over 10 years, would allay fears that interference with the present position would be so sudden as to be disruptive. It would give time for individuals, institutions and the economy to adjust and would avoid the series of reversals in policy at comparatively short intervals which have so disastrously prejudiced the development of a smoothly running housing programme in the past.

Thirdly, non-partisan agreement. A 10-year programme would inevitably involve at least one new parliament and possibly more and could mean a change of party in power. Housing, especially where public funds are involved, is too important to cease to be the vital concern of the body politic and in this sense it could not, or should not, be " taken out of politics." However, the experience of the last few years has encouraged less confidence in traditional confrontation policies and more willingness to work towards continuity and consensus. On certain issues, e.g. improvement of older areas and housing associations, an agreed non-partisan policy resulted in the provisions of the Housing Act 1974.

SPENDING

National measures

The most satisfactory measure of national spending is the annual value of " gross fixed capital formation " (GFCF) on housing, defined as the value of fresh housing added to the stock each year. A net annual figure would be obtained by deducting the value of housing lost by demolition, although precision is less easy on that basis.

The sheer size of housing's role in the economy is immediately apparent from such a measure. GFCF in dwellings was £4,084m. in 1975 or 36 per cent of all GFCF in all new construction (£11,309m.) or 20 per cent of GFCF of all kinds. GFCF in housing represented 4·38 per cent of the total gross domestic product (GDP) in 1975 (£93,146m.) (4, 5).

It must be recognised that, as with any overall measure, GFCF is not a perfect one. In the first place, only a small proportion of the value of improvement work is included. At a time when it is acknowledged that a shift towards rehabilitation in national policy is more appropriate than the previous emphasis on new building, there are no accurate national statistics which enable this policy trend to be measured and thus for the effectiveness of grant-aid to be tested.

Secondly, increases in overall value of GFCF may conceal changes in volume, cost or quality. For example, the costs of construction increased relatively faster than other prices during 1972 and 1975 in all sectors. Also, to meet market demand during this period in the private sector, builders tended to produce bigger and more expensive houses, as well as more houses.

Thirdly, international comparisons according to proportions of GDP, however tempting to make, especially in the interests of calling for an expansion of housing's share of the national cake, are unreliable. Statistical practice still differs between countries, especially on the amount of improvement work included. The UK inevitably emerges badly on this score because of the growing improvement content in total output and will do so increasingly during the remainder of this century.

Apart from these events, other countries may have to make up more ground in their housing conditions while the UK may be able to devote less to bricks and mortar and more to other costs which improve the quality of life.

The relatively *constant* value of housing production is nevertheless underlined by the GFCF measure.

At first, this constancy may seem extraordinary in view of the high priority given by all postwar governments both to increased housing expenditure in the public sector and special taxation concessions for housing costs in the owner-occupied sector. Whatever they have done, these stimuli do not seem to have been very effective in producing more housing as the following diagrams illustrate.

The graphs show that in *both* the principal housing sectors, we have had ever increasing subsidies but falling investment. Indeed,

Table 1. International Comparisons   per cent

GFCF in housing as a share of GNP:	1972	1973
United Kingdom	3·4	3·7
Belgium	4·7	*
France	6·7	6·7
Germany Fed. Rep.	6·5	*
Ireland	5·0	*
Italy	5·8	6·2
Netherlands	6·3	6·3
Norway	5·3	*
Sweden	4·8	*
USA	4·6	*

Source: *PQ Hansard*, 10 March 1975.
* Not available.

Table 2. Gross Fixed Capital Formation in housing (UK)
£ million at 1970 constant prices

	1966 £	1967 £	1968 £	1969 £	1970 £	1971 £	1972 £	1973 £	1974 £	1975 £
Public sector	756	869	911	891	802	747	712	710	821	859
Private sector	847	915	957	894	841	1,007	1,160	1,040	873	950
Total	1,603	1,784	1,868	1,785	1,643	1,754	1,872	1,750	1,694	1,809
Total as percentage of Gross Domestic Product *	4·07	4·41	4·46	4·19	3·78	3·94	4·14	3·65	3·52	3·81

Source: *Housing Stats.*, Vol. 18, Table XXI.
* At factor cost.

whereas only seven years ago for every £1m. in subsidies some £5m. worth of housing was being produced, for every £1m. in subsidies now we are producing some £2m. worth of houses and forecasts suggest that the ratio will narrow even further.

Table 3. More subsidies, less investment.

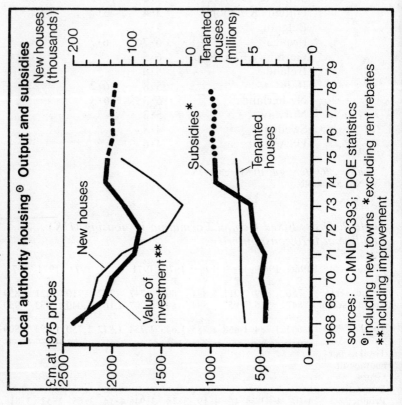

Local authority housing⊙ Output and subsidies

New houses (thousands)

Tenanted houses (millions)

£m at 1975 prices

New houses

Value of investment **

Subsidies *

Tenanted houses

sources: CMND 6393; DOE statistics

⊙including new towns   *excluding rent rebates
**including improvement

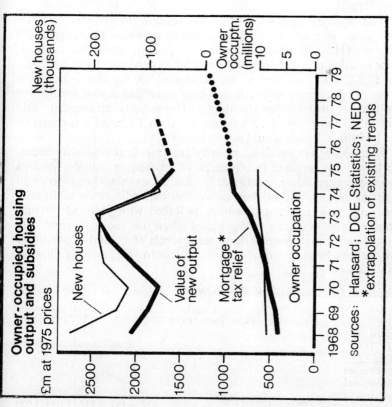

Owner-occupied housing output and subsidies
£m at 1975 prices

New houses (thousands)

Owner occuptn. (millions)

New houses

Value of new output

Mortgage* tax relief

Owner occupation

1968 69 70 71 72 73 74 75 76 77 78 79

sources: Hansard; DOE Statistics; NEDO
*extrapolation of existing trends

Reproduced from *Building*, 1 October 1976.

The top graph for public housing shows that between 1968 and 1975 subsidies more than doubled (from £477m. to £1,017m. at constant prices), while the value of annual investment actually fell by 15 per cent from £2,473m. to £2,113m. Hence the 1:5 ratio has become just over 1:2 and is forecast to become less. This increase in subsidies cannot be accounted for by the introduction of rent rebates—they are excluded here—nor because of an increase in the number of tenancies which rose by only some 16 per cent over the period (from 5·4 million to 6·2 million dwellings).

The bottom graph shows that tax revenue forgone as relief on mortgage interest more than doubled between 1968 and 1975 (from £411m. to £964m. at constant prices), while the value of new housing produced annually fell by 23 per cent (from £2,238m. to £1,722m.). This cannot be accounted for by the increase in owner-occupation—only 18 per cent over the period (from 8·9 million to 10·5 million dwellings). The subsidy/investment ratio has fallen here from 1 : 5 to even less than 1 : 2 and a forecast of 1 : 1 within a decade would not be fanciful.

If housing has received priority treatment, the priority seems to have been retained in the levels of Exchequer subsidy towards *current* expenditure, presumably that of existing households in existing houses, rather than on *capital* expenditure on additional housing. This, one must suspect, is linked with political circumstances. The suspicion is sharpened when one looks more closely at the relatively *constant* long term levels of capital expenditure which have been far from *even* from year to year, as the following table shows:

Table 4. Uneven Capital Expenditure   £ million at 1975 prices

				Actual					Forecast	
	1968	1969	1970	1971	1972	1973	1974	1975	1976	1977
PUBLIC SECTOR Housing Investment Value (incl. improvement, land etc.)	2,473	2,141	2,052	1,790	1,738	1,872	2,187	2,113	2,043	1,925
Change 1968=100	100	87	83	72	70	76	88	85	83	78
PRIVATE SECTOR New Housing (only) Output Value	2,238	2,051	1,894	2,215	2,511	2,647	1,942	1,717	1,850	1,953
Change 1968=100	100	92	85	99	112	118	87	77	83	87

Sources: Public Expenditure White Papers, H & C Stats, NEDO.

Housebuilding has obviously suffered from very marked cyclical changes in the economy (6). The causes vary as between each sector. In the private sector, they surely reflect builders' confidence, which itself is linked to a number of factors, such as the anticipated strength of demand in relation to level of over- or under-production in the preceding period and the availability of mortgage funds, itself closely linked to the money supply. In the public sector, they undoubtedly reflect the intentions of central and local government, particularly any periodic desire to cut public spending.

It is perhaps not sufficiently realised how easily both sectors over-react to underlying pressures. In the private sector, for instance, builders react with exaggerated caution when the market is weak because of the long production period. And the market weakness itself is easily exaggerated because the whole exchange process between buyers and sellers slows down as people find it difficult to move. In the public sector, of all public expenditure programmes, housing has the largest capital budget—being in 1976–77 some 62 per cent of its total—many times larger than in other sectors like health or education, for instance, where the bulk of spending goes on running costs, particularly salaries. As a result, the capital programme is an easy target for cuts.

This vulnerability is increased by the nature of the housing system because changes in housing programmes affect a minority. In any one year, only a little over 1 per cent of stock is replaced and some 10 per cent of households move. Therefore, fluctuations do not affect the majority of households who stay put and this is, in turn, reflected in public opinion of the majority which is primarily concerned with the level of housing payments.

Individual house costs

The broad subdivision of cost within a typical two-storey three-bedroom, five-person semi-detached house outside London on a flat site are shown in the following chart, as at April 1976. Construction costs are shown to be 77 per cent of total costs, the remainder being professional fees and land and legal costs. The superstructure constitutes less than a third of the total cost of a house. This illustrates the relatively small savings which are possible through reductions in Parker Morris standards. The extent of such savings are in any case sometimes exaggerated, it has been claimed (7).

It must be borne in mind that outlay costs, as explained in the next section, give a " two-dimensional " picture. A true " three-dimensional " picture can only be obtained by measuring costs over time, as affected by both running costs and funding arrangements.

Table 5. Individual House Costs

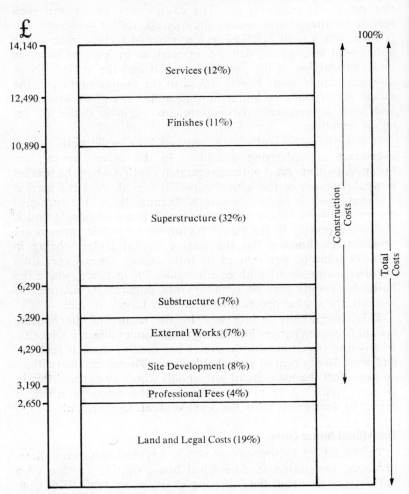

Source: "Trends in Housing and Construction." National Building Agency 1976.

FUNDING AND BORROWING

Generally

Houses are rarely paid for in cash for two reasons. They are too expensive and it obviously makes sense to spread costs over time on a "pay-as-you-use" principle. The original capital sum borrowed is therefore repaid in instalments of principal, together with an additional interest or "use" payment on the outstanding debt in order to compensate the lender for forgoing the use of the capital sum. Strictly speaking, rent is that use payment where the house is let and the asset paid for and retained by the landlord (the housing authority).

Borrowing periods have been evolved to suit each of the two most common situations. In the owner-occupied sector, the typical mortgage over 25 years suits the earning life of the individual. In the public sector, the 60 year loan term matches the notional life of the asset, the house.

It is about the resultant costs over time that differences of opinion (and misunderstandings) arise. It is generally accepted, so far as physical standards, materials, finishes or insulation are concerned, that to measure a house according to its capital cost gives an insufficient " two-dimensional " picture. A true " three-dimensional " perspective can only be obtained by measuring cost, however imprecisely, over time; capital savings may be offset by higher running costs, whether maintenance, management (e.g., transfers necessary) or fuel.

Measuring finance three-dimensionally over time is much more difficult to keep in perspective. It is quite common, for instance, to find calculations which contrast an original outlay cost of a house of, say, £10,000 with a " total cost " over time obtained by multiplying annual repayments by the number of years over which the sum is repaid. Thus, using a mortgage rate of 11 per cent, a sum of £66,126 over the 60 years of public housing is sometimes contrasted with a sum of £29,685 (gross) over the 25 years of a private mortgage; or similarly a sum of £19,363 paid via an insurance company " endowment " mortgage is sometimes contrasted with the sum of £23,255 paid on the standard building society mortgage, both with a term of 25 years and net of tax relief and with life cover; or it is contended that substantial savings in public expenditure could be made if housing was paid straight out of revenue (in cash) as battleships are; or, again, it is said that the interest payments which swell authorities' housing revenue accounts are simply " filling the pockets of financiers."

It is important that the fallacies of these arguments are understood. Firstly, military equipment may best be paid for out of cash because it is prudent to assume it has no life, because of the risk of obsolescence or destruction. Secondly, interest may be defined as the " opportunity cost," willingly paid by the borrower for deferring outright payment in favour of making periodic payments as he earns the money to meet them, or so as to make use of money left in hand. This money may earn an equal " opportunity benefit " by being put to alternative uses. In this way, the interests of borrowers and lenders are equally balanced at a particular rate of return. The present values of a stream of loan charges due over a period of time in the future should therefore be " discounted " to a worth *no more and no less* than the original capital sum. There is no financial difference between £100 in hand now and the expectation of a series of £10 owed or received over a period of *n* years, or £*n* received over a period of 25 years, the unknown *" n "* being determined by the interest rate. The interest rate is itself determined by the demand for borrowing and the expectation about money's real worth in the future (8, 9, 10).

Under conditions of inflation, a new phenomenon enters into the calculation—the more so the higher the inflation. The rate of interest rises and loan charges increase because of the prospect of a fall in the real value of money. In order to compensate himself, the lender naturally requires a higher rate to offset anticipated losses later. So the time pattern of repayments is shifted; " front-loading " occurs because the very high repayments which are required in the early years of mortgages and loans become negligible in relation to new money values in the later years (11, 12).

This explains one of the attractions of low-start mortgages in an inflationary period because they redress the time-pattern so that a slightly more constant proportion of income can be paid by the housebuyer over the initial period of his mortgage. It also explains why, following a period of hyper-inflation in 1974–75, the indexation of loans and mortgages has been widely advocated on principles used in the Netherlands and in Brazil. How much more, it is also argued, might such mechanisms be beneficial for an institution like a housing authority for whom interest charges represent some 63 per cent of annual revenue expenditure (13, 14).

However, the advantages of indexation are deceptive. For a variety of complex factors, the supply of capital funds for lending have for many years generally exceeded the demand for funds. Consequently, lenders have been forced to accept rates of return equal to, or even less than, the rate of inflation—in other words to accept *real rates of return which are negative;* their decisions on where to place their money (apart from such factors as convenience and the incidence of taxation) have tended to be based not so much on where it would earn most but on where it would lose least.

It is therefore possible to see in better perspective the strain caused on individual housebuyers or on housing revenue accounts by the recent ravages of inflation which have caused loan repayments to escalate. Except in the short-term, it is the building society investor and the local authority stockholder who are the losers and the building society borrower and the local authority (or effectively the tenant) who are the gainers. These conditions do, nevertheless, entail suffering in the short-term while we search for appropriate mechanisms to adjust to them.

Owner-occupied sector

House purchase loans are obtained from four main sources of which building societies account for the predominant share.

Table 6. Sources of New Mortgages (Gross)   per cent.

	Building Societies	Local Authorities	Insurance Companies	Banks	Total
	%	%	%	%	£ million
1975	82	14	4	not available	6,060
1976 (prov.)	94	4	2	„	not available

Source: H & C Stats, Table 35.

But this pattern has fluctuated very considerably.

Table 7. All New Mortgages 1970–75 (net)   £ million

	Building Societies	Local Authorities	Insurance Companies	Banks	Other Public	Total
1970	1,088	72	36	40	10	1,207
1971	1,600	107	13	90	12	1,748
1972	2,215	198	2	345	22	2,783
1973	1,999	355	121	310	46	2,831
1974	1,490	465	120	90	117	2,282
1975	2,760	618	67	60	200	3,712

Source: H & C Stats, Table 35.

The trends are of interest for three reasons, treated here in turn: *firstly* and most immediately, the pattern of lending practices; *secondly,* the link between the volume of funds and house prices; *thirdly,* the place of house purchase funds in the economy.

During the mortgage " famine " of 1974, the building society (BS) share was reduced to only 65 per cent of a much smaller total. The local authority (LA) share correspondingly increased to 20 per cent, in part as a result of government encouragement, as a counter-cyclical measure, to maintain some buoyancy in the housing market and in part spontaneously as first-time buyers, often buying more risky, older and unimproved properties and needing 100 per cent mortgages during a time of high prices, found BS mortgages more difficult to obtain. During the last decade, insurance companies have been trying to increase their share of the market through endowment-linked mortgages which are financially more favourable to higher taxpayers and which may look more attractive to all buyers if future repayments are shown at undiscounted levels (15).

Unfortunately, statistics are not collected on the volume of back street mortgage business, carrying penal interest rates, which thrives in the inner city, often immigrant, areas. Their borrowers cannot satisfy the requirements of BS's or LA's, either because of unstable income or the condition of their houses (disrepair, subletting). Clearly, LA's have an important role to develop in this part of the market as part of their comprehensive housing service (16, 17, 18) (See Chapter 3).

The " choosiness " of BS's is a constant source of debate. It is commonly alleged that they are evading their social responsibilities by concentrating their business on the easy end of the market, existing owners moving house, above-average incomes and good houses, whilst leaving the high-risk buyers and houses to the LA's. Although the statistics are not conclusive, broadly speaking it seems that BS's are still lending a fair proportion of their funds to low-income earners, but still chary of lending on older property (at least unimproved older property) (19, 20).

Several underlying complications in the statistics for sources of loans should also be noted. Firstly, the income figures tend to conceal a growing dependence on working wives (57 per cent with one major society's first-time buyers in 1974)—such is the difficulty of reaching the first rung of the home ownership ladder (21, 22). Secondly, as owner-occupation spreads, the number of existing owners buying and selling their houses obviously increases so that the proportion of funds needing to be allocated to the second-time purchase market increases as house prices increase in real terms. Thirdly, as BS's are favourably placed to lend at cheaper rates of interest—say, 10½ per cent (12¼ in late 1976) whereas LA's have little choice but to lend at 12 per cent (13½ in late 1976)—the loans market is weighted automatically in favour of the more fortunate. Fourthly, although it is often contended that the sale of council houses would produce a capital saving to the housing authority (and also to public expenditure) this does not eventuate because, in the majority of cases, sitting tenants in council houses find they have to look to their LA for a mortgage.

The government has been making determined efforts to reduce the volume of LA home loans, whose value (gross) accounted for a range of between 7 and 19 per cent of housing public expenditure (net) in the period 1968 to 1975, so as to increase the amounts available for other LA purposes, such as improvement of council houses. In 1975, it therefore began to negotiate an arrangement whereby LA's could nominate their prospective borrowers to BS's. An annual saving of some £100m. was envisaged for the years 1975–77 and of £146m. for 1977–78, this last being part of the

July 1976 cuts. It is too early to gauge the success of the nomination schemes although some LA's have alleged that BS's are not willing to relax their conditions sufficiently, the net result being likely to over-concentrate LA loans on the " last resort " end of the market. Meanwhile, BS's reply that accurate assessment is impossible because many mortgagors who would otherwise have gone to LA's are coming to BS's direct.

Whatever the truth of these allegations, others argue that nomination arrangements are bound to be an unsatisfactory compromise and that it would be more sensible for LA's to act as administering agents for on-lending BS funds—so extending the barely used " guarantee " powers which have been available to LA's for several years. Unfortunately, initiatives of this kind have been frustrated by a technical convention of the Treasury which classifies private borrowing funds used even in this on-lending fashion as an addition to, rather than a saving from, the public sector's borrowing requirement once it passes through the doors of the town hall!

From the humble self-help artisan building clubs of the Victorian age, BS's have evidently grown into a central controlling interest in the housing system and the economy. This development, coupled with their inability (or unwillingness) to take stabilising measures in the 1972–73 period and the envious eyes of LA's short of home loan funds during 1975 and 1976, has not surprisingly re-opened the argument for greater governmental control of BS operations. Some have suggested that a compulsory stabilisation fund should be set up and others, from further left, that BS's should be nationalised.

How seriously should these suggestions be taken? The achievement of BS's in defying financial convention by borrowing short and lending long on a grand scale (fittingly described by one writer as an invention which must rank with the invention of the steam engine in changing the face of Britain) is the envy of other countries (23). Although the multiplication of their high street offices has been criticised on the grounds that it adds unnecessarily to their administrative expenses and they are also helped by a favourable arrangement whereby tax is paid at a " composite " rate on behalf of investors (at 27·75 per cent during 1976–77 when standard rate tax was 35 per cent), their published figures still show them to be operating efficiently on very tight overhead margins (24). Against the accusation that they are evading their social responsibilities by preferring not to lend at the " high-risk " end, it must be borne in mind that they are mutual organisations which have to strike a balance between borrowers and investors. Although there are no statistics available on their borrowing profiles, BS's themselves acknowledge that they are operating as much more than a mere high street deposit bank for the small saver (having taken business from the clearing banks and national savings); they are now also attractive to larger investors who otherwise place their funds in local authority stock or in the equity share market if the differential in rates makes them more attractive (25).

The *second* live issue which has prompted closer government links with the BS's since 1973, via a joint consultative committee, has been the very evident connection between the amount of money lent for house purchase and the rate of change in house prices. In the period 1972–73, an expansion of the money supply in the economy, intended by the government to boost general production and employment, was quickly reflected in an increase in BS receipts. Because the period coincided with a bulge in the demand for house purchase, the BS's lent the funds on mortgages and so fuelled an explosion in house prices of unprecedented proportions. The boom in funds was followed by a recession in 1974 (again linked with general economic movements) when the volume of net receipts by BS's fell so severely that the government made £500m. available to BS's at preferential rates in order to prevent a rise in the (politically sensitive) mortgage interest rate and to maintain confidence and employment in the building industry. 1975 found the fortunes of BS's again in the ascendant with record inflows of funds as people confounded the forecasters by reacting to inflation by saving *greater* proportions of income than formerly (on average 14 per cent as against 8 per cent in 1968) (26). This time BS's resisted pleas, especially from the building industry, to increase their lending in proportion to their receipts. In part this was because they shared the government's apprehension about the risk of a further big house price increase and in part because they preferred to build up a reserve against the day when they feared greater competition for funds in 1976 and 1977. It should also be noted in passing that during 1975–76 BS's have been acting as important financial intermediaries supporting the government's own borrowing requirements because so much of their enlarged liquidity reserves have been held in government stock.

The success of the consultation machinery explains why the Labour Government has been willing to compromise over its intentions of intervening in BS activities and has agreed to allow BS's to build up their own informal stabilising funds.

A *third,* equally important, issue which has received less attention in view of these other immediate preoccupations is the steady long-term growth in the total mortgage debt outstanding. As owner-occupation has spread and house prices have increased in real terms, the demand for capital funds has grown steadily and so mortgage assets have grown much faster than the growth in assets of other personal saving institutions (24).

Table 8. Owner-Occupiers' Mortgage Debt Outstanding (UK) *

		£m.	per cent 1969=100
At end of December	1968	9,389	90
	1969	10,380	100
	1970	11,637	112
	1971	13,385	129
	1972	15,875	153
	1973	18,470	178
	1974	20,555	198
	1975 (prov.)	23,930	231

Source: H & C Stats, Table 35.
* With building societies, local authorities, insurance companies and banks.

In 1963, net new house purchase loan advances accounted for one quarter of the flows of funds into all financial institutions except banks (i.e., savings banks, investment and unit trusts, insurance companies, pension funds, property unit trusts, others including finance houses, building societies). *Within 10 years the proportion had increased to one third* (27, 28). Such an increase highlights two important features:

(a) BS's have increased their share of the savings market because their package of services has become more attractive to the small saver through the easily accessible facilities of high street branches and, more importantly, to the larger saver who needs a good rate of return and the advantages of liquidity;

(b) The increase in the volume of debt is far bigger than the increase in owner-occupation. In other words, the housing market is operating in such a way as to create a snow-balling demand for capital funds as existing houses and existing owners buy and sell at higher prices. The market has to rely on more than the " recycling " of existing funds.

Why should this matter? The volume of capital funds in the economy is not unlimited and therefore one would have expected sharper competition for funds if any " crowding out " was taking place. This has not happened over the last decade because demand from the main user of capital funds, industrial investment, has slackened (especially during the recession) at the same time as (especially during the inflation) people have been saving more.

Indeed, it is fair to say that there has been what amounts to a glut of capital. As soon as profitable prospects in the economy occur, funds pour into them as happened with the general (i.e. including commercial) property boom during 1972–73. Underlying these fluctuations there has been a steadily increasing flow of funds into private housing finance and into government stock, both of these being able to offer comparatively attractive returns and both enjoying taxation concessions.

If demand for industrial investment does revive, as is intended, and if the savings ratio declines to its more normal level, the competition for funds will obviously become keener. The beginnings of this problem may have begun to emerge in 1976 because the building societies are now finding that, in order to maintain sufficient funds to finance the normal volume of mortgage lending, some £200–£250m. of net receipts is necessary every month. However, this volume is only possible, it appears according to the BSA analysis, when the building societies' share rate is about one percentage point more generous than rates offered by other financial institutions, who borrow from the public on comparable conditions (the rate providing the best example of this being, according to this analysis, the local authority three month borrowing rates) (25). This obviously raises the question whether this comparative advantage can be justified, especially since it is partly maintained by two special taxation advantages: the composite tax rate paid by societies on investors' behalf and the interest relief received by mortgagors which enables mortgagors to pay higher borrowing rates than they could otherwise.

Local authority sector

Understanding how a LA funds the loans on the houses it builds is blurred by two special features which distinguish their loans from the usual mortgage which a private owner takes out on his own house.

Firstly, LA housing loans are usually repaid as if on a 60 year, not 25 or 30 year, mortgage to match the life of the asset and because (obviously) the longer the period over which the repayment is spread the less the annual level of loan charges—as private mortgagors know who have converted their 25 year mortgages into a 30 year term when the rate of interest has risen. However, lengthening the period has much less effect on the total annual payment when the rate of interest is high. When the rate is 7 per cent, a standard annuity mortgage on £10,000 over 60 years costs £713 p.a. and is considerably cheaper than one over 30 years costing £806 p.a. The difference reduces, as the rate of interest rises: between £1,103 p.a. and £1,151 p.a. respectively at 11 per cent and between £1,500 p.a. and £1,523 p.a. respectively at 15 per cent. Also, when it is remembered how much of a house needs renewal after 30 years, the 60 year life assumption becomes true only of non-renewable components such as the land and the house shell: otherwise " double-decker " loans might result.

Secondly, whilst housing loans are *accounted* for in an authority's books over a 60 year period, the unrepaid principal is actually *borrowed* by the authority's loans pool on much shorter terms. Indeed, on average, two-thirds of LA loans are for periods of five years or less (29). This is not surprising because short-term money is invariably cheaper than, say, 25 year money (30). Correspondingly in the private sector, building societies would not be so willing to lend for periods of as long as 25 years if they did not know that the average mortgage is in fact repaid after seven years when mortgagors move house (31). The financial attraction of LA short-term borrowing is reinforced by LA treasurers' tendency to borrow short in the expectation that the interest rate will fall. As the rate has in fact generally risen over time (although not always), one might ask why treasurers do not change their practice; the slight extra cost between 5 and 25 year money is so much offset by inflation as to be a bargain. Unfortunately, immediate financial pressures usually impose the short-term view.

None of these comparatively technical considerations explains why LA housing loans are so much in the limelight. An individual's mortgage is the predominant item in his outstanding capital commitments, far outweighing the debt on his furniture or motor car. Similarly, housing loans are the predominant item for local government where they account on average for 64 per cent of all its capital liabilities (i.e., liabilities on private home loans, improvement grants, as well as its rented housing stock), far outweighing the loan commitments outstanding on schools, roads, other buildings and plant (32). On a national basis, the total of all LA and new town housing loans outstanding still occupies the largest single item (32 per cent) in the long list of capital commitments which make up the national debt. This explains why housing ministers and housing committee chairmen are constantly under so much financial pressure, the more so when money is short. Sensible discussion is also often difficult because a feeling that debt is somehow a bad thing in itself persists in the layman's mind. Yet to finance capital spending by means of loans rather than in cash is always an advantage, unless the size and growth of loans are crowding out the possibility of investment elsewhere or if the cost of supporting interest payments cannot be covered from current income.

What of the size and growth of LA housing debt? At first glance its record is particularly vulnerable, having grown by 76 per cent over six years.

Table 9. Local Authority Housing Debt—England & Wales (only)

Outstanding on hsg.rev.acc. (only):	£ million	per cent Mar. 1970=100
At end of March 1970	7,190	100
1971	7,710	107
1972	8,143	113
1973	8,888	124
1974	9,840	137
1975	11,459	159
1976	12,619	176

Source: Local Government Financial Statistics (DOE) and Rate Support Grant Report (14).

However, as already remarked, over the same period the total mortgage debt outstanding on owner-occupied housing rose by 131 per cent. This highlights one important advantage of public sector housing. Its mortgage debt only grows when real investment, either in new houses or improvements, takes place. Although loans are continually having to be refinanced because so much borrowing is for short periods, the debt remains at the same historic cost although the market value of the assets would have increased—only interest payments on the debt rising to accommodate inflation. By contrast in private housing when, correspondingly, refinancing takes place as mortgagors move house and take out new mortgages—every seven years on average (31)—the total sum mortgaged is generally increased as houses change hands at higher prices. This explains why mortgage debt for private house purchase could go on increasing even if not a single new house were built, whereas in the public sector the total mortgage debt would decline because, when loans are repaid, they are repaid once and for all.

What of the cost of supporting that debt in interest charges? The advantages of LA pooled interest rates is well known. Even in the year 1976–77, this will produce a pooled rate of about 10·6* per cent on average whereas new funds have been borrowed at 13 per cent or more. This ability must be counted as much a national asset as the advantage which building societies have of being able to offer loans of 10½ per cent.

Unfortunately, during 1973–75, the advantages of LA loans pooling were undermined by the rapid inflation which worked its way through to interest rates: for a brief period LA's were paying up to 17 per cent on new money. They were not able to borrow so cheaply as building societies who could tap the savings

* Note: no revised estimate is available since the October 1976 increase in Minimum Lending Rate.

of the small investor in the high street. Societies could thus borrow overall at a rate of about 11¼ per cent (the gross equivalent of their then share rate of 7½ per cent tax paid). In themselves the high borrowing rates should still not have been painful to LA's because they were still less than the current rate of inflation and were therefore negative in real terms. The existence of loans pooling should have cushioned LA's from high marginal interest rates. However, interest rates on loans rose so fast that a " bunching " effect was experienced: the pooled rate commonly rose faster than the rate of inflation itself as earlier loans at 4 or 5 per cent were refinanced at between 13 and 16 per cent.

Because interest charges are the predominant item on housing authorities' revenue accounts and because wages and materials costs (management and maintenance) also rose faster than other prices, the overall effect was to produce an acute dilemma (33). Central and local government were faced with a choice between raising rents faster than inflation generally or raising Exchequer subsidies and rate contributions at a time when taxes and rates were having to bear unprecedented increases for other reasons. In the event, rents were held down by political decision for the sake of the social contract, although at the price in the following years of 1975–76–77 of cuts in housing capital programmes.

Eventually the " bunching " effect will even out and interest rates begin to fall in real terms. In the meantime, the perennial question will be posed: Why do LA's have to borrow at such high rates? As long ago as 1967, when interest rates were much lower, this question exercised the now defunct National Board of Prices and Incomes (NBPI). It thought then that there was no reason why LA's should not have greater access to the Public Works Loan Board (PWLB). Local authorities have, depending on their resources, only been able to borrow some 30–40 per cent of their loans from the PWLB. The NBPI thought this restriction was treating local authorities as second class customers (34).

However, the PWLB rates are no longer so favourable as they were then. In the 1960s, they were consistently lower than the building society mortgage rate. Since 1971, when the government decided to allow market pressures to have more effect on local authority borrowing as part of a general change of attitude as a result of the Bank of England's proposals in its paper *Competition and Credit Control*, PWLB rates have been consistently higher than the building society mortgage rate (35). That government influence still weighs strongly on the PWLB rate seems to be borne out by reports that ministerial pressure secured more favourable terms for a Greater London Council loan in 1975 (36).

The alternative to PWLB loans is capital which a local authority can raise by the issue of its own stock, now facilitated by the clearing house set up by the CIPFA loans bureau. LA stock had its most successful year in the 1974–75 period when the surplus in capital funds coincided with a fall-off in investment in private industry and in commercial property. During this time, local government was attracting money which, in normal times, would have gone to industry if it had had sufficient confidence to invest.

The availability and the price of funds for LA borrowing is unfortunately a long way from equilibrium. During the last decade, the balance of nature in the monetary jungle has been disturbed by the increase in the appetites of two younger and hitherto lesser species, the building societies and the local authorities. An otherwise inevitable clash of interests with the older and bigger species, the Treasury and industry, was avoided by the increase in the overall supply of money in 1973, the slackening of industry's demands, and a rise in the overall volume of savings.

If and when industry's demands do revive, competition for funds may be rendered more acute and raise questions as to the " rightful " share of each in the market. Strictly speaking, it seems more natural that local government should look to the same segment of the market as building societies—the funds of small and medium savers. This would require them to offer the same degree of high street convenience for deposits and withdrawals as building societies offer and also access to advantages equivalent to the composite tax rate which building societies have. In that case, the opportunity would be open to local authorities to fund some of their operations, such as their house purchase loans, on a self-sufficient basis.

Private landlords

It is very difficult to discuss the funding of this sector in the same terms as other sectors because it is declining rather than growing and therefore there is, practically speaking, no requirement for capital funds corresponding to the demand for owner-occupiers' mortgages or local authority housing loans.

Landlords letting as a business (as distinct from owner-occupiers letting off parts of their houses, i.e., " resident landlords ") would look for funds to quite different sources from those of other sectors. In the case of the small non-company landlord, bank loans would be provided by the clearing or secondary banks, but at least at the going rate (and often much higher), which is invariably above the building society mortgage rate and only available for comparatively short terms not exceeding five years. In the case of the company landlord, equity capital as well as bank loans would be available. In the case of either kind of landlord, however, the income from letting (even gross before deduction of tax) is unlikely to be sufficient to cover fixed interest on loans or to pay dividends. Only in exceptional cases (luxury category or speculative potential) would the residential property itself provide sufficient security for a loan—as, of course, is necessary for a mortgage. It is therefore not surprising that privately let property exhibits so often the two extremes of stagnation or speculation.

The capital structure of the privately let sector is quite different therefore from that of the owner-occupied or local authority sectors where the majority of assets are mortgaged. Although no figures are available for private landlords in the aggregate, it is a safe presumption that most of the property is held free of outstanding debt, the assets being held at historical book value and the corresponding liabilities on the balance sheet being held as capital reserved. It is an ironic reflection on the way the political scales have tipped, that that part of the housing system which makes least claim on capital funds is the one most heavily penalised.

Funds for developing the privately let sector have therefore usually been made available when purposes other than letting are involved: either when part residential provision is required as a condition of planning permission for commercial development or where speculative development has been contemplated, as in the break-up of London mansion blocks for sale or the conversion of town houses into self-contained flats for sale. The very high interest rates charged on borrowings in 1973 for these latter purposes (between 16 and 20 per cent), which came to light after a spate of bankruptcies following the collapse of this market from 1974 onwards, indicate just how speculative they were.

Strictly speaking, resident landlords, whose letting is only incidental to ownership, belong under the heading of owner-occupiers. Nevertheless, they are an important source of the total privately let pool. Again, it is worth emphasising that, in their case too, houses are generally being held debt-free because subletting is invariably forbidden in mortgage contracts. The exclusion of subletting by both building societies and local authorities is itself an issue worth review. A great deal of inner city (often immigrant) housing has not been acceptable to building societies for mortgage on grounds of its condition or other risk. Nor have its prospective owners been able to satisfy local authorities' requirements on income or other matters to qualify for mortgages (or anticipated that they would not). Purchasers have therefore resorted to the back-street mortgage. In order to meet the extortionate repayment rates which this involves, another vicious circle has been created in the housing system through subletting at high rents and under doubtful conditions. Here, obviously, is a clear role for house purchase loans by local authorities.

Developers

Builders and developers are bound to depend on continuous turnover for their operations to be self-financing on short pay-back periods. Otherwise, they incur high interest charges from fixed rate bank loans on capital tied up and, if they are companies, find it difficult to provide dividend for shareholders.

It is therefore little wonder, particularly given the structure of the building industry, with its multiplicity of small firms, that housebuilders' successes and failures follow the trade cycle in exaggerated form. The "spec" builder, much less than the contract builder who builds for a client (such as the local authority), is inevitably a quick victim to a decline in his own optimism about the housing market, or to a lack of optimism on the stock market—all conditions prevalent in the second half of 1976. Not surprisingly, builders as a group have been notorious for the frequency of bankruptcies, particularly during the recent 1974–76 recession.

In spite of their name, building societies have played a surprisingly minor role in the direct funding of housing construction and have almost entirely performed the role of house-owner societies, while an increasing proportion of their funds (now four-fifths) are simply refinancing the exchange of existing houses, the larger share of these being for existing owners.

It is sometimes said that this trend is reinforced because (simply) builders do not seek loans from building societies. In its evidence to the DOE Review, the HCT suggested a solution if the apprehensions of building societies (which are mutual institutions) about underwriting builders' risks were to blame. The problem might be resolved in certain circumstances if three-cornered arrangements could be agreed whereby building societies provided the loans, local authorities provided guarantees, and builders provided the houses. Similar arrangements had apparently been mooted to building societies in the past in general improvement areas (where market confidence at the outset may be lacking), but with no success.

Housing associations

It is most unfortunate that the " third arm " of housing has not opened a third avenue of funding. Indeed since the 1974 Act housing associations (HA's) are much less likely to look to the private market for sources of funds than previously. (37) The " take-off " of the housing association movement since 1974 has therefore been at the cost of an additional claim on public funds of astonishing proportions, at constant prices from some £74m. in 1970–71 to as much as a forecast of some £484m. in 1977–78. (38) Indeed, housing associations would then account for some 12 per cent of annual net public expenditure on housing. Associations will need to justify this increase with substantial increases in output.

Recourse to public funds is encouraged by the new system of grant. Instead of receiving annual subsidies during the life of the house as local authorities do, HA's now receive a once-and-for-all capital grant at the outset of each project they build or improve. This is calculated to wipe off the debt to an amount whose annual mortgage repayments are exactly matched by present rent income (net of running costs) for a 30 year term. On average the grant is about 75 per cent of cost, the amount to be covered by rent being only some 25 per cent.

The government is thus obliged to borrow three-quarters of the cost immediately on its own account whereas a revenue-based subsidy could encourage associations to make their own borrowing arrangements, so reducing the Exchequer's annual liability to a tenth of this 75 per cent sum. That lesser sum would have been sufficient to cover the HAs' deficit. Administratively, it is also much more convenient for HA's to borrow the outstanding 25 per cent from the local authority or from the Housing Corporation although it is open to HA's to seek a mortgage for this portion elsewhere. The 1974 Act has therefore caused the public sector borrowing requirement to carry practically the entire cost of HAs' annual investment programmes, cash down. When there is so much competition for other publicly funded programmes, a more short-sighted measure could hardly have been devised. (39)

When cash limits were imposed in April 1976 on HAs' capital expenditure (as on other publicly funded housing programmes), HA's not surprisingly began to fear that their expansion programmes might be thwarted. They therefore began to look for an alternative to government money for the 25 per cent residual component, perhaps from building societies, perhaps from other financial institutions such as pension funds. It is thought that sources such as the latter would be especially suitable when associations are participating in mixed developments (i.e., including shops and offices).

Conclusion

Unfortunately everyone seems to end an analysis of fund sources by casting an eye in the direction of pension funds, trade unions, or insurance companies. The fact of the matter is that our housing system is requiring more and more capital funds to create less and less housing. This is most true of owner-occupiers and housing associations; too large a proportion of funds is refinancing the revaluation of assets rather than real value added. It is ironical that the two sectors where this tendency has happened least—local authorities and private landlords (apart from municipalisation or the flat break-up market where comparatively small proportions are committed)—are the most popularly criticised.

Money to fund refinancing operations can only be attracted from elsewhere through any comparative advantage which building societies or government stock can offer. The volume of investment funds in the economy is not unlimited. It would be dangerous if we were to find we had reached the point where further subsidy or fiscal advantages were necessary to attract yet more money away from other productive uses into housing consumption.

PAYING FOR HOUSING

General

The obvious perhaps needs to be stated. So far as concerns the majority of households—whether owner-occupiers, tenants of councils or housing associations—what is not paid for by the individual consumer must be covered by central or local government, unless some cost is borne by an intermediate party such as the private landlord.

In the main, our attention must focus on the two main tenures, owner-occupation and council housing, which together house more than four-fifths of the nation's households. Seen from the point of view of government, subsidies to these two tenures alone are likely to exceed £2,200m. per year in 1976–77 or an equivalent of 13 per cent of income tax revenue. This figure has been increasing year by year in absolute terms (at constant prices after adjusting for inflation) and as a percentage of taxation. A reduction must inevitably involve an increase in personal contribution towards housing costs.

Admittedly in almost every country, housing subsidies are thought to be necessary if a civilised society is to overcome housing shortage. Yet the need for government funds, which ought eventually to be self-liquidating, has in the UK grown instead of diminishing—while, in some ways, the housing problem has intensified. The original framers of subsidies for public housing in 1919 must have believed that the need for such subsidies would disappear in time as good housing replaced bad. These same housebuilding subsidies (i.e., not including rent rebates or allowances for income maintenance), however, have been growing inexorably until in 1976–77 they will have amounted to some £1,100m. p.a. (40). Paradoxically, homelessness is increasing.

Similarly, the growth of owner-occupation from a level of 11 per cent of all dwellings in 1914 to 53 per cent in 1976 has surely been fostered in the belief that greater self-reliance would absolve the Exchequer from financial commitment. But this commitment, in revenue forgone as mortgage interest relief, has also been growing inexorably to a 1976–77 total which is also estimated to reach £1,100m. (41). Paradoxically *initial* gross mortgage repayments are requiring a higher proportion of average earnings (34 per cent in 1976 as against 23 in 1966) so that many would-be owners cannot afford to buy (25).

Housing subsidies have also been increasing at the same time as output has been falling in both sectors, during which time an overall national surplus of housing over households (42, 43) has developed and under-occupation in both sectors has increased. One is therefore forced to conclude that housing subsidies must be subsidising something other than housing production—perhaps other consumption or even perhaps indirectly the fuelling of price increases (44).

Paradoxically again, the average proportion of personal expenditure on housing has increased from 10 per cent in 1961 to just over 13 per cent in 1975 (2). The subsidy figures and the personal budget figures taken together seem to indicate that the defects lie in the way the benefits and burdens are shared out.

It is commonly asserted that the problem could be solved if everyone paid the economic cost of his housing. But what *is* economic cost? In the eyes of government, it must be apparent that practically no one, except the private tenant in the very best and very worst housing, is paying a sum anywhere near sufficient to cover the full replacement value of his housing, although the first-time buyer comes closest to doing so in his first year in a new house. The shortfall must inevitably be made up in overt or concealed forms of subsidy towards the mortgage (or loan) charges on the investment which individuals (or authorities) make in their housing (44). Even repair items which have traditionally been paid out of current income have, in the case of older houses, become eligible for improvement grant aid since 1969 and the 1974 Act has increased the subsidy on repairs still further (see Chapter 7).

It is sometimes contended that because subsidies ultimately come from the taxpayer, they are part of the "social wage" because the beneficiary and recipient are the same. However, the incidence of taxation and subsidy varies without good reason. For one thing, owner-occupiers paying the highest rate of tax or with the biggest mortgages receive most in tax relief; it is not the poorest tenants who get most subsidy. For another, taxation comes from companies as well as from individuals. Further, both constitutional and economic problems would ensue if it were not recognised, as has always been the case, that the tax revenue collected is a separate transaction from benefits disbursed—a point forgotten when it is contended, for example, that the cost of relief in revenue forgone in mortgage interest relief is balanced by the tax revenue collected from building society investors (45).

The fault may lie in the way subsidies are paid. Our society has concentrated on treating housing as a once-and-for-all investment. There is no corresponding provision for its costs in use and its costs of eventual replacement. Housing may last a long time, but it does not last for ever. A simplified bird's eye view of the national housing stock would be a one hundred year moving series of annual housing outputs, the oldest 1 per cent coming up for renewal every year (by redevelopment or improvement) and then going to the newest end of the queue. If our housing in all sectors were a self-financing operation then, once a national stock had been established, the extra cost of this annual 1 per cent renewed would be covered by a contribution from the remaining 99 per cent.

On a national scale, this would require our investment subsidies ultimately to be paid for out of levies on consumption: by existing households already housed paying for existing housing as it was " used up." Such a principle is no longer countenanced. Schedule " A " taxation, which provided for a method of doing so in the case of owner-occupiers, was abolished in 1963 and public sector tenants are not required to contribute directly towards replacement costs. As a result, investment subsidies (either to individuals or to authorities) are never returned by the housing system itself and therefore never diminish. Inevitably, they can only be met from increased proportions of general taxation.

A deceptively simple proposal for increasing the personal contribution towards housing cost is that the various proportions of income paid by different households " ought " to be brought more into line. Indeed, just how much housing is " politicised " is shown by the way it is so commonly discussed in terms of the " proper " proportion of income an individual should pay—much more so than are other basic essentials, such as food, clothing, health or education. This may reflect a popular recognition of how much government intervenes in the market to secure a reasonable standard of housing as a social right. Therefore, it is felt, if people ought to pay no more than some notional maximum, then correspondingly they ought to pay at least some notional minimum. Does that mean that actual costs are to be ignored and the pricing system for everyone's housing is to be based on a predetermined formula?

There is a fundamental snag in measuring proportions of income *paid*. What matters to the household is what is *left over* in relation to other needs and commitments, which vary enormously—hence the feeling that a " proportional " measure which applied to everyone would have to be balanced by universal housing allowances (see later section).

Even determining what proportions of income are actually paid is fraught with pitfalls. Therefore comparison between what *could* or *should* be paid must be treated with great reserve, bearing in mind all the qualifications which have to be taken into account.

Averages hide the range of incomes. The 9 per cent average proportion of head of household income paid by council tenants ranges from 20 per cent for incomes under £800 to 5 per cent for incomes over £3,600. The 12 per cent average for mortgagors ranges from 23 per cent for incomes under £1,550 to 11 per cent for incomes over £4,600 (46). Comparisons are too frequently made between extremes of these.

The next problem is that of reconciling these proportions paid by *buyers* with a mortgage with the proportions paid by all *owners*, including those owning outright, or again, of reconciling the proportions paid by *all* buyers with the proportions for *new* buyers in their first year because, as is well known, the proportions of income tend to fall as the years go by—mortgage interest and repayments cannot be evened out in the same way over a household's lifetime as rents for council tenants could be (47).

Again, household income frequently exceeds head of household income, but perhaps temporarily. The average earnings of first time buyers are usually quoted without taking into account the number with working wives (57 per cent with one major building society) (21). They can be misleadingly compared with the income of council tenants as a whole who include between 30 and 40 per cent of pensioner households in most authorities as well as the swollen earnings of households with two parental incomes and, for a period, earning children.

Equally, it must not be forgotten that usually the proportions for mortgagors are quoted gross before deduction of tax relief on their interest, yet net of rebates in the case of council tenants. Overall the total national deduction of tax relief amounts to some 37 per cent of all mortgagors' interest payments. Sometimes the way income figures are analysed, even in official data, gives the impression that housing subsidies are more generously distributed towards those on lower incomes than is the case (48). The differences are again to some extent offset by the inclusion within the rent of the costs of most management and maintenance (which will account for an average of 27 per cent of councils' expenditure in 1976–77 (17)); these costs are excluded from mortgagors' proportions.

Should proportions of income paid by mortgagors exceed proportions paid by tenants? If they are to reflect the differential in average (median) gross values for rating purposes, they presumably should: £201 in the case of the average LA house; £271 in the case of the average mortgaged house and £219 in the case of the average house owned outright (49); but public opinion expects that they should in any case, according to a NEDO special opinion survey (50). It is felt that the owner is acquiring a capital asset which, in old age, he can enjoy at less cost or realise upon, or use to trade up or down, pass on to his heirs and, in the meantime, upon which he can raise credit. By contrast, the tenant's lesser payment is for use and occupation only and continues indefinitely.

The same opinion survey confirmed earlier surveys that there is a clear majority preference among all householders, regardless of present tenure, to own their own homes, not only for reasons of taste or independence but also because, financially, to own a house is seen as a better bargain than renting. Does this highlight a contradiction at the core of our housing finance? In all commodities there is an eventual price equilibrium, however imprecise and volatile in the short term, between owning and renting as there is between hiring and buying a TV, an aircraft or a factory. This equilibrium has been lost in housing finance because the threshold costs of buying are now disproportionately higher than council renting, yet the eventual position is the reverse.

To sum up: if reform of housing finance is to be both equitable and efficient and at the same time allow freedom of choice, it must respect the whole range of commitments illustrated and not impose some theoretical straitjacket. There is no simple formula, according to proportions of income. Equally, as argued earlier, there would be problems if housing were to be charged according to real value or cost; that would run counter to the development of a subsidy system which has turned its back on recouping investment subsidies directly from the housing system via levies on housing consumption. On the other hand, more consistency is undoubtedly needed, including re-establishment of some clearer relationship between the costs of renting and owning.

In this situation, the HCT's *Evidence* felt a choice had to be made between three main options: to continue the present system of high investment subsidies, which appears unacceptable on grounds of cost and efficiency; to offset investment subsidies by taxing housing consumption, which however logical in the long term appears impractical as a basis for the immediate changes necessary; or to reduce investment subsidies selectively which it thought the best compromise for the short and medium term. These options, which affect four-fifths of the nation's households, need to be looked at against the circumstances of each of the two main tenures.

Owner-occupiers

As has been shown in Chapter 2, owner-occupiers are by far the larger of the two main tenure groups, being 53 per cent of the nation's 20 million households. In spite of the tendency, especially in the media, for owner-occupiers to be lumped together, the differences of financial circumstances *among* owner-occupiers are as important as differences between them and other tenures. These differences appear as soon as any practical decisions have to be made which take into account the extreme variations in costs which households face. For instance the Pay Board's *London Weighting Report* (51) found it impossible to cater for the variations, through some housing allowance, which would be appropriate for all owner-occupiers in London. It may be helpful therefore to recall certain distinctive features.

Firstly, the *margin* problems. Housing policy and any discussion of it tends to be preoccupied with changes at the margin of the existing stock: either with new houses completed although their annual number, which has ranged from 268,000 in 1975 to 414,000 in 1968, actually forms a little over 1 per cent of the stock or less when losses and demolitions are taken into account (31); or with first time buyers, although their numbers annually, which have ranged from 220,000 in 1974 to 394,000 in 1972 (19), represent less than 3 per cent of owner-occupiers. This preoccupation is a natural expression of attempts to eliminate shortage and to enable new households to realise their legitimate housing aspirations. It is obvious that this preoccupation has to be balanced by attention to what happens to the remaining 99 per cent of the stock owned and the 97 per cent of existing owners (52).

Secondly, the *threshold* problem. The full impact of prices and the interest rate affects only the minority of would-be buyers trying to cross the threshold of owner-occupation for the first time; these will be most vociferous and command the most sympathy. Gross repayments of first-time buyers as a proportion of their earnings in the first year of purchase have ranged between 19 per cent and 25 per cent during the last five years (47). Existing owners exchanging one house for another will obviously be cushioned by the proceeds from the sale of their existing house, the average proportion of income they pay in gross repayments on purchase ranging between 17 per cent and 23 per cent in the first year (53, 54). In some cases, existing owners are not so cushioned when they have to cross another price threshold which inhibits mobility, the regional one (e.g., house prices in London and the South East tend on average to be a third higher than in the Midlands)—although these buyers are a small minority because most moves are within a small radius (55).

Thirdly the *exchange* process. As owner-occupation spreads and as existing owners with mortgages move more often, every seven years on average, the proportion of buyers who are existing owners is inevitably rising and the proportion of first-time buyers correspondingly falling—from 63 per cent in 1969 to 47 per cent in 1975 (56). Thus, to some extent, the complaints that building societies are granting fewer mortgages to first-time buyers is an unreasonable one. Also, more and more owners are mortgagors: 58 per cent in 1975 as against 52 per cent in 1965 (57). Correspondingly fewer are outright owners and it is expected that the proportion of elderly owner-occupiers with mortgages will rise in future (57). This is contrary to the popular belief that as owner-occupation spreads, more owners will pass through the mortgage process to outright ownership. Equally important, more and more mortgages are bound to be on existing houses—less than one-fifth of new mortgages are on new houses now (1976) as against one-third in the early 1960s (58)—so that the link between mortgages (and subsidies on them) and the level of new housebuilding cannot but be an indirect one. Lastly, of the small number of fresh mortgages on new houses less than one-half are to first-time buyers. So, of all fresh mortgages, some 9 per cent are to first-time buyers buying new houses. Therefore, the link between policies to first-time buyers and new houses is even more remote (59).

To understand these three features—the *margin,* the *threshold* problem and the *exchange* process—is essential before appropriate reform of the financial system governing owner-occupation can be evolved. To be appropriate, reform must respect " the nature of the beast " it is dealing with and be tailored to the financial contours and movement of the sector itself. This means identifying the sector's strengths and maximising them, identifying its weaknesses and minimising them.

Strengths:

(a) Self-reliance. As owner-occupation spreads, the system should become independent of the need for public subsidy. This potential is enhanced by the inestimable success of building societies in providing cheap finance.

(b) Mortgage interest relief is timely. The most usual mortgage is repaid on the " constant annuity " system so as to produce a constant total paid annually, but consisting of higher amounts of interest and lower of principal in the early years and vice versa in the later years. So long as the mortgage is below £25,000, tax relief is payable on the interest. Tax reliefs are, therefore, highest in the early years, so offsetting the very high threshold repayments, e.g., on a mortgage of £10,000 at 11 per cent for 25 years annual repayments are always £1,188 but, at the standard tax rate of 35 per cent, relief declines over 25 years in a curved " staircase " from £385 in the first year, to £328 in the eleventh year, £168 in the twenty-first year and £34 in the last year. If the individual pays tax at higher than standard rate, the value of relief is higher.

(c) Easier later years. With inflation and rising income, and perhaps with interest rates which are effectively negative, repayments become a smaller proportion of income. The burden eases, therefore, as the family grows.

(d) Trading-up is possible. As the family grows and perhaps its income increases, it can use the proceeds from the sale of its first house to move to better housing.

Weaknesses:

(a) Independence of public funds is not in fact being realised. The total revenue forgone by the Exchequer in relief on mortgage interest is growing many times faster (250 per cent between 1968 and 1976) than the rate of owner-occupation (20 per cent between 1968 and 1976).

(b) The purchasing power of existing owners is boosted too much in conditions of inflation. For, when the proceeds from sale by an existing owner are added to the advance he can support from his enlarged income, the ability to gear up increases much faster. In the period 1971–75, the average mortgage advanced to first-time buyers and to existing owners moving increased almost exactly in step, in *both* cases doubling from about £4,000 to £8,000. The widening differences are to be found in the deposits paid, rising in the case of first-time buyers from about £1,000 in 1971 to £2,000 in 1975 (double) and in the case of existing owners moving from about £2,000 to £6,000 (triple). The purchasing power of existing owners can therefore set the pace of house prices to the detriment of the first-time buyer. Indeed, at the time of the fastest price increase, the price paid by existing owners moving has grown far faster than that paid by first-time buyers. In 1968 previous owner-occupiers paid about 30 per cent more than new owner-occupiers; the difference gradually increased from 1969 to 1971 and then grew rapidly in 1972, reaching around 50 per cent in the second half of 1972 and, after falling back in 1974, attained this differential again in 1976 (60). Whether this potential power is exercised depends on other factors of demand, especially from first-time buyers whose increased demand during 1971–73 reflected, among other things, the post-war bulge in the birth rate. In the years of slacker demand preceding 1971, existing owners were not under any pressure to exercise their purchasing power to the full. Analysis has shown that they put the " spare " proportion of their proceeds from sale into spending on consumption other than housing which, it is arguable, is equally inflationary or undesirable for other reasons (61, 62).

(c) The process is compounded by the Exchequer. Under the existing system, each time the existing owner moves he is entitled to maximise his interest relief on the tax relief " staircase " already referred to, as in some real-life game of " Monopoly " he goes back to " Go " again and collects a bonus. Not only does he receive a higher amount of relief if his new mortgage is higher, but he reverts to the full relief of the *first* year of a new (say) 25 year mortgage term. The average length of a mortgage is now less than seven years so the average mortgage outstanding is now less than 3½ years old and has only less than 3½ years to go. The average mortgage therefore tends both to reflect current high prices and to be always near the favourable top end of the tax relief staircase. An example in the HCT *Evidence* illustrates the way one owner can draw relief for 37 years using two moves to increase the relief he receives.

(d) First time buyers need more assistance. The comparative advantage of the existing owners coupled with higher interest rates causes the magic carpet of owner-occupation to hover higher above the reach of the first-time buyer. A variety of methods to assist him are therefore mooted, most of which would involve still extra cost to the Exchequer; otherwise he has to accept falling standards (smaller or older houses) or greater personal sacrifice (working wives).

(e) A snowballing claim on capital funds. As existing houses change hands at higher prices and more frequently, the demand for funds to finance the mortgage borrowing requirement increases faster than the rate of growth of owner-occupation, i.e., faster than funds can be " recycled ", as was shown earlier in the funding section. In financial terms, debt liabilities are increased without a corresponding increase in real assets (either in numbers of houses or in numbers of owners).

(f) No necessary encouragement to new building or improvement. As noted earlier, the Exchequer's bill in revenue foregone has been increasing quite independently of investment, which is falling. In spite of this, it is commonly believed that the house-building industry depends on the present system remaining unchanged.

In these circumstances there is a logical attraction to the reintroduction of some form of levy on housing consumption (similar to Schedule " A " taxation) in order to offset both the rising investment subsidies (in the form of mortgage interest relief) and the inequities and inefficiencies of the present system. It is contended that, by requiring all owners to contribute according to the value of the house they occupied and on the income in kind enjoyed, taxation on housing would be put back on to the same footing as on money income earned on other investments; otherwise distortion in the economy, especially in industrial investment, results. Indeed, the original justification for mortgage interest corresponded to the present taxation position of companies, who receive tax relief on loan interest paid on investments but pay tax on income received. At present, owner-occupied housing investment is in a unique position of a *double* taxation exemption and this provides a partial explanation for the decline of the private landlord who does not enjoy a corresponding advantage. Also, there is no automatic encouragement for housing maintenance as previously happened when house-holders' Schedule " A " assessment was reduced on proof of maintenance and improvement expenditure, which might be to the long term benefit of the housing stock and reduce the Exchequer's future liability in improvement and repair grants.

In the HCT's view, a consumption tax is ruled out for reasons of practicality for the immediate future. In any case, it could only be entertained in the long term after careful study and together with parallel changes in the local authority sector by charging rents according to replacement value. HCT therefore preferred the compromise option of reducing the generosity of investment subsidies in the short term, as explained below, supplemented perhaps by minor taxation changes on death or on capital gains or transfer in order to ensure the eventual return of some value of investment subsidies to the Exchequer.

HCT proposed several partial measures, as did some other bodies (63):

(a) lowering the mortgage ceiling eligible for relief below £25,000;

(b) standardising relief at 35 per cent (removing eligibility of higher relief for higher taxpayers);

(c) lowering the rate on which relief is paid to a representative rate less than the borrowing rate (then 11 per cent).

All these measures, however, have limitations. The first two would produce only small savings to the Exchequer, and none of them would tilt the balance of advantage away from the existing owner, because the mortgage sums advanced to existing owners are on average so similar to those advanced to first-time buyers. Reduction of relief to the standard rate is estimated to produce a saving to the Exchequer of only £120m (64) out of its total bill of some £1,100m. a year. Lowering of the ceiling on which relief is eligible does not produce a saving of over £100m (65) until a ceiling as low as some £8,000 is reached, at which point first-time buyers are likely to be heavily prejudiced too. A lower representative rate could, however, be introduced on a differential basis so as to bear less heavily on recent purchasers and more heavily on earlier purchasers whose repayments have fallen to a small proportion of their incomes.

HCT's novel and fourth proposition was also to introduce a differential treatment between first-time buyers and existing owners exchanging one house for another. Accordingly, a " one man, one mortgage " or " single annuity " principle was proposed (as illustrated in its *Evidence*). The principle is a simple one. Relief would be paid as now on the actual full interest paid each year on a first-time mortgage. The change was proposed when an owner moved, say, after seven years. He would still get more relief on a bigger mortgage for a more expensive house but not so generously as at present. His new relief would not be available as in the *first* year of a new 25-year term when relief is highest but as if in the eighth year or whatever number of years had run from the date of his original mortgage. Relief would always taper off, for whatever size of mortgage, to expire at the end of a set 25-year period.

The " single annuity " relief would, HCT contended, have several advantages of reducing the Exchequer bill substantially, while respecting the commitments of existing owners, because only fresh exchange transactions would be affected. Thus transition from the existing to the proposed system would be gradual and relatively painless, without prejudicing the first-time buyer at all. Relief on bigger mortgages would still be allowed so as to preserve mobility and the home-ownership ladder. Although the proposed system would gradually reduce the demand for larger and more expensive houses and increase it for smaller and cheaper ones, the building industry would have time to adjust without having to suffer a reduction in the overall value of housebuilding output, profits or employment.

Local authority housing

The second of the two main tenures, local authority (LA) housing, now houses as many as 31 per cent of the nation's 20 million households. By virtue of numbers, as well as spread of tenants' incomes, it therefore cannot be thought of as consisting only of a disadvantaged minority.

As we recalled earlier, subsidies to this sector have also apparently been rising inexorably. A great deal of publicity has focused on the subsidies on new or improved housing, which are now paid at a level of at least two-thirds of the cost of loan charges on them in the first year. Although these levels are to a great extent offset by the existence of a cost pooling system, the fact remains that rents (*excluding* rebates) now only contribute an average of some 53 per cent towards the expenditure on LAs' housing revenue accounts and have fallen to this level from a proportion of around 67–70 per cent over the last 10 years (66, 33).

Naturally in the case of high cost areas, where authorities feel it necessary to undertake large new housing or improvement programmes, the rent contribution is much lower than 53 per cent. Should rents be increased to bear a larger share of costs? After all, it is argued, a low rent philosophy is out of date because local authorities have been obliged since 1972 to provide rent rebates for income maintenance of the poorest tenants. Moreover, such a philosophy encourages the idea of " welfare housing " which would be resented by those it benefited as strongly as those it excluded.

Unfortunately, what a LA rent should be and how much it should be subsidised have proved just as elusive questions as what an owner-occupier should pay and how much he should be subsidised. It is often argued that many of our housing problems would be resolved if the public sector charged market rents but, upon investigation, market rents prove to be an elusive concept too. Increasingly during the twentieth century, because of both rent control and the favourable taxation treatment accorded to owner-occupiers, those landlords who have let ordinary housing on a systematic business basis have increasingly relied for their profits on the expectation of some eventual capital realisation on sale rather than on straightforward income from letting. If a market rent were to be defined as a sum sufficient to cover the total cost of funding the land and bricks for a house at a rate of return sufficient to match one from other investments, in central urban locations it could be more than the net income of a man in full employment occupying it.

Two alternative methods for rent fixing in LA housing have therefore been preferred. *Either* (a) " residual " method by which a level of subsidy thought sufficient to produce a " reasonable " rent is first fixed (supplemented by some contribution from the local rates, at times compulsory and, under recent legislation, optional. Rents are then fixed to cover outgoings, less subsidy. This has been the principle between the various methods in the long succession of public housing subsidy legislation since 1919 and is still used in the main in the current 1975 Act; *or* (b) a " formula " method by which rents are first fixed according to some predetermined approved yardstick of value in order to produce

" fair " rents, subsidies being paid on whatever deficit results. Used partially in the 1961 Act, this was the main basis of the (now repealed) 1972 Act. Many housing authorities continue to use rule-of-thumb formulae related to the 1972 method.

The predominance of " residual " rent fixing, together with the practice of pooling all subsidies and costs and rents in one balanced account, has meant that the major determinant of the level of local authority rents has been historical costs. These have therefore reflected the differing, and in many ways chance, circumstances of history or geography, thus producing variations in rent levels between one authority and another. In this sense, LA housing has suffered from drawbacks analogous to the problems of owner-occupied housing where the housing outgoings of next door neighbours can also reflect very different historical costs and variables depending on particular circumstances, such as age, dates of purchase and whether the present house has been bought with the proceeds from a previous one.

By contrast to the problem facing owner-occupiers, each local authority can, within its own boundary, even out the different costs which would otherwise face tenants occupying houses built at different dates. Indeed neither the " residual " method of " reasonable rents " nor the " formula " method of " fair rents " could have worked without using this cross-subsidisation, in use since 1935.

Levels of subsidy apart, the question arises as to whether LA rents should reflect historical cost as now or some recalculated formula such as " fair rents ". But fair rents were set according to levels in the smaller and declining private rented sector and would therefore become less and less appropriate. Alternative proposals have been made according to some multiple of capital or replacement values, as proposed as the basis for local rating by the Layfield Committee; but then LA rents would reflect the varying degrees of scarcity at the margin of each local house purchase market. Others have suggested, harking back to the arguments that rents should be based on proportions of income, that rents should be fixed according to some proportion of average regional earnings; but this risks " chicken and egg " complications, because earnings might be forced up by higher rents.

The danger, as with all formulae, is that what seems eminently logical and sophisticated to the specialist appears unreal to anyone else. It would not be clear why rents according to value should be different from (and sometimes more than) rents charged according to cost.

More fundamentally, if LA rents were based on capital or replacement values in order to ensure that high investment subsidies were returned to the Exchequer in some form of consumption levy, this would have to be matched by a parallel value-based system for owner-occupied housing (as Schedule " A " taxation) which, as was argued earlier, also suffers from serious practical difficulties.

As for owner-occupiers, the HCT felt that a compromise of reducing investment subsidies, coupled with some redistribution of the benefits and burdens of the existing system, would be more appropriate, at least in the short and medium term. Again, this would respect the " nature of the beast " if the strength of the existing system were maximised and its weaknesses minimised.

Strengths

(a) A priceless national asset. The most striking feature is the potential cheapness. The average debt outstanding on each council dwelling in England and Wales is not more than £2,750 for which an annual loan charge of £300 or just under £6 per week represents a break-even rate of return given pooled interest rates. All-in costs, including management and maintenance, are on average no more than £8·50 per week *without any subsidy or mortgage interest relief at all.* If subsidy were received automatically on the loan charges on the outstanding debt at the standard relief rate for owner-occupiers of 35 per cent, assuming an 11 per cent interest rate, the £8·50 cost rent would be reduced by between £2 to £2·50 a week. This is ignoring any additional " high cost " subsidy supplement and also ignoring the more generous tax relief received by higher rate taxpayers with mortgages.

(b) Cross-subsidisation evens out costs within each local authority. The high costs of adding to or renewing its stock can be offset by surpluses on an authority's not-so-new stock. By this process, which does not exist in the owner-occupied sector, rents can be kept within the reach of households at the threshold of setting up house for the first time.

(c) It is not "welfare housing." So far, the UK has avoided the tendency in some other countries, notably the US, of restricting public housing to a residual role of housing only the poor, the old and otherwise disadvantaged. A fair spread of socio-economic groups is of social benefit.

(d) Declining debt. As noticed earlier in the funding section, the outstanding debt on LA housing is not increased in the process of re-financing, as happens with owner-occupied housing as houses change hands. It remains at its historical level unless increased by real investment in new or improved housing.

Weaknesses

(a) High marginal costs deter investment. As the average cost of historic debt on houses within an authority's pool falls, so the cost of each new or improved house appears prohibitive.

(b) High subsidies add to the public expenditure burden. New or improved houses are eligible for subsidies of at least two-thirds of the cost, yet this level is still insufficient to bridge the cost gap between the new work and the rent paid for it. Nevertheless, the total amount of subsidies has grown so big that it has already begun to threaten the capital programme for supplying those houses.

(c) Lack of cross-subsidisation between authorities. Chances of history or geography are not shared. Those authorities who are fortunate enough to have satisfied their housing needs for the time being and to be able to reap the benefits of past subsidies cannot share their financial benefits with disadvantaged authorities who need a heavy programme of new building or improvement —even though the fortunes of surplus and deficit authorities will reverse in time.

(d) Financial pressures towards welfare housing. Is it not true that the lack of any objective system of rent fixing, whether according to " fair rent " or " reasonable rent " formulae, encourages the setting of rents by political bargaining? Does this not discredit the potential of public housing and suggest a condition of dependency for its tenants? Will not more generous subsidies be accompanied by greater scrutiny and greater insistence that the local authority and the tenant demonstrate housing need?

(e) Paying Paul may involve robbing Peter. Whilst it is impossible to generalise about all areas, this is one of the problems of the sale of council houses. A local authority may be attracted by the benefits of selling its houses because of a reduction in rate-funded contributions. In the long run, this may simply shift the burden to central government which, perhaps after a temporary reduction in subsidy, incurs a near perpetual liability in mortgage interest relief as houses are sold and re-mortgaged each time, instead of a steadily declining liability in subsidy if the house remains in the public sector.

(f) The type of subsidy may over-influence the form of development. Until recently at any rate, re-development was more generously subsidised than improvement, and some types of redevelopment or sizes of dwellings more generously subsidised than others.

The HCT, therefore, proposed to maximise the potential offered by cross-subsidisation through a system of national pooling of the mortgage (i.e., debt charges) element on all council housing in order to match the different and, over the years, changing needs of each authority to build or to improve. In this way the " life-cycle " of different authorities would be catered for. Over time, the pattern of cross-subsidies would vary because each authority's need to build or to improve occurs according to the different age profile of its stock and according to its varying housing needs in relation to its development.

Accordingly, the relationship to the pool would change: receiving authorities this year might become donating authorities in five years' time and vice-versa. This principle of a " revolving fund " would be in the self interest of authorities.

Subsidy would be paid centrally every year in the form of interest relief on this national mortgage total at a rate in line with the standard tax relief granted on an individual owner-occupier's mortgage (at present 35 per cent). The subsidy would be apportioned by balancing each authority's loan charges expenditure against its means to pay according to a " target income " formula. Each authority would be required to raise sufficient mortgage element in its rents to meet this target income. Where this was less than its actual loan charges, the national pool would cover the deficit; where more, the surplus would be paid into the pool. Maintenance and management charges would remain locally attributable and directly covered in rent.

Besides the incidental merit of simplicity, the formula which HCT proposed had been devised to possess two essential conditions. Each authority would retain the essential freedom and responsibility for setting individual rents. And the method of calculating the target income, by using the aggregate gross values (for rating purposes) of an authority's stock, was designed to avoid poorer areas from subsidising more prosperous ones. Gross values, it was thought, are still in the *aggregate* the best measure reflecting value, according to age, location and amenity, however anomalous they sometimes are between individual houses. If it were thought more appropriate, capital values could be substituted if the Layfield Committee proposals were adopted for rating purposes.

In addition, the division of the " service " from the " equity " element (loan charges) in the rent would leave all the options open for equity-sharing schemes or for schemes of sharing responsibility for management and maintenance costs.

In its evidence, the Trust calculated examples of the proposed system for the national pool, for the housing revenue account of an individual authority, and for an individual tenancy. If the original 1974–75 figures used in the evidence were to be updated with 1976–77 figures, the increase in rent needed under the proposals would eventually average some £1·50 per week (which would, of course, have to be phased). This level of increase, the Trust argued, would not be dissimilar from the levels of rent increases which are being required in any case under subsidy reductions in the public expenditure White Papers. It would, however, be made without the interference and cuts in capital programmes of new building and improvement involved by continuation of the existing system.

Private rented sector

The decline of private renting since 1914, when 90 per cent of all dwellings were so let, and an accelerated decline from 53 per cent in 1950 to 16 per cent in 1975 (all figures include housing associations) is well known. Even some Conservative politicians who might be thought to be traditionally in favour of private letting, believe the sector cannot be resuscitated (67).

However, its contribution is still too important to be ignored, even more so when the degree of concentration in particular areas is taken into account. It continues to provide flexibility in letting which other rented housing sources, local authorities and housing associations, have as yet been unable to match. Opinions vary therefore between those who feel that private letting is doomed and that its extinction should be made as quick and painless as possible for all concerned, those who feel its life can be temporarily prolonged, and those few who believe it can be rejuvenated.

Care must be taken to avoid two common pitfalls if its financial state is to be understood and appropriate reform proposed. Firstly, the range of types of house and of landlord is too heterogeneous, from Edwardian mansion blocks in Kensington to cramped or multi-occupied terraces in industrial towns, from students' rooms to businessmen's expensive *pied-à-terre,* to fit the single preconceived image each of us tends to have. Secondly, private letting is a frequent political scapegoat at both ends of the political spectrum: from popular Conservatism which sees it as counter to the emancipation offered by owner-occupation; to idealistic Socialism which feels the basic human need of shelter should be removed from the market place. These tendencies are reinforced by the conditions of squalor and scandal inevitable when obsolescent property in the inner fringes of our towns is left to itself.

One must not forget too that there are a number of small landlords who continue quite irrationally to let, perhaps content with a negligible rate of return, and simply relying on realising their capital asset one day. They offer a range of flexibility (short contracts, instant lettings, lettings above shops) and often provide management services for virtually nothing.

Although the sector's severe weaknesses are undeniable, it must be understood how these stem from the nature of the housing market itself. This differs from the market in other everyday commodities because its turnover in any one period is still relatively small in proportion to the whole stock and there is very little " homogeneity " which allows one house to be interchangeable with another, given the specific, fixed and local characteristics of each house. So the " reshuffling " process which we associate with the ideal operation of supply and demand cannot take place. In conditions of scarcity, this is even less so. It is inevitable that, with a limited supply of lettings available, prospective renters with the most means will be at the head of the queue and competition will be fiercest towards the end of the queue until the poorest 10 per cent of incomes compete for the last and worst 5 per cent of the accommodation left (68).

This explains why rent control and security of tenure is to be found in so many countries, in time reducing the landlord's income and ultimately creating a black market in rented housing at both the smart and the squalid extremes, conditions of overcrowding, poor maintenance and speculative pressure. While the income from letting may be sufficient to support a low and reducing historical debt, it would be insufficient to support the higher repayments or the replacement cost of the house. There is therefore, an inherent tendency for the sector to stagnate.

Rent control is not entirely to blame. Private letting in the twentieth century has been placed at a double disadvantage. From 1919, local authority subsidised rents were inevitably lower than private cost rents, controls apart. Owner-occupiers, already benefiting from cheaper loans from building societies (and mortgage interest relief), received increasingly favourable taxation treatment because Schedule A assessments were not revised from the 1930s onwards and were finally abolished in 1963, with the result that the value of owner-occupied houses has continued to rise faster than other prices. Landlords increasingly held property not for its letting income but eventually to realise its capital value for owner-occupation. Consequently, the periodic attempts to reduce rent control in the 1930s, in 1957 and in 1969, in order to remove the deterrent facing private landlords resulted not in more *letting* but in more *selling off*. As the differential between the two markets has evidenced, the investment value of houses has fallen if occupied and risen if vacant possession is secured: the stage was therefore set in high demand areas for the silver handshake, winkling, harassment and, at worst, Rachmanism.

It is important to understand why attempts to reverse this financial discrimination have proved so difficult and are likely to continue so. Attempts have been made to increase landlords' income by introducing the " fair rent " system under the 1965 Act for all new tenancies and, subject to phasing, progressively for most tenancies in legislation since. The basic principle underlying a fair rent, however, is one which could be agreed between willing parties *less* an amount representing a notional scarcity factor. In determining this somewhat elusive rent, the rent officer who registers it is bound by the wording of the Act to have more regard (in order to eliminate the effects of scarcity) to the rents of comparable accommodation previously agreed or previously registered in the district and less regard to whether the rate of return for the landlord on his investment is reasonable. The interpretation has since been confirmed in the appeal courts (69). Under steadily rising inflation, a system based on comparables has become less and less appropriate and has sharpened the contrast between the low income a landlord can expect and the potential value of his asset on a rising market for owner-occupation.

So far as taxation is concerned, the landlord has no entitlement to deduct an allowance for depreciation as an ordinary company has, for instance, in respect of its plant and machinery—houses are treated for taxation purposes as a non-depreciating asset (70). This may seem illogical in that a proportion of the growing commitment of government expenditure in improvement and repair grants surely represents the cost of depreciation stored up over time in the form of decaying property. On the other hand, landlords are liable for taxation on income from letting, either in corporation tax if companies or in income tax for Schedule D if individuals, whereas owner-occupiers no longer pay an equivalent income tax Schedule A on the income derived in kind from occupation (71, 72).

It is true that landlords are eligible for tax relief (i.e., against rental not all income) on loan interest as owner-occupiers are, but this relief is of far less value to them. Most privately let houses in any case do not have loans outstanding on them as is the case for most owner-occupied houses, which are constantly being refinanced as they change hands.

Within the context of their overall responsibilities towards the housing needs of a district, local authorities (and housing associations) face contradictory pressures. On the one hand, the landlord with an occupied house is likely to delay selling against the day when vacant possession can be realised—so the conditions deteriorate. On the other hand, authorities are under a statutory (or strong moral) obligation to rehouse private tenants in housing need. In doing so they may risk the loss of yet another house from the district's declining pool of rented accommodation which is still providing an essential function. Further, in order to make good the loss, authorities may in turn be faced with purchasing similar previously let but now vacated houses at high prices.

No comprehensive proposals for reform of housing finance in the privately rented sector have so far been put forward in detail, although the British Property Federation has listed some changes it regards as essential (70). The HCT has suggested some guidelines. These call for a more positive innovative approach than hitherto by recognising the important contribution which the privately rented sector still plays, by describing the present set of incentives and constraints facing private landlords as contradictory, and by questioning the cost-effectiveness of policies aimed at buying out the sector. The HCT's evidence does not question the need for reasonable security of tenure but calls (in outline only) for analysis of possible reform under three heads:

(a) Incentives. That, in the main, ways be investigated of compensating for the taxation disadvantages referred to above and of providing for more flexible use of improvement grants;

(b) Rents. That the principles of assessing fair rents be re-examined according to valuation formulae (rather than comparables) in order to strike an acceptable balance between income and capital growth. Consideration might also be given to some provision for coupling this with an option to sell to local authorities so as to give a measure of guarantee of realising capital value.

(c) New types of Landlordism. That examination be made of " sale and lease back " schemes between the landlord and the local authority, so enabling the landlord to realise capital values (not necessarily in cash) and yet remain letting. That part-equity schemes with local authorities, or purchase using annuities, all be investigated.

All of these aim at reducing the financial differential between private letting and other tenures. However, this differential could never be closed entirely unless both owner-occupiers and local authority tenants paid for housing according to some value-based system (rather than historical cost) and which, HCT has argued, could only come about after a decade of transitional measures.

Housing associations

The new system of finance for housing associations (HA's), its problems and possible directions of reform, must be understood within the context of attempts to launch a new " third arm " sector of substantial size. Although HA dwellings are only a small proportion of the national stock (under 2 per cent) and although, until recently, their annual development programmes were correspondingly small, their present annual programmes are now aiming at an annual UK production of some 50,000 dwellings. In England and Wales alone, their 1975–76 totals were 31,500 new and 18,500 improvement approvals for dwelling starts or an equivalent of some 26 per cent and 50 per cent respectively of local authority annual programmes of 118,629 new starts and 37,106 improvement approvals respectively in 1975. The all-party political support which this expansion drive has enjoyed (itself an encouraging omen in the field of housing finance) is an act of confidence that the HA's will be able to fill the vacuum left by the declining private landlord, particularly in areas of concentration, which are frequently stress areas in conurbations, and will also provide a third choice to prevent the tenure system polarising into the two monoliths of owner-occupation and council housing.

The wide variety of types of HA (described in Chapter 6) may be classified under three separate systems of financial arrangement as follows:

(a) "Fair rent" housing associations which offer a conventional periodic (usually weekly) tenancy and charge a fair rent registered by the rent officer at levels corresponding to the fair rents set for private landlords since the 1965 Act (fair rents were also set for local authorities for a short time under the now repealed 1972 Act). The central principle of HAs' subsidy legislation introduced by the 1974 Act is that, upon proof of a non-profit constitution, they may be registered with the Housing Corporation—so entitling them to receive Exchequer subsidies, access to loan finance from local authorities and the Corporation, and the same exemption which local authorities enjoy from the security of tenure provisions for their tenants.

HAs' subsidy system is composed of two simple components: Housing Association Grant (the capital-based grant already described in the funding section above) and a discretionary supplementary Revenue Deficit Grant if an association can show good reason why its management and maintenance and administration costs exceed its full permitted rent income. This system is immeasurably more workable and generous than the makeshift and inadequate system it replaced and which had been "scissors-and-pasted" on to original provisions in the 1967, 1969 and 1972 Acts. The 1974 Act has undeniably given associations far greater financial viability than before (although its initial high cost has already been criticised, particularly from the local authority quarter).

Nevertheless, where associations are purchasing and developing and managing older houses, the system is still framed with an emphasis on improvement of the housing stock, thus reflecting government concern with the rehabilitation drive. It remains to be seen whether HA's find this does not conflict with their other main interest of meeting personal housing need (rehousing of disadvantaged families, purchase of run-down occupied housing) for which short-term improvements of "soling and heeling" are often preferable solutions because limited resources can be spread further and families are less disrupted (39).

(b) Co-ownership housing associations. These are associations having members who enter into a joint agreement to repay (as rent) the net costs of a joint mortgage taken out on a particular housing project, most commonly for a 40 year term. The association is corporately entitled to the same mortgage interest relief as individual mortgagors are—usually option mortgage relief (see Chapters 5 and 6). Each member has a contract entitling him to share in the proportion of any capital appreciation which, subject to technical provisions, can be realised if the member leaves after, say, a five year period. Obviously, this is an advantage to members but has an offsetting disadvantage because, to cover the cost, the rent contributions by an incoming member are correspondingly higher.

Co-ownerships were originally fostered under legislation in the 1960s and the majority of those now in existence were set up then. In the late 1960s and early 1970s, the sharp rise in interest rates had the effect of reducing to negligible proportions the narrow financial advantages which co-ownership had enjoyed over conventional owner-occupation and thus increased the image of co-ownership as a second best alternative to it. This explains why the number of new associations has dwindled. Efforts are being made by the National Federation of Housing Associations and the Housing Corporation to preserve the original purpose in other forms such as " community leasehold " or " equity sharing," which are further discussed in Chapters 5, 6 and 11.

(c) Co-operative associations. Before the 1975 Act, these could be set up under financial provisions akin to those of co-ownership, the co-operative again being corporately eligible for mortgage interest relief, but with the difference that members held shares only on a par value, i.e., they were not entitled to participate in any capital appreciation, which would ultimately become the property of the association. Under the 1975 Act, the par value condition remains but co-operatives are now entitled to the far more generous grants of " fair rent " housing associations.

Possible directions of financial reform of co-ownership and co-operatives were explored by the first " Campbell " Report of 1976 (73); a second " Campbell " Report is due to make subsidy proposals. " Fair rent " housing associations have been looked at as part of the DOE's general review of housing finance and, therefore, there is speculation that the 1974 Act subsidies for them will prove to be as temporary as the 1975 Act subsidies for local authorities.

The market circumstances will make the choice for the future difficult. As recently as 1968–69, housing associations operating in the urban improvement field experienced very little difference between the cost rent and fair rents at then rates of interest, and after deducting any improvement grant to which an owner or landlord was automatically entitled (74). Instead of receiving a capital improvement grant, HA's were eligible for an exact annuity equivalent paid as an annual " contribution " and (where acquisition of existing housing was involved) an amount towards purchase costs otherwise aided by mortgage interest relief for the individual owner-occupier. Only in London was this contribution received at twice the national rate and even then the (discounted cash flow) values of HA subsidies were no more than, and some-times less than, the value of subsidies paid on comparable individual houses in the owner-occupied sector.

By contrast, current public expenditure figures now estimate that three-quarters of the capital cost of each housing association dwelling improved or built will have to be written off by grant. These figures are the national average. In some areas 90 per cent or more will be necessary. The differences which have developed in under a decade demonstrate the combined effects of an out-of-control housing market and controlled rent levels.

The disadvantages of the new capital-based grant system from the point of view of its public expenditure cost has already been described (under the funding section). There are two other disadvantages in the way these costs are accounted. Firstly, each project (house or group of houses developed at any one time) is treated in a self-contained way, so there is no built-in provision for cross-subsidisation with other, earlier projects elsewhere. Secondly, no distinction is made between the element of the cost attributable to the acquisition of the perpetual asset (the site) on behalf of the community and the building cost which is consumed by the tenant(s).

Because housing associations are expanding at a time of very high costs, the " threshold " costs facing each association in buying sites or houses and developing or improving them are extremely high. In time, the annual cost of funding the historical debt incurred would settle down, aided by interest rates which, however high, are still less than inflation and therefore effectively negative. If associations could develop some system of pooling costs, not many years would need to elapse before the movement as a whole would be self-financing with a subsidy no more generous than the 35 per cent interest relief subsidy now received by owner-occupiers with a mortgage. In the present circumstances, however, the whole burden of HA costs, including the purchase costs of perpetual assets, are " front-loaded " on to year one so requiring the 75 per cent subsidy. Needless to say, such Exchequer generosity is hedged with controls which can cramp the flexibility which associations need and the impression is given that the tenant is being inordinately subsidised.

There is clearly a strong case for alternatives to capital grants for HA's and for investigating the feasibility of a pooling system between associations so long as this preserves HAs' talent for innovation and a degree of parity with the levels of rent which local authorities charge.

Equity sharing

Both local authorities and housing associations have been investigating ways of achieving an intermediate hybrid tenure in order to combine the benefits of owning and renting. The basic principle is that, say, 50 per cent of the house is purchased and 50 per cent is proportionately rented at the normal local authority rent level, or " fair-rented " in the case of a housing association. The combined total outgoings are less than the outright purchase for the sake of the consumer who is helped on to the first rung of the home ownership ladder and require less subsidy for the sake of the Exchequer and the rate fund. Ultimately, such schemes aim to reduce the call on public capital funds provided building societies can be persuaded to act as mortgagees.

The 50/50 proportions can, of course, be varied. The owner-renter participates in the share of capital appreciation in capital value (in that sense akin to co-ownership) and retains the option to purchase the outstanding share when his means improve (in that case having the advantage of a low-start mortgage). That such a device should be necessary illustrates the extent of the gap which has now opened up between the artificially inflated costs of buying (not owning) and the artificially restrained costs of renting.

The first such scheme introduced by Birmingham Corporation for a new housing development has excited widespread interest. The resultant costs for an £11,000 house on a 30 year mortgage at 11 per cent are as follows:

	Gross monthly repayments £	Option mortgage repayments £
Ordinary Mortgage		
£11,000	105	75
' Half and Half '		
£5,500 mortgage	53	38
Half reasonable rent	14	14
	— 67	— 52

How commonly will equity-sharing schemes be adopted in the future? The Greater London Council is contemplating equity sharing on a large scale in the London Docklands, partly with a view to ensuring a wider social mix in the housing there. Some believe that such schemes could and should become the universal model for existing council housing. It has been argued in the HCT's *Evidence,* however, that the shared equity principle cannot be pursued in isolation from essential changes in the two dominant sectors of owner-occupation and council housing for several reasons (75):

(a) Essentially equity sharing schemes are designed to disguise a real rise in the cost of repayments of owner-occupied housing for the first-time buyer. Within the last decade this rise has absorbed a rising proportion of income and made joint husband and wife incomes a frequent necessity for buying. Now, in some places, only half a house is within a man's reach. Could there not be a danger that the price of half a house will eventually reach the price of a whole house as the automatic result of demand pressures?

(b) Such schemes have not yet solved the disadvantages of co-ownership schemes in that the appreciation in capital value, which is the attraction for the first buyer, raises the price to the occupier who replaces him (say after seven years) so that the scheme becomes less and less within the reach of the income group for whom it was originally designed.

(c) Although it is claimed that the Exchequer liability is less on the owned portion than on the rented portion, Exchequer liability on this portion remains and increases rather than diminishes with each change of ownership, as it does with owner-occupation of the full equity. Also, if prices or interest rates rise, Exchequer liability increases.

(d) There is no guarantee that shared equity schemes have " capital recycling " advantages for the Exchequer. Local authorities using public funds are likely to be the main mortgagees unless building societies show less reluctance to lend for shared equity schemes than they have shown for council house sales.

So far as concerns the more general arguments for the adoption of equity sharing schemes, including for existing houses, the objectives must be clearly analysed, distinguishing financial from other less definite attractions, particularly when the benefits of reforms which do not depart so radically from the existing structures could be tried more easily. Is the attraction of shared equity as a concept for council housing loosely associated with the search for solutions about the problems of " alienation " on many council estates? If so, this alienation may stem as much from other shortcomings in organisation, architecture, design or density. A change in the tenure or financial conditions will not necessarily offer a solution. Is some of the attraction the desire to pass as much of the cost and friction of management and maintenance on to the tenant in order to maximise do-it-yourself potential? If so, it may be that similar benefits might be brought about by changes in tenancy conditions, for example, a reduction in the service element in rent might be made in return for a reduction in landlord's responsibilities.

The sale of council houses

The sale of council houses is primarily seen as a political or social issue. This probably explains why central government has traditionally allowed local authorities discretion in sales (Chapter 3). However, the financial implications, which are not well documented (76, 77), are likely to come to the fore in the present economic climate. Not surprisingly, those implications mirror in miniature the issues of the whole housing finance system when analysed according to the interests of the following parties involved.

(a) *The individual purchaser.* Interviews (78) confirm that most tenants who have bought incurred a sharp rise in outgoings, often 50 per cent higher, as their mortgage repayments replaced rent, even more so when their new liability for maintenance is added in. But tenant purchasers invariably saw this as a fair bargain. They contrasted their fixed mortgage commitments with ever rising rents which they saw as " dead money "; their outgoings were now accumulating a capital asset (for trading-up, retirement, inheritance) which was a more worthwhile investment for their savings than other uses.

Surmounting the " threshold " of ownership will become even harder if house prices continue to increase faster than general inflation. This will, in turn, increase pressure for discounts on sale to be more generous than the 20 per cent below market value which the law allows. But a higher discount would be harder to justify on valuation grounds. For it is not, as is often supposed, given by virtue of the sitting tenancy since this does not lower the " investment value " as it does for the private landlord. It is given in return for the pre-emption condition obliging the purchaser to give the authority first refusal if he sells within five years. A larger discount could only be (and, in special cases, is) offered with a correspondingly longer pre-emption period, with the risk of spoiling the attraction of purchase. Larger discounts would also reduce the capital gain for authorities. In addition, they might be seen as offering tenants an unfair price advantage over normal home-buyers in similar financial circumstances and as reducing the demand for private developers' houses from ex-council tenants.

(b) *The local authority (representing community and ratepayers).* The attraction of immediate capital gains from sales is outweighed in practice because approximately four-fifths of mortgages are provided by the local authority; so there is no gain until the tenant purchaser eventually moves, maybe after several years.

The gain is received instead in annual revenue instalments because the mortgage interest and repayments which the authority receives after sale are almost certain to be more than the rent before sale. In addition, the management and maintenance liability is transferred to the purchaser. The size of the gain is a matter of calculation. It is usually larger in the case of older houses, which have a lower outstanding debt costing less to service, whereas their market value is not so much reduced by age. The gains from recently built houses are likely to be seriously offset by the ending of larger Exchequer subsidies.

The value of the initial gains must however be qualified according to projections of income and expenditure in succeeding years—most obviously if new houses have to be built at higher cost to replace those sold. Less obviously, projections may show that the *fixed* income from mortgage repayments on sold houses would have been overtaken by *rising* income from rents after, say, 5–15 years, depending on the rate of inflation (beware of glib assumptions!). A less familiar problem is what may happen when the tenant purchaser eventually moves and sells privately to a buyer who can only secure a mortgage from the authority. If by this time the value of the house has appreciated, the new mortgage will be far more than the authority's original debt on the house, so increasing the authority's own borrowing requirement in funding the new mortgage and causing competition with its other home loans.

(c) *Central government (representing the taxpayer and wider economic interests).* Do sales automatically reduce public expenditure? So far as concerns subsidies, the immediate cost to the Exchequer of mortgage relief on houses sold is likely to be less than the subsidy cost, especially on recently built houses. However, relief may exceed subsidy in the case of older houses.

Again, the pros and cons of sales can only be assessed by taking into account projections of future years so as to give a " three-dimensional " picture. For an unsold rented house, these may show a higher subsidy to start with but, because it is a fixed money sum, this declines steadily in real terms. In the case of the same house sold, Exchequer support (lower at first perhaps) will be re-injected in higher amounts each time the house is re-sold and re-mortgaged if its value appreciates.

Just as important is the public expenditure cost of loan finance because, at present, four-fifths of council houses sold are mortgaged by local authorities. Therefore, sales will continue to offer little immediate capital gain to the public sector borrowing requirement unless alternative sources are found. Building societies are unable to fill this need in any quantity, so committed are their funds to the financing of existing houses changing hands and of new houses built. This explains why many people suggest that alternative sources such as insurance or pension funds should be tapped. But, as argued in the funding section above, it is difficult to justify a further increase in funds devoted to house purchase because this may prejudice the claims of other investment purposes in the economy.

HOUSING ALLOWANCES

It is often said that housing subsidies should concentrate more on helping people and less on bricks. This section is concerned with ways in which a household's expenditure on housing is directly assisted according to *personal circumstances* rather than, as in the last section, indirectly via investment subsidies which are primarily aimed at increasing the national *housing provision* as an economic resource.

Housing allowances could be of two kinds: either an " ideal " universal system where, in future, *all* households could have their income adjusted to secure housing of some reasonable standard according to their means—and this would have to deal with all the intricate variations in proportions of income presently paid for housing; or a lesser system where, as now, deficiency payments are made on a *selective* basis only to those households whose means fall below a certain datum line.

THE PRESENT

Our present system is a means-tested one. Allowances are received under it for *income* maintenance and should be distinguished from the automatic *housing* subsidies which are received on the house regardless of personal circumstances.

The general conditions for allowances take two forms:

(a) rent rebates (and rent allowances) have been available since the 1972 Act to *all tenants* who are *in work*. (See also Chapter 3). There is no corresponding allowance system available to owner-occupiers;

(b) social security supplementary benefit payments (SB) available to *all households* irrespective of tenure (i.e., including

owner-occupiers) who are *not in work* (through unemployment, age, handicap or illness, family responsibilities, e.g.,
one parent families) and who can show that their income
would otherwise fall below subsistence level. Naturally, SB
payments replace rebates where appropriate; both are not
receivable at once. Eligibility for SB payment is more
rigorously tested, but there is correspondingly wider discretion exercised on payment. In December 1975 some
2,261,000, or 81 per cent of all 2,793,000 SB claimants,
were eligible for assistance with housing contributions (79).

Great care should be used in interpreting the figures. In the
case of supplementary benefit, it is not possible to distinguish a
specific amount for housing because entitlement is assessed
according to each household's total requirements. For instance,
the average rent assessed by the SBC as eligible for assistance in
1975–76 was £4·93 per week, but the SB *contribution* towards rent
is unspecified.

Owner-occupiers

Outright owners are only rarely eligible for SB payments
towards maintenance and repairs. Rates are eligible for separate
rebate. Mortgagors, on the other hand, are eligible for assistance
towards their interest payments (and repairs, maintenance, ground
rents and rates), but not their capital repayments. Interest is
treated as the equivalent of rent paid by tenants.

A mortgage is invariably conditional in the first place on a
regular income, and those who become eligible for SB payment
are likely to be victims of unemployment, marital breakdown or
bereavement. Naturally, therefore, the number is comparatively
small, i.e., in December 1975 391,000 households who were 6 per
cent of all mortgagors and 14 per cent of all SB claimants. The
eligible level of their housing outgoings was an average of £3·05
per week (79).

Is there a case for a more general scheme of assistance to
owners or mortgagors as of right and corresponding to rent
rebates/allowances? This would recognise that, as was not previously the case, owner-occupiers include poor households (particularly immigrant families) who have no other choice but to
buy; it would also recognise the concealed poverty of pensioners.
This question may be especially relevant for large areas of older
unimproved owner-occupied housing in, e.g., Wales and the North
West.

Doubts are sometimes expressed about the SB exclusion of
capital repayments (to prevent contributions towards the accumu-
lation of wealth) because it hits those households who rely on the

" back street " mortgages in the form of short term fixed principal loans.

It may be that these anxieties could only be catered for perfectly by some universal housing allowance scheme, given the wide range of costs which owner-occupiers face. Other remedies might be more readily available in the short term if local authorities were to promote more thoroughly the provisions already existing for grant-aided improvements and repairs, for interest-only loans, and for loans for house purchase on conditions which supplanted back street mortgages.

Local authority tenants

Council tenants are eligible for either rent rebates or SB payments. The term " rebate " is used because the rent is paid by the tenant net of rebate in one operation. Rebates in council housing were introduced universally and with the welcome of all political parties under the 1972 Act to replace a variety of rebate schemes then available in one form or another in only just less than 60 per cent of authorities (see also Chapter 3). The overall statistics are as follows:

(a) The annual value of rebates paid *direct* to LA tenants in 1975–76 for England and Wales was some £130m. affecting some 940,000 households or 20 per cent of LA tenants, an average of perhaps £2·85 per week per household (80, 81). To this total should be added some £130m. *indirect* rent rebates which were received by about 960,000 long-term SB claimants (after eight consecutive weeks claimed) and where local authorities reimburse the SB commission through block payments. The take-up of those eligible is estimated by the DOE to be of the order of 75–80 per cent. If the DOE estimate is correct—and this is sometimes challenged—and assuming that many of those who do not apply fall only just inside the eligibility limits, the scheme must therefore be reckoned a success and incidentally a reflection of sensitive housing management.

(b) Additionally, there is an unspecified amount of SB rent contributions to short-term SB claimants. The number of both short term and long term SB claimants who were LA tenants in December 1975 was some 1,297,000 or some 21 per cent of all LA tenants in GB (though some 24 per cent of LA tenants in England and Wales are in this category) and some 46 per cent of all SB claimants. The eligible level of their rent (i.e., *not* the actual contribution from SB) was an average of £5·79 per week (79).

From these figures stem several important implications about trends in the council house system in the present and as it might be after reform of housing finance. Firstly, as many as 44 per cent of LA tenants in England and Wales are in receipt of some form of income maintenance towards their housing expenditure. This demonstrates a concentration of poor families in council housing (" Jaguar-owning " tenants notwithstanding). This concentration is likely to increase as council housing rehouses private tenants via the normal process or takes over, through municipalisation purchases, the private rented sector which has so far had the highest concentrations of the poorest households. There are, therefore, strong arguments for preserving a spread of income groups within council housing in order to prevent a " welfare housing " concentration from developing in this country. In that case should the richest tenants be persuaded to move out after all?

Secondly, the raising of council house rents, however imperative, would not produce a straightforward saving. In financial terms it is reckoned that for the first £1 raised, central and local government would repay 25p in rebate, more for the second £1. In social terms, it might be feared that, if the numbers of rebated tenants rose beyond a certain proportion, this might increase the social segregation and indignity of council house tenants, generally thought of as a group in receipt of state charity. This kind of anxiety was revealed when the (repealed) 1972 Act was being put into effect because, according to its provisions, personal circumstances were to be excluded from the factors to be taken into account in assessing rent levels. Even so, a number of authorities, including e.g., Birmingham, secured reductions in fair rents on grounds that the rents set were too high a proportion of the average income of their districts.

Thirdly, because local authorities charge their tenants rents which are net of rebates, the rental income of housing authorities is frequently understated: unrebated rents contribute on average some 53 per cent of their housing expenditure whereas rebated rents reduce this proportion to 43 per cent, the difference being income maintenance and not housing subsidy. Unless the appropriate figure is used, the (undoubted) decline in the contribution which tenants make towards expenditure is exaggerated because it is often contrasted with the contribution of between 67 and 70 per cent made in the five years preceding the 1972 Act when rent rebates were introduced universally. In parallel, the average contribution net of subsidy which mortgagors have paid towards their interest repayments has also fallen (from some 74 per cent to some 62 per cent over the same period). The problem stems from the more general problems of the accelerated rises in interest rates in both sectors. At present, because subsidies are paid as a fixed proportion of interest payments, the Exchequer has been automatically locked in to an obligation to cushion both council tenants and owner-occupiers from the unpalatable facts of inflation, as has not been the case with transport and fuel costs.

Fourthly, the financial cost of rent rebates is shared between central and local government on a 75/25 basis (although the 25 per cent locally borne is also substantially reduced after rate support grant). On the grounds that rent rebates provide for income maintenance, many bodies, including HCT and the Layfield Committee, have recommended that central government should take full responsibility for them. For an indefinite period this principle has been accepted in the case of rent allowances paid by the local authorities to tenants of private landlords and housing associations.

Certain wider implications are raised by rent rebates. For instance, means-tested benefits are now so numerous (some 40 odd) that it has frequently been argued that rent rebates should be incorporated with other means-tested benefits—failing other more fundamental " tax credit " reforms.

Another perhaps more sinister issue might be raised in the context of the whole inner city problem of regional planning and employment. Are rent rebates in danger of creating an urban " poverty trap " ? For instance, housing authorities in London stress areas are obliged to house the poorest households (many of them pensioners and therefore not economically active) on land where purchase and development costs produce the most expensive housing. Although the unrebated rents do to some extent reflect these high values, the net rent revenue is correspondingly offset by rebates. To what extent therefore can it be said that the lowering of housing costs exacerbates housing problems? Or does this raise questions as to whether urban planning costs should be subvented in other ways by government or employers?

Private tenants

The tenants of private landlords are eligible for either rent allowances or SB payments if not in work. In their case, the tenant pays the full rent to his landlord and the claim for allowances is a private matter between the individual and the town hall, or in the case of SB payments, the local DHSS office.

Statistics for rent allowances to tenants of private landlords and of housing associations are unfortunately combined and therefore their value and success are not known precisely (81, 82).

(a) The annual cost of rent allowances and *some* SB payments to these two sectors together in 1975–76 was some £48m nationally for some 430,000 households (affecting one-sixth of private tenants) or an average of some £2·15p per household per week (79). It is true that the number of tenants eligible is reduced by the high proportion in the private sector whose rents are so low (controlled tenancies) or whose incomes are too high (in London mansion blocks). Nevertheless, the allowance take-up of those eligible is known to be very low at an estimated 30–35 per cent for private tenants and housing association tenants combined, and is a cause for concern because it remains low in spite of government publicity to make rent allowances more generally known. As the take-up rate is likely to be more successful in housing associations on account of more intensive housing management, the actual take-up rate for private tenants is even lower than the figures suggest, particularly in the case of furnished tenants. A similarly low take-up rate was previously recorded in Birmingham where the City had introduced its own private tenant rent allowance scheme before a universal scheme became available under the 1972 Act.

(b) More precise but still incomplete figures show that, in April 1975, 150,000 private unfurnished tenants and 11,000 private furnished tenants were receiving an average rent allowance of £2·41 and £2·80 per week respectively (80). SB claimants who were other than LA tenants numbered 573,000 in December 1975, or some 21 per cent of all SB claimants. The eligible level of their rent was an average of £4·26 per week (79).

The low take-up rates for rent allowances are yet another intractable aspect of the private rented sector, where so many problems, including bad housing conditions and poverty, are still concentrated. Such problems are likely to intensify if no positive measures by both central and local government are undertaken to ensure that the sector does not drift into a lingering demise.

Housing associations

It will be clear from the statistics just quoted that the tenants of housing associations are, generally speaking, treated on the same terms as private tenants. However, most of the larger housing associations have made special arrangements with local authorities in their areas for tenants to pay a net rebated rent and for the association to receive the allowances in bulk from the local authority on behalf of tenants. Subject to the proviso that some tenants still prefer the privacy of the allowance system and therefore that the figures are not completely accurate, it is fair to say that the proportions of tenants of " fair rent " housing associations in receipt of allowances are comparable to those of council tenants. Numbers will be swollen on the one hand by the high proportion of disadvantaged or pensioner households rehoused by associations in stress areas, and reduced on the other by the high proportion of (often elderly) sitting tenants in houses purchased subject to low controlled rents.

THE FUTURE

The logic of subsidising housing by means of housing allowances on a universal principle is an attractive one (83). They might resolve, it is felt, many of the unsatisfactory features of means-tested rent rebates and allowances, particularly the low take-up among private tenants, and replace the haphazard jungle of existing housing subsidies. Others suggest that an improved variant would incorporate a housing component into a universal tax credit system which would replace as many as possible of the 40 odd means-tested benefits. It would therefore form part of some more comprehensive programme of equitable income distribution at the same time as eliminating administrative complexities and, incidentally, the poverty trap (where, for a certain range of low incomes, pay rises are outweighed by loss of benefits).

When the ideas are analysed, it becomes clear why, in spite of the strong arguments for them to be considered as part of the long term strategy of achieving more consistency in the housing system (if political parties can agree), there are very considerable difficulties. Should, for instance, allowances be fully universal or should they replace existing social security schemes for certain (which?) groups? Should allowances be paid at a flat rate or be cost-related?

If allowances were to work side by side with the existing housing subsidy system, such is the range of housing costs faced by individuals that a " second tier " of supplementary means-tested allowances would still be needed. If, on the other hand, allowances were to replace the existing system, they would have to be extremely generous to cover the wide range of housing costs which individual households have, and therefore a correspondingly elaborate administrative mechanism would be needed to tax back the excess, as well as a method of ensuring that allowances were actually used for housing purposes.

It is arguable, therefore, that housing allowances would only be likely to succeed if more consistency existed within the housing system by, for instance, some more common denominator of housing costs being established according to value of housing occupied. Now it may be that such a development would be necessary in any case as part of the long term review of housing finance to overcome its other financial and economic distortions. This might be achieved if, as referred to earlier, a way of offsetting the Exchequer's inexorably rising bill in investment subsidies was established through, for instance, contributions from housing consumption, e.g., from value-related rents charged by local authorities and something akin to Schedule A taxation for owner-occupiers.

The ways suggested for financing universal housing allowances point in the same direction as the arguments for achieving consistency. Funds for financing an allowance scheme would have to come from: savings from supplementary benefit housing payments and rent rebates and allowances; from the taxation of income in kind from home ownership and from capital gains taxation to cover house value appreciation; from withdrawal of rent subsidies on public housing necessitating public sector rents being based on a nationally pooled basis; that is from the taxation of the housing system itself.

In other words, a scheme of universal housing allowances would in any case have to await changes elsewhere in the housing system. Similar, though not identical, changes are in the HCT's opinion necessary in their own right to overcome irregularities and inefficiencies in the housing system considered strictly from a resource point of view and can and should proceed independently —quite apart from the complications arising when personal circumstances are taken into account. Income distribution reform should be seen as a possible complement to, rather than an essential part of, such changes.

APPENDIX

Overall public and private expenditure on housing

The treatment of public expenditure (PE) has been relegated to an appendix because, in spite of the publicity with which its figures have been criticised, especially during 1975 and 1976, the form in which PE figures are presented makes them an inappropriate tool for analysing housing finance issues. These issues have therefore already been treated separately under each sector.

Comprehensive sets of figures which could be used without these qualifications are not available to form the basis of some strategic housing finance planning. As they are badly needed in both the public and private sectors, it is worth outlining the deficiencies of the present PE figures in order to aid the search for appropriate tools in the future (84).

Firstly, PE figures are published by the Treasury on a " cash flow " basis for the sake of its own (quite legitimate) convenience. As a result, the year's new capital commitments (corresponding to balance sheet items) as well as current expenditure (corresponding to income and expenditure account items) are added together (thus producing double counting) as would never be the case under normal accounting practice used by a statutory authority or commercial company. From an economic point of view, transfer payments, i.e., those sums which are simply the redistribution of revenue collected passing in and out of the public purse (as subsidies are) and without any intermediate economic process, are lumped together with direct expenditure which compete for real resources (labour, materials, capital) by creating goods (e.g., houses) or services (e.g., housing administration).

Using the PE totals as they are published, it is often said (quite correctly) that PE on housing now accounts for as much as 5 per cent of Gross Domestic Product as against half that figure a decade ago. Unfortunately, such ratios are of very limited value, except in a rough and ready way, and distract attention from very serious fundamental imbalances within housing finance. It would signify little if, by analogy, the total of one's personal cheques made out in the course of a year were expressed as a proportion of annual income. It would be equally meaningless if the "cash flow" sum totals of housing expenditure in the private sector—which, needless to say, would show a growth pattern very similar to the public sector's—were also expressed as a proportion of GDP.

Unfortunately, when there is a budgetary deficit, all government expenditure without distinction between capital and current or between direct and transfer, is somewhat crudely tarred with the same brush because it increases the public sector's borrowing requirement. Obviously, other vitally important issues in the context of financial and social policy, such as the effectiveness of the "social wage" or the burden of taxation, or the desirability of cushioning consumers' housing payments from the full effects of inflation, are still relevant. In the context of the economic policy of housing, however, unless careful distinction is made, cuts and curbs for the sake of the biggest immediate cash economies tend to fall on building programmes and house purchase loans rather than on subsidies—as was the case with the cuts of July 1976.

Secondly, it is not generally realised that, according to the distinction in the PE White Papers themselves, only between a fifth and a quarter of increases in the overall total between 1974 and 1975 was due to "policy" changes, the lion's share being due to "other" economic changes, notably inflation of course. Somewhat ironically indeed, these "other" increases arose particularly from subsidy commitments undertaken by a previous (Conservative) administration which were carried forward to a succeeding (Labour) administration and would almost certainly have been incurred whichever party had been in power.

Thirdly, the issues are complicated by the inclusion within the PE housing totals (gross) of a proportion, varying between 8 and

20 per cent, attributable to expenditure from the Exchequer on private housing—on improvement grants, option mortgage relief and loans for house purchase.

Fourthly, by tradition only cash expended and not revenue foregone in the form of tax allowances is included. The implication so far as housing is concerned is that interest relief on mortgage interest which is received by owner-occupiers (total some £1,100m in the year 1976–77) is not included unless it is actually paid out in cash in the form of option mortgage relief (value £100m).

Recently a belief has grown that a breakdown of the national PE figures could provide a tool for housing finance on a regional or local basis; we should be able to have local housing policies and programmes (HPP's) akin to the TPP's used in transportation policy. On this basis, it is argued, local authorities would be free to decide their own priorities within a block allocation. Unfortunately, without a number of additional measures, such freedom could be an instrument of instability because it assumes that all spending is roughly interchangeable on a purely *cash* basis, e.g., that there is no economic difference as between £1m spent on, say, municipalisation or on new building or improvement, whereas the bulk of the first simply finances existing houses and the second and the third create more housing and make a real demand on employment and materials, although again to differing extents.

When all these reservations are expressed, the fact remains that as a nation we are seriously lacking in strategic housing finance planning. Although there is no precise indication of how this can be established, it has been one of the major preoccupations of the DOE's housing finance review. It might be best fulfilled by an annual national Housing Policy Statement. Some possible principles outlined by the late Mr. Crosland in his policy speech quoted earlier, describing the objectives of the review, might be distilled as follows:

   (a) Such planning must apply to *all* housing especially the two principal tenures;
   (b) It must avoid over-emphasis on the *margin* of housing, the tip of the iceberg, such as new building, first-time buyers, etc., and be equally concerned with the care, consumption and use of the *existing* stock and the demands made by households already housed;
   (c) Ways of measuring the effectiveness of existing policy ought to be to hand.

A simple beginning with the last might be attempted by expressing the trends of national housing finance in ratio form as a corporation or company does when analysing its productivity or the optimum use of its capital funds. In particular, this would need to chart: firstly, the trends in subsidies and investment in both the principal sectors; secondly, the growth in outstanding loan debt in relation to assets (growth of stock or of households in that tenure). Both of these trends have already been described earlier in the sections on spending and on funding respectively; so have the features which emerge:

(a) ever-increasing subsidies but falling investment in *both* main sectors;

(b) outstanding loan liabilities growing very much faster than assets in the owner-occupied sector.

Other measures of improving our national data base would come in their turn, such as ways of measuring the value of improvement output in the owner-occupied sector (which we lack at present) and ways of measuring the offsetting costs of changes in rent levels, interest relief, or equity (part or whole) sales of houses.

ABBREVIATIONS

ACC, AMA	Association of County Councils, of Metropolitan Authorities
BS, BSA	Building Society, Building Societies Association
CIPFA	Chartered Institute of Public Finance and Accountancy
CSO	Central Statistical Office
CURS	Centre for Urban and Regional Studies, University of Birmingham
HCT	Housing Centre Trust
H & C Stats	DOE Housing and Construction Statistics, Quarterly
HMSO	Her Majesty's Stationery Office
IFS	Institute for Fiscal Studies
MoHLG	Ministry of Housing & Local Government (before 1970)
NBPI	National Board of Prices and Incomes
NEDO	National Economic Development Office
WA	Written Answer in Parliamentary Debates (*Hansard*)

General note

The chapter refers constantly to HCT's Evidence to the DOE's Review, *Housing Finance Review*, published November 1975 and obtainable from the HCT, price £1. For a fuller discussion of evidence submitted by other bodies to the DOE's *Housing Finance Review* see M. C. Baker, *Housing Review*, May–June 1976 and B. Kilroy, *Housing Review*, January–February 1977.

REFERENCES

(Many of these are not obtainable through an ordinary bookshop but through HCT)

1. *Housing Review*, September–October 1975.
2. *Social Trends,* 1973 (Table 67) and 1975 (Table 6.3), CSO.
3. *Local Government Trends,* Table 6.5, CIPFA, 1975.
4. *National Income and Expenditure*, 1965–75, CSO.
5. *H & C Stats*, Vol. 18, Table XXI.
6. The plea that stability is as important as volume of output in *Evidence to the DOE's Housing Finance Review,* NHBC, 1976.
7. E. F. Cantle, " Parker Morris Dwellings Common Sense Standards ", *Housing*, January 1977.
8. *The Decision to Build* (Chaps. 2 and 3), HMSO, 1970.
9. A. P. Robson, *Essential Accounting for Managers* (Chap. 3), Cassell, 1966.
10. *Circular 65/69,* Appendix B, MoHLG.
11. R. Harrington, " Helping the Would-be Owner-Occupier ", *Housing Review*, September–October 1974.
12. D. Webster, " What Has Really Happened to Public Expenditure on Housing?" *Housing Review*, November–December 1975.
13. *Housing Revenue Account Statistics*, CIPFA, annually.
14. *Rate Support Grant* (Seventh Period), Table 13, ACC, AMA, etc., 1976.
15. A. E. W. Laugherne, " Assessing the Gains from Endowment Loans ", *B.S. Gazette*, October 1971.
16. V. A. Karn, *Priorities for L.A. Mortgage Lending,* CURS, 1976.
17. P. Williams, *The Role of Financial Institutions and Estate Agents in the Private Housing Market,* CURS, 1976.
18. S. Clark, *Roof,* October 1976.
19. *Facts & Figures 8,* BSA, October 1976.
20. *20 Per Cent Sample of LA Mortgages,* DOE, 1976.
21. *Occ. Bulletin 124,* Nationwide BS, 1974.
22. *Voice of Anglia 15,* Anglia BS, 1976.
23. A. A. Nevitt, *Housing, Taxation and Subsidies* (p. 8), Nelson, 1966.
24. *Background,* Bristol & West BS Quarterly Bulletins.
25. *Facts & Figures 7,* BSA, July 1976.
26. *Economic Trends,* CSO (monthly).
27. *Finance for Investment* (Chap. 6), NEDO, 1975.
28. *Bank of England Quarterly Bulletin,* Table G.
29. *Local Government Trends* (Table 3.12), CIPFA, 1975.
30. *H & C Stats,* Table 43.
31. *Occ. Bulletin 134* (p. 5), Nationwide BS, 1976.
32. *Return of Outstanding Loan Debt,* CIPFA (annually).

33. *Housing Review Panel Report,* L. Boro' of Camden, 1976 (Appendix XI on the Housing Revenue Account by A. A. Nevitt).

34. *Bank Charges* (para. 92), NBPI, Cmnd. 3292 (1967).

35. M. Craig, *The Sterling Money Markets* (Chap. 5), Gower, 1976.

36. " Cuts Destroy London's Housing Plan ", *Roof,* October 1975.

37. *Housing Associations* (Chap. 6) (" Cohen Report "), HMSO, 1976.

38. Cmnd. 6393.

39. B. Kilroy, "Housing Association Finance ", *Housing Finance,* IFS, 1975.

40. *Hansard,* WA, 3 March 1976.

41. *Hansard,* WA, 20 October 1976.

42. op. cit., 33, Table 1.

43. D. C. Stafford, *National Westminster Bank Review,* November 1976.

44. J. Odling-Smee, " The Impact of the Fiscal System on Different Tenures ", *Housing Finance,* IFS, 1975.

45. *Evidence to DOE Housing Finance Review,* BSA, 1976.

46. *H & C Stats,* Vol. 15, Table XIII.

47. op. cit., 25, Tables C and D.

48. " Effect of Taxes and Benefits on Household Income ", *Economic Trends,* CSO, December 1976.

49. *H & C Stats,* Vol. 16, Table XXX.

50. *Survey of Attitudes Towards Current and Alternative Housing Policies,* NEDO, 1976.

51. *London Weighting* (paras. 88–89, 155), Pay Board, Cmnd. 5660, HMSO, 1974.

52. A. Murie, P. Niner, C. Watson, *Housing Policy and the Housing System,* Allen & Unwin, 1976.

53. op. cit., 31, Table 5.

54. *Five Per Cent Sample of BS Mortgages* (Table 4), CSO, 1975.

55. op. cit., 31, Table 4.

56. *H & C Stats,* Vol. 17, Table 39.

57. op. cit., 31, Table 1.

58. op. cit., 31, Table 2.

59. op. cit., 19, Table 5.

60. op. cit., 54, p. 6.

61. *Chains of Sales in Private Housing,* DOE/Housing Research Foundation, 1973 (also DOE press release, 9 July 1973).

62. D. C. Stafford, *Housing Review,* November–December 1976.

63. For a discussion of evidence to the DOE housing finance review see M. C. Baker, *Housing Review,* May–June 1976, and B. Kilroy, *Housing Review,* January–February 1977.

64. *Hansard,* WA, 27 October 1976.

65. *Hansard,* WA, 30 March 1976.

66. *Hansard,* WA, 30 July 1976.

67. N. Scott, MP, *Home Run,* Tory Reform Group, 1975.

68. A. A. Nevitt, *Fair Deal for Householders,* Fabian Society, 1972.

69. *Tomes Ltd.* v. *Landau and Others,* A.C. 9 July 1970.

70. *Policy for Housing,* British Property Federation, 1975.

71. *Royal Commission on the Taxation of Profits and Income* (Chap. 28), Cmnd. 9474, HMSO, 1955.

72. See also Finance Bill Committee, *Hansard,* 21 June 1960, 6 May 1963, 16 May 1963.

73. *Final Report of the Working Party on Housing Co-operatives,* HMSO, 1975.

74. op. cit., 37, para. 6.33.

75. S. Weir and B. Kilroy, " Equity-Sharing in Cheshunt," *Roof,* November 1976.

76. Sir Frank Griffin, *Selling More Council Houses,* Conservative Political Centre, 1971.

77. B. Kilroy, *Roof,* May 1977.

78. A. Murie, *The Sale of Council Houses* (Chap. 6), CURS, 1975.

79. *Supplementary Benefits Commission Annual Report* (Chap. 7), 1975 Cmnd 6615, HMSO.

80. *Hansard,* WA, 16 November 1976.

81. *H & C Stats,* Vol. 16, Table XXVII.

82. *Hansard,* WA, 17 June 1976, 6 August 1976.

83. " Housing Allowances for All?" S. Lansley, *Roof,* January 1976.

84. The issues have since been examined and some remedies proposed by the House of Commons in its " Ninth Report from the Expenditure Committee " HC 466, July 1977, HMSO.

CHAPTER 9

Planning and Land

Planning

Town and country planning as it affects housing

The aim of town and country planning has been described as " so to plan the use of all land as to meet the essential economic and social needs of the population in the most efficient manner possible, and thus to give to all the best possible environment in which to live and work and have their being " (R. L. Reiss). The national consciousness of the importance of town and country planning is, however, about a generation behind the national sense of responsibility for the good housing of the population.

The inter-war planning legislation was in effect little more than an extension of nineteenth century public health and housing controls. It was preoccupied with the need to avoid overcrowding and congestion of building which would be a danger to health, and with designing roads which avoided the main traffic hazards. Controls over open land, ripe for development, were extended by the Town and Country Planning Act 1932, which empowered local planning authorities to make planning schemes to cover all land, whether built up or not, and to control development which took place before such schemes became operative through Interim Development Orders. The Act was permissive only, and there was no statutory obligation for local authorities to plan. Control of housing development was often carried out through restrictions on density, as was exemplified by the many suburban developments which took place at a standard of 12 or fewer houses to the acre. The Restriction of Ribbon Development Act 1935 was designed to prevent houses being built along arterial roads carrying traffic. Efforts were made to control the unplanned sprawl of cities by the preservation of a green belt of open land around the built-up urban area, and also to control sporadic building which was wasteful of agricultural land and costly in the provision of services—water, gas, electricity, etc.

One of the main aims of the architects of planning machinery since the last war has been to devise a system which would create a total environment for good living. The Barlow Commission on the Distribution of the Industrial Population, in addition to its recommendations which led eventually to the

257

policy for new town development, advocated the planning of physical environment on a national scale in 1940 (see bibliography Chapter 1). New development and redevelopment of all land came under interim development control before the end of the war under the Town and Country Planning (Interim Development) Act 1943. The Town and Country Planning Act 1944, which dealt primarily with land acquisition, gave powers of acquiring land compulsorily (and in certain cases speedily) for a variety of purposes in areas of extensive war damage (blitzed areas) and also areas of bad layout and obsolete development (blighted areas) and their associated overspill areas. It has been described as introducing a new concept of positive town planning by empowering local planning authorities to undertake (subject to certain restrictions) the actual development of their own areas. It also introduced the " 1939 standard " for compensation payable, but this was abolished, by 1947, in favour of existing use value.

The Town and Country Planning Act 1947—an important landmark in planning legislation—made far-reaching changes affecting land ownership and development, and replaced the former system of planning through rigid schemes by a new one of control through flexible plans. It prohibited the carrying out of any kind of development without the consent of the local planning authority. It also introduced a new and much more fundamental approach to the problem of dealing with compensation for people adversely affected by planning, and the collection of betterment value from landowners who benefited from the action of the community as represented by local planning authorities. The new principle in effect removed from the landowner his right to develop or change the use of his land, and acquired these " development rights " for the state (7).

A sum of £300 million was to be used to compensate claimants for the loss of development rights; though land itself was not nationalised, development value in land was.

The financial provisions of the 1947 Act were repealed six years later in 1953, when the charges on development were abolished. It was held that this charge represented a 100 per cent tax on development and, as such, was inhibiting development from being carried out, and preventing land being put on the market. Moreover, payments from the £300 million fund, on which claims could be made for compensation for loss of development value, were considered to be inflationary. There were further amendments to town planning legislation dealing with compensation for land purchased compulsorily and other matters, and in 1962 a consolidated Town and Country Planning Act was passed which remained the principal planning Act for nearly a decade, although it too was amended several times, and quite substantially by the 1968 Act.

Prior to the Town and Country Planning Act 1947, and in some senses of well-nigh equal importance to post-war planned development in Britain, was the New Towns Act 1946. This empowered the Minister of Town and Country Planning to set up New Town Development Corporations with powers and finance to build new self-contained towns, primarily to accommodate population, industry and commerce decentralised from congested urban centres. The Town Development Act 1952 followed a few years later to encourage the expansion of existing small communities, again by the decentralisation of population and industry. It enabled the local authorities of large cities and conurbations to develop major new housing areas in collaboration with the smaller receiving authorities outside their areas. The cost of housing the population moving to such expanding towns was assisted by special subsidies to which the exporting authorities contributed. The legislation under which these new and expanded towns are developed and the achievements which have resulted, and which continue to contribute to housing progress, are dealt with in the special chapter on the subject, Chapter 4.

The Town and Country Planning Act 1968 was preceded by the report of the Minister's Planning and Advisory Group (PAG) (1) and a White Paper, *Town and Country Planning* (Cmnd. 3333, 1967), which assessed the major defects of the existing development plan system as being that it had become overloaded and procedures were slow and cumbersome, that there was inadequate participation by the citizen whose interests were not sufficiently regarded, and that it acted as a negative control preventing undesirable development, but did not stimulate the creation of a good environment. The new Act made provisions for more direct public involvement in the planning process, for the speeding up of procedures, and for the progressive introduction of a new type of " development " plan comprising a structure plan and a series of local plans; the first to deal with broad long-term strategy and the major policies for the whole of an area, and the second, which would conform to the general policies of the structure plan, to consist of a written statement with diagrams, illustrations and descriptive matter. A local plan is designed to give local residents an understanding of how it is proposed that their area should be developed, to explain to property owners how their interests might be affected, and to show developers what opportunities are being provided.

The authorities must publicise the structure and local plans and seek involvement of the public in a positive way. The report of another government advisory committee, the Skeffington

committee, *People and Planning* (1969), made recommendations
as to how this could be done to secure the participation of the
public at the formative stage in the making of development plans
for their area. These recommendations were a guide rather than
a rule book. They included suggestions for publicity at each stage
of the preparation of structure and local plans, the proposal
that a community development officer should be appointed to
involve people who do not join organisations, the suggestion
that local people, including students, should be recruited to help
with survey work, and general recommendations to improve
knowledge about planning (2).

The 1968 Act's major positive characteristic was that it
obliged local authorities to state their policies explicitly in
structure plans and to give these policies quasi-statutory status;
and its built-in flexibility allowed for frequent reviews and adaptations. Most important, perhaps, was the Act's insistence on full
public involvement in the planning process, as mentioned above,
which led to its being hailed as " a legislative framework of
planning designed to bring about a greater degree of citizen
participation " (Cullingworth, 1972).

One of the drawbacks of the Act was that the approach to the
new-style development was still predominantly physical; although
economic aspects were given greater emphasis, the Act made no
mention of social considerations. In an attempt to remedy this
defect, the Department of the Environment produced *The Social
Content of Development Plans* (1971) as supplementary advice
to the Development Plan Manual (*Development Plans. A
Manual on Form and Content* (London. HMSO, 1970)). Even so,
it is considered that we are still unlikely to achieve structure and
local plans, which, according to Mel Webster in *Explorations into
Urban Structure* (Philadelphia University Press, 1964), would
depict the city as a social process operating in space.

Also, in practice, structure planning has moved away from the
flexible essential planning policy statements intended by the
Planning and Advisory Group, referred to earlier, into an over-
complex statutory planning procedure which makes frequent
up-dating of structure plans difficult.

The 1968 Act and other legislation relating to planning were
consolidated in the Town and Country Planning Act 1971, which
contains the main body of planning law, and is the principal Act.
Subsequent legislation deals mainly with amenities, conservation
areas and land, which is considered later in this chapter. Its
Scottish equivalent, the Town and Country Planning (Scotland)
Act 1972, is in force except for provisions relating to structure
planning introduced after local government reorganisation.

Planning is concerned with conservation, rehabilitation and redevelopment, traffic and road arrangements, and commercial and industrial expansion. Planning systems seek to restrain urban sprawl and protect the countryside, to introduce more open space into living areas and promote new land uses, to set out and organise a highway pattern suited to a motorised society, and to distribute industry sensibly and economically, while at the same time providing pleasant living conditions embracing the whole complex of a civilised environment—services, recreation, open space, education and social facilities, and control of noise and pollution.

As mentioned in Chapter 2, the Department of the Environment was established in 1970 to combine the functions and services of housing, planning and transport departments in the government under one Secretary of State. After six years, however, during which the Department was developing a working integration of the three sectors to produce government policy which considered the environment as an entity rather than the sum of several isolated parts, cabinet changes in 1976 radically altered its structure. Transport policy was in future to be handled by a separate Ministry of Transport, and responsibility for planning, formerly with a planning minister, for development control and for land was given to the Minister formerly responsible for housing and construction only.

Planning procedures

The slowness of the planning application system, which produces planning blight and its attendant evils, was highlighted in the DOE's estimate, included in the Dobry report, *Review of the development control system. Final report* (HMSO, 1975), that during the three months before the publication of the report not much more than 50 per cent of applications in England were decided within the statutory limit of two months. The report's most striking recommendation concerned the simple, minor or uncontroversial planning applications received by local authorities. It recommended that these should be automatically approved after 42 days, provided that they had not been formally refused or transferred to a special category for controversial applications. Mr. George Dobry, QC, who chaired the committee which reviewed the planning system, said that the two-tier system for applications, in " minor " and " major " categories, would enable planning authorities, many of whom were desperately short staffed, to concentrate on the more important issues.

The committee's proposals had to be considered, however, in the light of the Community Land Act, discussed below, and its attempt to give a more positive character to public control over development, and most of the recommendations were subsequently rejected by the government. For instance, the suggestion that planning applications should be divided into two categories, each having a different set of time limits and criteria for approval, was rejected as impracticable. Plans did not fall neatly into the two classes and there was a danger of hasty and ill-considered judgments in order to meet strict time limits. The proposed general planning aid scheme was dismissed as being too costly to set up and operate, despite increased charges for planning considerations, and plans for reform of the system of planning appeal were also rejected. With regard to the committee's proposal for the extension of the planning permission requirements to the demolition of buildings as well as to their construction, the Secretary of State for the Environment (in 1975) felt that this would substantially delay the process of redevelopment, and that the problem often caused by demolition would largely be overcome by the provisions of the Community Land Act which would remove much of the incentive of developers to pull down buildings merely as a tactic to pressurise councils to give them permission to develop.

In March 1976, however, the House of Commons Expenditure Committee decided to set up an enquiry into planning procedures, their delays and the growing dissatisfaction with their operation. Although there is wide recognition that the planning procedure system, and the confusion since local government reorganisation, are unsatisfactory, it is also mooted that such an enquiry can discover nothing more than was revealed by the Dobry report. The specific terms of the enquiry are " to examine, in the light of recent legislation and reports, the system of land use planning and development control in England and Wales in relation to planning applications, appeal procedures and determination, with a view to identifying reasons for delays and the resource costs that such delays create ".

Conservation of amenities

Special legislation is concerned with the conservation of amenities in town and country. In 1967, the Civic Amenities Act gave statutory recognition for the first time to the fact that whole areas and not only individual buildings could be of special interest. In relation to this Act, local authorities are increasingly consulting with the public generally and civic societies in particular about planning applications before development control decisions are made. The interim report of the Dobry committee in 1975 reaffirmed this point.

The Town and Country Planning Act 1971 also required every planning authority from time to time to determine which parts of their area are areas of special architectural or historic interest, the character of which it is desirable to preserve or enhance, and to designate such areas as conservation areas. The Town and Country Planning (Amendment) Act 1972 strengthened powers to protect conservation areas by allowing local authorities (subject to the approval of the Secretary of State) to extend to unlisted buildings within conservation areas the same powers that already exist to control demolition of listed buildings. The same Act makes finance available from the Historic Buildings Council for schemes to enhance the character and appearance of conservation areas (i.e. not just buildings) which in the opinion of the Historic Buildings Council are outstanding.

The Town and Country Amenities Act 1974 made further provision for the control of development within conservation areas, including the demolition of buildings; the protection of trees and general enhancement of such areas; and the manner of serving urgent works for the preservation of unoccupied buildings as an amendment to powers under the 1971 Act. A further clause provided grant-aiding for the upkeep of a garden or other land " which appears to the Secretary of State to be of outstanding historic interest but which is not contiguous or adjacent to a building which appears to him to be of outstanding historic or architectural interest ".

The Countryside Act 1968 contained new powers to provide country parks, acquire and develop portions of land in or near certain commons, provide picnic and camping sites in the countryside, undertake tree planting, appoint wardens in countryside parks and picnic sites, and provide for wider access by the public. The powers of the National Parks Commission were extended by the Act, and the Commission was renamed the Countryside Commission (Committee for Wales). The need for close co-operation between authorities in city and urban areas and those in rural areas was stressed and this was provided for in both planning and financial matters. DOE Circular 4/76 and Welsh Office Circular 7/76 set out the government's policy for national parks, in response to the Sandford report (*Report of the National Park Policies Review Committee* (HMSO, 1974)). The government agreed with the report that in any conflict between the two purposes of the national parks—the preservation or enhancement of natural beauty and the promotion of public enjoyment—the first must be given priority. The circulars also deal with control of development in national parks, landscape, roads and traffic, and, in probably the most controversial section, reject the Sandford recommendation that touring caravan sites should be located outside or on the periphery of the national parks; although the policy of providing caravan sites inside the parks is subject to the overriding consideration that the capacity of the park must be able to absorb the increased traffic without environmental degradation.

Further measures for protection and improvement of the environment are contained in the Control of Pollution Act 1974, which in its six parts covers waste on land, pollution of water, noise, pollution of the atmosphere, supplementary provisions and miscellaneous. Circular 10/73, *Planning and Noise*, covered both the motor car and aircraft as a noise nuisance (3,4,5,6).

Since town and country planning is concerned with the total environment, it overflows into such matters as economic planning, and, for example, certain parts of the Industrial Development Act might be regarded within the town planning legislative code. The New Towns Act and the Town Development Act have already been mentioned—they are so closely associated with the " creation of a good environment " that they should certainly be included as a part of the legal framework of town and country planning. The Economic Planning Councils, which have been established in the regions and in Scotland and Wales, have published studies which must influence the shaping of physical environment. The interim report on the *Development of the strategic plan for the South-east*, initiated late in 1974 to update the original 1970 strategic plan, and published by the Department of the Environment in March 1976, for instance, notes the dramatic changes which have occurred both in Britain and the world since 1970, including the general decline in prosperity and world trade and the increased costs for energy and natural resources, all of which affect planning and the provision of housing. In the South-east particularly, basic assumptions in the initial plan have not proved to be correct. The substantial population growth predicted has turned out to be a nominal decline; the decline of London's population, which was expected to stabilise, has continued; and the general economic growth which was counted on has been sharply curtailed. Due to the difficulty in knowing what the future holds either economically or socially, the report advises that local authorities concentrate on rehabilitating areas which have been declining. Redevelopment requires areas of land which are not currently available without incurring large capital costs, and it might well prove misdirected in the future. The report also stresses the need for an " explicit regional dimension in resource allocation ".

Our Guide, however, is a Guide to Housing, and sources of further information on town and country planning issues as a whole are listed in the bibliography. This includes *The New*

Citizen's Guide to Town and Country Planning, published in 1974, which gives a concise and lucid account of the principles and practice of planning in Britain for the layman, in the same way as our Guide aims to give a clear and comprehensive background to the housing scene (7, 8, 9).

Not only would it be impossible to attempt the improvement of housing conditions without taking into account town and country planning considerations, but planning also imposes restraints on the individual citizen who may want to make physical changes to his own property. Before any such changes can be made, the permission of the local planning authority must be obtained. The safest course is to assume that permission is needed if it is proposed to make any material change of use in land or property, or to carry out any building or engineering works, or to alter materially the external appearance of a building. When in doubt as to what needs permission and what is exempt under town and country planning legislation, the guidance of the local authority should always be sought, as it is an offence to carry out most developments without permission and enforcement action can be taken by a local planning authority against unauthorised developments.

Housing is one of the most important elements in the development plan, whether it is the old type of plan or the new structure plan under the 1968 Act. Housing occupies a major proportion of the area of any city, town or village, and it generates the need for other elements in the environment, such as roads, schools, social facilities and open space for recreation. The improvement of housing may be the main consideration in indicating an area as an " action area " in a structure plan. (An action area is an area which the local planning authority selects for comprehensive treatment. General improvement areas, authorised by the Housing Act 1969, and housing action areas under the Housing Act 1974, are detailed in Chapter 7 on Rehabilitation.)

Social planning and the problems of inner city areas

Social aspects of housing are considered in Chapter 11, but it is relevant to emphasise here the increasing concern being shown generally about the social effects of planning and the means by which planning can reflect more closely the changing needs of society. Planning strategies for urban renewal, as set out in two government circulars, *Housing Act 1974; Renewal Strategies* (DOE Circular 13/75, WO 4/75) and *Housing Act 1974; Housing Action Areas, Priority Neighbourhoods, and General Improvement Areas* (DOE Circular 14/75), stress that gradual and sensitive renewal, framed " to meet the housing needs of the people in the area " (as the task of local authorities was defined in the Housing Act 1969) encourages local authorities to treat housing areas as " living urban organisms ", with schemes responsive to particular physical and social needs. The circulars are discussed further in Chapter 7.

There is growing concern too about the problems of inner city areas, where much of the country's poor housing is found, and where the major problem involves considerably more than the improvement of physical conditions. Multiple deprivation is often suffered by people living in these areas, a deprivation which encompasses significant economic and social factors. The need to strike the right balance between total redevelopment and rehabilitation, which was the theme of a Housing Centre Trust Conference in 1973, is particularly relevant to inner urban areas where slum clearance and redevelopment programmes in the past have failed to solve their problems; in fact, sometimes such programmes have substituted one set of problems for another, or shifted them elsewhere. Slum clearance and redevelopment have often reduced the supply of cheap and readily available accomodation in a city, thereby increasing overcrowding in the housing that remains, and it has caused a great deal of social disruption and stress. Many of the problems in city areas appear to result mainly from maldistribution of resources, and the need for studies in depth into this and other pressing problems of inner city areas was identified by the SNAP project in Liverpool (*Another Chance for Cities, SNAP, 1969-72*. Liverpool Shelter Neighbourhood Action Project, November 1972), in which past mistakes were revealed all too clearly. In March 1972 the Department of the Environment announced that three industrial towns had been selected for special study, sponsored jointly by the Department of the Environment and the local authority concerned, and aimed at an integrated approach.

Three firms of planning consultants were asked to conduct an action-research case study, each in a different inner urban area— in Birmingham, Lambeth and Liverpool. From these, the Department of the Environment hopes to discover better ways both to identify areas where residents suffer multiple deprivation, and to improve conditions in them, either by activity in the area itself or by changes in management structure, statutory powers, financial arrangements and in other matters. In pursuing these objectives, the consultants were instructed to adopt a total approach to the problems, which was interpreted as giving equal weight to environmental, social and economic considerations. Despite their common terms of reference, the case studies have evolved differently, depending on the nature of the study involved, the study area itself, and the consultants' own approach. Details of progress reports which summarise what has been learnt from each of the action projects promoted in the studies are given in the bibliography. The studies were due to be completed officially at the end of 1976 (10).

The Birmingham Inner Area Study, which is being carried out by Llewelyn-Davies, Weeks, Forestier-Walker and Bor is a combination of research into, amongst other things, housing policies, industrial employment, environmental care and urban renewal management, with 20 action projects. The study includes a housing action area case study, taking into account the new approach in the White Paper, *Better homes—the next priorities*, and an action project (SHAPE) which aims at the rehabilitation of short-life property, and describes the work of the young people involved. The consultants advocate the halting of the economic, social and physical decline by new industrial development initiatives and by re-allocating resources to housing and environmental improvements to people and areas in worst circumstances, by greater emphasis on housing associations, co-operatives and self-help, and by area management which ensures that corporate planning is more sensitive to local needs.

A programme of research and experimental action to improve and revitalise an inner area of Liverpool was laid down in a report by the consultants, Hugh Wilson and Lewis Womersley. The programme, also in its final stages, had two major elements: an experiment in area management by the council and immediate action to improve the study area. For the latter, 10 action projects were carried out in the study area in co-operation with the local authority, then the Liverpool Corporation; these were: maintenance of a small block of council housing; day centre, with emergency accommodation for single homeless; short-stay hostel for mobile young people at risk; accommodation and support for single parent families; social work with people with special housing needs; environmental care in a small part of the study area; neighbourhood care of the elderly and disabled; management of social work with young people at risk; co-ordination of youth facilities; and comparative provision of two different types of playground, fixed and adventure.

The Lambeth Inner Area Study is being carried out by Shankland Cox Partnership and two of their recommendations in a report published by the Department of the Environment, *London's inner areas: problems and possibilities*, IAS/LA/11, one of a series written by the consultants, are that more new housing projects should take the form of smaller schemes on smaller sites, and the cost yardstick should be altered to permit a greater variety in housing design. It is pointed out that existing techniques for building and land assembly encourage large scale housing developments " which people find oppressive ". The consultants condemn the pursuit of housing gain as a " fruitless quest ", leading to densities which are " far too high ", and which crowd children together and increase vandalism. For future housing policy, they recommend a balanced overspill programme, encouraging outmigration of the unskilled and the skilled, to both new towns and outer London suburbs, to reduce pressure on land and housing in Inner London.

Other steps taken towards developing a comprehensive approach which, it is hoped, will provide the basis for new policies towards the inner urban areas of our cities include urban aid and community development projects sponsored by the Home Office, the establishment of educational priority areas by the Department of Education and Science, and an increase in capital grants for public transport by the Department of the Environment. Reports which have a direct bearing on the planning process include *The Reports of the Urban Guideline Studies* (12), and particularly the one on Sunderland called the *Sunderland Study—Tackling Urban Problems: Basic Handbook*, which deals with the way authorities might tackle some multi-element problems.

In September 1976 the Secretary of State for the Environment announced that an overall review of policies for the inner city areas and for dispersal would be undertaken. He described two factors which had contributed to the present conditions of the inner urban areas. First, the population had not increased at anything like the early sixties forecasts, and the latest forecasts indicated that the country's population (though not the number of households) was likely to remain relatively static until the year 2000. Secondly, the *planned* efforts to decentralise and decongest the inner cities had been accompanied by a voluntary movement of people much greater than had been anticipated by the planners. Major factors too had affected industrial location—these included substantial advantages of peripheral locations on transport grounds alone, and the relative ease with which it had been possible to develop purpose built factories on green field sites, or to acquire factories developed on such sites by public bodies, in comparison with the difficulty of assembling land and obtaining planning permission in inner areas.

Measures which had been taken to help with the particular social and environmental problems of inner city areas, including the rate support grant, the special programmes mentioned above, the direction of much housing investment to the inner areas by encouraging general improvement areas and housing action areas, as previously mentioned, and, more recently, by the special designation of stress areas in Circular 80/76, referred to in Chapter 3, had to some extent dealt only with the symptoms and not the causes of the decline of the inner areas. The basic causes lie primarily in relative economic decline of the areas, major migration of people, often the most skilled, and massive reduction in the number of jobs which are left. The future and the wealth of the inner areas were bound up with the fortunes of the manufacturing industry and the government must seek ways of stemming the tide of manufacturing jobs moving out, and of reversing it.

The Secretary of State also pointed out that a close look had to be taken at the operation of the country's planning mechanisms. The post-war system of land use planning and development control had been a great success, but the system had introduced distortions which had strongly favoured development on peripheral sites at the expense of the inner areas, as indicated above. Zoning (for different land use) had also played its part, and there was now a need to re-assess the advantages of trying to squeeze out non-conforming users. There must also be consideration as to whether the incentives to industrial location could not be better tuned to assist the inner areas, without disturbing regional policy.

A change of policy with regard to inner city areas and dispersal will have important implications for future planning and land use and is considered further in Chapter 12.

London's Dockland and Covent Garden

London and other large conurbations present special planning and housing problems. In London, for instance, large-scale planning problems have been created by the need for comprehensive development of London's dockland area in a scheme appropriate to contemporary living. The decision of the Port of London Authority to close the East India, London and Surrey Docks, which presented the opportunty for planned comprehensive development of an area covering some eight square miles (20·72 km²) of land in east and south-east London, led to the setting up jointly by the DOE and the GLC of the Dockland Study Team. The report of the team, *Docklands: redevelopment proposals for east London* (GLC Information Centre, County Hall) considered five optional schemes for comprehensive development of the area which comprised decaying, sub-standard housing, declining industry and shrinking opportunities for either employment or enjoyment. After the Greater London Council passed into Labour control the five optional schemes prepared by the consultants were rejected, and the Dockland Joint Committee, made up of the GLC and the five dockland boroughs, was set up to prepare fresh plans for a radical improvement in the environmental, social and living conditions of the 50,000 people living in the area, and for the development of the river frontage for amenity and recreation.

In August 1975, however, the government made two decisions in a White Paper, *Redevelopment at the London docklands* (HMSO), which together appeared to end any hope for the coherent development of London's obsolete dockland. The first decision, that the government would not make any money available for the planning and development of the area (other than the normal transport and housing grants), meant that the cost of the development, expected to be about £1,000 million, would have to be paid for by the Dockland Joint Committee and could only proceed piecemeal as money was available; and the second decision, that the Dockland Joint Committee would stay in control of the development, finally quashed the possibility of handing the control of docklands over to a new town-type corporation.

In January 1976 the Port of London Authority announced that it intended to close by the following year Millbank and India Docks, two of the last remaining three docks that still operate in the dockland area. With the DJC already finding it difficult to attract jobs into the area, the future of the obsolete dockland, now nearly 24 km² is bleak. Peter Walker, the former Secretary of State for the Environment, and David Eversley, the former chief strategic planner for the GLC, both revived the idea at a conference at the RIBA in January 1976, *Urban renewal and the problem of paying in our cities*, organised by Built Environment, that the development of the area ought to be managed and financed by a new town-type corporation, and in the following March a motion was put in the House of Commons deploring the government's lack of initiative in developing dockland and calling for an East End New Town Corporation to be set up.

In April 1976 the Dockland Development Team, under the direction of Nigel Beard, produced a further draft strategic plan, *London docklands; a strategic plan. A draft for public consultation*, and sought to get the public to participate in its appraisal. Every household and business in the area received a summary of the proposals and a questionnaire; a mobile exhibition toured the area as a prelude to a series of public meetings; and people were given until 30 June 1976 to make their comments known to the development team, who would then submit the final strategy to the government. The draft plan claims that " docklands cannot in any sense be treated as an island unto itself, for ' development must blend into the surrounding urban areas physically, socially and economically ' and ' what is done must respect the life-style of people now living in the area ' ".

Another area of London presenting special large-scale planning problems is Covent Garden where the community association rejected the Greater London Council's proposals for redevelopment. Subsequently, although the overall cost of the development over the next 10 years (£65 million) remains as planned, emphasis was shifted to rehabilitation and the possibility of large scale office development rejected. The plans imply a doubling in the residential population over the next decade and a similar increase in jobs, with small craft and industrial units being encouraged.

The Greater London Council has agreed to revitalise many of the existing empty properties for housing and/or small businesses. One of the specific proposals is to utilise the central Jubilee building for the next five years by conversion to a sports hall; thereafter it will be demolished to make way for the construction of 200 council homes. The local association has said that it will continue to function and pay special regard to the GLC's letting policy on business premises; it will also carry on with its own plans for converting derelict property into flats.

Development, compensation and rehousing

The impact of development on the lives of the individuals who live in the areas where it takes place and on the amenities they enjoy there, has given rise to considerable concern and debate. Particularly in urban areas, schemes to improve the environment involve changes which disturb the existing community, and which, even when carried out sensitively to include rehabilitation where practicable as well as redevelopment, may not be fully acceptable to people living locally. The increasing number of protests against new schemes by amenity and action groups reflect fears that proposed developments will prove contrary to local and special interests. They also emphasise the need to enlist the participation in planning of people affected, so that their needs and wishes are met as far as possible.

Many have seen the provision of new and upgraded roads as the most disturbing development in towns; and the Urban Motorways Committee was set up in July 1969 to examine the current policy for fitting major roads into urban areas, to consider what changes would enable them to be related to their surroundings physically, visually and socially, and to examine the consequences of such changes. The committee submitted its report, *New Roads in Towns*, to the Secretary of State for the Environment in July 1972, and in it recommended a new approach which would treat the planning of new urban roads as an integral part of the planning of the urban area as a whole. It recommended the extension of the cost of building the road to cover the mitigation

272 GUIDE TO HOUSING

or remedy of adverse effects in the adjoining areas, and it concluded that the major adverse consequences of urban roads were noise, severance, visual effects, and the nuisance of the construction period.

The recommendations of the committee were largely incorporated in the White Paper, *Development and Compensation; Putting People First*, which set out a policy for greater recognition of the rights of the individual affected by development. The proposals in the White Paper were subsequently embodied in the Land Compensation Act 1973, where eight principles underlie the legislative and administrative changes. The harmful impact of public development on the immediate surroundings must be alleviated by comprehensive planning and remedial measures. Noisy and unattractive public developments must, by good planning, be separated from people and their homes. The damage to visual amenity must be minimised by good design. Noise, smell and other forms of pollution must be reduced at source, and, where practical, eliminated. Where in spite of these efforts, individual amenities are damaged, reasonable compensation must be made to those who suffer. The administrative processes of enquiry and decision, compulsory purchase and payment of compensation must be concentrated in time and planned to minimise blight and its resultant hardship. Time must not be lost either in carrying out development and remedial works, or in making compensation for injury where appropriate. Finally, people threatened by development or suffering from the effects of it must be fully informed about what is happening, about their rights, and about what help is available to them.

DOE Circular 103/72 (WO 231/72), *Compensation, Blight and Rehousing*, gave guidance to local authorities and other bodies about acquisitions then in train and works which seemed likely to involve new obligations under the proposals in the White Paper. Reference was made to previous recommendations in MHLG Circular 46/70 (WO 48/70) about blight acquisitions, and authorities who were not already operating these provisions, which enable action to be speeded up, were urged to do so in anticipation of the statutory backing to be given to them.

Part I of the Land Compensation Act 1973 (see also Chapter 3), creates in certain circumstances a new right to compensation for injurious affection of land caused by the use of public works. Part II provides for the insulation of buildings against noise caused by the construction and use of public works, for the carrying out of certain other amenity works, and for the acquisition of land for the purpose of mitigating the adverse effect of the existence and use of highways and other public works on their surroundings. Part III makes provision for home loss payments (after a minimum period of residence of five years), farm loss payments and disturbance payments to persons displaced from land in consequence of compulsory acquisition, or of a clearance, demolition or closing order, or an undertaking that a house will not be used for human habitation, passed or given under the Housing Acts. (The Housing Act 1974 extended the benefits of the Land Compensation Act 1973 to people displaced by rehabilitation; and Schedule 5 to the Housing Rents and Subsidies Act 1975 placed on housing associations the same obligation as that placed on local authorities by the Land Compensation Act to make payments to persons displaced by improvement or redevelopment.) Part IV amends the general law of compulsory purchase, and Part V the law relating to planning blight under which an owner may require the acquisition of his interest where he desires to sell and the market value of the interest has been substantially reduced by impending events of specified kinds; and Part VI deals with general interpretation and the commencement and scope of the Act.

Land

Positive planning depends on the availability of land for development or redevelopment; but in our small island land is limited in extent and our density of population is one of the highest in the world. Town planning legislation is essential, therefore, to ensure that land is being used, as far as possible, for the benefit of the community as a whole, and that the conflicting needs of agriculture, development, communications and recreation are reconciled to the best of our ability. Anyone who doubts the need for planning legislation to control development, as British law has been doing since the last war, has only to remember the congestion at the centre of old industrial towns, where back-to-back and crowded houses endangered health, or the sporadic building which laid waste the countryside and sprawled in ribbons along the new roads during the inter-war period, or to hear of the problems of " wild cat " shanty towns around many foreign cities.

For housing, it is important that new developments are located in the right place, and that houses are built to satisfactory densities. The cost of land is also a vital factor in all housing development, and this, in a free market, inevitably reflects scarcity value. Before the passing of the Community Land Act 1975, which is detailed later, such value could be derived from permission to develop having been given under planning legislation to certain sites and not to others, and, often, from the location of a site and its desirability or otherwise for development which would give a good economic return. Housing, and particularly low-cost housing, may be required in a particular area where its benefit cannot easily be assessed in economic terms.

The important issue was that good residential development, in whatever sector, should not be held to ransom by high scarcity prices for land because it was in a popular position or had planning permission for development; and the high cost of land bedevilled our housing economy for many years. Rises of up to 100 per cent. for building land occurred at auctions during the last six months of 1971, and there were further increases in 1972. Figures covering the second half of 1972 showed that the weighted average cost of an acre of private sector land in England and Wales was then £20,000, whereas in the second half of 1971 it had been £10,400. In the two years 1972 and 1973, the value of land in the United Kingdom rose by more than £50,000 million —equivalent to the entire gross national product; and most of the benefit went to a comparatively small number of companies and individuals. The cost of land, however, fell substantially during 1974 and 1975 due to inflation and the economic recession and the Community Land Act will also have an effect on land values. Shelter's information bulletin for 4 to 10 March 1976, referring to a DOE press notice, points out that for 1975 as a whole, average prices were about £1,840 per plot and £42,000 per hectare, 31 per cent. lower than in 1974. On a half-yearly basis, average prices fell by 22 per cent from the second half of 1974 to the first half of 1975 and a further 12 per cent. to the second half. The following tabulation is given, with a caution that the sample of transactions used as a basis amounted to only just over 1,100 instances, but the strength of the trend is clearly shown:

Year	Index of price per plot 1970—100	Weighted average price per plot £	Change over previous year %
1969	91	828	+25
1970	100	908	+10
1971	113	1,030	+13
1972	190	1,727	+68
1973	295	2,676	+55
1974	293	2,663	—
1975	203	1,839	−31

The problem of how to stop or recoup the large sums made by owners of land as a consequence of successful applications to develop, without deterring the private landowner from making more land available for building, has been recognised by all three political parties, and figured in all three manifestos in the election in 1974. Many ideas have been put forward to try to prevent the element of land costs in rent from prejudicing the type of development, and many of them are politically controversial. It was the " development value," derived, it was argued, from the whole environment of the site, and not from what the landowner alone had done to it, which was acquired by the State under the Town and Country Planning Act 1947, referred to earlier under Planning. This did not, however, make land any cheaper for the ordinary developer to buy, since he was charged a levy of the difference between the existing use value and the value with permission to develop. The repeal of the financial clauses of the 1947 Act, and the return to market value prices in 1954, even when land was bought by local authorities in the public interest, meant that the cost of housing land was often high, and rose higher in areas of population growth where land for development was scarce.

To help make land more readily available, the Land Commission was set up by the Land Commission Act 1967. The two main objects of the land policy initiated by this Act were to secure that the right land was available at the right time for the implementation of national, regional and local plans, and to ensure that a substantial part of the development value created by the community returned to the community. The latter was effected by the powers given to the Land Commission to collect a betterment levy of 40 per cent of the development value on all land when it was developed; and the Commission was given powers to acquire land compulsorily and hold it until it could be released for housing and other appropriate uses. The constitution and powers of the Commission, and in particular the betterment levy, were matters of political controversy; and the Land Commission was abolished by the Conservatives when they returned to power in 1970. The betterment levy was abandoned and development value realised from land transactions was dealt with through profits and capital gains taxes, and a development tax, introduced in December 1973, made certain capital gains arising from the disposal of land and building with development value chargeable as income (Finance Act 1973).

The Land Commission's powers for buying land enabled it to aggregate land in different ownership where development of large sites was required. On the other hand, under the Leasehold Reform Act 1967, holders of long leases were given the right to have them extended for a further 50 years, or to acquire the freehold, and, thus, estates let on such long ground rents were fragmented. The Act made provision, however, for schemes to be introduced to ensure good management of the estate as a whole under special conditions.

The abolition in 1970 of the Land Commission, charged with assembling land, meant that there was no comprehensive national machinery for securing a pool of land available for new development located in the right place to satisfy urgent housing needs. By early 1972, 640 acres, which had been assembled by the Land Commission, were being sold to house builders, and by the end of the year 900 acres had been disposed of in this way. The government tried to increase the supply of land, in an effort to check land and housing costs rising due to scarcity. A total of £80 millions was made available over two years to councils for loans with which they could assemble land for building by private developers, provided the land was promptly serviced with roads, sewers and other services. Other measures which were proposed were that local authorities should keep a " Domesday Book " on land release, and publish detailed information of the location and state of readiness of land to be allocated to housing in the ensuing five years; and a possible change in the system of planning permission to build on undeveloped land by which a developer would simply inscribe his proposal on a public register set up for the purpose and if the application were not challenged by a specified date it would go through automatically.

Derelict land

Although the Secretary of State for the Environment said he was neither deviating from green belt policy nor turning planning procedure upside down, immense pressures built up to allow development in green belts. It was recognised that there were derelict areas in green belts which did nothing to enhance local amenity, but any release of such land should only be allowed after a comprehensive and careful national survey. Ministers systematically examined with local authorities the areas vaguely designated as " proposed green belt " and firm decisions were taken so that councils and developers knew the boundaries of the protected land. As a result many marginal areas were freed for building.

In 1972, 5,360 acres of derelict land were restored in England, and this was an increase of 12 per cent over the 1971 figure of 4,792 acres and nearly 50 per cent over the 1970 figure of 3,645 acres. 74 per cent of the 1972 total was cleared with the aid of specific grants to local authorities; and some of the best progress was made in the worst affected areas of Durham, Lancashire, Northumberland, the West Riding of Yorkshire, Derbyshire, Nottinghamshire, Cumberland and Stoke-on-Trent where 3,875 acres were reclaimed in 1972 compared with 2,901 in 1971. The figures are taken from the 1972 survey of derelict land undertaken by local planning authorities in England at the request of the Department of the Environment. DOE Circular 56/73 dealt with reclamation of derelict land after local government reorganisation and emphasised the importance of the retention of specialist teams for derelict land reclamation.

The private sector

Ways which would permit and encourage the participation of private capital in providing new homes in areas of cities which could open up new horizons in urban renewal have been explored. *New Homes in the Cities* (1971), a report from a working party set up in 1968 by the National Economic Development Office for Building, considered the private housing aspects of urban renewal programmes. The report set out fairly the political, financial and social obstacles to private enterprise participation, including difficulties over acquiring compact sites in slum and twilight areas characterised by fragmented ownership, problems of meeting the financial gap between acquisition costs and re-use value of residential land, and possibly low marketability of housing on redevelopment sites because of the character of surrounding areas.

Special partnership schemes between private enterprise and local authorities to secure some of the major private housing developments needed in the South-east were proposed in the report of a government-appointed working party, published in October 1972, *Report of Working Party on Local Authority/Private Enterprise Partnership Schemes* (HMSO). The report, which was published without commitment by the government or the other participating bodies and was intended solely as a basis for discussion, pointed out a number of special problems in growth areas of the South-east where development was to be concentrated. Briefly, these were: (a) the need to bring large amounts of land into production fast enough to maintain high rates of building; (b) the need in such areas for better and more comprehensively planned developments than many of those deemed acceptable in the past; (c) the problems of land price increases in such areas arising from the prospects of growth; and (d) the effects of those on the costs of related public services, and the high costs, in many cases, of infrastructure provision. Partnership schemes, in the opinion of the working party, had a significant role in the promotion of private housing development. Subsequently, however, the country's economic recession has seriously affected activity on the part of developers, and the government's land policy, as enacted in the Community Land Act 1975, described below, is an important additional source of uncertainty for the development industry and for investors. An Advisory Group on Commercial Property Development under the chairmanship of Sir Dennis Pilcher was announced in Parliament in December 1974, and the remaining members were appointed in January 1975. The Group's first report, *Commercial Property Development,* presented in November 1975, was prepared while the Community Land Bill was being considered in Committee in the House of Commons, and is, therefore, discussed later.

Land availability

In October 1972 DOE Circular 102/72, *Land Availability for Housing,* reiterated earlier exhortations by the Secretary of State that more land should be released for development by the planning authorities, and offered some practical advice and help. One of the main controversies was whether land shortage had been exacerbated by delay in developing land for which planning permission had been obtained. It was held that some developers were hoarding land, and the government's scheme to prevent developers profiting from land hoarding was set out in the White Paper, *Widening the Choice: the next steps in housing* (Cmnd. 5280), where it was proposed that a land hoarding charge would be levied on land for which planning permission had been granted, but where there had been a failure within a specified period to complete the development. The White Paper went into considerable detail as to how the charge would operate to avoid hardship, but also to ensure that evasion was prevented. Doubts were expressed as to the effectiveness of such a provision and the difficulties of implementing it, and it was not proceeded with before the change of government in 1974.

In order to make more land available for house building, the White Paper promised new guidelines for the treatment of planning applications which would contain a general presumption in favour of housing development. Such guidelines were the subject of another DOE Circular on *Land Availability for Housing* (DOE Circular 122/73), issued in October 1973. Although the green belts, national parks and areas of outstanding beauty, as well as land of high agricultural value, were to be protected, the White Paper suggested that some give and take might be necessary so far as green belt land was concerned; it was also proposed that there should be more active policies for enhancing the amenity value of green belts. Circular 122/73 emphasised that, since most development plans were drawn up before requirements for housing land were fully appreciated, until local plans came into operation much development would have to be permitted on " white " land, that is, land for which no change of use had been envisaged in the development plans.

The White Paper also referred to the release for housing of land held by the government, nationalised industries and hospital authorities which was not required by them. In this connection, the British Rail Property Board, following a special review they had made of their land ownership in Greater London, made some 220 acres of land available for municipal use in 1972, and have disposed of many sites since then. Also, the Defence Lands Committee which, under the chairmanship of Lord Nugent of Guildford, had during 1971 to 1973 undertaken the first comprehensive review of the subject for 24 years, published its report, *Report of the Defence Lands Committee* (HMSO, 1971–73). The committee examined 629,000 acres out of a total of 757,000 acres held for defence purposes. Of these, 31,000 acres were recommended for release, in addition to 1,700 acres recommended for release previously. Only a very small proportion of the released land, however, was available for house building; the siting of many installations in areas far from centres of population probably rendered this situation inevitable, but the report showed that departments concerned with defence were not holding vast areas of housing land. In London, enough additional land for 24,400 dwellings in 1972–81 was identified by the Action Group on London Housing (a group of London local authority members and officers set up by the Minister for Housing and Construction) after visiting 14 London boroughs to follow up the land availability survey carried out for them in 1972.

During 1973, many solutions to the problems of land scarcity and high cost were put forward. At the annual general meeting of the Housing Centre in October 1973 Lord Greenwood of Rossendale, the Housing Centre Trust's president, referred to proposals for the creation of a land bank. The Town and Country Planning Association had put forward proposals for a public land bank, which had been endorsed by NALGO and had much in common with the Labour Party's proposals. The basis of both the Labour Party's and the TCPA's plans was that land required for major development should be bought at existing use value, rather than at the exorbitant market value it secured once building permission had been given.

The Community Land Act 1975

The Labour government's proposals for tackling the land crisis and for solving the " betterment " problem were set out in the White Paper, *Land,* released by the Department of the Environment in September 1974. This reiterated the government's objective as being " to establish a permanent means: (a) to enable the community to control the development of land in accordance with its needs and priorities; and (b) to restore to the community the increase in value of land arising from its efforts ". The first objective of the land policy was termed in the White Paper " positive planning "; and public ownership of land was viewed by the government as the key to giving to the local authorities not only the power to make plans for their areas, but also the power to see that they were implemented.

The government had pledged itself to nationalise enough building land to satisfy housing needs until the end of the century and its Community Land Bill was published in March 1975, which provided the framework for ensuring that, ultimately, virtually all development takes place on land that is in, or has passed through, community ownership; and it also permitted government acquisition of large, empty office blocks like Centre Point in London. During the legislation's passage through Parliament, many amendments were made after considerable consultation with interested parties. Briefly, the outline of the proposals for land acquisition in the Bill was that, to begin with, local authorities would be able to buy land at a price excluding the amount of development land tax that would have been payable had the land been sold privately, with the basis of compensation being market value. After the transitional period (and some of the most complex parts of the Bill were concerned with this), however, the basis of compensation would be changed to current use value.

The Community Land Act, which received the Royal Assent in November 1975, is long and complicated and only a brief outline can be given here. Readers who wish to consider the Act in detail are referred to explanatory publications listed in the bibliography (13, 14, 15, 16, 17, 18). The Act places additional responsibilities upon authorities with respect to the planning, acquisition and development of land, the authorities under the Act being local authorities and new town development corporations in England and Scotland, the Peak Park Joint Planning Board and the Lake District Special Planning Board; and in Wales the Land Authority for Wales, and new town development corporations. The first appointed day for the implementation of the Act was 6 April 1976, and the initial five year rolling programmes and land policy statements were to be submitted to the Secretary of State in May 1976. DOE circulars 121/75 and 128/75 gave guidance on how local authorities should operate the land scheme.

A fundamental objective of the Act is to secure positive implementation of planning polices by giving authorities wide powers and duties to control the supply of development land and initiate development in accordance with the needs of the community, rather than merely to react to proposals by private developers as hitherto. Consequently, in considering what is development land, authorities are to have regard, inter alia, to the provisions of the development plan; and programmes for the acquisition of development land must therefore be based on and suitably supported by authorities' planning policy. The Secretary of State has indicated that appropriate support would include any of the following: (a) a regional strategy which has been endorsed by the government; (b) an approved or draft structure plan; (c) a local or draft local plan; (d) an approved old-style development plan or a submitted amendment; (e) a non-statutory plan or policy adopted by the authority and publicly available, and which can be incorporated into a statutory plan as soon as practicable. Thus the Act is clearly intended to operate within the present planning framework, and the functions of authorities under the Act are placed in the context of authorities' planning responsibilities. The intention is that the planning framework will be a key element in the identification of development land.

The first task of the authorities in each county jointly is the preparation of "Land Acquisition and Management Schemes" (LAMS) for submission to the Secretary of State. These procedural schemes are to set out proposed arrangements for the execution of the authorities' function in connection with land acquisition; and the factors which must be considered are detailed in Schedule 5 to the Act. They cover such matters as the resources and experience of authorities, their functions under planning and housing law and arrangements for discharge of these functions, and any other matters which the Secretary of State may direct. In particular, authorities are required to consider in the preparation of LAMS the availability of suitably qualified staff. Circular 121/75 states that "Authorities should not contemplate the recruitment of additional staff until they have examined and exhausted all other possibilities", and other possibilities mentioned include "use of outside resources where appropriate, perhaps to meet specific short-term needs, and in specialised matters such as aspects of commercial development".

The tasks facing authorities operating the Act, apart from the preparation of LAMS, can be divided into four categories: (1) review of planning strategy; (2) responding to applications for planning permission; (3) acquisition of development land; and (4) development and disposal of land. With regard to the latter, once land has been brought into public ownership, authorities will either develop it themselves or make it available for development by private development agencies, and a combination of these methods may be used as expedient. Where authorities do not wish or are unable to implement development themselves, the land acquired will be disposed of on a leasehold basis to private developers. In the case of commercial development the leases would probably contain arrangements for equity sharing between the authority (the ground landlord) and the developer, and for the authority's participation in future increases in income. Land for private housing, however, will generally be made available freehold to the eventual houseowner, with the builder/developer operating under a building licence.

Under the Development Land Tax Act 1976, a development land tax will replace the development gains tax imposed by the Conservative government in the 1973 Finance Bill. Development land tax, which is a proposed new flat-rate tax on the development value of land whereby authorities will pay market value less the amount of DLT that would have been payable if the vendor had sold privately, is payable (a) when a project of material development commences and (b) upon a disposal where development value is realised. The rate will commence at 80 per cent and is intended to rise to 100 per cent, so restoring increases in development value to the community. During the bill's progress through the House of Commons, however, the proposed tax has been modified to meet fears from the building industry that it could cause cash flow problems and more general concern that it will create land starvation. Concessions have been made to the intention to impose a tax of 80 per cent on all development profit above £5000. The exemption limit has been raised to £10,000; then, for three years, the amount of tax to be paid between £10,000 and £150,000 will be 66⅔ per cent. Above £150,000, it will be 80 per cent.

Although the full implications of the Community Land Act will not be measured for some considerable time, it will affect housing development, particularly if it does result in owners of land or private developers being deterred by what might appear to be lack of incentives for making planning proposals, or threat of lack of profit owing to the land development tax. On the positive side, the Act does provide an opportunity for local authorities to ensure that their powers are used to exert more stringent controls over subsequent development than they are able to do through planning law as it now stands. Two successive DOE documents, Circular 26/76, *Land for private development: acquisition, management and disposal* (HMSO) and Development Advice Note 1 on residential development, *The development brief: residential development* (HMSO) (the first in a series of advice notes on planning and design drawn up in consultation with the Environmental Board), however, contain clear warnings to councils to avoid making exacting design requirements when disposing of publicly owned land for private development. Both

documents emphasise the need for " short and simple " development briefs. In the case of private housing, a short brief would
" encourage developers to make full use of their skills and
experience in designing, building and selling a product at a price
to meet market demand ". Such a brief would not stipulate the
market the housing should serve, nor space requirements or
standards of internal design. Rather it would spell out planning
policies for the area, including density, access, parking provision,
open spaces, and play areas. " Where an authority wished to
influence the appearance of a development ", the Development
Advice Note advises, " it would be better to do this by indicating
design objectives rather than offering specific solutions ". More
complex briefs would apply only to the development of more
sensitive sites, in or adjoining conservation areas, sites for
comprehensive development of housing and other land uses, and
where, because of physical characteristics, there are particularly
different problems of layout and design.

The DOE also urges councils to keep to a minimum the period
that they hold land, if possible no more than two or three years.
" Vacant buildings should be put to good use wherever this can
be done in the interim period." If a temporary use cannot be
found, local authorities should consider demolishing the building
and putting the cleared site to short term use with some low cost
landscaping.

The director of the House-Builders' Federation has predicted
that the Community Land Act and the proposed development
land tax will be the cause of a building recession in two years
which will make the 1974 slump " look like a boom ". He has
said that together the measures would combine to create a land
famine towards the end of 1977 when the housing demand
could again be at peak. If development land tax is finally set at
80 per cent, eventually rising to 100 per cent, no-one would
release land for development, and also, the director believes, local
authorities will not have the resources to acquire significant land
banks, a process anyway which would be subject to lengthy delays.

According to the report produced by the Advisory Group on
Commercial Development, mentioned earlier, the prospects for
commercial property are bleak. The report says that the current
activity is simply a spillover from projects started before the
collapse in property in the autumn of 1973. This the group sees as
progressively diminishing, " to be superseded by a virtual hiatus
of construction beginning within two or three years ". Although
the effects of the Community Land Act are considered, much of
the blame is laid on the adverse state of the overall economic
situation. Four factors are singled out: the doubling of building
costs between 1970 and 1974, the high cost of short and long term

finance, the failure of rental income to keep pace with soaring building costs, and the relative weakness of the investment market.

An overall strategy

Sensible, speedy and flexible procedures for provision of land where and when it is needed and for planning approvals play an important part in an overall housing strategy, based on the varying needs of different groups of people, in specifically identified towns and regions. In times of financial stringency, the best value for money must be obtained in the use of scarce resources to meet the most urgent social needs, and any delay which holds up the housing process is costly, in terms of finance and often of social stress. At the same time, a closer relationship between the providers and the consumers of housing, through sensible participation schemes and genuine co-operation and understanding, must be achieved in all aspects of housing, including planning and land provision.

CHAPTER 10

Design, Construction and Maintenance

Types of dwelling

Dwellings may be categorised according to their physical characteristics in many ways. One-family houses may be distinguished by their layout as detached, semi-detached or terraced, or by the number of storeys as bungalows, two, three or more storey houses. If they have an internal court they may be termed patio houses, or split-level houses if the rooms on different floors are not regular. Blocks of flats for the public sector may be built as " walk-ups " up to three storeys, but where the entrance door is four or more storeys above street level, lifts must be installed. In blocks of flats, each self-contained unit is normally on the same floor level, although multi-storey blocks of maisonettes are also built in which the dwellings are on two floors with an internal private staircase. There are also some less common and ingenious plan arrangements, such as the scissor plan where living and sleeping accommodation may be on different levels, but above or below similar accommodation in the other flats in the same block. Such plans may be evolved in order to minimise noise disturbance from rooms used for different purposes, to achieve a better orientation or aspect for certain rooms, or to enable more dwellings to be reached from wide access terraces and the lift stops to be at alternate or even every third storey. Scissor flats also have the advantage of allowing cross ventilation not possible in other double banked corridor access plans.

Blocks of flats may be planned with gallery or internal corridor access where many flats open off a common balcony, deck or passage on each floor. Such blocks usually take the form of long narrow slabs. Staircase access implies fewer flats, two or three on each floor, opening off a number of communal stairways in walk-up blocks. In high tower blocks, many of which were designed and built in the 1950s and '60s but which are no longer popular, as discussed below, about four flats on each floor are reached from a central core containing the lift shafts and emergency staircase. Housing estates are also frequently described as high or low rise or mixed, and are also differentiated by whether they are high or low density, or more exactly by the number of persons, or bedspaces, per acre or hectare, which they provide.

The choice of types of dwellings to be built on any site is influenced by many factors, and is often a compromise between the ideal mix of houses and flats to meet the requirements of the householders for whom the housing is being built and the price which they can afford to pay. This is true whether the housing is to be built for letting by a local authority or a housing association or if it is to be built for sale to owner-occupiers in which case the building owner makes his own assessment of the kinds and sizes of houses which will attract owner-occupiers at the price which he will charge in the particular location where he has land available. The Community Land Act 1975, however, discussed in Chapter 9, will influence housing development, although all schemes of up to about 12 houses are exempt from its main provisions. Since early 1975, also, government policy has been directed more towards meeting social needs and providing accommodation of the size and type which social and demographic research indicates to be necessary—and the Department of the Environment's second annual report on its research and development programme in October 1974 showed that expenditure on research and development was estimated at £25·2 million for the year 1974–75, compared with £19·8 million in 1973–74. Speaking at Sheffield in March 1975 the Minister for Housing and Construction claimed that in housing the "whole impressive legal, administrative, technical and financial apparatus of planning controls, mandatory standards, contracting procedures, financial controls, subsidies, and project control should be directed to and subordinate to one end: providing what people need, and providing it quickly". A much larger number of small houses and flats is needed, suitable for small households of all ages—only 14 per cent of the country's housing stock in 1975–76 is in units for one or two persons, whereas 50 per cent of households come into this category. This means, among other things, building at higher densities in the private sector. Provision of accommodation suitable for elderly persons and for the physically handicapped is also urgently needed. DOE Circular 24/75, *Housing Needs and Action*, emphasised that much greater attention ought to be given to the needs of small households, both by making fuller use of the existing housing stock and by devoting a larger proportion of new building to smaller dwellings. Local authorities were asked to give "a fair wind to innovations", especially those which might provide people with a chance of a first home. Local authorities should consider simple conversions of suitable three bedroom houses to provide accommodation for smaller households, and to give scope for the provision of mobile homes and other forms of housing which could be made available quickly in order to meet immediate needs. The circular also asked planning authorities to ensure that their policies and procedures would help people to get homes at a price they could afford, and referred to promising developments in the provision of starter and extendable homes for smaller households. Later, *The Need for Smaller Homes* (1) reinforced the points made in Circular 24/75, and the National Building Agency has demonstrated the practicability of extendable homes (2) in six proto-type houses for Sheffield Council where expansion can be achieved into the roof space.

With regard to mobile homes, a Shelter report, *Factory Built Houses: a Shelter report on the present and future use of caravans, mobile homes and prefabricated houses* (3), was sent to the Secretary of State for the Environment on the same day as a private members' bill on mobile homes was discussed in Parliament. Shelter saw an extremely useful role for mobile homes in slum clearance programmes and in improvement areas—such homes could overcome the key problems of local authorities having nowhere to decant tenants while clearing and redeveloping, and of keeping the existing community together—and the report made recommendations for improving conditions for mobile home dwellers. The Mobile Homes Act 1975 added to the protection afforded to mobile home residents by the 1968 Act, and the Department of the Environment produced an explanatory leaflet entitled *A Guide to the Provisions of the Caravan Sites Act 1968 and the Mobile Homes Act 1975 affecting residents of mobile homes and operators of mobile home sites in England, Wales and Scotland.* In February, 1976, the Government announced that it was monitoring the working of the Act and had a review of the mobile homes situation under way to consider the wider aspects of the problem.

Encouragement for the provision of small units for single people has been given by the government and the Housing Corporation. A circular on cost yardstick allowance in January 1976 referred to below, showed that the Government accepted in principle that the single were a growing proportion of the country's population and would have to be catered for. In April 1976 the Minister for Housing and Construction announced new initiatives to provide for the housing of single people, including students, as part of the general housing programmes of local authorities and housing associations. Housing schemes mainly to be occupied by students were to be eligible for subsidy or grants in areas where student demand impinged on the general housing market, particularly in areas of stress and pressure—provided they contributed directly or indirectly to meeting the general housing needs of the area. Such schemes should normally provide for at least a proportion of non-students but schemes for students only were also to be considered on their specific housing merits.

The Housing Corporation also announced in a press release in January 1976 that it intended to increase its financing of the building of homes for those with special needs, e.g., young people, the single, elderly or handicapped, or for those with other special requirements, like one-parent families. Housing for special needs is considered in greater detail in Chapter 11, which discusses the social aspects of housing, but it is relevant to note here increasing government involvement in influencing the choice of types of dwelling according to social needs. Socially many factors are shaping housing need, which must in turn shape the housing programme, so that special needs are met and the right sort of accommodation is built. The supply of housing must be organised and diversified so that actual needs—for single people, for young married couples setting up home for the first time, for the old and disabled, for large families, and for the relief of homelessness and bad housing in all sectors—are satisfied in the appropriate areas. The implications of current social trends on where and how houses should be built in the future are also considered in Chapter 11.

The cost and availability of land have always been important elements in the choice of types of dwelling, and in the final price or rent, and although there have been special subsidies available for public sector housing on sites of high value, or sites creating special difficulties in housing construction, broadly, the higher the land costs, the higher the densities have been so that the cost was distributed over a greater number of dwellings. As mentioned above, however, the Community Land Act 1975, and also the Development Land Tax Act, will materially affect the planning and provision of housing and the important implications of these Acts were considered in Chapter 9.

Layout is inevitably influenced by the topography of the site and by site conditions—and special subsidies for building on sites with features requiring expensive site works (or liable to sub-sidence) have been mentioned above. Special requirements may be laid down under town planning legislation, such as limitations on density, traffic and parking standards, and even tree preser-vation orders. Schemes for public housing must be planned in relation to the structure and types of household who will occupy them. To achieve balanced communities, a variety of accommo-dation is desirable with a variety of tenure—rented property (both public and private), housing association accommodation, owner-occupied dwellings and co-operative housing. Large housing *estates,* which make problems of oppression, segregation, van-dalism and inadequate maintenance and management more and more difficult to solve, are being increasingly condemned. As discussed in Chapter 9, new housing projects function more satisfactorily in the form of smaller schemes on smaller sites; and housing everywhere should be an integral part of the landscape with housing schemes regarded not as a threat to existing amenity but an enhancement of it.

Density

A housing site has to conform with the local planning authority's pattern of development in respect of design and density. The latter is a convenient way of measuring the number of dwellings on a site and was formerly usually quoted as a figure for houses to the acre. Between the wars much housing was carried out at 12 houses to the acre. Such a low density may still be reasonable in rural areas, but owing to pressure on land, rising costs, and the reduction in the size of gardens, it has become proper to increase densities, and, moreover, to plan for mixed development of houses and flats. This has led to the more common expression of densities as numbers of persons, that is, bedspaces per acre (hectare). For example, two sites may be developed as follows: —

	Site A	Site B
Area	13·7 acres	7·28 acres
Density bedspaces per acre	70	161
Occupancy Ratio (Average)	3·5	3·5
No. dwellings per acre	20	46
Total no. bedspaces	959	1172
Total no. dwellings	274	335

With the same occupancy rate it is possible to increase the number of dwellings and bedspaces by increasing the density.

Some local authorities, however, do not think of densities in terms of bedspaces but persons per habitable room, say from 0·9 to 1·5.

In cities, high densities have been permitted at 200 persons per acre. In general, however, experience advises that this covers the site with too much activity; for example, considerable concern has been expressed about the effect of high density living where there are young children who may be housed in high blocks, often with inadequate play facilities (4 and 5) and tower blocks are no longer popular. Even where land is scarce, densities above 140 persons per acre (345 persons per hectare) should seldom be necessary. There is usually little saving with high densities because the ancillary needs of the present-day population in the form of access and parking space for cars, refuse disposal units, and the essential open space is so great. The higher the density, the higher the cost of development. The disaster at

Ronan Point, where failure of the structure of a high-rise block of flats occurred after an internal gas explosion, added to the unpopularity of high rise building. More stringent structural requirements were subsequently introduced, both for high-rise building and low-rise dwellings, and these in turn increased the cost of construction. An additional subsidy is provided for high blocks.

The widely-held view that tower blocks are intrinsically bad has been questioned. Mr David Canter of the Department of Environmental Psychology, University of Surrey, for instance, pointed out at the annual conference of the British Association in 1975 that, apart from the difficulties associated with children's play, there were major advantages, such as quietness and a good view, and the main problem revealed by many social investigations was that of the unreliability of the lifts. The crux of Dr Canter's argument was that the original concept of tower blocks had been watered down by trying to pare costs to the bone rather than just being satisfied with the efficient use of land. He contended that high rise buildings should be conceived of as culs-de-sac on end as they have great advantages of no through traffic. Provided the buildings were planned as complete living systems, their problem would be neither greater nor less than those of low-rise systems, and solutions were beginning to emerge that were more imaginative than putting boxes on top of one another. The information officer of the RIBA has also pointed out that, although architects have, in recent years, made it clear that they have had a degree of responsibility for the social consequences of the tower block, the failure of the tower blocks designed in the '50s and '60s must be seen in the light of inadequate finance for the architect to design in sufficient services and facilities; lack of adequate finance to provide landscaping and other amenities at ground level; the failure of housing managers to ensure that the tower blocks had occupants most suited to them and finally to the insensitive programmes of local authorities who bound themselves to produce numbers of tower blocks using systems devised by contracting companies for speed of erection rather than aesthetic quality. (Shelter Information Bulletin, 16–22 January 1975.)

In September 1976 a draft circular to local authorities recommended slightly lower housing densities in inner cities, with higher densities being tolerated on the fringe of cities. A long-term programme was set out for reducing inner city densities and also the amount of good agricultural land being lost to housing developments with unnecessarily low densities. The circular said that both could be achieved by raising building densities in the suburbs and towns from the current 20–30 dwellings per hectare

(8–12/acre) to 33–38 dwellings per hectare (14–16/acre). The considerations for rural areas were also concerned with transport, for the government felt that it would be increasingly difficult to provide adequate transport facilities to sprawling areas, whereas if more people were in the villages, then not only land would be saved but also train and bus services could be supplied more efficiently.

The circular supported setting strict upper limits on densities in inner city areas. However, on conversions, the need to provide smaller dwellings, and the provision of such dwellings that would result from conversions was " likely to outweigh density considerations where the density effects are likely to be small and localised." Councils were also urged to support building schemes which provided smaller and lower priced homes at higher densities.

Local authorities appeared to welcome the circular. They did not see a danger that the call for higher densities might mean a return to endless building of high rise blocks as the call was only directed at suburban and rural areas. They agreed too that part of the character of the countryside was that communities were tightly bunched together to allow full use of surrounding agricultural land. The provisions of the circular, therefore, only conformed to the " policy " which had been running for many years.

The Architects Journal, 15 September 1976, saw the proposed policy in the circular as being " fundamental to the way the relationships between city and town, and between town and country develop in the future." It also pointed out the great importance of the density figures proposed— a minimum of 170 habitable rooms per hectare (70/acre) regarded as necessary to ensure the economical use of land; and a maximum figure for mixed housing of 240 per hectare (100/acre) with 200 (85) for predominantly family housing.

The Town and Country Planning Association welcomed the section in the circular which asked councils to concentrate on the provision of low-rise (two to three storeys) accommodation designed for families with children and with the provision of a garden. The association, however, criticised the discussion of density on the basis of a limited number of factors, viz., location, the falling size of households and the need to protect good agricultural land; and described the move to encourage builders to reapply for development already approved but at higher densities as " tantamount to offering them a guaranteed opportunity to make hefty windfall profits on their land transactions and amounts to bribing builders to go for densities higher than they themselves consider acceptable in normal terms ".

Standards and Design

Recommendations for post-war standards of accommodation and design were made by a sub-committee of the then Central Housing Advisory Committee in 1944. The Dudley report, named after the sub-committee's chairman, Lord Dudley, recommended an increase in overall area from the pre-war standard of 760 sq. ft. (70·6 m²) for a 3-bedroom, 5-person house with living-room (the non-parlour house) to a minimum of 900 sq. ft. (83·6 m²) for a 3-bedroom, 5-person house with two living-rooms.

Household activities were used as the basis on which to recommend standards of room arrangement, room sizes and equipment, particularly as they affect the kitchen-dining-living space relationship. To allow variety of arrangement the report recommended a minimum aggregate for living space of 330 sq. ft. (30·66 m²) for a 5-person house instead of fixing minimum areas for each room separately. This method of approach to design standards was new.

Many of the recommendations of the Dudley sub-committee were incorporated in the *Housing Manual 1944,* which was issued as a guide to local authorities by the Ministry of Health and also contained type plans, although both overall area and aggregate living space controls were not used. Five years later, the *Housing Manual 1949,* as well as stressing the need for much great variety in dwelling types, re-introduced overall area control, and set it at 900–950 sq. ft. (83·6–88·26 m²) for the 5-person house, leaving out the aggregate living space standard.

After three more years, another Manual, *Houses 1952,* was issued by the Ministry of Housing and Local Government. This coincided with an economy drive on the one hand and an effort by a new government to achieve a higher output of separate dwellings on the other. Space standards were reduced, but emphasis was laid on the necessity of using compact plans with little loss of convenience.

A fresh look at the design needs of the family was taken by another sub-committee of the Central Housing Advisory Committee set up in 1960 under the chairmanship of Sir Parker Morris " to consider the standards of design and equipment applicable to family dwellings and other forms of residential accommodation, whether provided by public authorities or by private enterprise, and to make recommendations ". The report of the committee, *Homes for Today and Tomorrow* (6), published in 1961, is realistic and practical.

The committee interpreted its brief on the broadest basis and set out in its report a new philosophy of house and environmental design, based on careful analysis of the user requirements of households at different stages in the family cycle.

The Parker Morris committee emphasised that more space should be provided to meet the needs of the future—more space for activities demanding privacy and quiet, for satisfactory circulation, for better storage generally; space to keep the new household machinery; and kitchens arranged for easy work with room in them in which to take at least some meals.

Overall floor areas required as minima were stated to be 800 sq. ft. (74·32 m²) for a 4-person intermediate terrace house with two storeys, and 910 sq. ft. (84·54 m²) for a 5-person intermediate terrace house, plus 50 sq. ft. (4·65 m²) of general storage space in both cases. This represented an increase of about 60 sq. ft. (5·57 m²). Recommended areas varied according to the number of people (bed spaces) for whom the house was designed and according to its type (number of storeys, etc.). Better use can be made of available space if all rooms are adequately heated, and the committee recommended that a considerably better heating installation should be adopted, and that installations which were an improvement on this basic standard should also be encouraged. The Parker Morris committee recommended that housing standards generally should be expressed in terms of the activity of the occupants rather than of the number and sizes of rooms; an approach which they regarded as an important means of releasing more of the creative energies of architects concerned with housing who should be able to explore new living arrangements to suit changing needs. Other recommendations relating to the internal equipment of the house included provision of a second w.c. in a 5-person and larger house (previously recommended by the Dudley committee but later not enforced as a standard), better kitchen fittings and bedroom cupboards and more electric socket outlets.

All the recommendations of the Parker Morris committee, however, were put forward as *minimum* standards which should be improved where possible.

Immediately following the publication of *Homes for Today and Tomorrow* (6), the Ministry of Housing and Local Government prepared Design Bulletin 6, *Space in the Home* (7), which was issued in 1963. This supplemented the main report by illustrating the family activities which have to be catered for, tabulating related space and furniture sizes; and providing a basis for analysis and appraisal of plans in terms of the spirit and standards of the report. In 1968, another Design Bulletin No. 14, *House Planning—a Guide to User Needs with a Check List* (8), set out a list of points to consider when appraising plan arrangements and house design; and also analysed different plan forms for houses recently completed.

The Housing Development Directorate (HDD) of the Department of the Environment has produced over the past five or six years a number of Design Bulletins, available from HMSO, on all manner of topics. Bulletins most relevant to the housing field include those concerned with the detailed design of accommodation for special needs, e.g., *Some Aspects of Designing for Old People* (9) and *Housing Single People 2: a design guide with a description of a scheme at Leicester* (10), those dealing with environmental matters, e.g., *The Estate Outside the Dwelling: reactions of residents to aspects of housing layout* (11), *Landscaping for Flats* (12), and *New Housing and Road Traffic Noise* (13), and those dealing with services for housing, e.g., *Services for Housing; sanitary plumbing and drainage* (14). These and others are listed in the bibliography.

Design and standards are also affected by building regulations and public health legislation. A set of building regulations under the *Public Health Act 1961* was issued in March 1972 as S.I. 317. The new regulations, which came into force on 1 June 1972 and were a consolidation of the 1965 regulations and subsequent amendments to them, apply to the whole of England and Wales, except the Inner London Boroughs where building work is subject to the London Building Acts 1930–39 and the Building (Constructional) By-laws made thereunder.

The very large number of accidents which take place in the home means that special attention should be given to points of design which minimise the risk. Design Bulletin, *Safety in the Home* (15), describes these features and also gives a check list of them. Safety of buildings is being given greater prominence since highly publicised failures such as Ronan Point. The Institution of Structural Engineers, for instance, has produced *Criteria for structural adequacy* and in April 1976 organised a conference with the statement " The primary responsibility of the structural engineer is to ensure that no structure he has designed will collapse " (16).

Generally, our conception of standards of fitness in housing is rising all the time, and as present day social aspirations are rising too, higher quality physical and social environment is required to cater for higher living standards, if much of the housing now being designed and built is not to be obsolescent for the major part of 60 years, the " normal " length of life for financing housing, although the whole financial structure of housing is now under review (See Chapter 8). Building to higher standards now will mean higher costs, but will be much cheaper than remedying obsolescence later on, as some local authorities who face problems in comparatively young houses are now finding.

Some economists believe that the majority of households in this country cannot afford Parker Morris standards, which are obligatory for public housing, and that, moreover, the country can ill afford to lock its capital up in projects designed for a hypothetical future population (*Subsidies and Social Needs,* by Adela A. Nevitt at the Housing Centre Conference, 1969, *Housing Review,* Vol. 18, No. 5). There is a school of thought, too, which believes that standards (Parker Morris) in public housing should be reduced to the level of private speculative houses which are presumably considered as acceptable by the people who buy them. The Housing Centre, however, has always maintained that we should build to meet the reasonable aspirations of the day and anything less than the current version of Parker Morris standards would be unacceptable for new building. Parker Morris standards were intended to be minimum standards, and we should be thinking now of higher, not lower, standards for all new housing, including that built privately for sale. If any standards *have* to be cut in times of financial stringency, then cuts should only be made in items which can be added back later, such as kitchen fittings, heating in bathrooms, and not in space standards which cannot be added satisfactorily and economically afterwards.

The National House Building Council places an obligation on builders in the private sector not to build below a standard defined by specification and provides for registration and discipline with removal from the register as the ultimate sanction, for periodic inspection of the house in course of erection; certification; a two-year guarantee against minor defects and a 10-year guarantee (supported by insurance cover) against major defects, which are essential pre-requisites for a building society mortgage and which about 1·25 million houses carry. In September 1975 the Council announced that it was introducing changes which would mean that higher standards were being required in the private sector. The new standard would add about £100 to the cost of a house, but it was claimed that the homes would be safer, easier to run, better-constructed and better insulated and better " finished ". From 1975 on, however, items under the 10-year guarantee would only be paid for at original prices at the time of purchase, not when the defect occurred, and the council advised special inflation-proof insurance cover to guard against this kind of eventuality, the cover involving a single payment of £20 to a council-nominated insurance company.

In February 1976 the Minister for Housing and Construction agreed to arrange a meeting between the RIBA and the Department of the Environment to discuss matters relating to the improvement of design standards in reducing delay and excessive costs. The RIBA had previously emphasised the "inter-dependence" of the public and private sectors in housing as "a necessary and continuing system of employing architectural resources", and, expressing satisfaction with the Minister's concern to improve standards of design, claimed that action along these lines would enable architects to come more closely to grips with the "real housing needs of people".

Environmental standards

The Parker Morris committee emphasised that the general appearance of the majority of housing layouts could and should be greatly improved. Under the heading, " The Home in its Setting ", it suggested ways of improving external appearance, arrangements for reasonable privacy in gardens and access from one side of terrace houses to the other, and of making adequate and satisfactory playspace available for children and sensible and realistic provision for cars.

Within the housing site, where cars take up a great deal of space and are dangerous, straight, through roads for fast traffic are generally no longer feasible. Most designers seek to segregate pedestrians from vehicular traffic. A form of layout called the Radburn system, after a pioneer American scheme, involving in residential areas separation of through traffic from local traffic, and car traffic from pedestrian walk-ways, has been advocated to achieve horizontal segregation, but has not always proved satisfactory as it may entail loss of privacy. The present tendency is still to give access to dwellings from pedestrian ways, making separate access to groups of garages, so that the cars do not interfere with pedestrians (17 and 18). Vehicular access to houses by means of garage courts leading to back gardens, however, is not always popular.

The planning authority sets the standard for car space provision. Designing for 1:1 ratio for car spaces was normal and local authorities still insist on it or even 2:1 parking standards, even though the evidence of existing development shows that this is not required. The Department of the Environment is producing a new bulletin on the design of estate roads which is most likely to reduce the high standards required by engineers, and an illustrated booklet, written by Bruno de Hamel, describing the problems of blending new roads into the landscape and how the Department of the Environment is tackling them, was published in March 1976. The author places special emphasis on the part played by the Secretary of State's Landscape Advisory Committee which celebrated its twentieth anniversary in April 1976 (19). In low density schemes, the choice is for a garage with the house, and/or garages in groups. In high density schemes, full provision at ground level would mean almost total absorption of the basement storey below the buildings—leading to a system of vertical segregation of pedestrians from vehicular traffic. Much experiment has been carried out in this form of layout, but underground car parks are very costly and create problems of nuisance unless continually supervised.

A desirable form of layout in high densities should help to clear the site of cars and leave it open for full use by occupiers. Play provision should be made for children of different ages (DOE Circular 79/72) and the open space designed for the use of all ages. Landscape architecture should exploit existing features of the site by retaining as many of the original trees as possible and providing for the planting of new trees, grass lawns, shrubs and flowers. Shared open spaces and the paved access areas which link them need to be carefully and skilfully designed, taking into account the pressures of everyday use imposed by residents and children. Here, as in all aspects of housing, good maintenance, care and the co-operation of all concerned are essential.

Vandalism is discussed in Chapter 11 which considers the social aspects of housing. However, conclusions from an examination in America of what aggregate in the mix of social and physical variables combine to produce stable residential communities are relevant to any consideration of design and layout of housing. Professor Oscar Newman, of the Centre for Residential Security Design in New York, at a conference of the National Association for the Care and Resettlement of Offenders, explained that a computer-aided analysis of 100,000 units of public housing in New York City revealed that social variables predicted crimes, vandalism and vagrancy rates much more strongly than did the physical variables of the project's design. The particular social variables which were identified as correlating highly with crime rate were, in order of importance: the percentage of welfare families with only one head of household (normally female); the number of teenage children; and the percentage of black residents—the correlations of black residents with female head of household and low income were very high. The physical variables that predicted crime rate most strongly were, in order of importance: the size of the project; the degree of territorial definition, i.e., the number of units sharing an entry, and the building height. It was, however, in the combination of the social and physical variables that the most dramatic predictions were obtained. The increase in the size and density of cities meant that people often found themselves living next to neighbours with whom they did not share a common geographical background, age, ethnicity or life-style, and, as a result, tended to confine their activities within the areas they controlled: the four walls which contained their dwelling and the places distant from their home where they worked. People identify only with their own " defensible space "; the old concept of community based on the geographical juxtaposition of families with shared ethnic origins has gone, and lack of identification with the neighbourhood has given rise to many social problems, including vandalism. Professor Newman theorised how a " community of interest " could be achieved, and presented excerpts from two current works: *Design Directives for Achieving Defensible Space in New Residential Areas* and *The Closed Streets in St. Louis*— the city which recently demolished a 2,740 unit project (20).

With good design it should be possible to obtain privacy at either low or high density while at the same time allowing for sociability—the opportunity to make contact fairly easily. To encourage good design, the former Ministry of Housing and Local Government, the Welsh Office and the Saltire Society in Scotland promoted annual awards for high standards of design and layout in housing schemes, and these are still awarded.

To secure improvement in the built environment, too, the government set up, in 1975, an Environmental Board to influence the quality of work done or authorised by local government. Its membership includes the Department of the Environment's chief planner, the director-general of design services in the Property Services Agency, the director-general highways, the deputy secretaries responsible for housing and the environmental group and the adviser on construction, together with " highly experienced persons from local government and private practice ". The board has the services of a senior multi-disciplinary team drawing together the planning, design and constructional skills which the Secretary of State for the Environment considered must combine to produce a high quality result. One of the board's first tasks was to advise on guidance to local authorities on how to make the most of the public ownership of development land, discussed in Chapter 9. A 13-man group was also set up under the chairmanship of the Minister for Housing and Construction to monitor the supply and demand situation in the building world.

Housing cost yardsticks

A " cost yardstick " which sets the maximum cost of dwellings for which Exchequer subsidies would be paid for any local authority (and now registered housing associations) scheme, was introduced by the then Minister of Housing and Local Government in April 1967. Housing standards based on the Parker Morris recommendations were made obligatory from 1 January 1969 for all council housing sanctioned (Circular 36/67). Floor space standards incorporated the detailed recommendations in *Homes for Today and Tomorrow* (6) and heating standards followed the

Parker Morris recommendations for an installation maintaining 13°C (55°F) in kitchens and circulation space and 18°C (65°F) in living and dining areas when the outside temperature was −1°C (30°F). Bedroom heating was not provided for in the cost limits and neither were built-in wardrobes and double glazing for windows. The Ministry claimed that other recommendations by the committee—for kitchen fitments, electric socket outlets and play spaces for children—would be within the reach of councils prepared to spend up to the new cost limits introduced by the Ministry.

Other design and construction features which were considered socially significant in new dwellings included: reduction of noise by better planning and improved sound insulation within the dwelling and careful planning of dwellings in relation to traffic and playgrounds outside; aspect and orientation with regard to daylight and sunlight; improved methods of refuse disposal to meet the problems created by rising, and changing, standards of living (e.g., new forms of disposable packaging for food, and changes in domestic heating arrangements which restrict burning of refuse); adequate storage space for equipment, and space for hobbies, recreation and informal activity, and efficient lift installations in blocks of flats.

The cost yardsticks which were set out in 1967 based on these standards were expressed in terms of building cost per person. They took account of variations in density, sizes of dwellings, geographical cost levels and number of car spaces. Changes in standards have been made since 1967, e.g., in the heat levels required for elderly persons housing, and the cost limits were to be reviewed annually (Circular 36/67, para. 2). The failure of the yardsticks to keep pace with realistic costs, however, has been a cause of complaint almost since their introduction, as has been the use of the yardsticks as a mandatory cost ceiling rather than as an aid to cost planning, as originally intended. Yardsticks were increased in 1969 (MoHLG Circular 31/69, *The Housing Cost Yardstick*) and again in 1971 (DOE Circular 18/71) when the largest increases were awarded to low density schemes and the allowances for dwellings specifically for old people were raised, and again in 1972. In 1974, the yardstick allowance was increased by 70 per cent for firm price tenders and 60 per cent for fluctuating ones, and the market allowance, used to close the financial gap between the cost limit and the lowest tender, would all but disappear. DOE Circular 61/75, W.O. 109/75, *The Housing Cost Yardstick*, brought changes in the cost control system including a 12 per cent increase in the basic housing cost yardstick, a new cost allowance for smaller dwellings and a quarterly review of tender prices to ensure that the cost yardstick was kept at a realistic level. The Minister for Housing and Construction also announced that he had invited the local authority associations to take part in a working party to examine and make recommendations on future arrangements for local authority housebuilding cost control. The first increase to result from the quarterly review of tender prices designed to ensure that the yardstick was maintained at a realistic level came in September 1975, when the Department of the Environment announced a 2 per cent increase. In January 1976 the circular on cost yardsticks already mentioned gave an increase to encourage the production of more small units, and by March 1976 the rise over the level set in June 1975, when the quarterly reviews were introduced, amounted to 5 per cent. Subsequently, DOE Circular 65/76, issued in June 1976, announced a further increase in the yardstick which brought the rise over the June 1975 level up to 6 per cent. However, the *Financial Times* pointed out that housing costs generally were calculated to have risen on average by about 15 per cent in the year ending May 1976.

Although it has been recognised that there was a need for some system of cost control for subsidised housing, designers had complained of the time and effort expended in trying to pare housing schemes to minimum standards and minimum costs and voiced fears that by reducing quality and standards, maintenance and running costs would be increased and the period during which contemporary standards would be acceptable would be shortened. The quarterly review of yardsticks has improved the situation for designers and at present, tenders generally are being received which are within yardstick. This is due primarily to the present slump in building, described below, but applies more to " green field " sites; small infill schemes which are becoming more socially desirable still prove very expensive.

A survey by the Chartered Institute of Public Finance and Accountancy of about three-quarters of authorities in England and Wales showed that the cost of providing and maintaining public housing would rise by 38 per cent in 1975–76. Debt charges were the largest item of expense and were expected to rise from £992 million to £1,287 million, the total estimated expenditure rising from £1,504 million to £1,918 million. On published budgets, the cost of supervision and management had risen by 25 per cent and maintenance and repairs by 25 per cent. Rents contributed 44 per cent of money towards housing costs compared with 49 per cent the previous year (*Housing Statistics, England and Wales —Housing Revenue Accounts 1974/75 and 1975/76 (Outturn)*, available from CIPFA, Buckingham Place, London, SW1. price £1·50). Housing finance is considered in greater detail in Chapter 8.

Relationship between design and maintenance

In any assessment of overall cost and functional effectiveness of a building, regard should be given to maintenance and operating costs. A report from the Department of the Environment, *The Relationship between Design and Maintenance*, set out to show the influence of design decisions on the subsequent maintenance of buildings, to illustrate with specific examples how design could reduce maintenance costs without necessarily increasing first cost, and to make recommendations for research to fill gaps in current knowledge of the subject. The report reviewed economic aspects of design, discussed major maintenance problems arising from water penetration, condensation, roof design, industrialised building, use of timber, movement joints and sealants, and dirt deposition, and considered the cleaning and maintenance implications of surface finishes and decoration, plumbing and drainage, which created the greatest demand for maintenance and environmental control. Reference was made to the lack of feed-back to the designer and to the inadequate use of information which was available. One of the first results of the many sensible suggestions put forward in the report was the setting-up of a maintenance cost information service based on an inter-disciplinary team at Bath University. The service had grown out of a pilot study sponsored by the former Ministry of Public Buildings and Works at the School of Architecture and Building Technology, and it enables subscribers, whether corporate or individual, to receive a regular series of data sheets and the benefit of other facilities.

Disturbing reports in March 1976 on failures in buildings completed within 20 years emphasised the need for a closer relationship between design and maintenance, for higher quality control on site during building operations and more intensive feedback between the architect and the consumer in future housing. A survey published in *Building Design* showed that some 40 local authorities alone, including some of the large urban districts, were spending more than £20 million in keeping modern homes habitable, without including what it cost to rehouse tenants if they had to be moved while repairs went on, loan charges, loss of rent, damage to furnishings and decorations, and time lost on administration. Recurring problems were condensation, water penetration through roofs, falling tiles, cracking walls and floors, leaking plumbing, sagging beams and crumbling concrete, and defective joints and window frames. *Building Design* claimed that many of the problems occurred in high rise buildings and centred on " the inability of the designers during the 50s to understand the fierceness of the elements above five storeys! ". Problems in two blocks built in 1957 in Birkenhead included condensation, faulty underfloor heating and other defects which made the flats unpopular. The blocks are to be demolished at a cost of £270,000, just over a third of the original cost of constructing them. Canterbury council completed an estate in 1975 on which it was discovered that severe water penetration necessitated the expenditure of £500,000 to make the houses reasonably habitable, while an estate in Southwark has various defects which will cost a total of £2,782,000 to remedy. The Department of the Environment has expressed " concern " about the scale of these failures, which have been so widespread that much of the money which should have been used by the local authorities to bring older accommodation up to date is being deflected to prevent new accommodation from disintegration.

Changes in methods of construction, the use of different materials and changes in living habits have combined with other factors to make condensation a recurring problem in dwellings, and control of condensation an essential if large maintenance bills are to be avoided. DOE *Condensation in dwellings, Part I Design Guide and Part 2 Remedial Measures, HMSO, 1971 (21),* set out good practice in this respect, and a British Standard in 1975, *B.S. 5250, 1975. Code of basic data for the design of buildings: the control of condensation,* provided a general discussion of thermal performance related to condensation and constructional means of achieving it in new and existing building. In April 1975 the DOE issued a circular letter to local authorities advising them that in most cases it would be possible to relax the Building Regulations to allow cavity wall insulation to be carried out and listed the criteria it would take into account when deciding when such relaxation would be advisable.

In 1974, council building programmes were reduced because of the cost of a huge emergency operation launched by local authorities to trace and test suspect cement in thousands of public and private buildings. The DOE had warned all local councils to check buildings for a type of quick drying cement, known as high alumina, after roof beams in which it had been used collapsed at an East London school. In August 1975 a government sub-committee accepted a report of the Building Research Establishment which concluded that basically the risks involved in using the cement were small, but still there. The report gave guidance for structural engineers on methods of checking buildings which had used HAC, but said that houses, maisonettes and flats using standard factory produced joists of up to 10 inches in depth could be considered safe, with some caveats with regard to height of the buildings, the span of beams, evidence of condensation or leakage and other matters. The House of Commons was told in April 1976 that the estimated cost to local authorities of remedial work on buildings affected by high alumina cement was £2·9 million for 1976–77 and £3·4 million in 1977–78 and subsequent years to 1979–80. In April 1976 too, emergency checks were ordered for details of buildings in which cancer-causing blue asbestos had been used after the discovery of asbestos dust in vandal-damaged ceilings on an estate at Deptford, SE London.

In 1976, the long summer drought brought a further maintenance and repair problem. It caused extensive drying and shrinkage of the clay subsoil on which many houses, mainly in the south of England, are built, resulting in movement of house foundations and cracking of walls. Information on cracking caused by foundation movement or other reasons is provided by BRE Digest 75, *Cracking in buildings*; and the Building Research Advisory Service, which has been giving advice on this problem, its causes and solutions, over the past 30 years, has produced a Technical Information Leaflet—TIL 43, *Damage to buildings on shrinkable clay sites*, which discusses the problem in detail. Other useful publications are the *Architects' Journal's* housing rehabilitation handbook, Technical study 4, *Structural stability* (Architects' Journal, 23 June 1976), and, for a more general treatment, the *AJ Handbook of building structure*, by Allan Hodgkinson (Architectural Press) (22).

National problems of energy conservation have led to work being undertaken on looking at housing as energy systems, at, for example, such establishments as the Building Science Section and the Project Office of the School of Architecture at Newcastle University. The space heating energy consumption of housing in the United Kingdom is probably the highest per dwelling in the whole of NW Europe. Of the total prime energy consumption in the UK, some 30 per cent is consumed in domestic buildings, where an analysis of house energy consumption shows that approximately 66 per cent is used in space heating, 21 per cent for water heating, 7 per cent for cooking and 6 per cent for lighting and power outlets. Heat losses in the average home are 25 per cent through the roof, 35 per cent through the walls, 10 per cent through the windows, 15 per cent by draughts and 15 per cent into the ground. Methods of reducing the energy used by buildings which could lead to a saving of up to 15 per cent of the total consumption of primary energy in the UK were described in a report of the Building Research Establishment working party on energy conservation (BRE CP 56/75). The working party estimated that by undertaking all the technically feasible options it should be possible to achieve an ultimate saving of over 15 per cent in the UK annual consumption of primary energy by measures in building services which would not impair environmental standards. Using only well established technologies, it should be possible to save about 6 per cent of the UK primary energy consumption by action in existing housing stock. The report was intended as a discussion paper, and assessed the potential, relative importance and economics of existing and possible future energy conservation technologies. It also outlined a methodology that would help the individual householder to determine whether particular energy saving measures are economic or not in his case. The outcome depends on a number of factors such as the amount he spends on fuel, how long he expects to stay in his dwelling and his view of the extent to which he can recoup any costs when he moves. The Housing Centre Trust's conference in Manchester on *Husbanding Resources in Housing* was reported in *Housing Review*, Vol. 24, No. 3.

Alternative approaches in the design of housing to reduce running costs are seen in eco-systems—self supporting structures, recycling waste, utilising methane from effluent, using complete solar heating systems for both space heating and water supply. The Cambridge House, designed by Alex Pike, to do all these things, was to be built with a grant from the Science Research Council and lived in by a normal family with measurements being taken to assess the performance of the house over a series of heating seasons. Also, the " house under glass " (HUG) proposal produced by Ted Nicklin and Malcolm Newton uses glass as an outer skin over a semi-traditional house to maximise and utilise solar heat. The initial cost of providing a solar energy system for heating houses in Southern France has been described as high initially, but it is claimed that the system should pay for itself in nine years. In England, a solar heating system is to be incorporated into a council house scheme in Lewisham. Twenty-nine small flats have been planned for completion in 1977 at a cost of £330,000, of which £13,000 will be for the solar heating which will supplement all domestic hot water heating and the heating of the flats themselves. Experiments are also being carried out in the use of heat pumps, which extract heat from a low temperature source such as air, river water or the ground and inject it into the dwelling, and into the potential of wind energy. Although the overall aim of experiment and research is to develop as simple and low capital cost systems as possible, it must also be emphasised that, as shown earlier in this chapter, a higher initial expenditure, for example, in measures to control condensation, can reduce a constant drain on maintenance.

Repairs and maintenance

The importance of repair and maintenance of existing stock has been increasingly recognised as a fundamental part of rehabilitation of older housing and preservation of a good environment.

Any consideration of present and future housing standards must take account of the areas of sub-standard housing which still exist in this country, and rehabilitation is considered in detail in Chapter 7.

The White Paper, *Better homes—the next priorities*, proposed special repairs-only grants, and already special payments were given for well-maintained houses in slum clearance areas. Part VII of the Housing Act 1974 provided for financial assistance by way of grants towards works of improvement, repair and conversion. The Defective Premises Act 1972, which came into force on 1 January 1974, altered the law with regard to responsibility for repair and maintenance in several respects. The law had formerly been that a purchaser bought at his own risk and had no right to compensation in the event of the dwelling he bought not being fit for habitation; under the 1972 Act, a duty was imposed upon those having control of the quality of the workmanship put into a dwelling to see that the work was done in a workmanlike or professional manner with proper materials so that the dwelling would be fit for habitation when the work was completed, including conversion work and the enlargement of dwellings. A right was thereby given upon which the person who orders the dwelling and every person who acquires an interest in it (including someone who is under a contract to purchase or who has entered into an agreement to take a tenancy) can sue. Also, if a landlord is under an obligation to a tenant to maintain or repair a property, e.g., in a lease for a term of less than seven years, a duty was imposed upon him to take care of everybody who might reasonably be expected to be affected by defects in the state of the property. This duty was established if the landlord ought in all circumstances to have known of a defect, so that if a landlord should have inspected the property but omitted to do so he will be deemed to have discovered the defect. The landlord is also deemed to be under an obligation to the tenant if he has a right to enter the premises to do repairs which the tenant is not obliged to do under the terms of his tenancy, whether or not the landlord has actually entered into a covenant to do them. It should be noted that where a landlord is under an obligation to repair or maintain the common parts of a building, he owes a duty to everybody who might reasonably be expected to be affected by defects in the state of the premises, and not only the tenant.

All kinds of skills and constant experiment and innovation are needed, not only to create the housing we want, but also to maintain what we have, and full advantage must be taken of advances in technical processes. Sections of the building industry mount valuable exhibitions of developments, including the use of new finishes, of plastics of all kinds, of glass fibres and other materials, and improvements in methods of water and space heating and in television and radio systems. The Department of the Environment has prepared a short series of building maintenance bibliographies giving details of sources of information on techniques, repairs, plant and management. Subjects dealt with include: cleaning buildings; design of buildings with a view to maintenance; management and economics of maintenance; building services engineering; deterioration and weathering of materials; and preservation and restoration of buildings.

The powers of local authorities to control statutory nuisances, dangerous structures, sanitary facilities and wants of repair are discussed in Chapter 3. With all the legislation, and powers under it, available, it may seem surprising that so many unremedied defects still exist; this may be due to the fact that so much of the law is still permissive, and also to ignorance of tenants of their rights. Moreover, in those areas where the law should be more fully used, local authorities trying to implement it all would be unable to do anything else.

Maintenance of housing standards, however, and indeed all the quantity and quality of repair and general maintenance work, depend to a great extent on the efficiency of the building industry and the availability of labour and materials.

The building industry

About one-eighth of the national output is used for construction and maintenance of the built environment. About four-fifths of the work done by contractors is on new building and works, of which two-fifths is housing. The direct labour departments of public authorities carry out about one-eighth of all building and civil engineering work, a large proportion of which is maintenance—direct labour is discussed more fully below.

The construction industry is one of the country's largest employers. It includes not only general contractors but also subcontractors of many specialisations, suppliers and manufacturers of building materials and components, many of whom serve other industries. The industry embraces very many firms, some of them very large, and very many, quite small. Much of the labour is engaged for specific projects and much of the equipment used on building sites is hired. This diversity makes the industry well suited to the variety of demands made on it, every project being unique at least in location, and almost always in size and design, while the total demands on the industry fluctuate with the strength of the economy. This very flexibility and fragmentation, however, do not make it easy for the industry to engage in continuous appraisal of performance and improvement in methods which might benefit more closely integrated industries.

While the demands on the industry, both in volume of work and in standards, are increasing, the industry's most vital resources—skilled men—cannot increase at the same rate. The national strike of building workers in 1972 caused widespread disruption on building sites throughout the country, delayed major projects by months and caused the loss to the industry of many thousands of operatives who have never returned to a site; altogether the size of the building force fell between 1966 and 1972 from 1,090,000 to 835,000. Increasing demands can only be met, therefore, by improving the industry's productivity. Many efforts are being made to this end, including ways of integrating design and production, mentioned below, but the major efforts, concerned with work on site, take the form of what has come to be called " industrialisation ".

The prefabrication of large parts of the superstructure of housing projects is one means of this industrialisation and in recent years development of technique has intensified. Prominent among these are the precasting of large concrete panels for walls and floors, which reduces the need for traditional craft work in constructing these elements, and can eliminate or reduce the need for craft work in finishing the surfaces, installing the services and in work such as erecting scaffolding and shuttering. For low rise housing, there is an increase in the use of timber framing, often prefabricated, in place of load-bearing masonry for walls, while the possibility of a wide choice of treatments for the elevations, including brick facing, is retained. Some steel frames are also used in this way.

Prefabricated techniques usually involve considerable investment in development work and in factories, and unless the plant is operated at nearly full capacity, and the cost of materials are carefully controlled—since the materials they replace in traditional solutions are relatively low in cost—competitive costs are difficult to achieve. For these reasons, the idea of authorities joining together in groups or consortia has developed in order to make full use of industrialised building methods. CLASP (Construction of Local Authorities Special Programme), which was mainly concerned with school building in Nottinghamshire and other counties, was followed by other consortia aiming to bring about an increase in quantity and quality of housing by the use of industrialised building techniques, examples are the Yorkshire Development Group and the Midlands Housing Consortium.

Industrialised techniques need not involve prefabrication in a factory, and some systems of construction use panels cast on the site. The majority of industrialised housing is not, in fact, prefabricated at all, but is built in " no-fines " concrete cast in framework, which can be used again. Technical innovation is not in itself essential to industrialisation and particularly in the field of low rise housing significant improvements in productivity are following systematic improvements in the detailed design when traditional techniques are used. These improvements are centred on simplifying the work on site, reducing the interference between trades and enabling each trade's work to be closely organised to ensure continuity of work.

Another means of harnessing industrial potential is by making use of standardised components which can be incorporated in individually designed projects. These may not necessarily be major parts of the superstructures, but if they are to have a wide market and thus be made competitively, they must be subject to disciplines of dimensional co-ordination in order that they are compatible with other components. Pre-finishing is sometimes practicable, on kitchen cabinets, for instance, and can reduce the work for painters on site and allow better quality treatments. The construction industry's resources are augmented when other industries develop products for it. For example, the sheet metal and plastics industries have made significant contributions in developing at competitive prices such items as sheet metal garage door units and plastic rainwater goods, which being lighter and self-finished can make for simpler and quicker operations in installation than with traditional products.

Industrialisation is also served by mechanising even traditional site operations and, above all, by improving the quality of management of work. Whatever techniques are used, productivity can be improved by systematic appraisal of achieved performance and applying the results in improved design and better management. The organisation of the demand itself is important in achieving continuity in the use of resources, both of production facilities and of teams of experienced operatives, and this can be influenced both by initiative by official bodies in combining programmes of work, and by the sales efforts of speculative builders. Criticism has been made against governmental use of the building industry as an " economic regulator ". Restrictions of building activity by government measures from time to time restrict the building industry's ability to make long-term plans for strengthening the organisation of firms and achieving higher efficiency. Using the industry as an economic regulator has meant that forms of pre-fabrication requiring massive investment are not economically viable because large programmes cannot be achieved. Also, every time there is a slump in the industry more skilled men leave and fewer apprentices join. Unfortunately, too, the building industry tends to attract more than its fair share of lower standard labour and output is not likely to rise until there is an economic incentive, as well as improved conditions of labour, including better pension schemes. Criticisms are made too that the country has spent too much time and effort on prefabrication and similar forms of industrialisation and not enough on seeing that management makes the best use of the simpler skills.

In January 1975 the Minister for Housing and Construction told a local government conference that local authorities and others building homes would have to consider the advantages of using unconventional construction methods in order to speed up the housing process. " An average of nearly two years to build a home is just not good enough and it is not necessary. The sorry fact is that housebuilding design and construction times are lengthening ". The Brick Development Association, however, challenged ministerial assumptions and completed a pair of semi-detached houses at Bottesford, on the Nottinghamshire-Leicestershire border, within 15 days.

In 1974, the construction industry was faced with the prospect of an 8 per cent decline in new work between 1973 and 1975. The Chancellor of the Exchequer announced a £120 million programme of spending in the public sector to help to sustain activity and employment in the building industry. Arrangements were made for expenditure of £100 million in 1975–76 and £20 million in 1976–77 to enable new orders to be placed as quickly as possible. £46 million of the total was made available to the Department of the Environment for capital works on water and sewage, new towns, local authorities and other environmental services and schemes.

Although housebuilding rose in 1975—according to the Department of the Environment's figures for the third quarter, public sector starts were a 22 per cent increase on the previous quarter; and private sector starts, although only a modest 4 per cent increase on the previous quarter, were 68 per cent up on the last year's third quarter—the industry as a whole is certainly not in a healthy state. New orders in the first six months of 1975 were down 15 per cent over the previous six months and verged on the low levels of the first half of 1974. Other evidence of the decline of the industry as a whole included the market reduction in the volume of inquiries; reports that both public and private clients were inviting an increasing number of contractors to tender for any one project; the relatively static level of tender prices compared with increased costs; and the increase in the number of unemployed, with special emphasis on the growing number of skilled men out of work. Some 350,000 building workers, including those normally working in the manufacture and distribution of materials, are out of work and small businesses are experiencing the worst recession in 50 years.

In November 1975 the government made a further £32 million available to local authorities to fund new work for the construction industry, the grant representing the final element in the £200 million programme announced to protect jobs during the winter and stimulate investment. According to government estimates, the programme was to create or avert the loss of 6,000 building jobs, the benefits to be spread among private employers, local authorities, direct labour organisations and other parts of the economy. England got £24 million, of which £12 million was to be spent on publicly owned housing, £4 million on the National Health Service, £4 million on education and £4 million on other local authorities services, e.g., improving fire precautions in old people's homes. Scotland got £3½ million, Wales £2½ million and Northern Ireland £2 million. Areas with the highest level of building jobless were given priority but the government also stated that it wanted money steered towards the inner city areas such as London. The overall emphasis will be on minor construction works as it is planned that the money will be used on projects to be completed by the end of the financial year 1976–77.

The initial reaction from the National Federation of Building Trades' Employers was that, while it welcomed the recognition and support for the stricken construction industry, it considered that the government's aid would only scratch the surface of the problem. In 1976, it directed a five-point plan to the Chancellor of the Exchequer, asking for: improved investment incentives for industrial and commercial buildings; extension of the VAT zero rating for construction work to include repair and maintenance work; suspension of industrial development certificate control for the duration of the current economic recession; some form of demolition grant for industrialists prepared to replace buildings; and an extension of direct incentives—such as cash grants for industrial building, which are often available only in assisted areas.

The Federation's president announced that a survey showed that builders were owed more than £1,200 million, about a third of the money being outstanding beyond the terms of the contract, and he blamed this late payment as being an " important factor " for the 50 per cent rise in building costs over the last two years.

Official DOE figures for August 1976 showed that the level of new orders in the industry continued to fall. In three months to August 1976, orders showed a 15 per cent fall off, even after making adjustments for seasonal variations. Orders for new council housing decreased by a massive 22 per cent, while the private housing sector suffered a 14 per cent drop. The National Council of Building Material Producers has stated that this fall off will continue and has predicted that between 1976 and 1978 new orders for council housing will decline by a further 27 per cent; the outlook for the whole industry, in their opinion, is one of decline at least until mid-1979.

Concern has also been expressed over the shortage of building materials in some areas despite the many thousands out of work and underworked throughout the industry. With regard to bricks, the Minister for Housing and Construction intends to study the issues which would arise in establishing a brick bank following the report which the Monopolies and Mergers Commission hopes to make within a few months on its investigation into the supply of bricks.

Considerable publicity was given at the beginning of 1973 to the adverse effects on house building and prices of the lump labour system which has bedevilled the building industry for over 25 years. At its worst, " the lump " means gangs of roving free-lances hawking themselves from site to site and paying no tax, insurance or training board levy; at best, it means permanently self-employed workers hired out by responsible agencies or working on their own behalf. Many employers prefer them, but others consider the system thoroughly bad because safety, health and welfare regulations are ignored, there is large-scale tax evasion and often the work done is shoddy. An attempt to rid the building industry of the system came in a Labour-only Sub-contracting Bill, introduced in the house of Commons by Mr Eric Heffer, MP, but the government declared the bill unacceptable as making the system illegal overnight would lead to short-term difficulties. In August 1975 tighter tax restrictions for building sub-contractors were announced by the Inland Revenue, whose estimated loss through the lump was at least £10 million a year. The Revenue's scheme incorporated a replacement of sub-contractors' existing tax certificates, new certificates only being issued to sub-contractors who have a clean tax record and a properly-constituted business. Subsequently, the Department of the Environment issued a circular (75/75) and a pamphlet on the setting up of a Demolition and Dismantling Industry Register, a voluntary register open to all firms who agree to abide by the following provisions: to observe the British Standard Code of Practice on Demolition, to observe the nationally agreed working rule agreements which contain a declaration of intent that all operatives should be in direct employment, and to operate appropriate safety training schemes. It was hoped that this voluntary method might abolish the use of lump labour in the trade as well as improve safety and working conditions and encourage training. There did not appear to be any moves to make the voluntary register of building firms mandatory; at present, this contains 1,300 companies but is considered too unrepresentative of the industry to justify imposing such a scheme.

In October 1975 the Department of the Environment set up a working party to examine the operations of direct labour departments of local councils with the intention of providing a sound basis for future policy on their development and ensuring that they played a " full and developing role " in the construction industry. In March 1976 the GLC (General Powers) Bill which would give direct labour departments in the GLC the power to compete with private builders for contracts both for new construction and for repairs and maintenance, was debated in Parliament. Arguments for and against the expansion of direct labour activities split along party lines, and after a division a press release from the Department of the Environment invited submissions of evidence on direct labour organisations to the working party. Two other bills, the West Midlands County Council Bill and the Tyne and Wear Bill, propose similar measures in their areas as the GLC Bill. In Parliament at the same time the idea of a state controlled building agency was discussed as a means of co-ordinating local authority activities with the construction industry.

With the possibility of government legislation on the subject of direct labour, expanding the role of council departments, the debate on the efficacy of such a proposal has received wider attention. Both the CBI and the National Federation of Building Trades Employers are against the expansion of direct labour organisations and would like to see their activities run down. They have submitted two papers to the Department of the Environment which, they have said, illustrate the inefficiency of the council operations. Weight was added to their arguments by Professor Denis O'Brien of Durham University who claimed that the main cause of the inefficiency within direct labour organisations was that they tended to hoard labour and employ more people than they need to cope with their workload; and, further, that they had an unfair advantage in that they obtained capital at favourable rates of interest, made no profit on their operations and had their bills paid more promptly.

In September 1976, 537 of the 548 local authorities and new town development corporations had direct labour departments, employing some 265,000 people to carry out work ranging from routine maintenance to new house building. The Fabian Society *Changing Prospects for Direct Labour* argued that expansion of direct labour organisations could reduce costs; and that, although many labour councils and councillors concerned themselves with fighting for increased council building, few thought about the way in which the houses were built or at what cost. Councils should expand their activities, within the current limitations, in order to prove that direct labour organisations could operate as, if not more, efficiently as private builders. Among others campaigning against direct labour organisations is the Federation of Civil Engineering Contractors, who claim that the output per man in direct labour is just half that of workers in the private construction industry, but the Association of Metropolitan Authorities has stated that they have plenty of evidence that direct labour gets jobs done more reliably than private contracts.

In October 1976 Mr Ernest Armstrong, Parliamentary Under-Secretary of State for the Environment, explained that the intention of the legislation would be to get value for money for the country's direct labour organisation and to make sure that that value for money is seen to be achieved by the people whom the council serves. It was proposed that a local authority should be able to undertake new construction work within the county for another local authority, and because of their importance in the housing programme, for new town development corporations and for registered housing associations; that a district should be able to do new construction work for a contiguous district of another county; and that authorities should be able to do improvement and maintenance work for owners of private houses in housing action areas and general improvement areas within the county. It was recognised that competition under fair and reasonable rules had an important part to play in stimulating efficiency, and the financial basis on which work could be carried out by direct labour organisations would be made clear in the legislation.

At the Housing Centre's national conference in June 1975, on *New Thinking in Housing*, Mr Roger Warren Evans, Industrial Adviser on Construction to the Department of the Environment, examined ways in which the construction of housing could be speeded up, and claimed that the traditional division between design and construction was a major drag on the construction industry, particularly in housing. Mr Evans described two levels in the use of design and construction methods (Design and Build contracts). At one level, the local authority decides what mix of house types is needed in its area and then asks a housebuilder for a complete tender for design and construction, the sketch design being discussed with the authority's architect at an early stage. The builder takes a high proportion of the design costs and the local authority buys the houses from the builder. At the second level, the whole characteristics of a scheme are designed by the local authority's architect, and the builder invited to tender for his own house types on the overall pattern of layout, with the advantage that new house types for every scheme are avoided and the builder is forced to concentrate on the total product. Design and Build contracts, which are allied to the former "package deals" whereby contracting firms undertook to handle both the design and the construction of the whole of a housing scheme, are not generally considered by architects to offer any advantages in practice over the traditional form of contract and can lead to the local authority department losing control over a project. The Minister for Housing and Construction has affirmed that the Department of the Environment is not specially favouring design and build types of contract, but has stated that procedures like design and build have " a part to play in helping us to improve the speed, efficiency and environmental quality of public sector housing."

At the Institute of Housing's annual conference in 1976, Mr R. Warren Evans pointed out that in local authority house production it was rare for any officer to have authority for the total production process, stretching from the key land acquisition and clearance functions, through the planning and design stages, through the construction period, and to the point of delivery. He claimed also that he had found no district authority which had analysed its total production costs for housing, taking into account the contract price, design and other professional overheads, general management overheads, the full cost of delays irrecoverable by contract, and of finance during construction; there was certainly, to his knowledge, no authority capable of expressing these costs as a total cost per unit. In the public sector, both the questions, " Who is in charge "? and " What does it cost "? needed urgent answers. Mr Evans claimed that by far the greatest contribution to high costs was antiquated methods of production, including lengthy procedures, accepted conventions, professional ethics and separate professional roles. A great deal of fresh thinking, however, had been done in alternative procedures in housing production and in management methods which would be available when DOE Circular 94/76 was completed.

The National Building Agency was set up to help and advise the former Ministry of Housing and Local Government and local authorities in the selection and use of industrialised methods, and Circular 21/65 explained the help which the Agency could give. The functions of the Agency included the appraisal of building systems and advice to local authorities on the appointment of professional consultants with experience of industrialised building, but the Agency now advises over a much wider field of the construction industry.

Self-build groups are being encouraged by the Department of the Environment and the Housing Corporation and these are considered under alternative approaches to housing and tenure in Chapter 11 on the social aspects of housing.

Metrication of housebuilding

The change to the metric system in the construction industry was programmed over the period from 1967 to 1972. The timing of the change in local authority housing was kept consistent with the programme, and all standards affecting house design were made available in metric terms. The Department of the Environment kept local authorities informed of the timetable for the use of metric components through circulars, and in 1968 issued Design Bulletin 16, *Co-ordination of Components in Housing— Metric Dimensional Framework*. All authorities were urged to make the fullest use of the opportunity provided by metrication for rationalising design, production and site operations by the use of standard housing components. A 300 mm planning grid was required for metric schemes. (*Metrication for Housing*. By Sylvester Bone. *Housing Review*, Vol. 18, No. 4.)

In 1969 (MoHLG Circular 69/69) local authorities were given a range of 21 house shells for two-storey houses designed in metric in rectangular form from which they had to choose to obtain loan sanction and subsidy. These allowed a wide variety of different plans (*Metric House Shells*, by Robert Purdew *Housing Review*, Vol. 19, No. 3). The National Building Agency, which monitored the change to metric, also provided an information service to local authorities on problems arising out of metrication, and published a series of relevant publications (23) and (24).

Staff

The design and supervision of the erection of a local authority housing scheme is in general the work of the officer, either an architect or a surveyor, appointed by the council, and housing association schemes are usually designed and supervised by an architect. Large local authorities have an architect's department, and some have a housing architect's department which specialises in housing work. Small authorities usually employ architects in private practice, and some larger authorities put work out to private architectural consultants with a view to achieving variety in schemes. In some cases, two or three councils undertake joint schemes for which a private architect has been appointed. The former Ministry of Housing and Local Government recommended that the fullest use should be made of architects in all housing work, and that borough architects should be appointed to authorities above a certain size. Architects' fees are regulated by the Royal Institute of British Architects. The RIBA has raised the difficulty faced by many architects who work for housing associations, that fees are only paid when the site is acquired; if the site is not acquired no design fees are forthcoming; and the matter is being raised with the Housing Corporation.

Reference has already been made to the need to utilise all kinds of skills to create satisfactory housing and to the importance of taking full advantage of advances in technical and sociological processes, in cost control and financial techniques. Constant experiment and innovation are also necessary to meet changing standards and changing needs. Ultimately, these needs will be satisfied functionally, aesthetically and socially, by architects, planners, engineers, surveyors, housing managers and builders and all who are concerned " on the ground " to see new and decent housing being built in a civilised environment, and carefully looked after when it is completed, and older housing rehabilitated and properly used.

The fullest use must be made of professional skill in all branches of housing, and development and continuity in the professions assured by sensible training schemes and facilities and by adequate financial reward, and at the same time public participation and co-operative housing schemes encouraged so that housing meets the wishes and aspirations of those who will live in it.

CHAPTER 11

Social Aspects of Housing

Demographic and social studies have shown that the truism, that the housing problem is not one problem but many, is as valid sociologically as geographically. Professor J. B. Cullingworth and others pointed out many years ago that crude statistics of numbers of people and numbers of rooms—even of numbers of households and numbers of dwellings—are little guide to our housing standard and adequacy, both physically and socially, unless dwellings match occupants in size and type and relate to the reasonable preferences and aspirations of those occupants. The fit must be right, not only in location, but also in respect of needs of special groups, and should be conducive to user satisfaction and contentment.

There is a growing awareness to-day of special housing needs in modern society, and a realisation that if these needs are to be catered for in a comprehensive way with limited resources, there must be greater flexibility in various aspects of housing provision. If it is accepted that to live independently is a social benefit to be extended to all those who desire it, then housing policies must be tailored to meet specific categories of need. The dwindling supply of both furnished and unfurnished accommodation in the private sector, traditionally providing accommodation suited to many special needs, must mean the expansion of local authority and housing association activity to include more of these categories. This in turn must mean more flexible allocation procedures to allow the best use of existing stock in the public sector, if necessary adjusted across borough and district boundaries, so that under and over occupation may be remedied; together with increased cohesiveness of the housing association movement and genuine co-operation between the movement and the local authority, to ensure that the activities of all housing associations in an area are co-ordinated within the strategies of the local authority and full advantage is taken of the particular skills of some of them in meeting specialist needs. Integration of housing aid and pro-vision, with all agencies contributing to the solution of housing problems, especially in urban regions, is essential if limited resources are to be allocated in the most socially desirable way, and if our housing service is to help people with the immediate housing difficulties which confront them, in the way best suited to their particular circumstances.

317

There is a growing awareness, too, that a policy for the provision, management and encouragement of good housing and environment, which has been a major factor in most national and local elections since 1919, has a greater impact than merely a basic expectation of every individual: it can be the key to the realisation of many other social policies. The Cullingworth committee (1969) argued that the allocation of council housing should be as much on the grounds of social need as on the traditional housing management concept of housing need. The Cullingworth report commented: " Our review of current local policies convinces us that local authorities need to have a clearer, deeper and more detailed understanding of the changing housing situation in their areas . . . without this, local authorities will repeatedly find that they are catering for needs which have already been met, or are ignoring other needs which have not come to their attention." (1: 17) An article, "Alternative Approaches to Assessing Housing Need ", *Housing*, June 1976, based on research work carried out by staff within the Scottish Development Department, points out too, " Moreover, the housing situation in different parts of the country varies considerably so that priorities must be established on the basis of local needs and cannot be assumed. Above all, the social nature of housing policy must be recognised. Progress cannot be measured purely in terms of bricks and mortar—levels of new buildings, and demolition—but has to take account of their impact on different sections of the community." (See also Chapter 3, regarding needs assessments.)

On the other hand, an increasingly important sociological question posed is how the housing stock can be managed to the greater satisfaction of the occupants. There is a growing polarisation between owner-occupiers on the one hand and council tenants on the other, and there is also a deep and growing gulf between good and bad council estates. A serious problem is that of steeply rising cost—and increasing criticism—of management and maintenance. A number of local authorities now find that the cost of these services is greater than their total rent income, yet tenant dissatisfaction mounts and rent arrears, vandalism and other social problems increase. More involvement by tenants in the provision, management and control of housing is seen as a possible solution to some of these problems, and serious consideration of alternative approaches in housing, e.g., housing co-operatives, " self-build " societies, development leasehold housing, and shared equity schemes, is a salient and welcome feature of the modern complex and critical housing scene.

This chapter discusses housing for special needs, including the elderly, the disabled, students and single people, the homeless, single parent families, the problem families, newcomers and immigrants, and gypsies. It outlines the incidence of social problems in housing and discusses tenant participation, variety of choice in housing and alternative tenures, comprehensive management functions and co-operation between all agencies and professions concerned with housing and social welfare.

Housing for the elderly

The largest and most generally recognised " special group " of households is that of the elderly. People of 65 and over formed 12·9 per cent of the population of Great Britain in 1971, and their numbers and proportion will go on increasing until the early 1990s. The Government Actuary's department estimates of future population trends indicate that the number of elderly people, i.e., those over pensionable age, is likely to increase by the order of 10 per cent during the next 10 years; more significantly, however, the population over 70 is likely to rise by something like 20 per cent over the same period. In *Population projections No. 4, 1973–2013* (Office of Population Censuses and Surveys, HMSO, 1974), forecasts are as follows:

1973	1991	2001	2011
9·3m	9·9m	9·5m	10·0m

" The very old (80 and over) increase particularly rapidly over the next 20 years but thereafter become almost stationary in numbers at around 3 per cent of the population " (*Ibid.*).

Although most elderly people do not require specially designed forms of housing and continue to live in normal households, often in the housing they occupied before reaching retirement age, about one and a half million older people live alone, the great majority of them women, and it has been estimated that about 300,000 elderly people need accommodation suited to a minor degree of frailty. Further, there are nearly one million council houses of five or more rooms occupied by one or two pensioners. No-one should ever be forced out of these under-occupied houses, but if the right alternative could be offered—smaller, more convenient accommodation within or near the same neighbourhood— then more elderly people would move than do at present, when the only alternative is usually to move out of a familiar neighbourhood away from family and friends.

Housing suited to older people is, therefore, one of our most pressing needs. Design standards for such housing are currently governed by MoHLG Circular 82/69 issued five years ago. Considerable experience of provision to these standards has been achieved since that date. There is a wealth of advice and information available on the accommodation needs of old people, much of which is listed in the bibliography, and the Department of the Environment has the standards currently under review.

Basically, what the majority of people reaching retirement age will ask for are small easily-managed dwellings on one level, with constant warmth not involving complicated heating appliances; convenient to shops and services and with group activities nearby to provide a stimulus for getting out of the home; to be part of the community in order to avoid the feeling of isolation, but not to be integrated too closely with families containing the age groups from 3 to 18 years. In case of emergency they like the availability of an " S.O.S." service. At this stage they do not usually object to living in large groups of their own age, and it is of interest that there are successful very large schemes of old people's housing in other countries (1).

To provide small homes to modern standards is proportionately more costly than building larger ones, because the kitchen, bathroom and essential equipment of a self-contained dwelling—the expensive core of the house—costs almost as much for a one-room dwelling as for one with two or three bedrooms. Moreover, a higher standard of heating is needed for dwellings for old people, since warmth is more important for them than for younger, more active households. In order to enable old people's dwellings to be built in the public sector and to be let at appropriate rents, additions to the cost yardstick are available, conditional on the provision of additional standards which include a higher heating standard and some other special fittings (MoHLG Circular 82/69), as detailed below.

Old age pensioners are, of course, able to claim supplementary benefits to meet their rent, and if they are living in council or housing association housing, will almost certainly be encouraged to claim them if they are eligible. There was some uncertainty as to how far the Supplementary Benefits Commission would cover high rents, but in 1970 an arrangement was made which means that virtually all rents in the public sector are covered by them in full.

Special purpose housing for old people takes different forms. Some, who need constant care and attention and are too frail or infirm to look after themselves, must live in residential homes if they are not looked after by their own families. Such homes are built and run by the social service authorities under the National Assistance Act 1948 and are not dealt with here since they are not regarded as a part of normal housing provision. Since the 1950s, the Department of the Environment has encouraged the building of flatlet schemes and other grouped dwellings with a warden for old people who will keep in touch with the tenants and help them in an emergency. Such schemes are sometimes referred to as

" sheltered housing ". There are a number of variations on how many amenities are shared: in some, there is no sharing and the presence of the warden is the only significant difference from any other housing. There are also many completely self-contained small bungalows and flats scattered among larger dwellings intended for, and usually occupied by, older tenants. To describe an interesting development, the Housing Development Directorate of the Department of the Environment has published a paper (HDD Occasional Paper 1/76), *Housing the elderly: how successful are Granny Annexes?*, evaluating schemes by some local authorities of " Granny Annexes ", which are self-contained homes attached to family houses, and which are already quite common in the owner-occupied sector. The paper shows that the extended family, and even unrelated neighbours, often give the kind of emergency help a warden provides and often more help in the home than any warden could, whether the old people's housing is adjoining or just nearby, and the old people in the survey seem to be often as old and frail as many in sheltered housing. It also emphasises the importance of flexible allocation policies mentioned earlier in this chapter.

Two categories of old people's housing were recognised in 1969 by the Ministry of Housing and Local Government for additional subsidy (Circular 82/69). These are self-contained dwellings designed to Parker Morris standards, and grouped flatlets with warden's supervision. In Category 1, dwellings must have handrails, special locks, higher standards of heating (an installation capable of maintaining 21°C throughout when the outside temperature is $-°1C$) and a refrigerator or ventilated, cool cupboard if they are to qualify for a small addition to the yardstick subsidy. Optional extras for grouped schemes of self-contained dwellings in Category 1, which may or may not have a warden, include limited communal facilities, such as a common-room with kitchen and WC, an emergency alarm system and a guest room. The additional subsidy is related to the extras provided and varies according to whether the scheme is for less than 20 old people or for 20 or more.

Category 2 includes flatlet schemes with a warden. Mandatory standards cover the floor areas, which are slightly lower than those mandatory for Category 1 dwellings because of the communal provision. It is also necessary to provide individual cookers designed for safety as well as the mandatory special equipment for the self-contained dwellings. Flatlet schemes must have a self-contained warden's dwelling, an emergency alarm system by means of which tenants can communicate with the warden, a common-room with provision for light refreshments and cloakroom accommodation, a laundry room, a telephone for use by the tenant, and storage and facilities for deliveries. All communal accommodation must be accessible from the flatlets by enclosed and heated circulation space. Guest accommodation and a warden's office are optional extras.

Other mandatory standards for old people's housing follow broadly the same lines as for all public sector housing, but in blocks of flats for old people two storeys only may be provided without a lift instead of three storeys as in family housing, and access to dwellings from a lift above four storeys high must be enclosed.

There are special considerations to be borne in mind when choosing the best site for groups of dwellings for old people. Since elderly people may have difficulty in walking long distances, particularly on hilly ground, easy access to the post office where pensions are collected, bus stops, shops, churches and communal facilities is important, as mentioned earlier. Access to and from the dwellings should be by easy gradients; difficult steps or slopes likely to become slippery in bad weather should be avoided. People who spend much time sitting at home enjoy an interesting and lively outlook, although most appreciate protection from unpleasant noise or the activities of children which may become too boisterous. Since visits from and to younger relations are important for elderly people, their homes are best sited in the neighbourhood of family housing, and single or small groups of bungalows or flats may be interspersed in housing estates. It is usually held that grouped flatlet schemes should comprise about 30 units to avoid the institutional atmosphere which can easily arise in large schemes, but there are successful projects in this country with over a hundred dwellings for the old, and, as mentioned above, in Europe and America schemes for two or three hundred are not uncommon. A group of about 30 units can be looked after by a single permanent warden with temporary relief, but some of the larger schemes in other countries allow a higher standard of communal provision and care to be provided economically.

In a memorandum on *Design Standards for Old People's Housing*, submitted to the Department of the Environment in 1975, the Housing Centre emphasised that there was as much variation in the housing needs and preferences of old people as of other households and the utmost flexibility should be fostered to allow for variation in provision. The Centre's main recommendations may be summarised as follows:

(a) For sheltered housing, the two categories identified in MoHLG Circular 82/69 should be merged into one category of grouped housing for old people with a warden. The present mandatory higher standards within dwellings for old people should continue to rank for additions to the yardstick, whether such dwellings are grouped and there is a warden, or not.

(b) Standards of space within the dwelling should be those of the current Category 1 dwellings.

(c) Standard provision should be two person one-bedroom type dwellings, even for single person households.

(d) A proposition of two-bedroom types should be included in schemes as appropriate. The second bedroom should have full heating standards for old people's housing and this should rank for an additional allowance on the yardstick.

(e) Subject to the maximum possible flexibility, mandatory and optional communal facilities ranking for additional yardstick allowances should be: mandatory—warden's dwelling, alarm system, a guest room or more, communal TV aerials and GPO conduits, telephone kiosk, office accomodation, two lifts in schemes of three storeys and over for which it should be made clear that additional allowances to the yardstick will be available, and heated access corridors and stairs; optional—laundries, common rooms, hobbies rooms, gossip corners, handrails in corridors, lifts in two-storey schemes, and communal showers.

(f) Baths should be provided in all dwellings.

(g) Arrangements should be made for heating installations to take account of economical running costs, even at the expense of higher capital costs. Background heating should preferably be under landlord control.

(h) The cost yardstick should be revised six monthly (subsequently a quarterly review has been made), and be more generous, particularly for low density development, small and awkward sites, and to allow standards which will reduce running costs to landlord and tenant. Fixed sum allowances for mandatory and optional extras should be more generous, particularly for alarm systems, and to allow finishes and furnishing of common rooms, and landscaping.

(i) Requirements as to accessibility of kitchen window openings or other ventilation should be included in the check list as mandatory. In other respects, the existing check list of mandatory items is endorsed.

(j) Yardstick allowances for car parking should be adequate to cover the standard required by the planning authority in each case, or planning authorities should be required to accept a national standard for old people's housing. Some arguments supporting the recommendations and suggestions and comments likely to be of general interest were given in the main body of the memorandum.

The appointment of a warden to visit and give help in an emergency to old people seems to have developed originally from agreements between the housing and social service authorities or these two departments of the same all-purpose authority. A contribution from the social services authority was made under section 126 of the Local Government Act 1948 (later, section 126 of the Local Government Act 1958) to the cost of services which prevent people having to be taken into homes for care and attention when they could continue to live independently if given some support. The special additions to the yardstick in 1969 are considered adequate to cover the extra cost of the warden's accommodation and salary as a housing service, although contributions under the Local Government Act 1958 may still be made if appropriate. Additions to the yardsticks to cover rising costs since 1969 are noted elsewhere (Chapter 10).

Normally the duties of wardens involve visiting tenants each day, responding to the bells or telecommunication system connecting their individual dwellings with that of the warden for use in emergency, in some cases helping with shopping and other necessary missions for tenants who are temporarily confined to their homes through minor illness or bad weather, helping tenants who fall ill to get the attention they need but not themselves carrying out nursing duties, and being responsible for the functioning of communal heating and the cleaning of communal accommodation, though not necessarily doing cleaning work themselves.

In large schemes a deputy warden may be appointed, and in smaller ones arrangements for relief of the warden during holidays and off-duty periods by temporary and part-time appointments often include the designation of an active resident to stand in.

Wardens are provided with a self-contained house or flat to Parker Morris standards which is usually large enough for a married woman or man. Wardens are usually women, but men or married couples are also appointed. They are sometimes people with nursing experience, but a kind, cheerful, patient and practical disposition is regarded of primary importance for a job which involves the care of other people who are normally self-supporting without appearing to interfere with their independence. Tenants of schemes where there is a warden are expected to be able to maintain their own homes, with the help of relatives and such services as " home helps " and " meals on wheels " where appropriate. Where tenants suffer serious or prolonged illness, or become too frail in mind or body to manage alone without constant care, they move to a hospital or residential home. Occupants in these schemes are, however, usually able to carry on in them for the rest of their lives and may only suffer a short terminal illness.

The provision of grouped flatlets with warden service for elderly people has been encouraged officially for years now, but it has been suggested in some quarters that in their present form they are not in fact the universal solution and the time has come to re-define the needs and perhaps to adopt other methods. For example, evidence from a small survey conducted in Leeds and Oxfordshire, with the help of the Nuffield Centre for Health Service Studies, to ascertain what elderly people want, showed that sheltered housing did not provide the accommodation the majority of elderly people favoured. Many felt they were not " old " and did not need supervision—the majority wished to stay in the house they were occupying, their family home, but if they had to move they would have liked to stay in the same street or neighbourhood. Small dwellings built to mobility housing standards (see below), with a proportion of wheelchair housing, in single units and groups of two, four, six and eight throughout the community would be suitable for elderly people or younger small households whose housing problems local authorities and housing associations are now starting to tackle, as discussed later in this chapter. Tenants could look after one another and family and neighbours would help. " Elderly people are not different because of their age, which ranges from 65 to 110. Their difference is forced upon them by virtue of their low income and immobility. For some people, Category II is heaven. For others, it is a haven, but no more satisfactory a haven than would be provided by a well-designed, small dwelling with a few elderly or not-so-elderly neighbours giving each other support. Elderly people have much they can give to young people. For others, Category II housing carries a stigma and they feel that segregation means ghetto-isation " (2).

Here, as in other housing spheres, there must be diverse solutions to allow real choice. " The construction of suitable accommodation for old people is not simply dependent on analysing physical needs, calculating the scale of the provisions and assembling in economic fashion an aggregate of parts. It depends much more on learning how old people live, how they interact, what they want to make of their lives and then translating the knowledge into an effective and sympathetic physical solution." (Quoted from " Accommodation for old people: two schemes at Norwich," *Architects' Journal*, 28 January 1970—compiled by Selwyn Goldsmith).

Age Concern, in a memorandum on a Consultation Paper, *Housing for Old People*, issued by the Department of the Environment, the Department of Health and Social Security and the Welsh Office, and others concerned with the welfare of the aged, have also advocated a wider range of types of accommodation being provided by local authorities and housing associations. If there is to be a switch of capital resources from residential and hospital provision for the old to housing within the community, and from housing for families to housing for old people, there should also be an assessment of the adequacy of domiciliary health and social services. The links between such services and housing services must be close, and also between statutory and voluntary services. This is important, too, in relation to provision for " extra care," which is increasingly needed as longevity of the population increases. For example, people often live so long in sheltered housing that the average age and disability grow and wardens are called upon to do too much; Anchor, for example, are putting in bigger kitchens to their common rooms to allow for lunch clubs, and extra care facilities in sheltered houses are being considered by interested bodies.

Old people often find difficulty in getting access to council housing, if they wish to move to be nearer younger members of their family on retirement, either because they do not have a residential qualification or because they are owner-occupiers. Easier access for the elderly to council housing could help in solving many problems.

Choice of the type of housing available to the elderly has also been limited because, as has been indicated, under Circular 82/69, Category I and II bungalows and flats have become the stereotyped form of provision by many local authorities. In advocating a wider range of types, Age Concern and others presumably have in mind housing where there is some meal and other supporting services. Many housing associations, they point out, can already contribute specialist expertise in particular forms of accommodation.

Regret has been expressed that sheltered housing schemes by private developers and by housing associations operating without subsidy on a tenant investment basis have run into cost difficulties under present economic conditions. The possibility of using private and public capital resources jointly to overcome this, and also of arranging co-operative and other forms of tenure for the elderly should be considered.

Many elderly people live in substandard houses and houses lacking the standard amenities. Help should be given to increase applications for improvement grant from the old and the granting of maturity loans for elderly owner-occupiers should be encouraged. Positive encouragement to use grants towards the cost of roof insulation even where no other improvement is planned would be helpful, as well as making grants for repairs only and other insulation work more widely available and with fewer conditions attached than at present. (See also Chapter 7).

Although many of the housing difficulties of the old could be alleviated by help and advice, Age Concern have found indications that many housing aid centres do not attract enquiries from them. Some HACs give, or are thought to give, advice only on council tenancies or disputes between landlord and tenant. Better training of staff as to old people's housing needs would help and, since HACs are not available or accessible to all old people, publicity material widely distributed through all channels, including voluntary organisations, is recommended.

Housing for the disabled

Housing for the disabled, where design details are of special importance, can ensure privacy and independence for handicapped persons. The Chronically Sick and Disabled Persons Act 1970 gave close attention to the planning of buildings, and section 3 dealt with the duties of housing authorities. A circular (DHSS 12/70) on the implementation of the Act was sent to all local authorities; for the section on housing in the Act the circular referred to the now outdated MoHLG circular 54/64, *Flats for the Disabled*, and to *Designing for the Disabled*. Ad hoc yardsticks were used; currently, DOE Circular 92/75 gives the special allowances for wheelchair housing and mobility housing and HDD 2/75 the standards. There is a considerable difference in the standards and yardstick allowances between wheelchair housing and mobility housing.

There is now a Minister for the Disabled; a special provision under the Land Compensation Act 1973, relating to disturbance payments, was introduced to allow payment of the expenses of modifying a dwelling for a disabled person who has to move from one which has been adapted for his needs; in the assessment of a fair rent, features which may be necessary for a disabled tenant such as special WCs, bathrooms and kitchens do not necessarily increase the value of dwellings, as they may not be an asset to the able-bodied occupant; and the computation of the needs allowance for rent rebates and allowances includes arrangements for persons who are registered in pursuance of provisions under section 29 (1) of the National Assistance Act 1948 (welfare arrangements for handicapped persons).

Since the middle of 1974, the concept of " mobility housing " has been promoted by the Department of the Environment with the issuing of two government circulars and two Housing Development Directorate Occasional Papers: *Housing for People who are Physically Handicapped* (DOE Circular 74/74) and *Wheelchair and Mobility Housing: Standards and Costs* (Circular 92/75 referred to above); Selwyn Goldsmith, " Mobility Housing " in *Architect's Journal*, 3 July 1974, later issued by the DOE as Housing Development Directorate Occasional Paper 2/74; Selwyn Goldsmith, *Wheelchair Housing*, Housing Development Directorate Occasional Paper 2/75, DOE. It is suggested in an article " Mobility Housing—More Flexibility in Housing for the Disabled," in *Housing*, June 1976, that the " mobility housing " concept should become a fundamental principle in housing provision and necessitate a re-design of house plans and site layouts; it could also mean a total re-appraisal of the traditional types and level of housing provision for the physically handicapped. The article discusses the implications for local authorities from both an architectural and housing and social services point of view, and the experience of one authority, Wakefield MDC, in adjusting to the new concept. The authors of the article, E. F. Cantle, BSc (Soc) Hons, and N. A. Sharp, ARIBA, point out that mobility housing provides for a more flexible approach to provision for the physically handicapped and recognises the range of disability; it will almost certainly be catering for the *majority* of physically handicapped persons if taken up by local authorities.

The Department of the Environment consider that certain *essential* features should be incorporated into the design of mobility housing: (i) the entrance door is at least 900 mm wide and has a level or ramped approach (accessible by wheelchair); (ii) internal doors and corridors are at least 900 mm wide (allowing for easy movement by ambulant handicapped people, including those with wheelchairs but not totally chairbound); and (iii) the bathroom, WC and at least one bedroom are at entrance level (ground floor flats and bungalows are therefore most suitable). There are various other features which are considered desirable and indeed the possibilities go beyond those suggested by the Department of the Environment. For example, it is possible to design bathrooms so that a wheelchair can be placed alongside the WC; hang doors to facilitate wheelchair movement (or sliding doors); ensure there are no threshold sills or doormat wells; and provide socket outlets, light switches, and coin-in-slot meters within the reach of a seated person.

It is important to note, however, that all this must be done without increasing dwelling size, or significantly increasing costs (Circular 92/75 creates an allowance of only £50 per dwelling.) The point of this is to ensure that mobility housing is regarded as normal housing and retains its flexibility as an all-purpose unit.

The third edition of Selwyn Goldsmith's *Designing for the Disabled* (RIBA Publications Ltd.) (3) gives comprehensive information and advice on all aspects of disability. Housing is dealt with in a section completely revised to take into account the publication of the DOE, HDD papers 2/74 on mobility housing, and 2/75 on wheelchair housing, mentioned earlier, and which also considers adaptations, home dialysis and cost allowances.

Special housing for the physically disabled may be associated with housing for old people. Some old people become partially disabled, or at least less active, and simple aids, such as hand grips for baths and WC's, stair rails, handles, switches and cupboards which can be manipulated easily and reached without stooping or climbing on a chair all help anyone with a disability; but people who cannot move about except in a wheelchair or with the aid of crutches or elaborate walking aids, particularly if they are members of a young household, have different housing requirements.

Some adaptation to the special needs of each disabled person is likely to be necessary, and in many cases the adaptation of an ordinary dwelling may be the best way of helping a disabled person to live at home, go out to work and carry on the usual household activities. Often the solution to the problems of a disabled person may be found in allocation or transfer of the household to a dwelling where access and interior arrangements are, or can be made, suitable. Some local authorities and housing associations have built special dwellings for wheelchair cases with level access to the dwelling and all accommodation within it used by the disabled person, with wide doorways and corridors which allow the chair to be manoeuvred, with kitchen equipment with clearance below the working surfaces for the chair and with storage accessible from a sitting position. Sometimes details may have to be adjusted for severely disabled people after the dwelling has been allocated to a particular case and the two stage approach of the DOE papers is intended to encourage this.

The integration of the disabled into the general community has been stressed by some authorities and housing associations. For example, a pioneer scheme in North London carried out by the Habinteg Housing Association accommodates severely disabled people within a large housing scheme; and Friendship House, on the south coast, is another example of grouped accommodation which allows the maximum independence to severely disabled people. (*Housing Review*, Vol. 22, No. 3.)

Reports on the disabled include *Registered as Disabled*, by Sally Sainsbury, G. Bell & Sons Ltd., 1970, which describes the actual needs of individual disabled people compiled from interviews with them, and *Four Architectural Movement Studies for the Wheelchair and Ambulant Disabled*, by Felix Walter (Disabled Living Foundation, 1971) which analyses the space requirements of disabled people with varying degrees of mobility. Other publications concerning the disabled are listed in the bibliography (4, 5, 6).

Housing for students and single people

The Homeless of the 1980s, the verbatim report of a student Co-operative Dwellings conference, 1971, pointed out that by 1981 there would be over five million people in the 18 to 24 years age group in England and Wales. The vast majority of these would not qualify for council housing nor would they be able to afford to buy their own houses. Unless some positive action was taken, their only refuge would be in privately rented accommodation, which, by 1981, was likely to be halved to less than a million dwellings, grossly overcrowded in the housing stress areas, and much of it squalid and expensive. Control over furnished lettings since the Rent Act 1974 has further decreased the supply of furnished accommodation available for students and single people. In some areas, for example in stress areas and near universities and training institutions, students compete for scarce family accommodation.

John Hands points out in *Housing Co-operatives* that the young and mobile form a growing but largely unrecognised housing need: young workers, trainees, nurses, apprentices, teachers, students and others living away from the parental home before settling down and taking roots. If their housing needs are ignored, they will increasingly struggle with low income families for a share in the diminishing private rented market; and urban centres will find growing shortages of teachers, transport staff, local authority employees and other service workers.

"The example of 'young and mobile' which most readily springs to mind is the student. But this is because students are, not surprisingly, one of the most studied occupational groups. In fact, there are only half a million registered full-time students of the five million people aged 18 to 24 in England and Wales. What research has been done suggests that less than 25 per cent of this whole group live with their parents, and the proportion is falling rapidly.

Three million of this group are single. There are 3·5 million single people aged 25 to pensionable age and 2 million single old age pensioners, producing a total of 8·5 million single adults. Yet the number of one and two-room dwellings in the country is around three-quarters of a million, of which a quarter million is rented furnished (just less than half the total furnished stock). These people do not show up on published statistics as single person households for the chief reason that there is not the stock of single person dwellings for them to occupy exclusively even if they could afford it." (7)

The physical needs of the young and mobile are categorised as: cheapness, mobility and, as a consequence of their income, mobility and life style, the provision of certain amenities such as clothes-washing facilities or access to a launderette. Their social needs are grouped into three categories: privacy—not to be confused with the isolation often experienced in a completely self-contained single-person dwelling unit; sociability—a need for a facility for easy and natural social interaction at varying levels of intimacy, both within their own group and, importantly, with those outside, but not the artificial introverted and enforced socialisation of a traditional hostel or student hall of residence; and control—the ability to control their own life styles, not to be confused with independence, as the three social needs taken together call for an interdependence.

Before the seventies, there had been little special new building to meet the needs of these groups, but examples began to reach completion in 1972 to 1974. Many young people and students require furnished accommodation, and this, though previously unusual in council provision, is being provided in some of their special schemes, and in schemes promoted by voluntary organisations. Older single people probably prefer to have their own things around them in unfurnished dwellings. The standard of residences which universities were able to provide and which could result in unsatisfactory living conditions were considered in *Student Housing: Architectural and Social Aspects,* by William Mullins and Phyllis Allen (8), which discussed, in three sections, all aspects of student housing, including individual needs, such as a high level of heating and good natural and artificial lighting; optimum group sizes and arrangements, shared facilities, staffing and the necessity for good management; and loan finance for low cost student housing. Design Bulletin 23 of the Department of the Environment, *Housing Single People 1: How they live at present,* 1971 (9), which confirmed that the demand for single person accommodation generally was increasing, concentrated on two groups—the low-paid middle aged, and the relatively better off mobile working young—and reviewed purpose-built accommodation provided for them. The conclusions reached were tested in the high-rise block for 160 single people designed by the Housing Research and Development Division of the Department of the Environment for Leicester City Council, and a Design Bulletin No. 29 (10) on them issued in January 1976, following on from Design Bulletin No. 23.

This block, completed in 1973, included a variety of flats and grouped flatlets to cater for young people, together with some communal facilities (*Housing Review,* Vol. 22, No. 3). In 1973 also, Student Co-operative Dwellings, now the Society for Co-operative Dwellings (SCD), announced what was described as a breakthrough in tackling the worsening housing crisis for students and other young low-income people in urban areas. After five years of intensive lobbying, including all-party amendments tabled to two Housing Bills, administrative consent was given by the Department of the Environment to proceed with the project in January 1973. SCD registered a local housing co-operative society, Sanford Co-operative Dwellings, acquired a one acre site on a 75 year lease from the London Borough of Lewisham for £40,000, and contracted the design and building based on the SCD design brief in co-operation with its professional consultants. Half the cost of lease purchase and development was borrowed from the Housing Corporation, and half from an insurance company, both loans repayable over 40 years, with the insurance company having first security on land and buildings. The variable rate of interest, currently 11 per cent, was reduced by the option mortgage subsidy to a corresponding level of 7·3 per cent pa. A grant sufficient to cover the cost of furnishing the scheme was negotiated with the Inner London Education Authority in return for the Sanford Co-op agreeing to ensure that at least 57 of its members were students of ILEA colleges.

The scheme was opened on 1 October 1974. It consists of 14 self-contained houses, each designed for 10 single people, and six self-contained bed-sitter flats for couples. Each communal house is on three floors and contains 10 bedrooms, each with its own handbasin, two bathrooms, three WC's and a farmhouse kitchen. The houses and flats are furnished, carpeted and centrally-heated throughout. Full details of the scheme are given in the book, *Housing Co-operatives*. SCD are following this successful scheme with other similar projects.

The Department of the Environment, through its Housing Development Directorate, is encouraging local authorities to build for single people. As already mentioned in Chapter 10, DOE Circular 24/75, *Housing Needs and Action*, emphasised that much greater attention ought to be given to the needs of small households, and *The Need for Smaller Homes* reinforced the points made in the circular. In January 1976 DOE circular 12/76 (WO 14/76) set out yardstick allowances for accommodation for dwellings designed for single working people on the lines recommended in Design Bulletin No. 29 and in April 1976 the Minister of Housing and Construction announced new initiatives to provide for the housing of single people, including students, as part of the general housing programmes of local authorities and housing associations (see Chapter 10—Types of dwelling). In January 1976 also the Housing Corporation announced that it intended to increase its financing of the building of homes for those with special needs, which included the young, single and handicapped.

For the first time a London borough council is planning to provide council accommodation for single people and childless couples under pensionable age. Richmond Council is developing 105 acres of former nursery land at Hampton in which will be included a number of bed-sitting-rooms and one-roomed flats for occupation by the single. The site is a mixed one of council development, housing association work and private building, but the council will have nomination rights on much of the property to be provided by bodies other than themselves, and will be able to ensure that single people get a fairer deal. The acquisition of the site will be the subject of a public enquiry when the council applies for compulsory purchase orders.

Provision must be made for other groups of single persons, such as those suffering from mental illness or personality defect who need a measure of social support and who cannot find stability of accommodation in the private sector, and the Campaign for the Mentally Handicapped in their submission to a government committee in March 1976 argued that the establishment of the concept of ordinary housing for the mentally handicapped is the major breakthrough needed in their care. Housing authorities can assist in dealing with these needs by making sites available, not only to social service departments for their statutory provision of hostels, but also to voluntary associations who specialise in running hostels and other housing for single deprived persons and also by direct provision of suitable accommodation, including for the rehabilitation of persons after mental illness.

The National Association for the Care and Resettlement of Offenders has also called upon local authorities and housing associations to provide a small proportion of their housing for offenders, as part of a strategy for treating inadequates which, the director of the Association has claimed, could help to cut the number of men put into prison by a fifth and the number of women by three-tenths.

The homeless

The increase in numbers of people without a home at all has evoked growing public interest and concern for several years. In April 1969 the Department of Health and Social Security, acting for the Secretary of State for Social Services, invited Professor John Greve to lead an investigation into homelessness in London, and the resultant research and report, published by the Scotland Academic Press in 1971, under the title *Homelessness in London*, revealed much new information about the scale of the problem and about the characteristics of the homeless. The report maintained that homelessness in London would continue to worsen until the shortage of decent accommodation at reasonable rents was overcome; and considered that the situation demanded a regional housing authority in London, with large subsidies to local authorities and housing associations, and less distinction by officials between the " deserving " and " undeserving " (11). A study of homelessness in South Wales and the West of England (*Homeless Near a Thousand Homes* by Bryan Glastonbury) also found a tendency to think of homeless persons in terms of "deserving" and "undeserving" while administrative boundaries exacerbated the problem (12).

DHSS Circular 37/72, *Homeless Single Persons in Need of Care and Support*, sent to all local authority social service departments in England and Wales, drew attention to the rapid increase in single homelessness and asked local authorities to experiment with a variety of small units of accommodation in their areas. The circular stressed the need for supportive social work in many units, and encouraged local authorities to co-operate with voluntary organisations who, it was recognised, had considerable experience in this work. Voluntary bodies welcomed the circular as marking a real step forward in government recognition of both the size of the problem and the need for new and humane homes to replace the disappearing Victorian lodging houses; and signalling the beginning of a clear definition by the government of the responsibilities of local authorities towards single homeless men and women. Local authorities were asked to submit programmes for their supportive services for the years 1973–83, including financial estimates for the expansion in provision they expected to undertake. Plans were submitted early in 1973 and considerable revisions were undertaken.

The Campaign for the Homeless and Rootless (CHAR) carried out a survey to monitor the response of key local authorities to circular 37/72 and to examine the plans of the authorities for the next 10 years for single homeless people. The survey concluded that the need of single people for a wide range of non-specialist accommodation was not being met; it did, however, report that local authorities were increasingly aware of the needs of discharged psychiatric hospital patients in their areas, and were using more widely their powers under the Mental Health Act 1959 to give them supportive housing. The survey pointed out that, as things were, it was easier for a single homeless man with a psychiatric history to obtain a roof over his head than for any other single person to do so, whatever his circumstances.

The statutory position at the end of 1976 with regard to homelessness is that housing authorities, i.e., the councils of districts (Metropolitan and non-Metropolitan), the GLC, London Boroughs and the Common Council of the City of London, have a general duty and adequate powers under the Housing Act 1957 to provide and furnish whatever accommodation is required to meet the housing needs arising in their areas. No specific duty in regard to homelessness is placed on housing authorities but, since homelessness is the most extreme form of housing need, they should have regard to its incidence in assessing the general housing need of their areas. Housing authorities have no powers to pay for hotel accommodation. Any hostel accommodation they might provide, including that for homeless people, will, under section 106 of the Housing Act 1974, be included in housing revenue accounts as from 1 April 1975 and will be eligible for subsidy in the same way as self-contained dwellings. Social service authorities, i.e., the councils of non-Metropolitan counties, Metropolitan districts, London Boroughs and the Common Council of the City of London, were, prior to April 1974, required by section 21 (1) (*b*) of the National Assistance Act 1948 to prepare schemes for providing temporary accommodation for persons who are in urgent need thereof, being need arising in circumstances which could not reasonably have been foreseen, or in such other circumstances as the authority may in any particular case determine. Section 195 (3) of and Schedule 23 to the Local Government Act 1972 replaced, as from April 1974, the duty to make a scheme by a power to make arrangements, but the power was subject to directions by the Secretaries of State for Social Services and for Wales. The then Secretaries of State for Social Services and for Wales, in accordance with previous undertakings, made directions in February 1974. Thus social service authorities continue, as before 1 April 1974, to be under a duty to provide temporary accommodation in accordance with the 1948 Act.

The circular on homelessness, issued jointly by the three Departments concerned in February 1974, (DOE 18/74, DHSS 4/74, WO 34/74), promoted a fresh approach by local authorities to homelessness but made no changes in statutory responsibilities. The circular was based upon authoritative advice, including the Seebohm report of 1968, the Greve and Glastonbury reports published in 1971, and the report of the joint central and local government working parties which followed the latter publications. Three main objects were emphasised—(a) to clarify the priorities to be accorded to the homeless; (b) to stress the responsibilities of local government as a whole and the need for local authorities to use their combined resources: to bring out— as a major change of practical responsibility between the housing and social service authorities—that housing authorities should undertake increasingly the prime responsibility for homeless people and their accommodation: to indicate the steps which the authorities should be taking to implement the changes outlined in the circular; and (c) to set out the range of ways by which local authorities can prevent and tackle homelessness. As already mentioned in Chapter 3, the circular pointed out that although all homeless people, whether families with children, adult families, or single people, should be helped, even if the homelessness seems to have been self-inflicted, in areas of housing stress there must be priority groups who must have first claim on the resources of local government. These groups, for whom local authorities should provide accommodation themselves or help those concerned to find accommodation in the private sector, are families with dependent children living with them or in care; and adult families without children, or individuals who become homeless in an emergency, such as a fire or flooding, and are temporarily unable to fend for themselves; or who are vulnerable because of old age, disability, pregnancy or other special reason. The prevention and relief of homelessness is regarded as a function of local government as a whole and not of either housing authorities or of social services alone.

Nationally, official homelessness statistics were compiled by the DHSS until June 1974, when the DOE took over the task of collecting them. An interim report, published in August 1976, after a long period of delay, showed that, taking applications to local authorities by families as the measure of homelessness, the first half of 1975 saw 25,120 families asking for help. This is an increase from under 20,000 in the same period in the previous year and represents a doubling in the level of applications since 1970. Although the number of families resident in temporary accommodation at any one time has risen, the increase is less striking, which would imply that authorities have been improving the rate at which they have provided permanent rehousing. The Department stress throughout the interim report that the figures are not directly comparable with those previously collected by the DHSS on H41 forms, but the reasons for this non-comparability are not detailed.

A consultation Paper on homelessness issued by the Department of the Environment, Department of Health and Social Security and the Welsh Office in 1975, sought views on the general approach to homelessness and on particular points raised in the paper, i.e., legislation to clarify the roles of housing and social services authorities and to secure that local authorities carry them out; legislation relating to housing authorities; legislation relating to homelessness arising in a disaster or emergency; legislation relating to residential care; legislation relating to other forms of social support including financial help; the need for new powers to enable housing authorities to incur expenditure on voluntary or private accommodation, including hotels; and ideas for improving the organisation and administration relating to homelessness.

In a memorandum on homelessness, the Housing Centre agreed with other published views that the housing department of a local authority should be responsible for homelessness, but stopped short of saying that housing authorities must provide a council tenancy for all homeless in their area. The Centre recognised that areas differ in their ability to cope with homeless families and that some—as in London—most burdened with housing stress cannot be expected to absorb all comers. However, all housing authorities should provide short-stay temporary accommodation for those accepted as homeless and this should be backed up by the full range of supportive social and housing advisory services.

The Centre acknowledged that in some cases the best solution would be the offer of a tenancy by the local authority; in many other cases, however, permanent resettlement might involve for the homeless returning or moving to another area and, for the housing staff, painstaking negotiations with appropriate organisations to secure the most suitable accommodation. The Centre advocated a network of advice officers in all housing departments and machinery for communication between them to facilitate exchanges of information and better use of all available resources. It also saw great value in regular meetings of housing and social service staff on a county basis.

In its memorandum, the Centre considered the causes of housing shortage and homelessness in some depth and made recommendations, including the following: the need for closer scrutiny of the relationship between housing and employment; more liberal policies concerning allocations, and transfers from one size and type of tenure to another; a call for examination of schemes to help the private rented sectors in those areas where private lettings form a high proportion of the housing available; powers to requisition empty houses in certain areas; more help and guidance from the Department of the Environment for local authorities in their housing management functions, including the establishment at headquarters of a strong housing management advisory service.

Although no measure to make the relief of homelessness a specific *housing* function of local authorities was forecast in the Queen's speech opening Parliament in November 1976, the Secretary of State for the Environment indicated to the House of Commons shortly afterwards that he would take any opportunity presented to introduce such a measure. The Minister for Housing and Construction emphasised that housing authorities would have to ensure that accommodation was available for the priority homeless. Such groups would be spelt out by order and subject to Parliamentary scrutiny although they could be reviewed and changed: the Bill to tackle the problem of homelessness would make clear that the practice of splitting families as a way of meeting their accommodation problems should end. (See also Chapter 12.)

Problem tenants

What constitutes a problem tenant or family? Broadly, any tenant or family who creates a problem for society—and the housing department. This depends on what society—and the housing department—regards as a problem. Irregular rent payments, dirty or destructive habits, hooliganism and misuse of property and fittings, rowdyism and nuisance to neighbours, and other deviations from accepted social standards of behaviour; all housing managers could add others to the list and will know that problems are not confined to any one age or section of the community. " Problem tenant or family " is indeed an unsuitable name —most people and families have problems of one sort or another at different times and at different stages of family development— and the description attempts to put into one category a whole variety of tenants and families each with very different and complex problems. Generally, however, the term " problem family " has come to mean an " undesirable " family, and the Cullingworth committee were concerned that under this heading applicants for council housing might be graded according to an interpretation of their desert in the eyes of the housing department (1.17). The report suggested that the assessment of need should take into account both housing conditions and the ability of individual households to cope with the conditions. The highest priority for public sector housing should go to those households in bad conditions with which they are unable to cope and where the potential ability to improve this situation themselves is low. If indeed these households are not helped, they will probably deteriorate still further and eventually disintegrate, the children may scatter and become delinquent, ending up a burden on the state with children of their own in care. The circle is a vicious one and in economic, social and humanitarian terms society benefits in the long run from keeping such households together. Realistic social support is essential for such households because good housing on its own is rarely the panacea for the ills such families suffer.

Very large families, particularly with low income. The large, low-income family may face the problem of obtaining a dwelling which is suitable in size and price. Such families are often at risk of becoming homeless since privately let accommodation of the kind needed is in very short supply, and local authorities cannot always themselves find suitable houses for them. The move to place the main responsibility for the homeless on housing as opposed to social service may highlight the need for more big, comparatively cheap dwellings. Housing associations have been active in providing for families in stress areas by the acquisition and improvement of older houses, but improvement grants under the Housing Act 1969 encouraged the sub-division of large houses into a large number of small units. However, the ceilings of grants to housing associations were varied in 1973 so that higher amounts were available for larger units in order to encourage the provision by conversion of some larger family units, and the Housing Act 1974 has further facilitated such work by housing associations.

Part of the reluctance by housing authorities to provide large units is caused by the increasing importance given to the national major decline in household size and the consequent deficit of small dwellings. Percentage-wise this trend is important and is rightly taken into account in forward-planning housing programmes, but the immediate need for large units can be met in ways other than by building a disproportionate number of four or five bedroom houses which may not be required in 15 years time. A policy can be pursued of acquiring individual houses in improvement areas, for immediate single family occupation but suitable for conversion into smaller units in the future; end-of-terrace houses existing on council estates can often have an additional room built on; or two adjoining houses (usually very small if pre-war) can be combined. If new building is necessary, the design should provide for flexible conversion into smaller units in future and if in deciding on priorities of large families the expense of building is a limiting factor, the cost yardstick might well be re-examined, e.g., a more equitable basis of calculation would be capital cost per person, instead of the more usual cost per unit (1).

Single parent families. Here again, these families often have complex problems. The report of the National Council for One-Parent Families (1975) says that there are 650,000 lone parents looking after over a million children. In November 1974 265,000 were claiming supplementary benefit, which amounts to nearly half of them being on the poverty line, and a most disturbing fact is that the number who are homeless or living in squalid housing is on the increase.

The main problem here again is one of ability to obtain a suitably priced home. Segregation of this group is not generally regarded as desirable, and housing provision in specially built blocks or grouped flatlets could destroy the family's opportunity to live a normal life by mixing with the community. Special provision has, however, been made to a limited extent for mothers of young children in conversions, and in one case in a purpose-built scheme by a housing association particular facilities were provided to enable the mother to work. (*Housing Review,* Vol. 21, No. 6, November 1972).

The proposals in the Finer report for helping one-parent families have not been fully implemented because of the financial crisis. The Minister of Housing and Construction announced in October

1975, however, that he would initiate a drive to secure better housing provision for these families. The aim would be to improve their housing conditions through consultations, guidance by circular, personal visits and contact through the DOE's regional offices with local authorities, housing associations and new town corporations. In particular, local authorities would be encouraged to adjust their managerial and allocation systems to take full account of the particular situations of single parent families—there were still far too many cases where, consciously or unconsciously, such families were being discriminated against in practice because the way in which the points systems operated did not take sufficient account of the absence of a husband, mother or wife in the family situation.

Newcomers and immigrants

The increasing mobility of the population, which is desirable from the point of view of employment, puts at a disadvantage people who want council housing in areas where a residential qualification is operated. As mentioned in Chapter 3, in spite of recommendations by the Cullingworth committee in *Council Housing; Purposes, Procedures and Priorities, 1969*, (1.17) and official encouragement to authorities to open housing lists to those in need regardless of their former residence, authorities in areas of acute housing shortage still feel they must give preference to local residents. Section 22 of the London Government Act 1963, for instance, was quite explicit in forbidding the practice of requiring prior residential qualification before an application for housing could be made, but all London Boroughs adopted a formula which circumvented its intentions, although the London Borough of Hammersmith abandoned the practice in 1975. In the new towns, the industrial selection scheme also often has the effect of making it difficult for unskilled people without a job to move there from areas of housing stress. Restrictions of this kind militate against immigrants, and in spite of the safeguards of the Race Relations Act 1968 may seem to make particularly difficult the housing problems of coloured immigrants.

Some local authorities are still somewhat ambivalent about the advisability of recording the race of their applicants and tenants, although the Cullingworth Committee felt it was important in order to ensure that allocations were in fact not prejudiced, a view supported by the Select Committee on Immigration and Race Relations, 1975. Further, three reports which suggest that black families go to the poorer areas of the community—*Race and Council Housing in London* from the Runnymede Trust, *People, Housing and District,* the DOE Lambeth Inner Area Study, and the Report of PEP on the subject—back up Cullingworth, for without the availability of information the patterns revealed could not have been established.

The Race Relations Board has been studying policies for the dispersal of coloured tenants, to avoid the formation of city ghettos, and in a statement issued in January 1975, after three years of discussion with Birmingham City Council, the Board concluded that such policies could legally be pursued by local authorities as long as the tenants themselves agreed. Full agreement had been reached with Birmingham's housing department on the principles which must be followed to avoid discrimination. Birmingham pledged that their policy would be conducted with " full respect for the wishes of the individuals concerned ". The Board has said that it would like to secure similar agreements with other local housing authorities. " Dispersal is a matter for local decision, but whatever is decided must comply with the law as laid down in the Race Relations Act 1968." All tenants must be treated equally and given a free choice of available accommodation. On treatment of tenants, the guidance paper says, " Tenants must not be treated less favourably than others on the grounds of colour or race. The normal rules of management, such as property maintenance, tenancy conditions, transfers, the service of notices to quit etc. must be applied equally to all occupiers." It also says, " Existing tenants who incited a housing department to transfer a coloured family because they objected to the colour or race of the family would contravene section 12 of the Act. The local authority would also act unlawfully if they gave in to pressure." Policy guidelines are laid down in a document distributed to Birmingham's staff which emphasises " The compulsory dispersal of any group on the grounds of their colour, race or origin is unlawful." It would be unlawful to withhold from coloured applicants details of accommodation that would be offered to others, or to discriminate in the handling of the waiting lists, awarding of priorities or selection of tenants.

Social aspects figure largely, too, in the Community Relations Commission's report, *Housing in Multi-Racial Areas*, which is concerned with those groups which migrated to the UK from the New Commonwealth. It is pointed out that, although many households from ethnic minorities now seem to have solved their housing problems satisfactorily and enjoy adequate space and amenity standards, a high proportion do not; moreover, the minority population is highly localised in areas of housing stress. Rehabilitated housing, especially improved acquisitions from the private sector, as well as accommodation in new developments, may be appropriate to the special needs in multi-racial areas, e.g., large families requiring four bedroom accommodation and larger (they may be nuclear families with a large number of children, or may be three generation families where grandparents want to live with their married children); one-parent families; elderly people; and Asian women alone.

The report recommends that among ethnic minority house-owners, house improvement work needs to be increased. There is often considerable interest in improvement grants on the part of these house-owners and take-up in some areas is very good. For example, in Bradford between December 1974 and February 1976 a third of the improvement grants approved were to Asian families. However, because of the difficulties that are already occurring, particularly in stress areas, this may not be general and the report emphasises that the situation needs to be kept under review at national and local level to ensure that minorities are benefitting from and participating in renewal policies.

It is pointed out that dealing with multi-occupied property in some areas is a delicate matter which greatly affects race relations. The report recommends that authorities consider a co-ordinated approach from the planning, environmental health and housing services to formulate a policy which recognises the role of houses in multiple occupation and uses all the available positive powers to improve conditions of repair, amenity and management.

Travellers with mobile homes

In formulating policies for these mobile home dwellers, usually still referred to as gypsies, who are nomadic by nature and not usually by force of circumstances, local authorities have duties under the Caravan Sites Act 1968. Exemption has been claimed by a large number of authorities on the grounds that suitable sites were not available, or that the numbers of families resorting to their area were too small to warrant provision being made. Unfortunately, many families, amounting to an estimated 25,000 persons, many of them children, are without standard amenities and often create a health hazard and a nuisance.

There are difficulties in providing sites of a permanent nature and transit sites. Cost is an important factor as this is met out of the " locally determined sector " and, therefore, is very vulnerable when capital programmes are cut. Local prejudice has also to be overcome, and as the problem must be tackled on a regional basis, collaboration between several authorities is essential. Some authorities are, however, providing very successful sites, and as the need for many more exists, it must be evaluated and the new authorities should be prepared to make land available for this purpose in the same way as for any other housing need (1).

Other groups

Other groups for whom housing may have to be provided as a matter of urgency to prevent actual homelessness include all those whose accommodation is of a service nature, e.g., prison officers, police, agricultural workers, HMF servicemen, caretakers, etc. who retire on age or health grounds; and tenants who have no security of tenure, e.g., certain tenants and subtenants of unfurnished and furnished lettings. A local authority has to consider each case on its merits, but more comprehensive housing advice might provide an alternative to a council allocation, e.g., service gratuities could provide a down-payment for purchase of a house if a local authority mortgage were granted, and job vacancies for particular skills may exist in areas of no housing shortage or with accommodation available (1).

In 1975, the government announced plans to abolish the system of tied cottages, that is accommodation let or occupied as part of a service contract. In September 1975 a survey of 300 farmworkers in six different areas revealed that only 5·3 per cent of them were in favour of tied accommodation in agriculture, their main grievance being the lack of security in tied cottages. 55 per cent expressed fears in this direction. The report of the survey was part of a document prepared by Moira Constable, author of the Shelter report on tied accommodation (13) on behalf of the Arthur Rank Centre associated with the Royal Agricultural Society of England. The government issued a consultation paper on their proposals for abolition, and submissions were considered.

The Rent (Agriculture) Act 1976 implemented the proposals to give security of tenure. It was brought into operation on 1 January 1977 (SI No. 2124 (C58)), thereby virtually abolishing tied dwellings, other than hostel accommodation, for agricultural workers. Forestry workers are to be brought under the legislation by a subsequent order.

The Act has the effect of giving security of tenure, similar to that afforded by the Rent Acts, to workers employed whole-time in agriculture for two years and who are living in a service tenancy. If they cease to work for the owner of the dwelling, they become statutory tenants and the provisions of the Act cover the terms of the tenancy, for which not more than a rent fixed by the rent officer may be charged. Provisions cover the passing of the tenancy to a successor, a widow, widower, or member of the family, on death.

An owner may obtain possession if the accommodation is required in the interests of agriculture as well as through the courts on the grounds available under the Rent Acts, but excluding that enabling him to do so if the dwelling is required for another employee. If possession is required in the interests of agriculture, the owner may apply to the local authority to rehouse the occupier. If the authority is satisfied that the dwelling is so required, they have a duty to use their best endeavours to rehouse.

Agriculture Dwelling-House Advisory Committees are to be established under the Act to advise local authorities on agricultural need and the degree of urgency. The Act was passed through Parliament somewhat hurriedly under the guillotine, and a drafting error was made, necessitating the introduction of a further Bill later in January 1977 to impose time limits on local authorities to notify their decisions as to rehousing.

The problem of battered wives has been gaining prominence since the opening of a hostel by Chiswick Women's Aid, a pioneer in the field of hostels for battered wives. The interim report of the Commons Select Committee on *Violence in Marriage* (HMSO) concluded that urgent action is needed to alleviate the plight of many women and children. Recommendations include that local authorities should be more ready to provide housing for battered wives and their children, and that 24-hour family crisis centres should be opened in all towns with a population of over 50,000 to provide immediate help to those forced out of the house by the extent of the violence perpetrated on them.

Social welfare

The great majority of occupiers of housing in all sectors are quite capable of running their own homes and affairs, and in the rented sector it is certainly the object of good management to help them to do so. There are, however, in modern society many households who may need help, temporarily or permanently, from social service departments, and these will include the elderly, the disabled, the poor, the problem families and immigrants when in areas of housing stress, as has been discussed above. Housing, therefore, will often include a strong welfare element, although paternalism, condescension and any idea of " welfare housing " are strongly condemned. The Cullingworth committee stressed that in the local authority sector more weight should be given to social need in the allocation of housing and in rehousing; and in the private sector, where there is housing distress, close co-operation between the tenant, the local authority housing department and the social agencies is essential. Reference has been made in the chapter on local authority housing to the recommendation of the Seebohm committee and the establishment of housing aid centres. Where the local authority accepts this role of responsibility for housing help for all sections of the community, for tenants in the public and private sector, as well as owner-occupiers, it should be able to prevent seemingly small social welfare problems from developing into crises by contacting the appropriate statutory or voluntary services in the area, and to forestall evictions by liaison with courts and rent tribunals.

Social planning

The need for planning to reflect more closely the changing needs of society has become a recurrent theme of architecture and social study. The value of Octavia Hill's simple statement, " You cannot deal with people and their homes separately," is being increasingly recognised, although its simplicity is often cloaked in ecological and other currently fashionable terms. The inter-relation of people and their homes and environment is fundamental and it is surprising that the obvious truth that physical plans should serve social needs should have been often overlooked. The failure of some housing projects to meet the needs of those who live in them is borne out by several reports, including those on the undesirable results of housing families with small children in flats, *e.g.* the survey, *Two to Five in High Flats*; the NSPCC's survey, *Children in Flats, a Family Study* (14); and the report of the former Ministry of Housing and Local Government's research and development group after a survey of housewives' reactions in three high-density estates: Ebor Gardens, Leeds; Everton Heights, Liverpool; and Loughborough Estate, Brixton, London (15).

In housing schemes there is often no comprehensive service which makes a social plan in the same way as the city planner makes a physical plan. Coupled with the actual building and design of houses and their environment, there must be a careful study of their social effects, a matter which was too long delayed, for example, in the case of multi-storey housing. Although high density schemes as such may be an almost inevitable development in view of urbanisation, population growth, the increase in the number of small households and other factors, the need to pack more people into less space would seem to run counter to certain of to-day's social trends. Affluence, improved education and increased leisure all suggest that people will aim at *more* space in which to operate. In redevelopment schemes, a comprehensive service should make a social plan; and observation and recording of a community's social development should be put in hand as soon as the physical development of the community is completed, so that valuable pointers to future planning may be obtained.

It has been slowly recognised that social disaster can occur when areas of housing are demolished wholesale and families decanted to estates far away from familiar surroundings. Total redevelopment can cause the break-up of valid community life and inflict hardship on families forced to move to estates on the outskirts of cities. Not enough is known (or known widely enough) about what has been called " community dynamics," about the social effects on people left in areas of debris and demolition; about the psychological effects of wholesale transportation of families to new neighbourhoods, or about the effect of new developments on the traditional social structure of the area and the effect of this social devastation on the individual people.

The change in official policy with regard to urban renewal has been described in Chapter 7. Briefly, the Housing Act 1974 and subsequent circulars (DOE Circular 13/75, WO 4/75 and DOE Circular 14/75) stressed that gradual and sensitive renewal, framed " to meet the housing needs of the people in the area," encouraged local authorities to treat housing areas as " living urban organisms, with schemes responsive to particular physical and social needs. In cities where large redevelopment and rehabilitation schemes are in progress or even at planning stage, many people may live in derelict conditions outside their control. These are the citizens who have experienced at first hand the environmental consequences of national programmes, designed to improve their lot—slum clearance, new roads, new housing, new schools, development, re-development and rehabilitation. Those who continue to live in these areas have survived a physical and community upheaval which may have left them better provided with housing accommodation, but may have done little, if anything, to improve the local environment outside their front doors. The local authority has a responsibility in this respect—different areas have very different forms of dereliction and the best value for money and the best satisfaction for local people can be obtained by a special and local selection of those jobs most needing to be done. Further, there is a danger that circumstances in the housing field over the last few years, which have encouraged many people into owner-occupation who really cannot afford it at present prices and rates, may produce more dereliction.

At the same time, social dilemmas are often inherent in rehabilitation schemes where working-class areas may be invaded by middle-class house hunters, and a conflict arise between demands for architectural conservation and the housing needs of the poor people. Families who have lived in the area for many years may resent what they call the middle-class attempt to rescue their neighbourhood from its " twilight " state; they may fear that as landlords become anxious to sell with vacant possession there will be an increase in harassment and other forms of pressure on tenants, and that an introduction of higher rents and improvements will drive other working-class tenants and residents out. Whether house improvement is a help or hindrance to the poor is considered in detail in the Catholic Housing Aid Society's Occasional Paper, *The Housing Poor—a new appraisal,* by Alison Ravetz (16).

In modern times, when local authorities and private developers have the power to destroy whole communities and to create environments intended to satisfy a multiple of explicit goals and having far-reaching effects on the many human beings who will live in them, a concern for people before bricks and mortar is all-important to any solution to our housing problems.

Squatters and empty property

The problem of empty property, for instance—property empty for many reasons, including planned decanting programmes prior to rehabilitation or redevelopment; owners away on business, often abroad; and purely speculative reasons—at a time of a shrinking private rented sector and an often overloaded public sector, has produced an increasing incidence of squatting. Some housing authorities, recognising that for many people in dire housing need squatting may seem a " viable " means of providing themselves with accommodation, have arranged licensing agreements with squatting groups—the GLC, for example, currently have agreements with approximately 2,000 squatters in some of their empty property. Irresponsible squatting, sometimes for political ends, has led to difficulties and violence in some areas, as well as damage and destruction of property, and the Law Commission is considering changes in the law regarding trespass and conspiracy. The DOE has sent out a consultation paper to local authorities with the object of getting " an agreed approach to the squatting problem by local housing authorities and the Department and to develop a joint policy," and has recommended that " at a time of housing shortage it is important to consider whether some form of licensed or authorised squatting can acceptably secure the use of empty property for which no immediate use is planned. There is scope for giving individual squatters or responsible organisations a licence to occupy such properties." In a report, *Squatting: trespass and civil liberties*, the National Council for Civil Liberties claim that the problems of squatting are not such that they would be solved by amendments to the law, least of all to the criminal law, and call for an improved housing programme, including a clear and broad responsibility towards the homeless, as the only ultimate solution to squatting. Other publications relating to squatting are listed in the bibliography.

Housing associations have assisted in schemes for making temporary use of vacant property to help people in dire housing need, and some local authorities have arranged to take over temporarily empty property in the private sector. The London Borough of Westminster, for instance, launched a scheme to take over the management of homes that are empty for short periods of time, with the co-operation of the owners of the properties. The temporary tenancies will last for at least six months and are primarily for single people. Landlords have the right to vet the tenants, and the council, which will entirely manage the scheme, have the obligation to hand back the property " in no worse condition " than when it was taken over.

In order to make empty properties which are awaiting clearance habitable even for a short term it is usually necessary to carry out some repair work. This means that local authorities and housing associations who are to manage such shortlife dwellings must assess the economic viability of the project in relation to the cost of work and the expected length of life of the dwelling. Some practical aspects of the subject, based on experience in Birmingham, were discussed in an article, *Short Life Residential Property—Problems and Policies* by Nick Morton and John Tate in *Housing Review*, October–December 1976, Vol. 25 No. 5.

Social problems

Social problems on housing estates in the public sector were mentioned at the beginning of this chapter. Considerable trouble is being experienced through vandalism and a generally irresponsive and irresponsible attitude by some tenants on some estates, especially in large towns and conurbations; it was reported in 1974 that Liverpool had devoted 58 per cent of its maintenance budget to repairs after vandalism on council estates, and a pamphlet produced by the National Association for the Care and Resettlement of Offenders, *Vandalism: an approach through consultation*, claimed in 1976 that vandalism was becoming a normal form of behaviour for large numbers of children between the ages of 12 and 16 who live in big council estates. The study of the causes of vandalism, and of possible solutions to it, has increased in the last few years, often in the narrow context of the point of view of one practitioner only, *e.g.*, a sociologist or a designer. A Bristol conference on vandalism, sponsored by the Design and Industries Association in conjunction with the University of Bristol in November 1976, presented a broader view by considering social causes and effects, environmental attitudes and creations of architects and planners, design problems and the importance of sensible housing allocation and good management. Reference has been made in Chapter 10 to the work of Professor Oscar Newman who suggests in his treatise on *Defensible Space* that vandalism increases where areas of access in buildings are very public so that no one can identify with the space immediately outside his dwelling. Other studies and reports on vandalism are listed in the bibliography.

The council housing maintenance service generally has a poor image and low consumer confidence, even though standards are often better than those provided for the private rented sector. Rent arrears are rising in many areas—a report by the National

Consumer Council, *Behind with the Rent,* showed figures from only half the local authorities in England and Wales for 1974–75 of £27·5m in owed rent, and in London alone the total reached £12m by mid-1976. Often local authorities find it difficult to instil in many council tenants a sense of pride in the possession and occupation of their council dwellings extending beyond the dwellings. This is particularly evident in many high density estates, with a large element of sharing of access, refuse disposal, garaging, open space and other services, and it is often necessary to provide a high standard of local management and maintenance, usually with a residential caretaker, in order to preserve a good appearance and desirable image.

Tenant participation

More tenant involvement in the management of publicly-owned housing, and possibly ultimately the passing of control of housing and its environment to the users, where this is practicable and, most important, genuinely desired by them, is being increasingly advocated as a solution to some of our housing problems. In his book, *Tenants Take Over* (3: 6) Colin Ward foreshadowed a situation in which existing municipal housing would be transferred from the council to tenant co-operatives. He considered it was desperately necessary that the status of the municipal tenant should be changed into one which gives him at least some of the benefits which the owner-occupier takes for granted. Although every country in the western world, and the eastern world too, gives some kind of public aid to housing, in Britain we have, without actually intending to, drifted into a situation which encourages dependency; it does not encourage or assist people to help themselves, except for those in the individual " home owner-ship " sector, which is, in England and Wales, actually the major sector in the housing market, thus establishing the housing norm: the standard from which the other sectors are judged.

The Housing Act 1974 emphasises the need for public participation in housing programmes, and as mentioned earlier, alternative approaches in housing are being seriously considered, both by the government and elsewhere. At the Housing Centre conference in June 1975, on *New Thinking in Housing,* various examples of public participation in housing were described, including the tenant involvement in the design process in the Byker redevelopment at Newcastle upon Tyne, the scheme for self-help rehabilitation at Black Road, Macclesfield, and the establishment of Holloway Tenants Co-operative. The report of the government working party on housing co-operatives, under the chairmanship of Harold Campbell, has been published, together with a circular outlining the government's reactions to the recommendations, and has opened the way to a number of co-operative initiatives. The Housing Corporation has set up a Co-operative Housing Agency, with John Hands as its Director, with the broad brief recommended by the Campbell report, namely to advise, assist and finance co-operatives and other bodies providing sponsorship and support services for co-operative housing projects. A new co-operative scheme in the Midlands has been financed by the Corporation—the first phase was completed with the aid of a £1,035,000 loan from the Corporation by the South Midlands Coalfield Co-operative Housing Association Ltd. The formal structure and legal aspects of housing co-operatives, with a description of the district features of co-operatives, are included in the book, *Housing Co-operatives*, by John Hands (7).

Other developing approaches in housing to give variety of tenure, more choice in housing and greater participation and control by the users, include equity sharing schemes operated by Birmingham, and by the GLC in Hertfordshire, a housing scheme by Lewisham Council using a self-build system and proposals for development leasehold housing. Advice on how "self-build" housing societies can be helped and encouraged, especially in improving older property, was given in a circular *Housing Act 1974: Part I—Self-build Societies* (DOE Circular 118/75, WO 210/75).

The social divisions bred in society by the narrowing of choice, imposed by the current financial structure, to two distinct tenures —public sector housing and owner-occupation—have serious implications for housing and social policy. Acceptance of alternative approaches in housing—in finance, design, tenure and social commitment—involves radical rethinking and reassessment of priorities, especially at a time of financial stringency, unemployment and industrial setback. If alternative approaches are seen as development in response to changing standards, increasing sensitivity and greater social awareness, and experiments in new forms are carried out in a spirit of co-operation and not confrontation, then real progress towards a healthier, happier housing situation may be achieved.

Housing management

Housing management has been discussed in Chapter 3. The foregoing summary of social problems in housing today indicates the need for a " positive " housing service whereby provision can be made for all types of housing need, a variety of solutions to people's housing difficulties can be explored, alternative approaches to housing tenure can be considered and flexible management policies practised. At the same time, the housing service must be seen as part of a comprehensive programme to improve standards of housing environment and community life within the planned availability of resources—financial, physical and social. This calls for a continuous appraisal and adapting of housing management methods and training procedures to meet changing social needs and for a sympathetic understanding of the objectives and constraints of other services—planning, architectural, environmental health and social service—together with an ability to work closely together to achieve a joint success (17).

Although no one can be complacent about housing, there has been encouraging evidence that housing and environmental problems are gradually being looked at comprehensively and humanely: the Cullingworth (1 : 17), Skeffington (9 : 2) and Seebohm (11 : 18) reports all advocated a comprehensive approach to housing, planning and the social services, with an emphasis on social needs; alternative approaches to design and tenure are being implemented, and the government is seeking to channel limited public funds into areas of housing stress. We are as a nation slowly realising that to satisfy housing, environmental and aesthetic needs in the widest context, we must find out what human beings want and how they are affected by different facets of housing deficiency in different districts, learn how they respond in different settings, and then produce buildings and environments and a financial framework to meet these requirements, rather than the other way round. Only by linking physical, social and economic planning in a total context will we be able to bridge satisfactorily the gap between them (the providers) and us (the consumers), and to create homes in balanced communities which will satisfy socially and financially real human needs of all sections of society.

CHAPTER 12

The Future

The foregoing chapters show the complex background to the housing situation in this country—the mass of legislation affecting housing; the many reports on different aspects of housing deficiency and on social problems allied to housing; the involved system of controls on where and how housing is built; the complicated financial arrangements under which it is provided and let by various agencies, and, more recently, in a time of unprecedented financial stringency, efforts to maximise the allocation of resources in terms of improving the overall housing stock and meeting social need. Yet the basic problem remains unsolved—how housing can best be produced within a sensible, realistic economic framework, in the right place and of an adequate standard, both in condition and in social and physical environment, which will give satisfaction to those who live in it.

"Solving the housing problem" must surely be one of the most hackneyed phrases in sociological and political treatises since the Second World War. Unfortunately, the term "housing" is often so overcharged with emotion, hedged with misunderstanding and shrouded in political mists that anyone who dares to suggest that there are some areas of the country where there is now no housing shortage is likely to be accused of complacency and smugness; and the same applies to anyone who emphasises the considerable improvement in the living conditions of the vast majority of the population since the war. No-one genuinely concerned about housing *can* be complacent while we have congested and decaying areas with slum conditions internally and poor environment externally, while we have families overcrowded in sub-standard tenements, distress and deprivation in housing, especially for minorities, often culminating in homelessness and worsening social problems, such as vandalism, violence and racial discord; and, on the other hand, while we have in some districts good housing available but at too high a price for those most in need, despite subsidies, rent rebates and allowances and tax relief on mortgages, and accommodation standing vacant for long periods. It is now, however, increasingly recognised that it is unrealistic to talk of "the housing problem" which any one political party or any one housing policy will spirit away. Rather, specific solutions are needed to specific problems which affect different groups of people in different parts of the country in different ways; and continuous research and reappraisal in the housing field must ensure that available resources are directed to where they will yield the maximum social and economic benefit, and that housing policy and practice are really appropriate to housing need.

Although since the publication of the original Guide in 1971 progress has been made in relieving some of the social pressures in housing, e.g., financial aid may be obtained where levels of rent and rates cause hardship in all sectors, security of tenure has been extended to all private tenants (with very few exceptions) and penalties for harassment have been increased, the basic facts still show that unsatisfactory housing to-day results from four main factors. The first is the shortage of dwellings in the congested areas of London and the other conurbations, exacerbated by scarcity and high cost of land. Secondly, a large number of old dwellings have become unfit and lack basic amenities: as existing houses grow older and standards rise, more houses become obsolete, so that replacement is a continuous process, Thirdly, there is a lack of fit between households and dwellings of the right size, cost and in the right place. Fourthly, there is increasing dissatisfaction by the occupants of tenanted housing, especially on local authority estates, with management and maintenance, which leads to a demand for more tenant participation and involvement in design and management.

An overall housing strategy, therefore, which sets out to remedy housing deficiencies must secure (a) sufficient land for housing in the right places, related to location of industry and transport, and to national and regional development, and at a fair price, (b) the production of dwellings to a standard which will give reasonable satisfaction and good value, now and in the future, in sufficient variety of type and form of tenure to afford a choice, (c) an equitable financial structure which will enable a good standard of living to be maintained in all sections of housing and, at the same time, recognise and take account of the implications of rising costs, and (d) urgent attention to social problems in housing. It is perhaps the housing finance system which is the key to future progress in housing. This was no doubt why the late Anthony Crosland, when Secretary of State for the Environment, stated, when he instigated the government's review of housing finance in 1974, that it was to be fundamental. This review has since been extended to embrace housing policy as a whole, but at the date of going to press the government's promised green paper based on it is still to be published.* It is to be hoped that it will not only look forward to lines of policy to be followed by the government of the day but also, in view of the long-term nature of housing, will outline policies which

---

* But see Supplement added during printing.

could become a broadly acceptable basis for future governments. It is not the object of a factual guide such as this to speculate on what these policies will, or should, be, but to set out information which must be taken into account when they are being assessed. This chapter therefore indicates the direction of some current trends and also refers to some of the most recent reports and statements on special aspects of housing currently under consideration.

(a) *Land*

Statistics given in Chapter 2 show that overall, in numerical terms, there is already a sufficient stock of dwellings to accommodate all households, and, therefore, generally additional land is needed to allow for improved space standards, better amenities and new facilities in both redevelopment and improvement schemes to keep pace with rising living standards. The Community Land Act, described in Chapter 9, was passed to ensure that this land would become available as and when required. Although at present restricted finance will hold up the full implementation of the Act and realisation of its aims, the Minister for Housing and Construction told the House of Commons in May 1977: " despite the background of a difficult economic climate, the land scheme made a good start. In the first year of the Act, local authorities bought 1,571 acres at a cost of £12·1m."

The annual expenditure white paper in 1976 allowed for about £25m, including administrative costs, to be spent on an estimated 1,200 acres. Councils in some parts of the country have acquired their new holdings for much lower prices than expected, although the provisional £12m excludes staff and administration costs. Of last year's acquisitions, 832 acres have been bought to accelerate private housing development, 730 acres for industry and 9 acres for commerce. London councils spent £1·35m on 15 acres, an average price of about £90,000 per acre.

In overcrowded areas of housing stress, such as London and the other conurbations, where a plentiful supply of land is urgently needed for housing, the Community Land Act will be of limited and protracted benefit. Here sites remain vacant for various reasons, including high acquisition costs arising from notional site values, based on land use rights, which could not be realised on the open market, and efforts to involve the private sector in redevelopment of inner city areas have not so far been successful. In a section of the final report of the Liverpool inner area study, *Change or Decay* (1), the consultants attack over-ambitious planning for the huge amounts of vacant derelict land, amounting to 11 per cent of the study area in March 1975. More than 75 per cent was owned by Liverpool City—about half had been vacant for at least two years and as much as three-quarters was likely then to be vacant still after five years. The problem is one of long-standing, and the report comments, " Despite the persistence of vast amounts of derelict land, the estates department does not maintain a comprehensive or up-to-date record of vacant land in the city. Nor is the city estates surveyor charged with assessing the economic or social costs of holding land vacant."

In a report based on research on the amount of vacant land in 30 of our largest cities, published in the *Architects' Journal* of 18 May 1977, it is claimed that the basic answer to the question of why there is land vacancy is that there is a mismatch between the location and type of the large amount of land becoming vacant in cities and the land use demands of city activities in recent decades. In addition, the resources needed to develop land, most notably capital, are scarcer than land itself. The best use of total resources, of labour, capital and time, in the best interests of the whole community, may not necessarily require the full utilisation of all city land at any one point in time.

With regard to derelict land grants, their scope is being considered in the Secretary of State for the Environment's review of the needs of inner cities. At present, 100 per cent grants are payable to local authorities for the reclamation of derelict land in areas designated by the Secretary of State for industry as development, intermediate or derelict land clearance areas. Elsewhere the grants are restricted to 50 per cent by section 9 of the Local Government Act 1966.

As figures on the amount of vacant land in this country are mainly unreliable as representing a true picture of land wastage, more research is needed on how much vacant land local authorities have within their jurisdiction and the true cost of holding it vacant. Such research, together with a revision of planning policies and a programme of forward-thinking schemes to attract finance to inner city areas, is needed if housing shortage and related social problems are to be tackled effectively.

Inner city areas. The government's policies for inner city areas have been discussed in Chapter 9 and reference made to the three action-research case studies, sponsored jointly by the Department of the Environment and the local authority concerned, in three industrial towns—London, Birmingham and Liverpool. Nearly 40 reports have been produced over the past four years and summaries of the findings in some of the areas were put together and published by the Department of the Environment (*Inner Area Studies: Liverpool, Birmingham and Lambeth— Summaries of consultants' final reports* (9:11)). A circular was produced in conjunction with the report which said that the government's immediate concern was to encourage public debate of the issues raised in order to help them to formulate a definitive policy.

All the reports emphasised the importance of social influences, as well as economic, in the making of deprivation; and future policy for regeneration of economic activity and improvement of the physical environment must be framed within a social context. The problems of Liverpool were seen to be the results of divorcing economic policy from housing policy. As a result of huge slum clearance programmes, the population in the study area fell from 725,000 in 1921 to 300,000 in 1971, and widespread physical decay, with one-tenth of the land vacant, was created. Declining environmental conditions led to professional and skilled workers moving out. The major necessity in inner Liverpool is to promote economic development and to create jobs, but an important recommendation is " improving access for housing for disadvantaged groups " by " making better use of existing council property through conversion and better management; providing furnished flats, sheltered accommodation and housing advice; and by providing mortgages for those on low incomes." The report also recommends tenant participation and methods of " renewing private housing incorporating greater local control."

In Small Heath, Birmingham, where the population fell from 50,000 in 1951 to 32,000 in 1977, the report proposes setting up a " task force " to establish industrial estates in the inner city; switching investment from new municipal housing development to rehabilitation and local employment; and encouragement of community organisations which should be given greater responsibility.

In Lambeth, housing is seen as central to the decline of the area, with low income workers caught in a " housing trap " which makes it impossible for them to buy houses while being unable to obtain access to council housing. Symptoms of population pressure are relatively high house prices, high densities, widespread multi-occupation, long council waiting lists, squatting and homelessness. The survey showed that between one-quarter and one-third of the households would move if they could, and the report proposes policies to enable these people to move if they want to.

Subsequently, the final reports on the inner area studies were published separately by the Stationery Office—*Unequal City—Final report of the Birmingham Inner Area Study* (2); *Change or Decay: Final report of the Liverpool inner area study* (1); *Inner London: Policies for dispersal and balance. Final report of the Lambeth inner area study* (3).

In 1977, the urban programme, formerly administered by the Home Office, was made the responsibility of the Department of the Environment and recast to cover economic and environmental as well as social projects. Its annual allowance was increased from under £30m to £125m in addition to the £80m which the Chancellor had made available in the budget. In April, the Secretary of State for the Environment announced a scheme for "special partnerships" between government and inner-city authorities in an attempt to "shift the emphasis of government policy and bring about a change in the attitude of local authorities". There will be joint preparation of inner area programmes to which grant aid will be related. Such partnerships will be offered, in the first instance, to Liverpool, Birmingham, Manchester/Salford, and London's Lambeth and dockland. Others can also apply, but the inner areas will get priority, especially in the early years. A total of £83m is to be made available for construction work in English inner cities. Birmingham, Liverpool and Manchester/Salford will get £11m each; London docklands will get £17m; the London Borough of Lambeth £5m; and the Inner London Education Authority another £2m to be spent in the docklands area and in Lambeth. The disposal of the remaining £26m earmarked for the English cities and the £17m allocated to Northern Ireland, Scotland and Wales has yet to be decided. A white paper *Policy for the Inner Cities* with details of the proposals (Cmnd. 6845), was laid before Parliament in June, 1977. (4).

Closer working contact between central and local government may be advantageous to both, but the local authority are concerned about the allocation of inner-city aid. The Association of District Councils has pointed out that there are equally pressing problems in other big cities beside the conurbations, in smaller towns and in country areas.

The Association of Metropolitan Authorities has asked the government to press for a bigger and more widely applicable European Regional Development Fund in order that grants may be made from the fund to help to improve the environment and to develop industry in the deprived inner-city areas. According to the AMA, Britain's current interpretation of the fund's regulations ensures that aid is concentrated in the special development areas of Northern England, but new criteria should be adopted so that inner-city areas can be helped. The fund's rules should be changed to make specific provision for helping to tackle obsolescence and dereliction in old industrial areas.

New towns. Reappraisal of new town policy referred to in Chapter 4 has resulted in less severe cutbacks than were feared. The scheme for Central Lancashire New Town is to continue, although with a severely reduced programme envisaging an extra 23,000 inhabitants instead of the 100,000 planned.

Other changes in long-term targets (including induced and natural growth) are: Milton Keynes loses 50,000 from its original target of 250,000; Northampton drops 50,000 from 230,000; Peterborough loses 20,000 from its original 180,000; Telford loses 70,000 from the intended 200,000; and Warrington loses 35,000 from 205,000. The government will be having a consultation period on the precise population targets before final decisions are made by the summer recess.

The extension plans for Bracknell, Skelmersdale, Redditch, Basildon, Corby, Runcorn, Harlow and Stevenage are to be shelved, and the development corporations in these eight areas will be wound up in the next five years.

In describing the background to the need for this reappraisal, the Secretary of State for the Environment particularly mentioned changes in population forecasts since the mid 1960s when the third generation new towns were planned on the assumption that the population of England and Wales would grow to 60 millions by 1991; recent trends, however, indicate that the population will only reach 51 millions by that date. Other factors taken into account were the continued increase in the number of households, the need to balance industrial and employment requirements of the inner areas with the need economically for industrial growth points outside, the amount of infrastructure already provided and under-used in new towns and the importance of these communities becoming balanced and viable places.

Housing Review of March/April 1977 looked realistically at the present situation and pointed out that the country was not dealing with the simple but formidable question of inner-city regeneration or further development of existing new and expanded towns. " It has always been an interlocking relationship, and it is surely correct to say that this continues to be so." Reference was also made to an address at the Housing Centre's Newcastle conference in November 1976 by Mr. Wyndham Thomas, General Manager of Peterborough, who said that the ongoing new towns should be encouraged to complete their programmes to make a direct and vitally important contribution to meeting the housing and environmental needs of deprived families now living in the inner cities, particularly as the inner cities " cannot go it alone ". Only thus could the inner city cope and eventually win through.

In the meantime, the implementation of the New Towns (Amendment) Act 1976, designed to enable existing dwellings and related assets to be transferred from the new town development corporations and the Commission for the New Towns to appropriate district councils in England and Wales, is proceeding. DOE Circular 5/77 on transfer schemes under the provisions of the Act and three new town staff circulars have been issued; and schemes for the first towns to be involved in the transfer— Crawley, Hemel Hempstead, Hatfield, Welwyn Garden City, Aycliffe, Basildon, Bracknell, Corby, Cwmbran, Harlow, Peterlee, Skelmersdale and Stevenage—become effective on 1 April 1978. Separate legislation exists for Scotland.

(b) *Production of dwellings*

Figures for numbers of dwellings built and rehabilitated have been given in previous chapters. New orders in the public housing sector dropped from December 1976 to February 1977 by 13 per cent as compared with the previous three months, and by 39 per cent compared with the same period a year earlier. *The Government's expenditure plans,* (5) published in March 1977 showed that the government had increased funds for local authority house improvement by an extra £100m, which is an increase of 40 per cent in 1977–78 and of over 50 per cent in 1978–79. Local authority expenditure on new dwellings, however, is projected to decline from £1,293m this year to £1,092m in 1977–78 to £1,035m in 1978–79.

Owing to the high cost of new building, contracts in the private sector are falling, and speculative builders might have to explore various equity sharing and co-operative schemes to ensure a continuing market for their product. At the same time, falling interest rates and a flow of money back into the building societies might induce a revival in the private sector.

The depressed state of the building industry has been discussed in Chapter 10. The first report, *Trends in construction activity,* from the newly-formed Joint Economic Advisory Panel, which includes representatives of both the National Joint Consultative Committee and of the Construction Programme Policy Group, is extremely critical of the succession of public expenditure cuts the industry suffered throughout 1976 and points out that an analysis of the white paper referred to above shows new construction to have been cut by some 17 per cent whereas other forms of public expenditure have suffered cutbacks of less than 2 per cent. Unemployment in the industry is now spread much wider than the 220,000 in the building and contracting sectors; and it is claimed that the money this represents in unemployment benefits would be enough to build some 20,000 dwellings annually. Ancillary industries, such as furniture and floor-coverings, are also suffering unemployment.

Further, figures in a RIBA regional chairmen's survey, released in April 1977, show that over 2,500 architects have been laid off in the preceding 12 months. The private sector was by far the hardest hit, accounting for over 90 per cent of the total number of staff discharged. The survey covered 2,141 private offices, 41 per cent of which reduced their staff during the year. Staff levels are down by 30 per cent compared with the end of 1974 and are likely to go down still further as the workload continues to fall. In the public sector, 37 per cent of offices reduced their staff, but only 5 per cent of employees have been laid off. The RIBA considers that the findings of the survey reinforces its view that the construction industry as a whole is now in a desperate position from which it may never recover. With craftsmen leaving the industry and design teams breaking up, the outlook for house construction, maintenance and improvement is bleak, and the government's concession in the form of construction work in inner-city areas described above is seen by the industry as minimal—the equivalent of half a day's work for the industry, according to the National Federation of Building Trades Employers.

While the country has housing problems—and the will to solve them—a healthy building industry is vital. The report referred to above is not only critical of the government's action in using the construction industry as a " convenient general economic regulator ", it also recognises on the other hand that " the industry . . . will henceforward need to exercise all its ingenuity in improving its flexibility and productivity". Concern with the improvement of management processes and with the contributions to these processes that each of the industry's sectors can make is essential. The report concludes by urging the government to examine more closely the possibility of attracting private funds to finance, at no cost to the public purse, works of a public nature that would not otherwise be started.

The development of serious defects in comparatively new properties has been discussed in Chapter 10. There is an urgent need for more investigation into the causes of these defects and into the influence of design decisions on the subsequent maintenance of buildings; for more advantage to be taken by the whole building industry—both designers and operatives—of the very fast pace of development of technology and new materials and for provision of higher standards of sound and heat insulation and of energy conservation generally. At the same time, more adequate and realistic " feed back " from consumer to designer and more intensive use of technical and sociological information already available would lead to greater consumer satisfaction in housing.

The Housing Corporation, through the housing association movement, will fund over 30,000 new and improved homes in

England and Wales in 1977, mostly to let at fair rents—almost 7,000 are to be provided by registered housing associations in London, and some 1,500 by associations in Wales. At a time when the private rented sector has declined to about 7 to 8 per cent of forms of tenure—and there is no immediate prospect of its recovery although attempts may be made to slow up its rate of decline—the work of housing associations brings flexibility into housing provision and provides an alternative form of tenure. Housing association tenancies will probably continue to increase—possibly to some 5 to 10 per cent of public sector tenancies in 10 years' time.

Figures emerging from the 1976 house condition survey, described in Chapter 2, show that there has been a substantial drop in the number of unfit houses since 1971. There are now about 900,000 such houses in England and Wales and about 1 million properties which are fit for habitation but still lack either a bathroom, indoor WC or hot water supply. In 1971, it was estimated that there were 1·244 million unfit houses and 2·866 million properties without one of the basic amenities. Clearance rates are now likely to be much lower because most of the major slum programmes are ending and also because of restricted finance. It is estimated that a further 50,000 to 60,000 properties are likely to become unfit each year.

A discussion document prepared by the National Home Improvement Council, *Improvement in United Kingdom Housing— A Reappraisal,* (6) reviews the housing stock position in relation to lack of amenity and serious disrepair, and puts forward proposals for improvement of the existing stock, whatever its ownership and present condition. It sees the problem for the next decade as the continuous upgrading of the existing housing stock within a total housing requirement which is expanding relatively slowly; and recognises that achievement of a significant reduction of sub-standard stock within an acceptable period of time, together with a steady upgrading of all homes, will require new approaches, new attitudes, new ideas and plenty of discussion. The main proposals for examination, some of which raise controversial issues, are summarised under the headings: activity levels, which include a target of 250,000 improved dwellings as a minimum annual requirement; reappraisal of grant scheme, including the establishment of a " minimum habitability standard " to combine unfitness, lack of amenity, serious disrepair and essential replacement, and mandatory aid for improvement of all sub-standard property to this new standard; resuscitation of the private rented sector, which includes proposals for a definition of " tenancy standards " for grant aid, " tenant allowance " for landlord improvement to this standard and a local authority register of landlords receiving aid with property to this standard; loan availability for low income applicants improving older property, including a revision of local authority improvement " guarantee " rules, loan availability for all " sub-standard " improvement and advisory centres for aiding negotiation of new tenancy forms, tenant purchase and related finance; and encouragement for repair and maintenance, general improvement and replacement, including avoiding discouragement by penal re-rating, saving for home investment via a new home saving bond, and zero rating for VAT on works of repair and maintenance. The Council makes the point referred to earlier that money would be better spent on construction work—in this case rehabilitation rather than new building—than on unemployment benefit.

(c) *Financial structure*

The urgent need for reform of housing finance has been clearly demonstrated in Chapter 8; and the enormous amount of material submitted to the government's housing finance review group by many bodies and individuals in the housing and allied fields provided the government with weighty evidence of this need and contained many recommendations.

Local authorities. The government's proposals for housing finance reform are still awaited. In order to give local authorities greater flexibility in the use of resources for capital finance, block allocations are being introduced to enable them " to respond more flexibly to unforeseen changes in local circumstances " (Circular 18/77). Block allocations are split into four groups: (1) new building, (2) acquisition, improvement and slum clearance; (3) improvement grants and loans for mortgages and improvement; and (4) housing associations. Circular 18/77, *Housing Capital Expenditure: Arrangements for the Financial Year 1977/78,* states that these " would require comprehensive assessments by local authorities of housing needs and the formulation of proposals to deal with them by a rolling programme of capital expenditure." They would have to ensure that they are fully informed on the total housing situation in their areas so that they know where and what the urgent local needs really are and can base local policies and spending on an up-to-date understanding of the problems of individual areas and the context in which they arise.

For the financial year 1977–78, the Secretary of State has introduced an element of flexibility by enabling authorities to switch a proportion of the expenditure from one programme to another (virement) and also to carry forward or anticipate expenditure within a defined limit (tolerance). There are restrictions in the new arrangements; local authorities can transfer only 25 per cent in and out of any particular group; and national cash limits must be adhered to. For England, these limits are £1,400m for new building and land (£950m and £90m respectively); £391m for municipalisation, council improvements and slum clearance (£60m, £29m and £35m); £172m for private improvement grants and mortgages (£72m and £100m); and £22m for lending to housing associations. Authorities will be free to carry forward to the succeeding year any underspending up to 10 per cent of the allocation or capital payments forecast for the expenditure block; or to bring forward from the succeeding year and spend in the current year an extra amount up to that limit. (The virement and tolerance arrangements are set out in Annex A and exemplified in the appendix to the Annex of Circular 18/77). A close check will be kept by central government on local government use of the new powers, and the compilation of the necessary statistics is likely to introduce further complications into housing finance.

For new building, the *pro-forma* sent out to local authorities to enable them to state their case for the allocation in this group emphasises that the DOE regards as committed expenditure in this area only those schemes where the contract has already been let. No special provision will be made for other schemes which are uncommitted expenditure. Fees for planning and design work already carried out by independent architects, however, will have to come out of the allocation for new building (or from 25 per cent moved into this group from one of the other groups), thus reducing the money allocated for specific projects.

With regard to allocations for housing associations, too, the cost of rehabilitation work where contracts have not been let cannot be regarded as committed expenditure, although the house purchase on a mortgage will have been completed. The association will be paying interest on a mortgage and will not qualify for HAG grant until improvement work is completed.

These restrictions and reductions, together with central government control for the first time over housing action area and general improvement area improvements, and improvement grants for owner occupiers and landlords in the private sector, have caused some local authorities to claim that the new arrangements are likely to slow down housing expenditure rather than achieve more flexibility.

The Scottish Office has published the final report of its working party on housing. Under the new system, each of Scotland's 56 districts and islands authorities will prepare a five-year plan for housing in its area covering the needs to be met in public and private sectors, and the policies it proposes for meeting them.

It will also include a programme of capital investment which the authority itself proposes to make over the five years.

These plans—and the first is required by the Scottish Office by July 1977—will be rolled forward each year and submitted to the Secretary of State who will assess each authority's spending programme against the needs and policies in its plan and authorise in advance the capital spending to finance the first year of the programme.

Eventually the authorities will be allocated a single block of capital spending to cover new building, modernisation, and all other aspects of building work, and the present project-by-project Scottish Office scrutiny will be removed. Meanwhile, there will be two spending blocks covering spending carried to the housing revenue account and all other spending. This contrasts with the four categories mentioned above which apply in England and Wales during the same transitional period.

Capital programmes should distinguish between committed and uncommitted expenditure. During the first year, authorities will need the Department's approval to move resources from one of the two sectors to the other, but within the block authorities will have complete freedom of allocation. However, the Secretary of State will have the power to make " strong reservations " about any respects in which he feels that policies and programmes may fall short of the needs of the area.

The new block grant system will mean an end to the housing cost yardstick, though the report suggests that the Department should continue to prepare housing cost indicators " as a guide to local authorities in preparing their capital programmes ".

The report also suggests that, subject only to conforming to statutory building regulation standards, authorities should be free to choose the standards to apply to individual schemes—which could mean abandoning Parker Morris standards in favour of the lower standards at present permitted only for the private sector.

Meanwhile, Chapter 8 has dealt with the important issues in housing finance generally and the subsidisation of local authority housing. As has been pointed out, some two-thirds of the cost of public housing is now being met out of Exchequer monies raised by taxation and only about 30 per cent out of rents paid by council tenants. Together with tax relief on mortgage interest this means that most households are not only benefiting from some form of subsidy towards their housing costs but are also paying through taxes, and sometimes also rates, towards that subsidy. Criticism is levelled against such general subsidies because they do not seem to be meeting the most urgent housing needs. Moreover, because public expenditure on housing is so high, programmes of new building and rehabilitation tend to become the casualties of economic crises, and many believe an increase in direct payments by occupiers towards the housing they enjoy could ultimately lead to higher housing standards. The issues, however, are controversial and governments and political parties fear the unpopularity of introducing increases in rent and loan charges. The background to the present housing finance system has been dealt with in earlier chapters of the *Guide,* and it only remains here to stress again the importance of assessing new policies, when they are announced, for their relevance to housing progress rather than any narrow sectional interest.

The drastic reductions in the allocation of funds for local authority loans for house purchase will increase the difficulties of those looking to authorities for mortgages. Local authorities have concentrated their lending on borrowers who have difficulty in raising a mortgage from a building society or private source because they present a higher risk, for example because their income is low or they can only buy an older and cheaper property. Thus it is these people, many of whom may be young married couples embarking on house purchase for the first time, who are most likely to suffer from the cuts. In the House of Commons, the Minister for Housing and Construction quoted figures for local authority lending which highlighted the sad story in this area: " at 1976 survey prices, reported lending in 1974–75 totalled £686m; the allocation for 1977–78 is £100m." (" 1976 survey prices " is the term used by the public expenditure committee as a base for establishing housing expenditure in 1976—or any given year. The " survey price " is based on the actual expenditure up to the November of the preceding year). To mitigate the effect of the cuts, an arrangement was made whereby the building societies agreed to advance £100m to borrowers sponsored by local authorities. Despite this and the claims of the societies that they are in fact lending extensively to first time buyers, buyers with comparatively low incomes and those purchasing older houses, they are often criticised for their reluctance to lend on poorer-type houses.

In 1977, building societies have been able to reduce their rates of interest on borrowing in line with the reduction in interest rates generally, without reducing the inflow of funds for lending. This means that they have been able to reduce their lending rates also, which will help potential purchasers. There are fears that house prices will escalate if too much money is available for lending on easier terms, as happened in the early 1970s, but it is hoped that the machinery set up for monitoring will provide warning of such dangers and the situation will be kept under control through the co-operation of the societies with the government.

Housing associations. The following breakdown of the £300m cuts in housing expenditure for the year 1978–79, at 1976 survey prices, given by the Minister for Housing and Construction to the House of Commons on 1 April 1977, shows that the activities of the housing association movement, which expanded at such an impressive rate after the passing of the Housing Act 1974, will be restricted in the future:

	£m
England	
Housing association (grant and loans)	94
Local authority investment	
(a) Land	50
(b) Acquisitions	70
New town investment	41
	255
Scotland and Wales	45
	£ 300m

In England and Wales, an extra £30m was allocated to housing authorities and housing associations for improvement and reno-vation. However, although increased administrative and other costs incurred in housing association activities are currently being met by revenue deficit grants, which cover the difference between the rent a housing association is permitted to charge and its outgoings, the question must arise on how long this commitment—and the present system of generous capital grants—will be main-tained at a time of continuing financial stringency.

The Housing Corporation's budget for the current financial year was reduced by £57m at the end of 1976. In April 1977, however, the Corporation received approval from the Treasury and the DOE to borrow £25m from banking sources; and it has set up a private company for this purpose with the Corporation holding the controlling interest. It is hoped that a further £25m will be raised during 1978–79.

By seeking alternative forms of finance for its operations, the Corporation will be able to continue its valuable work of promot-ing the activities of more than 2,000 registered housing associa-tions to bring flexibility and choice into housing provision and provide an alternative form of tenure and landlord.

The private sector. At the end of January 1977 the government issued a consultation paper on the review of the Rent Acts which sets out in detail some of the main issues to be studied and con-tains a questionnaire. The review necessarily covers social as well as financial issues, and its particular objectives are set out as follows:

(a) to safeguard the interests of existing private tenants, many of whom are elderly, poor or for other reasons have difficulty in finding adequate accommodation;

(b) to ensure (without imposing unreasonable burdens on landlords, many of whom are of limited means) that fit private rented houses are properly maintained and kept in repair and do not deteriorate prematurely so that there is no alternative to clearance;

(c) to promote the efficient use of housing, particularly to meet needs not otherwise adequately catered for (for instance, lettings to the young, single and mobile) and to encourage the use of property which might be available for letting for limited periods only;

(d) to ensure that the methods and criteria for the determination of rents are tailored to meet the difficulties faced by both landlords and tenants;

(e) to simplify the law on private renting and the administrative machinery, and to make for a speedier and more effective resolution of disputes between landlord and tenant; and

(f) in general to provide a legislative framework which maintains a fair balance between the interests of tenants and landlords so that private rented accommodation can contribute effectively to meeting housing needs and choices and evolve into social forms of housing involving and acceptable to existing landlords and their tenants.

The Housing Centre Trust has welcomed the wide scope of the review to cover all aspects of housing provision by private landlords, and has submitted a memorandum to the Department of the Environment. (7)

Consideration of the longer term future of the private sector reflected the diversity of views, disciplines and interests of Housing Centre members. Some members felt that the aim should be for all rented housing to come into social ownership (i.e. local authority, housing association and co-operative ownership) and would like to see this take place as rapidly as possible. Others felt that the sector should continue to provide a useful service to existing tenants and to those who could not get access to local authority housing, including the young and mobile, and who could not afford to buy or did not wish to do so. It was generally recognised that to transfer the whole privately rented sector rapidly to social ownership would be beyond the nation's current resources in public money and manpower and more costly to the taxpayer than the modest tax reliefs or subsidies needed to improve the current position. Acquisition would also be a considerable burden on the public borrowing requirement. Although some felt that confidence in letting had already been so far eroded that there was little hope of resuscitating the sector, or even reversing the trend towards its decline, it was generally agreed that policy should be designed to hold the position and to improve conditions to an extent which would enable the sector to contribute usefully to general housing needs.

Proposals in the memorandum cover the question whether different treatment for different categories within the private rented sector would be justified. The three broad divisions identified in the consultation paper are:

(a) the older dwellings mainly let unfurnished often to elderly poor tenants and owned by small landlords:

(b) the more modern dwellings owned by larger business landlords, both furnished and unfurnished;

(c) accommodation mainly let furnished by resident landlords or owner occupiers during temporary absence, etc., including accommodation which might be so let if conditions were more favourable.

There was pessimism about the possibility of improving the housing conditions in category (a) in that much of it will need redevelopment anyway, and it was thought that available resources for bringing any private property into social ownership should be concentrated first on the oldest and least viable properties. At the same time, some ameliorative measures for use as a holding operation were suggested in the answers to the questionnaire.

Category (b) would be most amenable to improvement through the general financial incentives proposed in the memorandum; and there is scope for transferring parts of it to forms of co-operatives and equity sharing tenures without making calls on public funds.

Owners in category (c), whose property by its nature must remain mostly in private ownership, should be encouraged to let it by some relaxation of restrictions provided these can be made compatible with the avoidance of abuses which create hardship for occupiers.

It was recognised that the problems in these sectors were different, but the consensus view was that there should be one basic legal code covering rent regulation and security of tenure for (a) and (b), but that (c) as now should be more readily entitled to possession within the contract.

With regard to security of tenure, although consideration had been given by the Housing Centre to whether the differences in the degree of demand for rented dwellings in relation to supply justified different treatment in different parts of the country, the consensus of opinion was strongly in favour of maintaining security of tenure, as most members' experience was in areas of shortage where freedom from controls is most likely to be abused.

The memorandum recognised that the financial system under which the private sector operates in relation to other sectors is the key to its future, and this system has been considered in detail in Chapter 8.

It is suggested that modified proposals for changing the tax system under which landlords operate should be investigated. Some Housing Centre members had argued that landlords were not looking for a rate of return on capital after allowing for management and maintenance costs equal to current rates of interest on fixed interest bonds, but, in view of the appreciating value of their asset, would be content with considerably lower rates of return. If this contention proves correct, then astronomical rent rises in real terms would not be necessary. Necessary rent levels calculated on the basis of the rents required to finance a local authority or housing association scheme without subsidy do not support this view, but the Centre suggests that the removal or amelioration of tax disincentives which affect the private landlord should be examined in greater depth and detail.

An important point emphasised in the memorandum is that if the private sector is to survive it will not be solely by improved financial incentives for landlords alone, important as these are. What is also needed is an improvement in confidence throughout the sector—confidence on the part of landlords that future governments will honour any commitments entered into, enough confidence to induce landlords to let their property, to repair it and improve it. Equally important is to find some way of moving away from the confrontation of landlord and tenant. There must be, throughout the country, thousands of satisfactory relationships between landlords and tenants, despite all the difficulties dealt with in the consultation paper. Some way must be found to put the difficulties into perspective and thus to present a fairer and more balanced picture of the sector.

The Housing Centre points out that the system of rent fixing introduced by the Rent Act 1965 had much to recommend it at the time it was introduced, but in the conditions of galloping inflation which have developed since, the three-year interval before rent revision inevitably appears unfair to owners. Other difficulties are the use as a basis of comparables with rents which become quickly out of date, as well as the disappearance of any relationship to a free market, since virtually none exists. It is considered, however, that the present system of discounting any scarcity element in the market rent should continue and should be applied to any valuation for rent however arrived at.

The memorandum points out that, in the new system of rent control proposed for Northern Ireland, multipliers of rateable values are to be used in preference to the fair rent system of England and Wales because of the time and expense involved in moving to fair rents (*Section O. The Private Rented Sector in Northern Ireland, The Government's Proposals, October 1976*). Multipliers of rateable values are commonly used for local authority housing in England and Wales. Although serious anomalies exist between rateable values of houses on the one hand and flats on the other, as well as between rateable values of individual houses, because of the " broad brush " approach adopted by the Inland Revenue, this may be said to be an argument for improving the system of rating assessments rather than rejecting the idea altogether, or of combining it with the present system of appeals to rent assessment committees. If rateable values were used as a basis, however, the proviso above regarding scarcity values would have to be taken into account. In Northern Ireland, rent assessment committees, identical in composition to the rent assessment committees in England and Wales, are proposed to examine appeals against rents set by reference to rateable values. There could be administration savings in such a system over the present one. It would seem worth while investigating whether the two sets of administrative machinery in England and Wales, one for rating purposes and the other for private rents (both of which are theoretically related) can be combined.

To prevent the erosion of regulated rents by inflation, probably the main cause of dissatisfaction to landlords under present inflationary conditions, it is suggested that annual indexing of rents is worthy of sympathetic consideration, even if the present system of rent setting by the rent officer with appeal to the rent assessment committee is continued. As a general principle, in all sectors frequent small increases in rent are more acceptable than less frequent larger ones. They are also likely to be of more value to the landlord since he would be able to collect a small increase, without phasing, immediately after it is made. A recent form of indexation, introduced by the Netherlands government in 1976, merits examination to see if its provisions could be applied in this country, especially to the institutional landlord.

The memorandum considers the very important matter of publicity and information. There is a limit to what can be done to make complicated material simple enough to be understood by landlords or potential landlords in general, including immigrant landlords. Continued support of citizens' advice bureaux and housing aid centres is important, and in addition to help dispensed by the mainly office-bound staff of such bureaux and centres, there is a need for more peripatetic advisors than are at present available in most areas so that small landlords in particular can have the benefit of more in situ advice on repairs, improvements, grants available, planning consents needed, publicity material available and so on.

In May 1977 a consultation paper in connection with the review of the Scottish Rent Acts was issued. This describes briefly conditions in the private rented sector in Scotland and raises both general issues and questions of a more technical nature which have arisen on the Rent Acts. It was stated in the House of Commons that the document was written within the framework of existing policies and did not attempt to anticipate any conclusions which may result from the review of housing policy and finance.

Rates. A green paper, *Local Government Finance,* (8) was published in May 1977 as the government's preliminary response to the Layfield report, referred to in Chapter 3. Local income tax is rejected, Exchequer support is to be simplified and the current system of rating is to be retained. A number of changes are proposed, however, to meet detailed criticisms that have been made of the system and to improve and strengthen it.

Capital values instead of rental values are accepted as the basis for the valuation of domestic property, and legislation is to be introduced to implement this. The earliest date by which the revaluation could take place on the new basis would be 1982–83, and the government say that they intend that this timetable should be achieved. The impact of the change will be softened by phasing arrangements and it is accepted by the government that there may be a need for more permanent modifications.

Changes of detail proposed for the rating system include an extension to non-domestic ratepayers of the right to pay rates by instalments and a different method of giving domestic rate relief to ratepayers who occupy mixed commercial and domestic properties; and it is understood that other changes are to be made in the administration and operation of rating and the appeals machinery.

(d) *Social Aspects*

Housing policy and practice must reflect closely the changing needs of society. The social aspects of housing in modern society were considered in detail in Chapter 11, where reference was made to encouraging evidence of increasing recognition of the need for a comprehensive, humane and flexible approach to housing, planning and the social services. Some more recent developments in the progress towards this overall approach are summarised here.

Homelessness. The continuing magnitude of the problem of homelessness was illustrated by DOE figures for the first half of

1976, published in April 1977. In that period, 26,140 households applied for help on the grounds of being or being about to become homeless. Local authorities accepted responsibility to secure accommodation for 17,120 of these and were able to provide accommodation for about 12,570; a further 2,220 found accommodation themselves. A report published by the Liverpool Inner Area Study Group, *Single and Homeless,* (9: 10) assesses the problem in one particular area for one particular group and describes a project which attempts to meet the social need locally.

The government has given its support to the Housing (Homeless Persons) Bill, proposed by Stephen Ross MP. The main purpose of the Bill is defined as " to replace the limited duty of local social services authorities to provide temporary accommodation for those in urgent need, in certain circumstances by duties to be placed on local housing authorities to provide, secure or help secure accommodation for homeless persons and those threatened with homelessness ". The Housing Centre, whose memorandum on homelessness is summarised in Chapter 11, the Institute of Housing and others, including the seven charities who have been working for the introduction of homelessness legislation, have welcomed the Bill in principle, particularly as it establishes the statutory definition of a local authority's responsibilities towards the homeless, and secures the transfer of these responsibilities to housing authorities, but certain amendments have been proposed. Further, the chairman of the housing committee of the Association of District Councils has expressed concern that the Bill " goes far beyond a mere transfer of responsibility. It imposes an entirely new duty on authorities by creating a right to accommodation. This in itself will encourage homelessness. Even worse, the financial memorandum to the Bill pretends that there will be no net addition to public expenditure. Of course, such additional responsibilities will add to costs." Similar misgivings were expressed on the Conservative side in the House of Commons where speakers felt that the Bill went too far and, if left unamended, would become a charter for rent-dodgers, scroungers and an encouragement to home-leavers, and that it tackled the effect of the social problem but not the cause, and in that respect was defective.

Seaside towns, led by Bournemouth, have also sought amendments to the Bill. While there is no complaint about the main intents of the Bill, there is concern that no residential qualification is proposed—anybody who can prove homelessness and who falls into one of the priority groups for housing, to be determined by the DOE, will have to be housed by the authority approached. Bournemouth DC wants the Bill amended so that it applies only to people who are normally resident in the area where they become homeless. It fears that people will go to seaside towns seeking holiday accommodation, find there is none and then go as homeless to the local authority. If they have no permanent home and they fall within one of the priority groups, the local authority will be legally bound to give them accommodation while it investigates the case, if clause 2 of the Bill passes into the Act unchanged.

A national policy on homelessness, within a legislative framework, is urgently needed, but only a flexible and sensitive approach by local authorities in implementing this policy—and the provision of the necessary resources, especially manpower—will ultimately alleviate the problem. Further, many people who become homeless misunderstand or are unaware of their housing rights or opportunities and do not know where to turn for help or guidance. So often the right kind of help at the right time by the right people can avert disaster. The kind of help which is urgently needed can be produced if there is speedy and effective training of housing advisers to staff more centres for housing aid and guidance, as recommended by the Seebohm committee, and close co-operation between housing departments and social services acting on a case-work basis.

The disabled. Attention was drawn at the annual meeting of the Centre on Environment for the Handicapped (CEH) in April 1977 to the gradual drying-up of sources of philanthropy and the need for the government to allocate money more wisely and equitably for the good of most handicapped people, including the disabled, the mentally ill and the elderly infirm. A case study in *The Architects' Journal* of 20 April 1977 points out that about two people in a thousand use wheelchairs in the home, and probably a quarter of these are effectively chairbound. Since disabled people tend to be poorer than average, they are likely to be found in housing requiring rehabilitation. The study concentrates, therefore, on characteristics of houses for wheelchair users particular to rehabilitation. Selwyn Goldsmith's *Designing for the disabled,* which gives full coverage of wheelchair housing and the special problems of the disabled, has already been mentioned in Chapter 11.

If scarce resources are to be used effectively to meet the needs of the handicapped, more information with guidance on tailoring rehabilitation to their special requirements is essential. It is understood that the Housing Corporation intends to publish, for the use of housing associations, a design guidance on housing the disabled, and the Department of the Environment should be able to provide appraisals of schemes carried out by a few pioneering local authorities for use as guidelines and pointers to design.

The provision of adequate housing for disabled people can be delayed by arguments over who pays for what. The DHSS/DOE consultative paper, *Adaptations to housing for people who are physically handicapped,* on joint funding in rehabilitation for the disabled, calls attention to this and points the sensible way— at present, DOE pays for " rehabilitation " and DHSS for " adaptations ", but common sense and correct priorities must ensure agreement to achieve speedy solutions to particular social problems.

Race relations. It is generally recognised that race relations are an extremely delicate and pressing social issue, and the Commission for Racial Equality has finally been established. The idea of such a Commission, conceived about three years ago, was published about two years ago and passed as law in 1976. The complete list of the Commission was published in April 1977 and work was to start formally at the end of that month.

Various reports and recommendations on race relations have been described in Chapter 11, and the advisability of local authorities' recording the race of their applicants and tenants, which the Cullingworth Committee felt was important to ensure that allocations were in fact not prejudiced, discussed. A further report, *Race and local authority housing; information on ethnic groups,* (9) prepared by a working party of the London Housing Research Group, which also included personnel from the Department of the Environment and the Community Relations Commission, has claimed that " indirect discrimination " could be proved against housing authorities that fail to keep ethnic records. Under the Race Relations Act 1976, " it would not be easy for a local authority to show that it had fulfilled its general duty to eliminate racial discrimination and secure equality of opportunity if it had not collected information or carried out special studies to measure the effects of its policies and activities ". With the Act's new concept of " indirect discrimination ", such discrimination could be alleged against authorities whose allocation policies resulted in the concentration of a disproportionate number of ethnic minority families on poor estates.

Lord Pitt, the Community Relations Commission's chairman, drawing attention to the " disturbing evidence " in the report that " in several areas black families have tended to get the worst housing ", commended the report's detailed guidelines for authorities on how to monitor the situation.

Another CRC publication, however, *Housing choice and ethnic concentration; an attitude study,* based on a survey of 1,700 people, 1,000 of them black, and 700 white, living in Lambeth, Haringey, Bradford and Leicester, points out that in many areas ethnic concentration results from the preference of the inhabitants themselves.

The survey shows that a large proportion of the white residents of multi-racial areas were over 65, whereas adult members of the minority community were mainly aged between 30 and 50. The report suggests that much of the resulting friction is in fact due to changes in the age profile or economic character of the area, but is perceived in racial terms. In those survey areas where the white population was younger, respondents were less likely to attribute the decline of the area to the presence of immigrants. Further, older people are less able to carry out home improvements, and so were often worse off in their housing conditions than the new black population.

Although the report supports measures to prevent a build up of black families on poor estates, it also calls on authorities to " discuss and encourage the growth of viable minority communities on their council estates ". It is argued that members of minority groups value the social support and cultural amenities available from their own community in multi-racial areas; and, the survey shows, there is no evidence that dispersal reduces hostility of white residents towards black.

Indeed, in a report published by Wandsworth Council for Community Relations, it is claimed that the hostility which can arise from moving black families to better council homes in the suburbs demands remedy. Black families may be accepted in poorer, inner city areas, but are often decidedly unwelcome in newer and better estates—and their movement to these estates is likely to increase.

Present housing allocation policies, based on need, often work against the provision of a mixed, balanced community. Because the homeless are given high priority, a disproportionately high number of immigrant families are moving on to the estates, and if these should include problem families, white families may tend to classify all black families as problem families.

The report urges housing authorities to look at the possibility of allocating some places for the second generation of local parents on the estates.

Speaking at an Institute of Housing London regional seminar, organised by the London Branch, on *Housing in Multi-Racial Areas*, discussed in Chapter 11, the Minister for Housing and Construction referred to this sensitive question of concentration or dispersal. He felt that many of the arguments over this issue were redundant. People should be free to make up their own mind whether or not to move into or from established communities. They should not be confined to an estate or area—nor compelled to leave it—on grounds of the colour of their skin or their racial origin. The way forward was to remove obstacles to movement—transfer policies had a major role to play in this field; it was effective equality of access and choice that was needed.

The Minister had emphasised that the latest estimates showed the total number of people with direct or family origins from the new Commonwealth and Pakistan who lived in Great Britain to be about one and three-quarter million, about 3·2 per cent of the total population. Forty per cent of these so-called " immigrants " were born in this country. It was pointed out that, as time passes, the proportion of newcomers to this country will grow smaller and smaller and we must become increasingly concerned with the needs of people born here and who have never known another home. This, Mr. Freeson claimed, underlined why we must root out discrimination and fight prejudice—if for no other reason that they were serious obstacles to solving the social and economic problems which we all faced, particularly in the hearts of our cities.

Evidence showed that ethnic minorities were often less well informed about the housing system—and council housing in particular—than the rest of the population. The problem of communication was a difficult one as the transmission of information could occur in a variety of ways. The DOE were considering the possibility of translating more of their leaflets and posters into minority languages, and also whether any of their films on housing could be dubbed. The Department was also looking at research into the ways in which housing information was put across to members of ethnic minority groups, the use they made of available opportunities and how they fared when they had taken advantage of these opportunities. It was hoped that authorities in multi-racial areas would consider what more they could do to make similar local arrangements, perhaps in co-ordination with a housing advice group or voluntary group. The Housing Services Advisory Group were considering the subject of training in the housing service, and would be looking at the question of a race relations element in training. It was important that authorities with large ethnic minority populations should be aware how particular policies affected them. Without the necessary information, authorities faced substantial difficulties in ensuring that their housing policy was going to be soundly based.

The Department of the Environment is consulting with local authorities and representatives of ethnic groups on the question of ethnic records, to ascertain whether keeping records and information in relation to housing members of ethnic groups can help authorities in developing a fuller understanding of the overall housing situation and needs of those who live in their areas, and whether the decision to keep records should be a matter solely for each authority in the light of their assessment of the size and composition of the various ethnic groups and of the overall housing and social circumstances of their districts. The Minister reminded local authorities that whatever final conclusions were reached, there was no doubt about the need for local authorities to collate more information on the total situation in their areas as the basis of policy decisions.

Gypsies. Reference was made in Chapter 11 to the duties of local authorities under the Caravan Sites Act 1968, which provided in Part II (only enforced in 1970) for the establishment of sites for the use of gypsies and other persons of nomadic habit, and for the control in certain areas of the unauthorised occupation of land by them. A network of sites throughout England and Wales was envisaged, in recognition of the gypsies' right of legal abode.

During nearly seven years of the Act's operation, however, councils have provided only 133 sites with pitches for 2,131 caravans—enough to accommodate little more than a quarter of gypsy families—probably as many as 6,000 families still have nowhere they can camp legally. Because the Act was not meeting the social need to provide accommodation for gypsies, in February 1976 the Minister for Planning and Local Government asked Mr. John Cripps, chairman of the Countryside Commission, to carry out a study with the following terms of reference: " To consider the effectiveness of the arrangements to secure adequate accommodation for gypsies in England and Wales, as required by Part II of the Caravan Sites Act 1968, with special reference to:

(a) the financial and administrative arrangements for the implementation of the Act, and
(b) the provisions for the exemption of local authorities and the designation of their areas; and to report."

Pending the publication of the report, the government issued a circular at the end of March 1977 reminding local authorities that evicting gypsies from illegal sites was an expensive waste of time if there were no legal sites they could move to. The circular pointed out, "It may be that curtailment of indiscriminate eviction—costly to carry out and fruitless in effect—could release resources for the provision of emergency stopping places equipped to a minimum level of facilities." It also suggested that councils should eke out scarce resources by helping gypsies to provide and equip sites for themselves. Where gypsies have bought and equipped their own sites—and failed to get planning permission —the authorities " might not consider it expedient to take enforcement action " until alternative sites are available. There had been a spate of evictions of gypsies over Christmas, but the circular highlighted the sad position that the unauthorised encampments which the Caravan Sites Act 1968 was designed to eradicate were as numerous and widespread as ever, not only causing serious worry and offence to the settled population but often barely tolerable living conditions for the gypsies themselves.

Accommodation for Gypsies, (10) published at the beginning of April 1977, describes very clearly how gypsies are very much the victims of general trends in society and of events taking place without regard to or for them. The growing complexity of laws and regulations, with a concomitant increase in form-filling, often baffles and exasperates them, while a series of Town and Country Planning, Public Health, Local Government, Caravan and Private Acts, and the bylaws they permit, have steadily eroded their choice of habitation. In particular, the number of stopping places has been drastically reduced over a period of three or four decades during which the travelling population has been on the increase.

The report does not underestimate the difficult social problems, especially that of worsening relations with the rest of the community. " The violence remains sporadic, but seems likely to grow. Behind it is an immense amount of personal distress and misery for house-dwellers and gypsies alike. It would be idle to attribute blame. The behaviour of one group conditions another's reactions, which aggravate it; so the antagonisms build up. Communal conflict arises because gypsies form an easily identified minority divorced from our society by culture, tradition and contemporary attitudes and behaviour; their manner of living conflicts at many points with that of house-dwellers. . . . The conflict is exacerbated by the denial, to large numbers of gypsies, of the right of legal abode." At the same time, the report emphasises that the problem must be kept in perspective. " It must surely be possible, in two countries with a combined population of 49 million, for the majority to come to terms with a minority, albeit non-conforming, who number less than 50,000, if gypsies now living in houses are excluded. Certainly it is in the interest of the majority to do this rather than to perpetuate the distress which they, in part, bring upon themselves, and to incur the avoidable cost of evictions, fencing and trenching, and make-shift arrangements to the tune of hundreds of thousands of pounds annually." Figures quoted in an appendix show that in 1975–76 one metropolitan borough spent £7,700 on fencing and £8,000 on trenching and estimated the cost of officials' time at £2,300—a total of £18,000; while the estimates of another included an item of £10,000, plus £5,000 for " manpower ", as the cost of dealing with gypsies. The amount of time now being spent by government officials, by members and officers of local government, by the courts and members of the police and probation services, and by individuals in numerous capacities is out of all relation to the size of the problem. Further, the eviction of men, women and children with nowhere else to go is increasingly distasteful to the men who are expected to use force, if necessary, against them.

The recommendations include that the government should demonstrate a much higher level of commitment to achieving rapidly the purposes of the 1968 Act by (a) giving to accommodation for gypsies the same priority as has been given to housing for non-gypsies; (b) seeking statutory authority for the payment of Exchequer grants to cover the capital cost of sites at a rate of 100 per cent for a period of five years; and (c) increasing the staffs of the Departments dealing with gypsy matters to enable them to perform the additional functions recommended for them. Also, it is recommended that local authorities should help gypsies to buy or lease land for their own use; that, where appropriate, the Property Services Agency should sell land to local authorities for this purpose, or, exceptionally, to gypsies direct; that families so assisted should be credited to an authority in the fulfilment of their quota; and that local authorities should be mindful of their statutory duties to provide accommodation for gypsies when considering applications for planning permission and site licences. Proposals are made for every non-metropolitan county, and metropolitan and London borough council in whose area gypsies reside or resort, to appoint or nominate a gypsy (liaison) officer, to be employed full-time as such where the size of the area and the number of gypsies warrant it, and for the Secretaries of State to appoint a national advisory body, at least four members of which are to be gypsies, to promote improvements in relations between house-dwellers and gypsies as a non-conforming minority, and to advise on all matters relating to these relations and on such matters as the Secretaries of State may refer to them.

The under-lying obstacle to meeting the need for suitable accommodation for gypsies, however, is not government intransigence, but usually the most determined and organised local opposition to any proposal for the provision of a gypsy caravan site in an area—and local government members are not likely to want to antagonise electors by espousing an unpopular cause. According to the report, upwards of 300 sites, together with transit sites and stopping places, are now required—at a probable cost at current prices of £30 million. At the present time of restricted finance, the government may well put provision for gypsies at this cost low in their list of priorities, but, even if the money were forthcoming, a change of attitude at local level would be an essential prerequisite to the production of the required 300 sites.

Tenant involvement. Tenant dissatisfaction with their homes and environment and with the management and maintenance of properties and estates; and the increasing incidence of rent arrears, vandalism and other problems were referred to in Chapter 11 as pressing social questions. Greater tenant involvement in the provision, management and control of housing was mentioned as a possible solution to some of the problems.

A report by the Housing Services Advisory Group on local authority tenancy agreements, (11) published in May 1977, calls for a " fundamental change " in the relationship between public-sector landlords and their tenants. Many tenancy agreements are seen as unnecessarily restrictive, in that they relate to duties and responsibilities already adequately covered by law or imply a code of conduct that is entirely foreign to the great majority of tenants. New agreements should set out the rights and duties of both parties in simple, plain language and, if this course of action were adopted, local authorities would no longer be able to insist on their own restrictive ideas of proper behaviour. Instead, reliance would be put on a general requirement for tenants to act in a reasonable way with regard to property and attitude to neighbours. The report stresses that tenancy conditions adopted by individual local authorities should be revised periodically in consultation with tenants.

The Minister for Housing and Construction hoped the report would encourage local authorities to take a thorough and critical look at their policies. The aim was not only to remove petty restrictions but also to encourage greater responsibility and initiative on the part of the tenants. There was no intention of allowing councils to evade their responsibilities, but there were many cases where tenants were able and willing to make and pay for improvements to their homes, and that sort of involvement should be encouraged.

The report is in favour of security of tenure, but with four exceptions: positive breach of the agreement; necessary repossession to carry out major rehabilitation; on divorce, the reallocation of the home, if necessary, to the person who has responsibility for children; and the restoration of private property to its owner at the end of a fixed lease.

The council's responsibilities should cover the maintenance and repair of the building and arrangements for consultation if it should prove necessary to end a tenancy. Tenants' responsibilities should relate to the payment of rent and other charges, provisions relating to any transfer to sub-tenants, building alterations, and overall conduct or behaviour. Married tenants should be allowed to opt for a joint tenancy.

Responsibility for decoration will vary in different areas, but applications for permission to carry out personal painting or to have lodgers should not be unreasonably withheld.

New forms of tenure. At a press conference to mark the publication of the report, the Minister for Housing and Construction said the government intended to give local authorities powers to license private landlords, and that tenants would be given the right to buy their homes on a co-operative basis when the owner proposed to sell the property " over their heads ". Other developments envisaged were the encouragement of landlord-tenant co-ownership or shared equity; the sponsorship by housing associations of full home ownership, and similar shared equity at the bottom end of the market as well as the formation of co-operatives; the extension of tenants' rights to take out a long lease or purchase properties which councils have bought in housing action or general improvement areas; and the right to form tenant co-operatives in the public sector.

New forms of tenure, therefore, such as co-ownership schemes, co-operative schemes and others similar to the Birmingham " half and half " scheme referred to in Chapter 11, are likely to account for an increasing share of housing provision in the future as they help to meet the desire of people to live in dwellings which they feel are their own. This may slow down the rate of growth of the traditional public sector proportion of housing, although there is a danger that an overwhelmingly owner-occupied society could result in only the poorest section of the community living in rented housing, creating " welfare housing " similar to that in America and which this country has moved away from over the last hundred years.

Following consultation between the Department of the Environment, the National Federation of Housing Associations and the Building Societies' Association, the Housing Corporation also hopes to proceed with the two principal versions of equity-sharing: co-ownership (equity sharing) and community leasehold.

Under co-ownership (equity sharing) it is hoped that half the capital cost will be financed by a block building society option mortgage, around a third will be funded by housing association grant, and the remainder financed by the Corporation on second mortgage. The Corporation will retain the freehold of the land or property, and that part of the equity funded by the housing association grant will always remain in social ownership. Any outgoing co-owner will be able to take out 50 per cent of any appreciation in the value of the property, provided he has lived there for at least a year, and there is a guarantee of no financial loss.

The other part of the pilot programme will consist of homes where the occupier will buy an individual lease for a proportion (initially set at 50 per cent) of the total value of the home and will benefit from its increasing value—if he paid half the initial value, he will get half the new value when he decides to leave. In community leasehold designed primarily for young couples in housing need, it is expected that the occupiers will take out individual building society mortgages to cover the purchase of the lease. In leasehold schemes for the elderly, sheltered housing would be provided for those of retirement age and the occupiers' contribution comes in the form of a lump sum; generally, this will result from the sale of their previous homes, now too large for their needs. In both these schemes, that part of the costs not raised by the individual's contribution will be covered by public funds, and the occupier will pay a " rent " for this portion.

The Secretary of State for Scotland, in a circular issued by the Scottish Development Department in April 1977, has asked housing authorities to take steps to improve the social and physical condition of housing estates, including the establishment, where conditions are right, of co-operatives to take over management duties.

An initial appraisal period before authorities commit themselves to the co-operative approach is called for, but a pilot scheme is proceeding in Glasgow at Summerston. The Glasgow development, which will eventually include 240 homes, has a management committee, elected by tenants, with powers to allocate houses, approve transfers, settle disputes and initiate eviction proceedings against unsocial tenants.

The Scottish Special Housing Association, Scotland's largest public landlord, holding exploratory discussions with tenants on two schemes, reported difficulty in sustaining interest. Aberdeen is concentrating on working with tenants' associations and has no immediate plans for co-operatives. Elsewhere, Edinburgh District Council has been threatened with legal action by tenants in traditionally managed estates if condensation problems in their flats do not improve; and in Arbroath, tenants suffering from similar dampness problems have called for a thoroughgoing review of the system of housing maintenance.

Future housing strategy. The housing scene in the seventies has been shown to be one of extraordinary complexity and wide divergence in condition and provision. To achieve the social aim of providing everyone with a decent home who needs it—surely a basic requirement in any civilised country—a well-worked out, overall housing strategy, based on the varying and particular needs of different groups of people in widely-differing towns and regions, is desperately needed. Short-term solutions to immediate problems in the past have created a chain reaction of further crises, and will continue to do so in the future unless a sensible, comprehensive and continuing strategy directs policies. Priorities must be established so that limited resources are directed to where they are most needed, and enthusiasm, dedication and political will, both nationally and locally, must implement and sustain policies once they have been decided upon. The government's housing investment programmes have made a start on enabling local authorities to direct their resources to areas of greatest need, physical and social; and, at national level, the setting-up of a parliamentary select committee drawn from all parties is surely long overdue to ensure that changes of government do not halt much-needed reforms and measures generally agreed by the three major parties. It must be the responsibility of central and local government, irrespective of political persuasion, and of all housing agencies to see that the nation's investment in housing is used to produce a comprehensive housing service which will give a fair deal economically and socially to all members of the community.

Review of Housing Policy in England and Wales

The government's long-awaited Green Paper, *Housing Policy: A consultative document.* Cmnd 6851 (Stationery Office £2·50.) was published in June 1977, together with two volumes of descriptive and analytical material, *Housing Policy: technical volume, Part I* (£3·50) and *Housing Policy: technical volume, Part II* (£3·00); the third and final part of the technical volume was expected to follow shortly. In a foreword, the Secretary of State for the Environment and the Secretary of State for Wales expressed the hope that the Green Paper and supporting material would provide a basis for a better informed debate on housing policy than ever before.

As has been pointed out in the *Guide,* the review, initiated by the late Anthony Crosland in 1974, was at first confined to financial issues. Its scope was subsequently widened to include social aspects of housing while an examination of the private rented sector was conducted separately. (See Chapter 12 for discussion on the consultative paper on the Rent Acts.) The *Guide* has also emphasised the need for an integrated approach to the formulation of a housing policy which must reflect the changing needs of society and be related to transport, employment and a wide range of other planning, economic, environmental and social issues. The Green Paper refers to several official studies of relevance to housing policy which will be taken into account in moving towards conclusions on future housing policy later in 1977. These are: the Green Paper, *Local Government Finance* (12: 8), published in May, 1977; the White Paper, *Policy for the Inner Cities* (12: 4), published in June 1977; a statement to the House of Commons on the reappraisal of new town programmes in April 1977; and a White Paper on transport policy published in June 1977. (1) The first three have been discussed in Chapter 12 of the *Guide;* the fourth emphasises that transport planning must be linked to energy and land use planning; that the aim of a future transport policy should be to decrease absolute dependence on transport and to plan more consciously for those who walk as well as use mechanical transport; and that more responsibility for meeting local transport needs should be devolved to local government.

The Green Paper does not propose any revolutionary changes in housing finance, either in the present system of tax relief on mortgages or to the methods of fixing council rents, but it does give an extremely comprehensive account of housing policy and housing conditions in England and Wales in Parts I and II, summarised below, and sets out specific proposals for the future in Part III. The notes below on Part III indicate the ground covered and paraphrase and quote from the Green Paper, in particular from its own summary of conclusions and proposals. The government announced it intended to hold consultations on the main proposals with all the major interested parties, and comments on them were invited. This supplement concludes with some of the first reactions immediately after publication.

Part I. The Framework for a Housing Policy

A summary of directions in housing policy since March 1974, and a survey of the present situation provide the background to the government's housing objectives. Factors which have been taken into account in formulating the objectives include the significant improvement in general living conditions revealed by the results of the 1976 house condition survey. These indicate a reduction between 1971 and 1976 of more than two-fifths in the number of unfit homes and those lacking one or more of the five basic amenities, but 2·7 million households in England and Wales are still living in unsatisfactory conditions or sharing accommodation. Other factors considered were the widening gap between the majority living in housing of good standard and the substantial, but diminishing, number living in poor conditions; the paradox nationally of sharply-rising housing expenditure with the continuance of persistent and seemingly intractable problems; the increase in average payments by householders in line with or faster than prices—though not normally as much as earnings—despite big increases in general assistance, i.e. tax relief on mortgage interest or option mortgage subsidy for house purchase; Exchequer housing subsidies to the public sector which are not directly related to tenants' incomes; and general rate fund contributions to local authorities' housing revenue accounts.

The government emphasises that objectives of housing policy must reflect " present realities ", as well as being rooted " in the traditions and reasonable objectives of the nation ". It is proposed, therefore, that policy for housing over the next decade should be directed towards the following eight objectives:

(i) The traditional aim of a decent home for all families at a price within their means must remain the primary objective. It no longer makes sense to think about national totals of those living in unsatisfactory housing conditions, a national approach may draw attention and resources away from the areas with most pressing needs.

(ii)   A better balance should be secured between investment in new houses and the improvement and repair of older houses, with regard to the needs of the individual and the community, as well as to the cost.

(iii) Housing costs should be a reasonably stable element in family finances. The 20 million or so householders in Great Britain—home owners and tenants—who have shaped their household budgets around certain broad expectations about housing costs, should not have to face sharp and disruptive increases in costs totally disproportionate to changes in their ability to pay.

(iv)   The housing needs of groups, such as frail elderly people, the disabled and the handicapped must be met. People with special problems should as far as possible be enabled to live in the community rather than in special residential care. In some cases the need is for specially designed or adapted housing, in others it is for help in obtaining ordinary housing.

(v)   A reasonable degree of priority of access to public rented sector housing and home ownership must be secured for people in housing need who in the past have been at the end of the queue, for example, some one-parent families, and middle-aged people with modest incomes.

(vi)   The scope for mobility in housing must be increased. It is essential, in a period of industrial change, that workers should be able to move house to change their job.

(vii) People should find it easier to obtain the tenure they want. A proper first concern for those who are badly housed should not lead to disregard for the reasonable housing ambitions of the community in general.

(viii) The independence of tenants must be safeguarded. All families have a right to expect a reasonable degree of freedom from interference in the way they use their homes.

Housing investment must continue to be supported by general assistance so that an adequate supply of housing of acceptable standards may be secured at a price within the reach of all families. Housing strategies, however, are to be developed locally within the framework of a national housing policy. The government considers that such local housing strategies will enable investment to be channelled in such a way that better progress is made in dealing with the needs of the most vulnerable households and the worst concentrations of bad housing, which are often found in the inner cities; and reinforce the trend towards gradual renewal by a careful combination of renovation and rebuilding which reflects the needs and wishes of individuals.

In the use of housing, there should be greater opportunity for home ownership; further development of " intermediate " forms of tenure such as co-operative, co-ownership and equity sharing; and the continuing provision of public rented sector housing for a wide cross-section of the population, with a charter for tenants to strengthen their rights and freedoms.

Part II. Past and Present

It is claimed at the beginning of Part II that housing in England and Wales seems to be as good as in comparable countries, and there has been rapid and sustained progress since the war in improving housing conditions. Housing problems persist, however, and to provide some explanation of the present situation, the following areas of housing policy are considered in detail, with some supporting statistical material: the size and quality of the housing stock in relation to the households to be accommodated; the effect of changes in housing tenure; and the relevant financial and economic trends.

These areas have been covered in the *Guide* where reference has frequently been made to the need for better and more up to date information. The Green Paper recognises this need, especially in such matters as the rate of household formation, changes in household composition, changes in the number of households sharing, vacant houses, and the composition and distribution of the private rented sector, and the differences between housing conditions in different areas. More up to date and comprehensive information is to be obtained from a new national housing survey and a survey of vacant dwellings to be launched later in 1977; and the DOE intends to establish a special unit to analyse information about housing and to monitor progress.

Subsequently, the House of Commons was told, in a written answer, that the dwellings and housing survey referred to above would provide up to date information on housing circumstances in England at national and regional level and in the larger areas of housing stress. About 375,000 households would be interviewed. In each of the London boroughs and in areas of housing stress outside London sample sizes would average about 7,000 households. First results were likely to be available by summer 1978 and the total estimated cost for the survey was £2m to £2½m.

Part III. The Future

The housing policy designed to achieve the stated objectives
" must be flexible enough to withstand the strain of unforeseen
developments and to accommodate a wide range of other social
and economic policies. The individual parts of a national housing
policy must also be closely interrelated."

The 74 proposals in the Green Paper, therefore, cover financial
and social needs, within a programme of local housing strategies,
a substantial level of housing investment, financial stability,
measures to widen the opportunities for home ownership, action
within the private sector to compensate for the loss of accommodation and to prevent the decay of houses, improvements in the
local authority housing service, extension of renewal schemes
in a careful mixture of renovation and new building, with renovation budgets being concentrated on basic improvements to
fundamentally sound houses rather than on high quality renovation of relatively small numbers of houses, encouragement of
new forms of tenure and closer attention to provision of housing
for special needs.

Local housing strategies

Local authorities will be asked to prepare comprehensive local
housing strategies. The strategies will be based on assessments of
the full range of housing needs in each area, taking account of
policies in other fields—such as transport and employment, health
and social services—within the broad framework of development
plans. Local housing strategies will involve a wide variety of
action in both public and private sectors, and will call for further
development of existing working relationships between local
authorities and all other bodies concerned with housing in their
areas, such as the Housing Corporation, registered housing
associations, local housebuilders, building societies, new town
corporations, county councils, and tenants' and community
organisations.

It is emphasised that the role of registered housing associations
should continue to grow and be integrated in local housing
strategies, and local housing and planning authorities will need
to ensure within the overall local strategy that requirements for
widely differing types of housing are met. Consideration should
be given by local authorities to taking more leases of empty
privately owned houses; and government procedures for dealing
with compulsory purchase orders on empty houses will be speeded
up. Local authorities should reduce vacancy periods within their
own stock to a minimum, and should review existing procedures
with this in mind.

A Housing Consultative Council for England is to be established, under the chairmanship of the Secretary of State for the Environment, to consider all major issues of concern to local authorities in the performance of their housing duties. Existing consultative machinery involving other bodies concerned with housing such as building societies and housebuilders will be maintained. In Wales, the existing relationship with the Council of the Principality will be developed.

Housing investment

It is recognised that a substantial level of housing investment will be needed in both the public and private sectors to help deal with poor housing conditions and special housing needs, and to provide for future growth in the number of households. However, the public sector will continue to play the major part in dealing with the most pressing housing problems, but public resources must be used economically and efficiently and applied where most needed.

The government proposes, therefore, to institute and develop a system of local authority housing investment programmes (HIPs). Local authorities in England will be asked to draw up housing investment programmes—related to their local housing strategy—covering their own capital expenditure for the coming four years on clearance and demolition, renovation, conversion, home loans, improvement grants to private householders, acquisition and new building, and related to the expected activity of other public housing bodies in the area and private housebuilders. The HIPs will be revised each year. The government will make capital spending allocations to each authority on the basis of its plans. A similar approach will be developed in Wales.

After the publication of the Green Paper, the government issued DOE Circular 63/77 to introduce the new system of HIPs as from 1978/79, as part of the general move towards allowing local authorities greater flexibility and autonomy over their own housing programmes. It is hoped that the system will achieve the following objects:

(i) increase the scope for each local authority to have a mix of spending which, while within the framework of national policies, reflects the different needs and priorities of the housing situation in its own area;

(ii) make more explicit the choices between alternative ways of meeting objectives;

(iii) provide greater flexibility and adaptability in the use of time, resources and cash if circumstances change in the course of the financial year; and

(iv)   help local authorities relate their own proposals more
explicitly to the housing contribution likely to be made
by the private sector and other agencies.

The government considers that in the course of the next decade
a growing number of local authorities should have very largely
dealt with their backlog of bad housing conditions. As this occurs,
the overall level of public sector housing investment should decline in response to changing circumstances. The danger of
coming to premature and false conclusions, based on inadequate
information, about the appropriate level of investment will be
avoided by the regular monitoring of progress under local housing strategies and housing investment programmes.

Financial stability

Rapid inflation and large rises in interest rates will upset any
housing policy unless the overall financial structure can withstand
such strains.

For the public sector, the government proposes to hold consultations with the local authority representatives and other
bodies about replacement of the present interim arrangements
by a new public sector subsidy system, which is described in
Chapter 9 of the Green Paper. It is considered that a more
effective and fairer use of subsidy can be achieved through a
system which concentrates subsidy on authorities with pressing
housing needs—who will consequently have large investment
programmes—and avoids the need for irregular and sharp changes
in rent levels. Local authorities are to be left their present freedom
to fix rents and make rate fund contributions, but the government
considers that over a run of years, rents should keep broadly in
line with changes in money incomes. Briefly, subject to consultations with the local authority representatives, the arrangements
for the new subsidy system are to run on the following lines:

(i)   the starting point of the calculation of subsidy would
be an authority's entitlement to subsidy in the previous
year (starting with the last year of the current system);

(ii)   each year a basis for the calculation of extra expenditure
admissible for subsidy—including extra costs of management and maintenance assessed on an appropriate formula
—would be settled for the coming year in consultation
with local authorities;

(iii)   each year an appropriate level of increase in the "local
contribution" to costs, from rents and rates, would be
determined for the coming year, also in consultation with
local authorities;

(iv) if the extra admissible expenditure of an authority exceeded the increase in the " local contribution ", subsidy entitlement would be increased. If on the other hand, the extra local contribution exceeded this extra expenditure subsidy entitlement would be correspondingly reduced.

Under this system, the rate of increase in the " local contribution "—rents and general rate fund contribution—would be perhaps the most important decision to be taken annually. It would be the predominant factor in determining the total Exchequer subsidy bill and it would also be likely to influence the size of local authority rent increases, though the balance between rents and general rate fund contributions, and the fixing of individual rents, would remain a matter for local discretion.

In general, the government considers that a system on these lines would tend to ensure that authorities with the biggest " gap " between their housing costs and their local resources would receive a rather greater proportion of total national subsidy payments than now, while authorities with relatively small investment programmes and correspondingly smaller needs would receive less.

In the owner-occupied sector, mortgage tax relief and option mortgage subsidy are to be maintained and measures taken to secure as far as possible a supply of mortgage funds which is not subject to sharp short-term fluctuations, and which increases sufficiently over the years to meet fresh demands.

Proposals for radical changes in the structure of general assistance, including those made by the Housing Centre Trust (see Chapter 8 of the *Guide*), are discussed in the Green Paper, but the government, after considering all the arguments very carefully, does not consider that there is a case on grounds of housing policy for an alteration to present arrangements governing tax relief on mortgage interest and option mortgage subsidy. The limit, at present £25,000, on that part of loans for house purchase admissible for tax relief, which has to be fixed annually, will be maintained, but will be kept under review. As regards Schedule A type or imputed income taxation, the government sees the gravest administrative difficulties about reintroducing it. Apart from these difficulties, however, and the question of public acceptability, such a tax would be incompatible in the government's view with its strategy for the growth of home ownership detailed below.

To prevent short-term disruptions of the private housing market that are harmful both to householders and to the housebuilding industry the government intends to develop the present arrangements with the building societies for stabilising the supply of mortgage funds. To guard against the risk that in the years ahead societies may not be able to secure all the finance that they need directly from the personal sector, the government wishes to discuss with the societies the possibility of their securing fresh sources of funds, possibly through a financial intermediary. The views of the Committee to Review Financial Institutions (the Wilson Committee) will be sought on this proposal in due course.

Home ownership

An increasing number of people want to own rather than rent their homes. The government welcomes this trend as reducing the demands on the public sector and helping job mobility. Various recommendations to promote and support home ownership, therefore, are put forward in the Green Paper.

Building societies should make low-start mortgages more widely available and, in particular, offer the choice of a low-start mortgage to those borrowers who select the option mortgage subsidy in preference to tax relief on interest. The societies should also make higher percentage loans more readily available. It is considered that this should be possible now that the Building Societies Association have arranged for guarantees to cover such loans to be extended. Building societies make significantly lower average advances as a percentage of purchase price than local authorities. In 1975, the average advance by building societies to first-time house-buyers was about £7,300 (76 per cent of average purchase price), while the average advance by local authorities was about £6,400 (90 per cent of average purchase price). These figures suggest that societies might be able to make more higher percentage loans than hitherto, although it must be remembered that building societies lend to far more people than local authorities, and local authorities lend to applicants with lower incomes.

More building society lending on older properties, including both unimproved and converted properties, is seen as an essential part of local housing strategies. Although the building societies lend large amounts in total on older houses—28 per cent of their loans on second-hand houses in 1976 were on pre-1919 property— these houses may often have been the more substantial kind of modernised older property in areas which are not declining. There is a need for more loans to be made on houses in which first-time buyers might be interested that are in a poor state of repair or lack one or more of the standard amenities such as an indoor WC or separate bathroom and which, if left empty, are likely to deteriorate.

Greater co-operation between building societies and local authorities is recommended, based on the foundation for working partnerships between them provided by experience with support lending. Local authorities should complement the work of the societies by providing topping-up loans, by providing improvement and repair grants in respect of older houses bought for home ownership, and by guarantees. They should keep the societies informed about their local housing strategies, and this should reduce " red-lining " (the designation of areas in which a building society is not prepared to lend on mortgage because values are believed to be declining) and help revitalise inner city areas.

For first-time buyers, the government proposes, after consulting the institutions concerned, to introduce new savings bonus and loans schemes. The savings bonus would be broadly equivalent to income tax at the basic rate on the aggregate of interest on up to £1,000 of qualifying savings. The loan—subject to house price limits—would be £500 for each first-time buyer who saved a matching sum under the savings bonus scheme over at least two years; it would be interest-free for the first five years.

A special difficulty has arisen in the last few years in relation to the mortgage rates charged for local authority lending, where some authorities have had to charge rates above that recommended by the Building Societies Association to its member societies. Legislation is to be introduced to enable local authorities to charge such rates as may be determined by the Secretary of State from time to time; the intention being that this rate shall be that recommended by the BSA. Any deficit on the local authority mortgage account would be charged to the general rate fund; any surplus would be credited to the fund.

In the implementation of its measures to widen access to home ownership, the government hopes that building societies will, within the limits of acceptable and reasonable commercial risks, give due weight to social factors when deciding what priority to give to applications for mortgages.

The growth of home ownership makes the supply of mortgage funds a matter of ever-increasing importance. The Green Paper points out that greater stability in the volume of mortgage lending can be achieved by development of the voluntary arrangement between the government and the building societies through the Joint Advisory Committee. The building societies should:

(a) build up their stabilisation " funds " to higher levels when possible;
(b) keep their structure of interest rates paid to investors more in line with the market;
(c) adopt a more flexible relationship between the rate paid by mortgagors and the rate paid to investors;
(d) be prepared to raise short-term loans on the money market.

To avoid losses to building societies resulting from the stabilisation arrangements, the government might accept part of the stabilisation funds for investment in the National Loans Fund, subject to agreement on the size of mortgage lending and of stabilisation funds. The government would also be prepared in exceptional circumstances to consider short-term loans from public funds.

Fresh sources of funds for building societies might well have to be tapped, and building societies might well both be able and prefer to deal direct with financial institutions. The idea is put forward, however, that a special financial intermediary might be considered to raise funds from institutions—in particular, life and pension funds—and on-lend them to building societies. Such an agency could also help with raising short-term loans to stabilise the flow of funds to societies. The intermediary could be a public or private body, but it is again recognised that the societies might prefer to develop any necessary machinery themselves.

With regard to the size of individual loans for house purchase, the government considers that the building societies should extend the practice of requiring an existing mortgagor to " plough back " net proceeds of the sale of an existing house into the purchase of the next, so that available mortage funds can be spread among a larger number of borrowers.

Building societies are seen as occupying a pivotal position in the growth of home ownership as they supply most of the finance for house purchase, but it is pointed out that extension of home ownership does not mean less social emphasis in housing policy. On the contrary, the widening of entry into home ownership for people with modest incomes can help to solve housing problems formerly faced largely by the public sector, as well as satisfying deep-seated social aspirations. The government hopes and expects that the building societies will be ready to shoulder still greater responsibility. In turn, further development of arrangements to stabilise the flow of mortgage funds should enable building societies to go further in providing advance mortgage " quotas " for housebuilders. Local authorities, in fulfilling their duties under the Community Land Act, must have regard to the housebuilders' need for a steady supply of land.

The private rented sector

The government's conclusions on the review of the Rent Acts (the consultation paper, issued in January 1977, is considered in Chapter 12 of the *Guide*) are expected to be announced by the end of 1977. The commitment to the broad principle that private tenants of non-resident landlords should enjoy security of tenure, with rents restricted to reasonable levels, is to be maintained. Three measures which could help to alleviate the problems created by the contraction of the private sector are, however, suggested in the Green Paper. First, letting by resident landlords and temporarily absent home owners should be encouraged by speeding up the procedures for obtaining possession. Secondly, lettings of flats over shops and other accommodation normally let with a business should not in future attract full security of tenure. Thirdly, an investigation is proposed into the possibility of a new type of rented accommodation, publicly accountable but backed by private money. Initial rents could be lower than initial costs of home ownership, but would be higher than rents for public sector housing.

Local authority housing service

(i) Accounting

A new method of cost control for local authority housebuilding, based on a fixed level of costs eligible for subsidy, instead of the present housing cost yardstick, will be developed in consultation with local authorities.

The government intends to discuss with local authorities new forms of accounts to assist effective financial management, and to explore the case for reintroducing statutory repairs accounts, linked with the new subsidy system already described. The treatment of general rate fund contributions for rate support grant purposes will also be discussed in the light of the proposals in the Green Paper on *Local Government Finance* (12: 8). The idea of a " subsidy floor " for individual authorities related to tax relief at the basic rate is put forward for public discussion as a means of achieving a greater sense of fairness between local authority tenants and home owners. Local authorities will be given greater freedom to vary the loan repayment period for investment without loss of subsidy entitlement.

Local authorities are advised that, in allocating the resources available to them, they should take account of the opportunities to meet housing need by building new houses—and consider the scope for converting or rehabilitating existing houses—for sale or for the newer " intermediate " forms of tenure mentioned below.

Income-related rent rebates and rent allowances are to be continued, but the scope and coverage of the present schemes are under review. Exchequer subsidy payable on the cost of rent rebates and rent allowances will be standardised at 90 per cent. Reimbursement by local authorities to the Department of Health and Social Security of the cost of rent rebates and allowances in respect of tenants receiving Supplementary Benefit will be ended.

(ii) Standards

It is recognised that the increasing range of housing requirement will make new demands on the public sector and will make it necessary to ensure that housing standards are not drawn up in a way that discourages variety of provision. The Department of the Environment and the Welsh Office are reviewing the scope for introducing greater flexibility into public sector standards, and will be consulting local authority representatives.

(iii) *Waiting lists and allocation policies*

The government shares the view of the Cullingworth Committee that it is " fundamental that no one should be precluded from applying for, or being considered for, a council tenancy on any ground whatsoever ". Now, eight years after the Cullingworth report, the practice of requiring a period of residence is still widespread. The case for legislation to prohibit residential or other qualifications for entry to local authority waiting lists is to be considered.

With regard to allocation policies, a local authority's methods must be seen as fair, and the government will introduce legislation requiring allocation schemes to be published.

(iv) *Relations with tenants*

A code of principles and practices designed to protect the freedom and rights of public sector tenants will be introduced (and consideration will be given to similar improvements in the rights of private tenants). Tenants should be permitted and encouraged to carry out improvements to their homes subject to reimbursement for substantial improvement when the tenancy ends and to sub-let rooms.

Legislation will be introduced to give public sector tenants security of tenure and the right to a written tenancy agreement. The Department of the Environment intends to issue guidance on tenancy agreements in the public sector designed to provide a better balance between the rights and obligations of landlords and tenants.

Tenants should be able to expect better management and maintenance of their homes. Consideration is, therefore, being given to the possibility of a more selective treatment of management and maintenance expenditure in the new subsidy system to take account of the needs of authorities with problem estates.

Emphasis is laid on giving tenants greater say in the running of their estates, and on enabling them to participate formally or informally in management decisions; such arrangements could be taken a stage further through the formation of housing co-operatives.

(v) *Sale of council houses*

The government considers that an authority's proposals to sell should be seen as part of the total approach to housing for its areas, including in particular its proposals for meeting demands for rented accommodation of the right type and quality. The general consent to the sale of council houses will be allowed to stand for the present, but will be considered in the light of emerging local strategies, housing investment programmes, and rates of sales.

The scope for greater use of building society mortgages to finance the purchase of council houses (as well as " intermediate " forms of tenure and building for sale) will be considered by the government with the local authority associations and the BSA.

Renovation policies

The government believes that a change in emphasis in renovation policy is now called for. Work on the renovation of older houses should be directed more at bringing larger numbers of houses up to a decent basic standard rather than on higher standard improvements of a smaller number of houses. A less rigid approach to the administration of improvement grants will be encouraged by the government in order to stimulate improvements to a basic standard. Consideration will be given to increases in existing cost and rateable value limits for improvement grants.

Subsequently, the Secretary of State for the Environment announced that the limit for discretionary grants paid under the Housing Act 1974 is to be raised from £3,200 to £5,000. For intermediate, repair and special grants, the new limits will be £2,700, £1,500 and £1,200 respectively—increases of between 70 and 80 per cent on the present limits.

The rateable-value limit for discretionary grants to owner-occupiers is also to be raised. In London it will be increased from £300 to £400; elsewhere, the ceiling of £175 will be raised to £225. These increases will bring more houses within the scope of the grant provisions.

The government intend to examine the possibility of allowing private tenants to apply for grants towards the improvement of the houses they occupy, with no increase in rent resulting from the improvement to the property. " Repairs only " grants will be made more widely available, and grant will be made available towards the cost of repairs to houses in multiple occupation, as for other houses. Consideration will be given to the introduction of mandatory grants towards the cost of installation of basic amenities for houses in multiple occupation.

Local authorities' powers to compel improvement and repair of unsatisfactory houses will be examined with a view to making them simpler and more effective. Provision will be made to remove the present ban on payment of improvement grants to owner-occupiers of houses in special areas which have been let within the preceding 12 months.

Housing associations

The Green Paper stresses that the government wishes to see a continuing growth of the activities of registered housing associations, who will play their part within the local strategies. With the growing importance of their role, housing associations should normally publish their allocation schemes.

The case for introducing similar arrangements to the proposed new local authority subsidy scheme to housing associations, and the arrangements for fixing housing association rents, are to be considered in consultation with the Housing Corporation and the National Federation of Housing Associations.

New towns

The proposed new local authority subsidy system can be applied to new towns, with appropriate adjustments. The Green Paper also draws attention to the need for new towns to house increasing numbers of the elderly and disadvantaged people who are willing to move from the inner cities, and to meet the growing demand for home ownership.

Newer forms of tenure

The formation of co-operatives in the housing association movement will receive continued support from the government through the Co-operative Housing Agency, and legislation will be introduced to remove obstacles to this policy. The scope for giving private tenants the right to purchase their homes on a co-operative basis, where blocks are up for sale, will be considered. The government intends to revive co-ownership housing, and current legislation will be amended to permit housing associations to build for sale, either outright or on an equity-sharing basis.

The spread and development of equity-sharing schemes in the local authority and housing association spheres, and of further ventures in " intermediate " forms of tenure in both private and public sectors, will be encouraged.

Special needs

Chapter 12 of the Green Paper, which considers individual housing needs, points out that, in the last analysis, the effectiveness of any national housing policy and local housing strategy is likely to be judged by how far it helps those facing the most pressing housing problems. It is recognised that the groups of people who may face special difficulties in getting suitable housing necessarily overlap and often have problems which go much wider than housing. Concerted help, through central government policies, and through services provided locally by different departments of a local authority or by co-operation between different authorities, is needed. Within this context, the following proposals are made in the Green Paper.

The homeless

The Housing (Homeless Persons) Bill now before Parliament should result in a real advance in dealing with problems of homelessness by placing the primary responsibility for this on local housing authorities, as part of their housing functions, although social services staff will continue to have an important part to play in helping people who are homeless or threatened with homelessness.

One-parent families

The report of the Finer Committee on one-parent families drew attention to the housing difficulties faced by single parents, particularly women whose husbands had died or who were divorced or separated. The committee estimated that in 1971 there were 620,000 one-parent families, with a total of just over a million dependent children in Great Britain. Over 500,000 of these families were fatherless. A third of families accepted as homeless are one-parent families, though one-parent families make up only a tenth of all families.

The government will be issuing guidance to local authorities on the housing problem of one-parent families; and the Building Societies Association have agreed to give further guidance to their members.

Battered women

Local authorities will be asked to provide information about the scale of the problem of battered women in their areas, and will be encouraged to help with the provision of accommodation.

Disabled and handicapped people

The government will consider legislative changes giving local authorities discretion to waive rateable value limits for improvement grants where disabled people are affected, and will continue to encourage greater provision of housing for disabled and handicapped people.

Old people

It is pointed out that in 1975 there were nearly 7 million people aged 65 or over (2·5 million over 75) in England and Wales— 14 per cent of the total population. Between 1975 and 1986 an increase of 450,000 (6½ per cent) is expected in the number of people aged 65 and over; but for people aged 75 and over the increase is put at 570,000 (23 per cent). This is one of the most significant of contemporary demographic trends, and the government intends that its policy of enabling elderly people to remain in the community as long as possible will be maintained. Comprehensive guidance will be issued on housing and other services for old people.

Single people

Single people—working or in further education—should benefit from various measures proposed in the Green Paper for improving the supply of and access to housing. Subject to availability of resources, local authorities should ensure that adequate accommodation for single people is included in their investment provision.

Mobile workers

Many of the policies which will help single people will also help mobile workers. Local authorities can also improve their arrangements for transfers and exchanges.

Ethnic minorities

The government will ensure that special problems faced by ethnic minorities are taken fully into account in housing policies and programmes, in consultation with the new Commission for Racial Equality (see Chapter 12 of the *Guide*).

Lower income householders

This group, which will overlap all the groups previously mentioned, will be helped by the continuance of the income-related rent rebates and rent allowances schemes. Special concessions are made in areas where rents are exceptionally high; and local authorities have some discretion to make extra payments in special cases. The Green Paper recognises that these schemes face the same difficulties as other forms of income-related assistance. One is the general problem of the poverty trap, although this is perhaps less acute with the rent assistance schemes than with many other income-related schemes, because of the gentle taper of the eligibility limits.

The inner city

The White Paper, *Policy for the Inner Cities* (Cmnd. 6845) (12: 4) promised a new and sustained attack on the social and economic problems of the inner city areas. As has been detailed in Chapter 12 of the *Guide,* in order to concentrate attention and resources on cities where the problems are at their worst, partnership arrangements between central and local government are being offered in the first instance to Liverpool, Birmingham, Manchester/Salford, and in London to Lambeth and Docklands. The problems of the inner cities are discussed in Chapter 13 of the Green Paper. In particular, it is pointed out that the development of local housing strategies will enable inner city authorities to look at their housing needs as a whole—as part of a wider strategy for regeneration—and the arrangements for public sector housing investment and subsidy will ensure that high priority is given to inner city areas with severe housing problems.

Reactions

The government's approach in the Green Paper has been generally welcomed as offering some promise of more stability in housing policy in the future and as introducing more flexibility into housing procedures, for example, in housing standards and cost control, in public sector landlord/tenant relationships and in building society operations. Further, the prospect of an increase to 90 per cent in the Exchequer subsidy payable on the cost of rent rebates and rent allowances has pleased the Association of District Councils, who have also endorsed the idea of a housing consultative council and the proposed abolition of the cost yardstick. The Institute of Housing has welcomed the setting up of a national housing survey and the drawing up of local housing strategies by local authorities, and has pointed out that the Green Paper underlines the need for a comprehensive approach to the housing problems of this country. The Institute hopes to see an added impetus within the housing service to enable its members to take an even more significant role in improving housing conditions, especially for people in special housing need such as the elderly and infirm.

The proposals on housing finance in the Green Paper, however, have been criticised for not facing up to the main issues and problems. When the review of housing finance was set up, it was hoped that some radical reforms would be produced for public discussion, but the government has decided to continue the present system of tax relief on mortgages and general assistance to the public sector based on existing methods of fixing council rents.

The Green Paper accepts the need to " make the most of available resources " which " will always be limited ". It recognises the disadvantage of the present system under which housing subsidies have been increasing at a much faster rate than investment—in the six years up to 1975, subsidies increased by 122 per cent but investment by only 35 per cent. It is argued that the average proportion of disposable income paid for housing is too low and the Green Paper refers to the contention that unnecessarily high subsidies lead to overconsumption. Those, including the Housing Centre Trust, who thought that only the fundamental reform of the housing finance system would remedy these defects and achieve the desired aims, have expressed doubts as to whether the proposals put forward in the Green Paper would go far enough.

The Housing Centre Trust's main proposals (see *Evidence: Housing Finance Review,* Chapter 8 of the *Guide*) were for reductions in subsidies, hitherto achieved by cuts in investment in new building and improvements, to be made in a way which would redirect the money still available into investment, while at the same time avoiding too much disruption to household budgets. This it was thought could be done by making better use of existing housing assets. The single annuity system proposed would ensure that the value of an existing owner-occupier's house was used to help him pay for a new one when he moved, while the value of existing council housing would be used to the best advantage through national rent pooling. These two specific proposals are considered and rejected by the government in the Green Paper—the single annuity system mainly on the grounds that it was administratively very difficult and might restrict mobility. The government are relying on encouragement to " plough back " the proceeds of a sale voluntarily into a new purchase. National rent pooling was dismissed because it would allow some authorities to produce a surplus on their housing accounts to benefit tenants of another authority. However, this form of cross-subsidy is to continue to be encouraged within a single local authority. The Green Paper's proposals claim similar advantages in assisting most the areas of greatest need and at the time of writing they are being studied by the Housing Centre Trust and others who intend submitting follow-up comments as invited by the government.

The Association of District Councils has also expressed concern at the new deficit subsidy plans, especially at the prospect of annual charges, and by the increased and possibly arbitrary central control which the proposed new system at first sight involves. The chairman of the Association has claimed that local authorities should know where they stand before making commitments.

Chapter 4 of the Green Paper sets out clearly the shortcomings of the present system of housing finance in this country, which indicate that fundamental changes are necessary. If it is difficult for any government to make changes which are likely to be electorally unpopular, then there may be a case for an independent body, or a parliamentary select committee, as proposed in Chapter 12 of the *Guide,* to examine the position and ensure that much-needed reforms and measures are carried through.

Scotland

A Scottish Green Paper on housing has also been published. As in England and Wales, the overall shortage of housing is over and varying problems need local rather than national solutions.

Arrangements have been agreed for housing authorities to devise strategies based on local needs. Accordingly, all authorities will be submitting their first " housing plans " to the Secretary of State for Scotland this summer to cover the five years beginning 1978–79.

The government will continue to give substantial support for authorities' housing expenditure, but the support will be distributed in a way which will reflect fairly the different burden in different areas, under new arrangements which should begin to operate in 1979. The level of assistance envisaged will enable the local contribution to housing costs (rents and rate fund contributions) to keep broadly in line with changes in money income.

The Green Paper advocates increased home ownership and suggests a possible home ownership forum to co-ordinate the efforts of public and private sectors in securing stable development. Further, the special measures to help first-time buyers set out in the Green Paper for England and Wales—the savings bonus and loans scheme—will apply equally in Scotland. At the same time, alternative forms of tenure—equity-sharing schemes, tenant co-operatives and other proposals—will be encouraged to meet the demand for a wider choice of tenures.

The development of a model agreement for tenants will be explored with the local authorities so that the responsibilities of both tenant and the authority are clearly set out. Public sector tenants should be secure in their homes and should not have to suffer outmoded and irritating restrictions, but they should be able to take on more responsibility, if they wish, for the management and maintenance of their homes.

References and Further Reading

CHAPTER 1: Historical Background

(1) *A Report on the Sanitary Conditions of the Labouring Population of Great Britain 1842*, Edwin Chadwick, ed., by M. W. Flinn. 1965. £3·50

(2) *Garden Cities of Tomorrow*, Ebenezer Howard. Rep. 1970. £1·20

(3) *Octavia Hill: A Biography*, E. Moberly Bell. 1942. An excellent biography of the Victorian pioneer of good housing management

(4) *Report of the Committee to Consider Questions of Building Construction with the Provision of Dwellings for the Working Classes*, Tudor Walters Report. 1918

(5) *Report of the Royal Commission on the Distribution of the Industrial Population*, Barlow Report. 1940. Cmnd. 6153

(6) *Final Report of the Expert Committee on Compensation and Betterment*, Uthwatt Report. 1942. Cmnd. 6386

(7) *Report of the Committee on Land Utilisation in Rural Areas*, Scott Report. 1942. Cmnd. 6378

(8) *County of London Plan*, J. H. Forshaw and Patrick Abercrombie. 1943

(9) *Greater London Plan*, Patrick Abercrombie. 1944

(10) *Design of Dwellings*, Dudley Report. 1944. Report of the Design of Dwellings Sub-Committee of the Central Housing Advisory Committee and of a Study Group on Site Planning and Layout in relation to Housing

(11) *Housing and Local Government*, J. B. Cullingworth. 1966. £2·25

(12) *Report of the Committee on Housing in Greater London*, Milner Holland Report. 1965. £2·70

(13) *Homes for Today and Tomorrow*, Parker Morris Report. Ministry of Housing and Local Government. 1961. 60p

(14) *Report of the Committee on the Rent Acts*, Francis Report. Cmnd. 4609. 1971. £2·85

(15) *Housing Subsidies Vol. I.* 1969. Report of the findings of the Estimates Committee of Members of Parliament

(16) *Fair Deal for Housing*, Cmnd. 4728. 1971. 22½p. A White Paper on Government policy for a new system of housing finance

(17) *Council Housing, Purposes, Procedures and Priorities*, Cullingworth Committee. CHAC. 1969. £1·45.

CHAPTER 1 : Historical Background—*continued*

(18) *Report of the Committee on Local Authority and Allied Personal Social Services*, Seebohm Report. Cmnd. 3703. 1968. £2·10
(19) *Our Older Homes—A Call For Action*, Denington Report. MoHLG. 1966. 25p. The report makes recommendations for standards of fitness, maintenance and improvements
Working Class Housing in 19th Century Britain, J. N. Tarn, 1971. £3·75 card, £5·25 cloth
Five Per Cent Philanthropy: An Account of Housing in Urban Areas Between 1840 and 1914, J. N. Tarn. 1973. £8·00
Trends in Population, Housing and Occupancy Rates, 1861–1961, W. V. Hole and M. T. Pountney. 1971. 80p. Long term trends in housing standards and provision

CHAPTER 2: The Present Position

(1) *Towards Freedom in Housing*, The Bow Group. 1975. 40p
(2) *The Housing Programme 1965/70*, Cmnd. 2838. 1965

CHAPTER 3: The Local Authority Housing Service

(1) *Local Housing Needs and Strategies—A Case Study of the Dundee Sub-Region*, Scottish Development Department (R. A. Grant, B. W. Thomson, J. K. Dible and J. N. Randall). 1976. £3·80
(2) *Estimating Local Housing Needs: A Case Study and Discussion of Methods*. CURS Occasional Paper No. 24, C. J. Watson, Pat Niner, Gillian R. Vale and Barbara M. D. Smith. 1973, reprint 1974. £1·75
(3) *Report on Programmes of Social Ownership and Renovation of Council Dwellings*, Department of the Environment Study Group. 1976
(4) *The Management of Municipal Housing Estates*, Sub Committee of the former Central Housing Advisory Committee. 1938
(5) *The New Local Authorities: Management and Structure*, The Bains Report. Report of a Study Group on Local Authority Management Structure 1972. £2·50 (reprint)
(6) *Tenants Take Over*, Colin Ward. 1974. £2·75
(7) *Final Report of the Working Party on Housing Co-operatives*, Department of the Environment. 1975. £2·00
(8) *Housing Advice Centres*, M. Harloe, R. Minns, and J. Stoker. 1976. 70p

CHAPTER 3: The Local Authority Housing Service—*continued*

(9) *Local Government Finance,* Report of the Committee of Enquiry, Layfield Report. 1976. Cmnd. 6453. £5·75
(10) *Housing Revenue Accounts,* Ministry of Housing and Local Government and Welsh Office. 1969. 62½p. This report of a Working Party reviews the subject and contains guidance on the use of Housing Revenue Accounts
(11) *Manual on Local Authority Housing Subsidies and Accounting,* Department of the Environment and the Welsh Office. 1975. £2·00. This manual explains the subsidy and accounting provisions of the Housing Rents and Subsidies Act 1975 and the continuing provisions of earlier legislation
(12) *Local Authority Housing Policy and Practice: A Case Study Approach,* Pat Niner. CURS Occasional Paper No. 31. 1975. £4·00
(13) *Winchester Housing Needs Study 1971–72,* CURS Research Memorandum No. 13. 1972
(14) *Cheltenham Housing Study,* CURS Research Memorandum No. 48. 1975. £1·50
(15) *Planning for Housing Needs: Pointers Towards a Comprehensive Approach,* SDD Scottish Housing Advisory Committee. 1972. 42p
(16) *The Sale of Council Housing: A Study in Social Policy,* Alan Murie. CURS Occasional Paper No. 35. 1975. £4·00

CHAPTER 4: New Towns

(1) *The South East Study 1961–81,* Department of the Environment. 1964. 75p
(2) *Ownership and Management of Housing in the New Towns,* J. B. Cullingworth and V. A. Karn, A report to the Ministry of Housing and Local Government. 1968. 87½p
New Towns: The British Experience, Peter Self, ed. Hazel Evans. 1972. £5·50
The New Towns: The Answer to Megalopolis, Frederic J. Osborn and Arnold Whittick. 1969. 2nd ed. £8·75
The New Town Story, Frank Schaffer. 1972. 75p
The New Towns of Britain, Central Office of Information. 5th ed. 1974. 65p
Perspectives on New Town Development, Ray Thomas. Open University. 1976. Conference of the New Towns Study Unit and Regional Studies Association. 1975
London's New Towns: A Study of Self-contained and Balanced Communities, PEP 1969. £1·00
Aycliffe to Cumbernauld: A Study of Seven New Towns, PEP 1969. £1·00

CHAPTER 4: New Towns—*continued*

" Reith Reports," Ministry of Town and Country Planning and Department of Health for Scotland. Reports of the New Towns Committee. Interim Report Cmnd. 6759. 2nd Interim Report Cmnd. 6794. Final Report Cmnd. 6876. 1946 *Reports of the Development Corporations* 31 March 1975, Aycliffe, Basildon, Bracknell, Central Lancashire New Town, Corby, Harlow, Milton Keynes, Northampton, Peterborough, Peterlee, Redditch, Runcorn, Skelmersdale, Stevenage, Telford, Warrington, Washington. £6·50 (Published annually)

CHAPTER 5: The Private Sector in Housing

(1) *Homelessness in London,* John and Stella Greve and Dilys Page. 1971. £3·25

CHAPTER 6: Housing Associations

(1) *Housing Associations,* Charles V. Baker. 1976. £7·50. The most comprehensive reference text on the subject
(2) *A Guide to Housing Associations,* NFHA. 1975. 35p. Brief notes on the formation, constitution and work of housing associations
(3) *Housing Associations—Some Basic Information,* NFHA. 20p
(4) *Housing Associations. Housing Centre Reference Sheet No. 4,* HCT. 1975 (revised periodically). 10p
(5) *Housing Associations. A Working Paper of the Central Housing Advisory Committee,* DOE. 1971. A summary of evidence to the Cohen Committee
(6) *People Need Roots. The Story of the St. Pancras Housing Association,* Irene Barclay. 1976. £2·50 hardback, £1·50 paperback. An account of the work of a London housing association from its foundation between the wars until the present day
(7) *Housing Act 1974. The Relevance of the Act to Housing Associations,* NFHA. 1975. £1·00
(8) *Practice Notes for Housing Associations,* The Housing Corporation. Revised 1976. 60p. Practice and procedure for projects seeking Housing Corporation loans
(9) *Recommended Form of Published Accounts for Housing Associations,* The Housing Corporation. 1976. £1·00
(10) *The Community Land Act 1975: The Development Land Tax Act 1976: The Implications for Housing Associations,* Andrew Williamson for NFHA, 1976. £1·00

CHAPTER 6: Housing Associations—*continued*

(11) *New Development by Housing Associations,* NFHA, 1977. £3·50. An excellent guide for housing associations, and any other housing developer, and their consultants, from start to finish of a new building project

(12) *Self Build. A Manual for Self Build Housing Associations,* NFHA, NBA and the Housing Corporation. 1975. £2·00. Comprehensive guidance for housing associations formed by people who set out to build their own homes using their own skills

(13) *Co-operative Housing Handbook,* David Page for NFHA. 1975. 75p. A guide to the formation, constitution and work of housing co-operatives

(14) *Final Report of the Working Party on Housing Co-operatives,* DOE. 1975. £2·00
Report of the Campbell Working Party.

(15) *Housing Co-operatives,* John Hands. 1975. £1·50. A comprehensive international review of the subject, practical advice for housing co-operatives in Britain, and a discussion of future development

(16) *Tenants Take Over,* Colin Ward. 1974. £2·75. The arguments for tenant involvement, including tenant co-operatives, as a counter to alienation on housing estates

(17) *Co-ownership Housing Associations,* NFHA. 1975. 25p

(18) *Co-ownership Housing. What is it?* Housing Corporation. Undated. Free. A brief explanation of co-ownership societies operating under 1964 Act rules

CHAPTER 7: Rehabilitation

(1) *Our Older Homes: A Call for Action,* Denington Report. Ministry of Housing and Local Government. 1966. 25p. The report makes recommendations for standards of fitness, maintenance and improvements

(2) *Scotland's Older Houses,* The Cullingworth Report of the Scottish Housing Advisory Committee. Scottish Development Department. 1967. 53p. The report contains comprehensive information on the condition of Scotland's housing and recommendations

(3) *House Improvement Grants,* Tenth Report of the Expenditure Committee. Vol. I Report. 1973

(4) *The Deeplish Study: Improvement Possibilities in a District of Rochdale,* Ministry of Housing and Local Government. 1966. A survey of a twilight area and recommendations for improvements to the houses and their surroundings, later implemented in a pilot project

CHAPTER 7: Rehabilitation—*continued*

(5) AREA IMPROVEMENT NOTES NOS. 1–11, Department of the Environment and the Welsh Office

1. *Sample House Condition Survey.* 1971. 40p
2. *House Condition Survey Within a Potential GIA.* 1971. 40p
3. *Improving the Environment.* 1971. 30p
4. *House Improvement and Conversion.* 1972. £1·30
5. *Environmental Design in Four GIAs.* 1972 £1·50
6. *The Design of Streets and other Spaces in GIAs.* 1973 45p
7. *Parking and Garaging in GIAs.* 1973. 30p
8. *Public Participation in GIAs.* 1973. 65p
9. *Traffic in GIAs.* 1974. 75p
10. *The Use of Indicators for Area Action: Housing Act 1974.* 1975. £1·75
11. *Networks for House and Area Improvement.* 1976. £1·50

(6) NATIONAL BUILDING AGENCY PUBLICATIONS

Conversion Schemes: Review of Time and Cost. 1974. 50p
Decanting: for Improvement and Conversion. 1974. 50p
Increasing Conversion Capability: A Management Study for One Housing Association. 1974. 50p
Planning Portfolio Rehabilitation: Two Housing Association Case Studies. 1976. 50p

(7) SCOTTISH LOCAL AUTHORITIES SPECIAL HOUSING GROUP (SLASH)

Rehabilitation and Modernisation Advisory Note 1. 1974. £2·00
Rehabilitation and Modernisation Advisory Note 2. 1975. £2·00

(8) *Improving Your Home,* National Home Improvement Council. 1976. 35p

(9) *Housing Improvement Handbook: A Self-help Approach for Residents' Groups,* Manchester University Extra Mural Course Group. 1976. £1·50
General Improvement Areas, J. Trevor Roberts. 1976. £5·95
House Conversion and Renewal, Peter Collymore. 1976. £8·95. The book examines the architect's technical and legal obligation in conversion work and includes 30 case studies
The Housing Rehabilitation Handbook, Barry Evans. 1977. £8·95. This book, for the architect, is concerned with the rehabilitation of housing originally built from the mid-Georgian period to 1914 (plus some consideration of inter-war buildings)

CHAPTER 8: Housing Finance

(See end of Chapter)

CHAPTER 9: Planning and Land

(1) *The Future of Development Plans*, Report of the Planning Advisory Group of the Ministry of Housing and Local Government, Ministry of Transport and Scottish Development Department. 1965. 50p
(2) *People and Planning*, Report of the Committee on Public Participation in Planning, Skeffington Report. Ministry of Housing and Local Government, Scottish Development Department and the Welsh Office. 1969. 75p
(3) *Planning and Noise*, DOE Circular 10/73 (WO16/73). 1973. 13p
(4) *Calculation of Road Traffic Noise*, Department of the Environment and the Welsh Office. 1975. £1·70
(5) *Noise Units*, Reports by a Working Party for the Research Sub Committee of the Noise Advisory Council. 1975. 29p
(6) *Land Compensation Act 1973, The Noise Regulations 1975*, DOE Circular 114/75 (WO 196/75). 28p
(7) *The New Citizen's Guide to Town and Country Planning*, John Ardill. 1974. £3·25
(8) *Summary of Town and Country Planning Law*, A. J. Lomnicki. 1973. £3·95 hard, £2·25 soft
(9) *Town and Country Planning in Britain*, J. B. Cullingworth. 1974. £2·95 5th ed.
(10) INNER AREA STUDIES
    Birmingham IAS/B/Nos. 1–11
    Lambeth IAS/LA/Nos. 1–18
    Liverpool IAS/LI/Nos. 1–19
    List available from Housing Centre Bookshop
(11) Summaries of Consultants' Final Reports. 1977. £1·50
(12) MAKING TOWNS BETTER: Reports of the Urban Guideline Studies
    The Oldham Study: Environmental Planning and Management. 1973. 47p
    The Rotherham Study: 1. A General Approach to Improving the Physical Environment. 1973. 57p
    The Rotherham Study: 2. Technical Appendices. 1973. 47p
    The Sunderland Study: 1. Tackling Urban Problems: A Basic Handbook. 1973. 60p
    The Sunderland Study: 2. Tackling Urban Problems: A Working Guide. 1973. £1·00

CHAPTER 9: Planning and Land—*continued*

(13) COMMUNITY LAND ACT 1975
Department of the Environment Circulars
1. General Introduction and Priorities. 121/75. 35p
2. Community Land Accounts 1975–6. 128/75. 20p
3. Scheme of Accounts for Land Bought for Private Development. 5/76. 28p
4. Community Land (Prescribed Forms) (England). Regulations. 22/76. 20p
5. Planning Applications and Permission for Relevant Development. 23/76. 28p
6. Land for Private Development: Acquisition, Management and Disposal. 26/76. 75p
7. Compulsory Purchase Procedures. 30/76. 35p
8. Development Advice Notes. 31/76. 8p
9. The Community Land (Register of Land Holdings) Regulations 1976. 36/76. 12p
10. Accounts Directions. 98/76. 50p

(14) *The Community Land Act Explained*, The Boisot Waters Cohen Partnership. 1976. £5·95
(15) *Community Land Act 1975*, a reprint of articles from the Local Government Chronicle 1976. £1·50
(16) *Community Land—The New Act*, V. Moore. 1976. £2·75
(17) *The Community Land Act 1975*, W. G. Nutley and C. H. Beaumont. 1976. £8·50
(18) *Land Policy: An Exploration of the Nature of Land in Society*, John Ratcliffe. 1976. £3·75 hard, also available in soft back
(19) *Community Land Bill: Consultative Documents*. Obtainable from Department of the Environment

CHAPTER 10: Design, Construction and Maintenance

(1) *The Need for Smaller Homes*, Department of the Environment. 1975. Free
(2) *Starter and Extendible Homes*, Department of the Environment. 1975. Free
(3) *Factory Built Houses*, Moira Constable. 1975. 35p
(4) *Families Living at High Density*, Design Bulletin 21. 1970. 60p
(5) *High Living*, Stevenson, Martin & O'Neil. 1967. £2·25
(6) *Homes for Today and Tomorrow*, Parker Morris Report. Ministry of Housing and Local Government. 1961. 60p

CHAPTER 10: Design, Construction and Maintenance—*continued*

(7) *Space in the Home*, Design Bulletin 6. 1968. 43p
(8) *House Planning*, Design Bulletin 14. Reprinted 1976. £1·00
(9) *Some Aspects of Designing for Old People*, Design Bulletin 1. 1968. 30p
(10) *Housing Single People 2*, Design Bulletin 29. 1974. 75p
(11) *The Estate Outside the Dwelling*, Design Bulletin 25. 1972. £1·75
(12) *Landscaping for Flats*, Design Bulletin 5. 1967. 78½p
(13) *New Housing and Road Traffic Noise*, Design Bulletin 26. 1972. 27p
(14) *Services for Housing: Sanitary Plumbing and Drainage*. 1974. 60p
(15) *Safety in the Home*, Design Bulletin 13. Reprinted 1976. 66p
(16) *Criteria for Structural Adequacy*, The Institution of Structural Engineers. 1976. £6·00
(17) *Cars in Housing 1*, Design Bulletin 10. 1966.
(18) *Cars in Housing 2*, Design Bulletin 12. Reprinted 1971. 30p
(19) *Roads and the Environment*, Bruno de Hamel. 1976. £1·50
(20) *People and Design in the Violent City*, Oscar Newman. 1976. £3·95
(21) *Condensation in Dwellings, Part I and Part II*, Department of the Environment. Part I £1·00. Part II £1·25.
(22) *AJ Handbook of Building Structures*, Allan Hodgkinson, 1974. £4·95.
(23) *Metric House Shells—2 Storey Plans*, National Building Agency. 1969. £2·00.
(24) *Single Storey Housing Design Guide*, National Building Agency. 1971. £3·00.

CHAPTER 11: Social Aspects of Housing

(1) *Housing for Special Needs*, Frances M. Cook. Lecture given at PTRC Autumn Course, 1975, on Housing—Forward Planning and Management
(2) *Housing for Elderly People*, J. A. Muir Gray, *Housing*, June 1976
(3) *Designing for the Disabled*, Selwyn Goldsmith. 1976. £20·00
(4) *Housing for Special Needs, Part One, The Physically Handicapped*, SLASH. 1974. £2·50
(5) *Towards a Housing Policy for Disabled People*, Central Council for the Disabled. 1976. £1·00
(6) *Handbook of Housing for Disabled People*, London Housing Consortium. 1976. £2·00
(7) *Housing Co-operatives*, John Hands. 1975. £1·50

CHAPTER 11 : Social Aspects of Housing—*continued*

(8) *Student Housing: Architectural and Social Aspects,* Phyllis G. Allen & William F. Mullins. 1971. £6·00
(9) *Housing Single People 1,* Design Bulletin 23. 1971. 60p
(10) *Housing Single People 2,* Design Bulletin 29. 1974. 75p
(11) *Homelessness in London,* John Greve, Dilys Page & Stella Greve. 1971. £3·25
(12) *Homeless Near a Thousand Homes,* Bryan Glastonbury. 1971. £1·95
(13) *Tied Accommodation,* Moira Constable. 1974. 50p
(14) *Children in Flats, A Family Study,* NSPCC
(15) *Families Living at High Density,* Design Bulletin 21. 1970. 60p
(16) *The Housing Poor,* Alison Ravetz. CHAS Occasional Papers 3. 1976. 60p
(17) *Local Authority Housing Management,* Derek Fox, *Housing,* April 1976
(18) *Report of the Committee on Local Authority and Allied Personal Social Services,* Seebohm Report. Cmnd. 3703. 1968. £2·10

CHAPTER 12: The Future

(1) *Change or Decay,* Final report of the Liverpool inner area study. 1977. £6·00
(2) *Unequal City,* Final report of the Birmingham inner area study. 1977. £9·00
(3) *Inner London: Policies for Dispersal and Balance,* Final Report of the Lambeth inner area study. 1977. £6·00 £6·00
(4) *Policy for the Inner Cities,* Cmnd. 6845. 1977. 60p
(5) *The Government's Expenditure Plans,* Volume 1 (general account), Cmnd. 6721–1. 60p; Volume 2 (details of individual expenditure programmes), Cmnd. 6721–11. £2·35
(6) *Improvement in United Kingdom Housing—A Reappraisal,* National Home Improvement Council. 1977. £8·00
(7) *Memorandum on Review of the Rent Acts,* Housing Centre Trust. 1977. 40p
(8) *Local Government Finance,* Cmnd. 6813. 1977. 70p
(9) *Race and Local Authority Housing,* Community Relations Commission. 1977
(10) *Accommodation for Gypsies,* 1977. £1·00
(11) *Tenancy Agreements,* DOE Housing Services Advisory Group. 1977

SUPPLEMENT

(1) *Transport Policy,* Cmnd. 6836. HMSO. 1977. £1·35
(2) *Housing Policy. A Consultative Document.* Presented to Parliament by the Secretary of State for the Environment and the Secretary of State for Wales. Cmnd. 6851. 1977. £2·50
(3) *Housing Policy. Technical Volume* Part I £3·50; Part II £3·00 Part III £3·25
(4) *Scottish Housing. A Consultative Document* Cmnd. 6852. 1977. £1·75
(5) *Green Paper Response 1: Housing Finance Memorandum* Housing Centre Trust 1977. 40p

Index

White Papers referred to in the text are indexed under their titles. The main, but not all, references to statutes are indexed under the title of the particular Act with an indication of the subject to which reference is made. Principal government committee reports are indexed both under their titles and also the name of the chairman. Principal government circulars after 1971 are listed chronologically under DOE Circulars, together with equivalent WO numbers where applicable. Other publications referred to are either included in the bibliography or must be sought through the relevant subject heading. The most common abbreviations are listed alphabetically in the index with their full meaning, except in the case of Chapter 8, which has its own list of abbreviations and references on pages 253–256.

417